ULTIMATE COMICS SPIDER-MAN

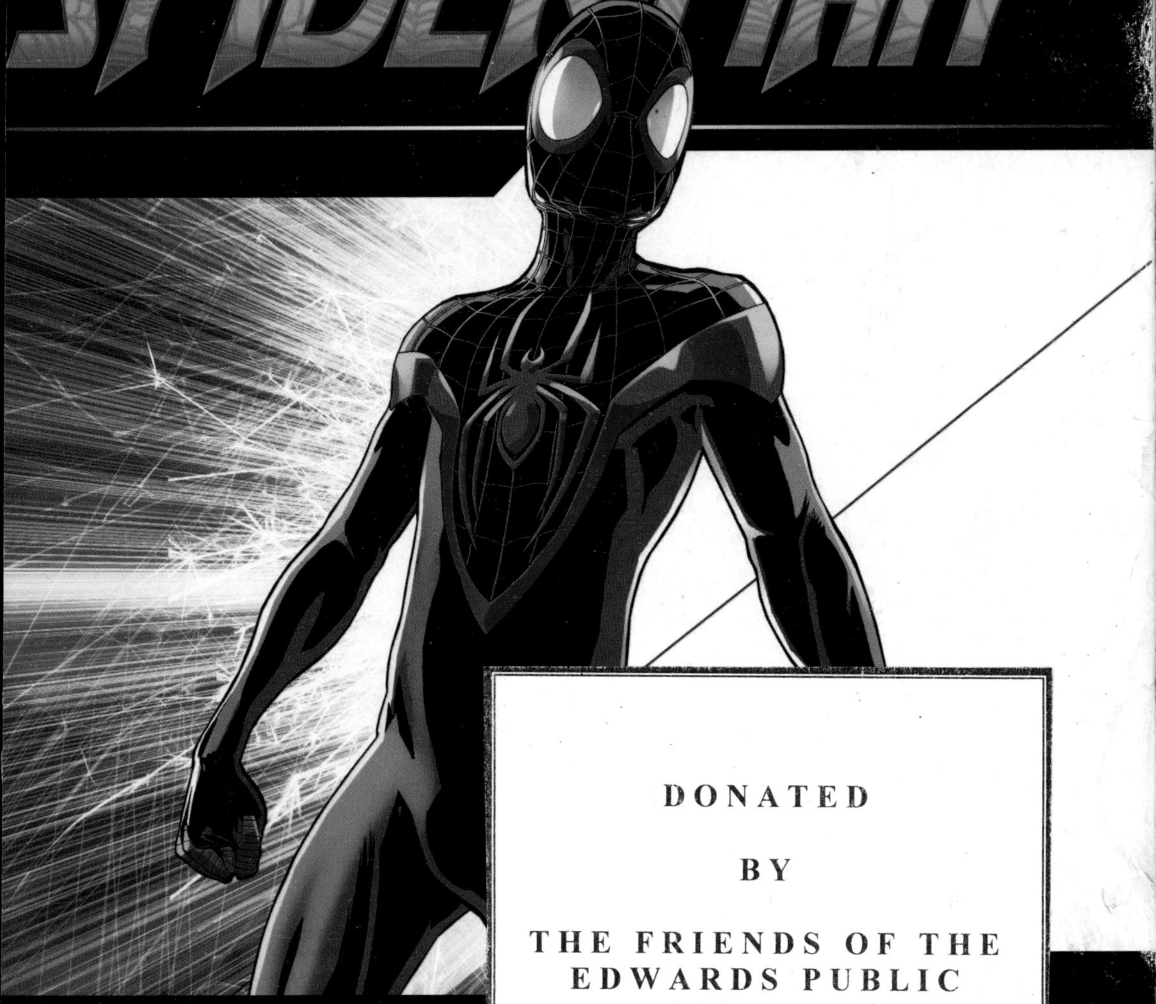

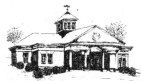

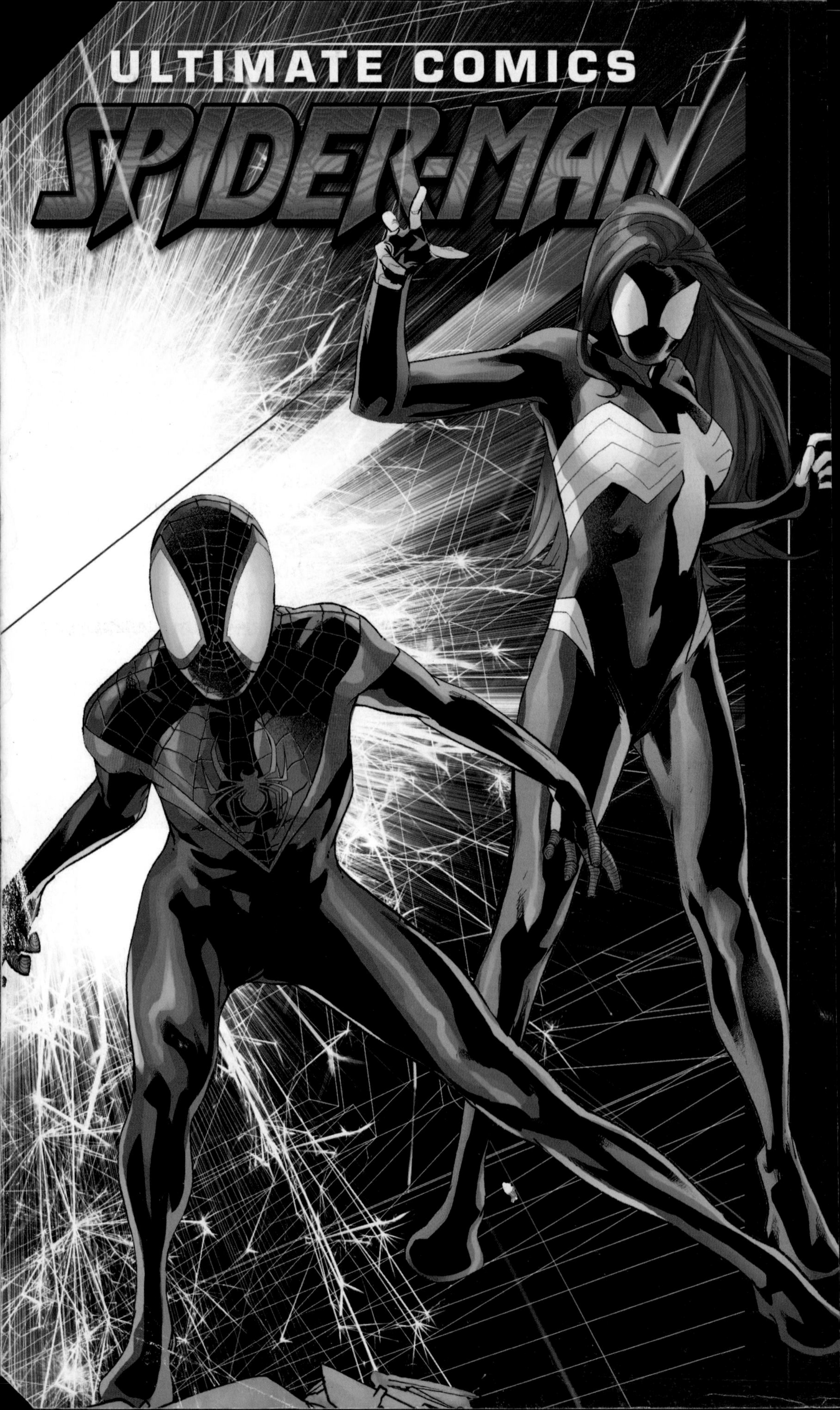
ULTIMATE COMICS
SPIDER-MAN

WRITER: **BRIAN MICHAEL BENDIS**

ARTISTS: **DAVID MARQUEZ** (#11-15 & #18)

& **PEPE LARRAZ** (#16-17)

COLOR ARTIST: **JUSTIN PONSOR**

LETTERER: **VC'S CORY PETIT**

COVER ART: **KAARE ANDREWS** (#11), **JORGE MOLINA** (#12-15); **DAVID MARQUEZ** & **RAINIER BEREDO** (#16 & #18) AND **SARA PICHELLI** & **RAINIER BEREDO** (#17)

ASSISTANT EDITORS: **JON MOISAN** & **EMILY SHAW**

ASSOCIATE EDITOR: **SANA AMANAT**

EDITOR: **MARK PANICCIA**

- -

COLLECTION EDITOR: **JENNIFER GRÜNWALD**

ASSISTANT EDITORS: **ALEX STARBUCK** & **NELSON RIBEIRO**

EDITOR, SPECIAL PROJECTS: **MARK D. BEAZLEY**

SENIOR EDITOR, SPECIAL PROJECTS: **JEFF YOUNGQUIST**

SENIOR VICE PRESIDENT OF SALES: **DAVID GABRIEL**

SVP OF BRAND PLANNING & COMMUNICATIONS: **MICHAEL PASCIULLO**

BOOK DESIGNER: **RODOLFO MURAGUCHI**

- -

EDITOR IN CHIEF: **AXEL ALONSO**

CHIEF CREATIVE OFFICER: **JOE QUESADA**

PUBLISHER: **DAN BUCKLEY**

EXECUTIVE PRODUCER: **ALAN FINE**

SPIDER-MAN BY BRIAN MICHAEL BENDIS VOL. 3. Contains material originally published in magazine form as ULTIMATE COMICS SPIDER-MAN #11-18. First printing 2012. Hardcover ISBN# . Softcover ISBN# 978-0-7851-6176-9. Published by MARVEL WORLDWIDE, INC., a subsidiary of MARVEL ENTERTAINMENT, LLC. OFFICE OF PUBLICATION: 135 West 50th Street, New York, NY 2012 and 2013 Marvel Characters, Inc. All rights reserved. Hardcover: $24.99 per copy in the U.S. and $27.99 in Canada (GST #R127032852). Softcover: $19.99 per copy in the U.S. and $21.99 27032852). Canadian Agreement #40668537. All characters featured in this issue and the distinctive names and likenesses thereof, and all related indicia are trademarks of Marvel Characters, ween any of the names, characters, persons, and/or institutions in this magazine with those of any living or dead person or institution is intended, and any such similarity which may exist is Printed in the U.S.A. ALAN FINE, EVP - Office of the President, Marvel Worldwide, Inc. and EVP & CMO Marvel Characters B.V.; DAN BUCKLEY, Publisher & President - Print, Animation & Digital ADA, Chief Creative Officer; TOM BREVOORT, SVP of Publishing; DAVID BOGART, SVP of Operations & Procurement, Publishing; RUWAN JAYATILLEKE, SVP & Associate Publisher, Publishing; C.B. eator & Content Development; DAVID GABRIEL, SVP of Publishing Sales & Circulation; MICHAEL PASCIULLO, SVP of Brand Planning & Communications; JIM O'KEEFE, VP of Operations & Logistics; e Director of Publishing Technology; SUSAN CRESPI, Editorial Operations Manager; ALEX MORALES, Publishing Operations Manager; STAN LEE, Chairman Emeritus. For information regarding el Comics or on Marvel.com, please contact Niza Disla, Director of Marvel Partnerships, at ndisla@marvel.com. For Marvel subscription inquiries, please call 800-217-9158. Manufactured 2 and 12/3/2012 (hardcover), and 10/22/2012 and 4/22/2013 (softcover), by R.R. DONNELLEY, INC., SALEM, VA, USA.

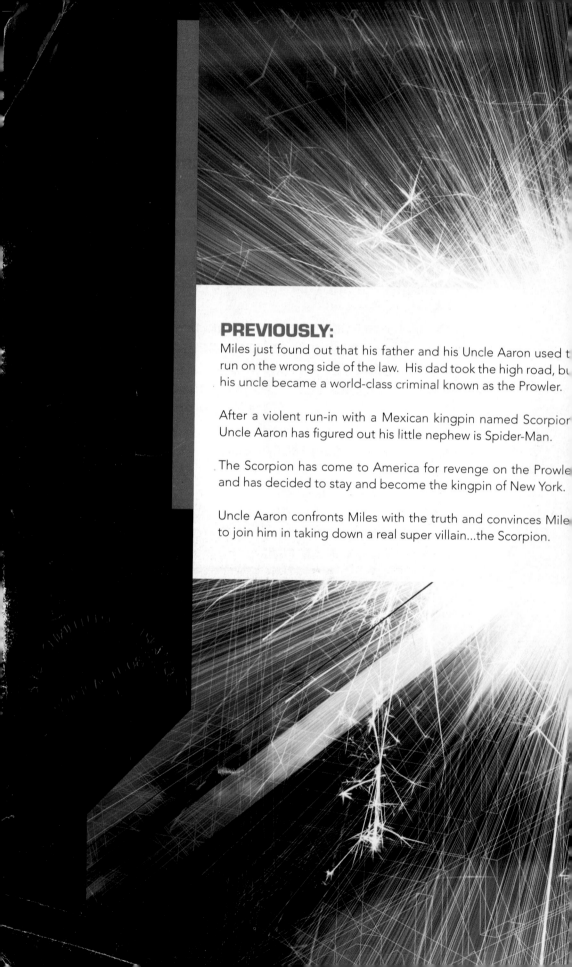

PREVIOUSLY:

Miles just found out that his father and his Uncle Aaron used t run on the wrong side of the law. His dad took the high road, bu his uncle became a world-class criminal known as the Prowler.

After a violent run-in with a Mexican kingpin named Scorpior Uncle Aaron has figured out his little nephew is Spider-Man.

The Scorpion has come to America for revenge on the Prowle and has decided to stay and become the kingpin of New York.

Uncle Aaron confronts Miles with the truth and convinces Mile to join him in taking down a real super villain...the Scorpion.

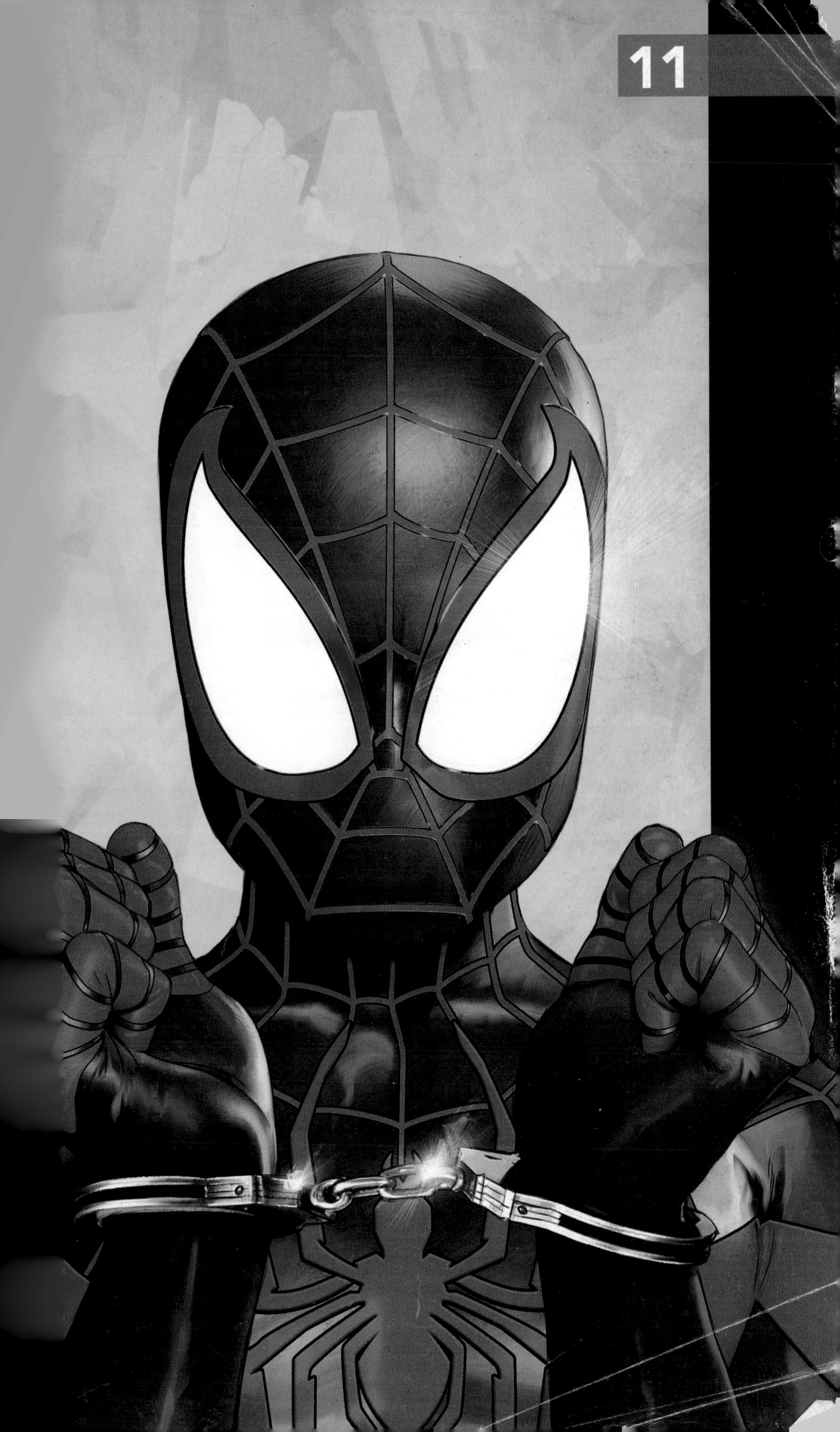

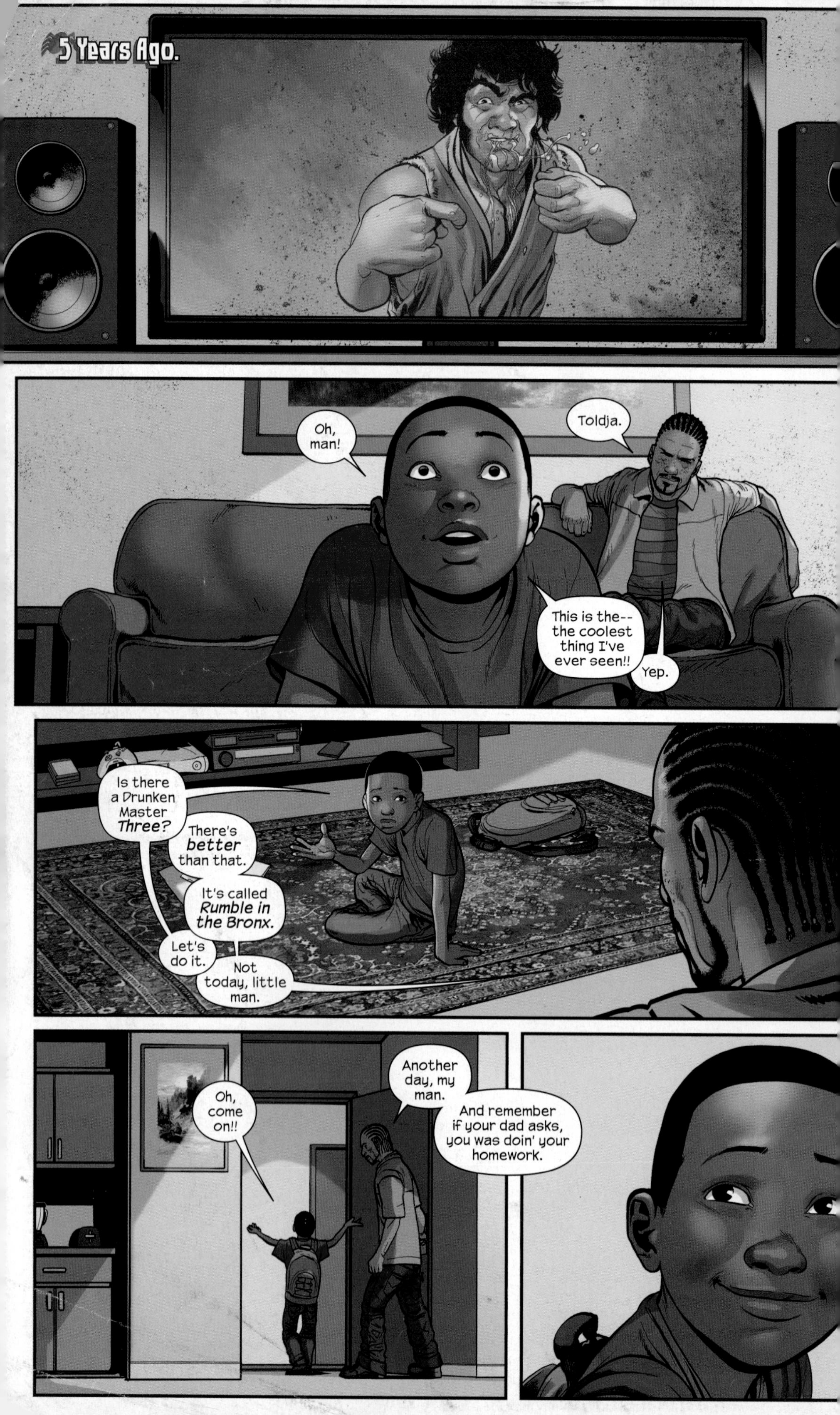
5 Years Ago.
Oh, man!
Toldja.
This is the-- the coolest thing I've ever seen!!
Yep.
Is there a Drunken Master *Three?*
There's *better* than that.
It's called *Rumble in the Bronx.*
Let's do it.
Not today, little man.
Oh, come on!!
Another day, my man.
And remember if your dad asks, you was doin' your homework.

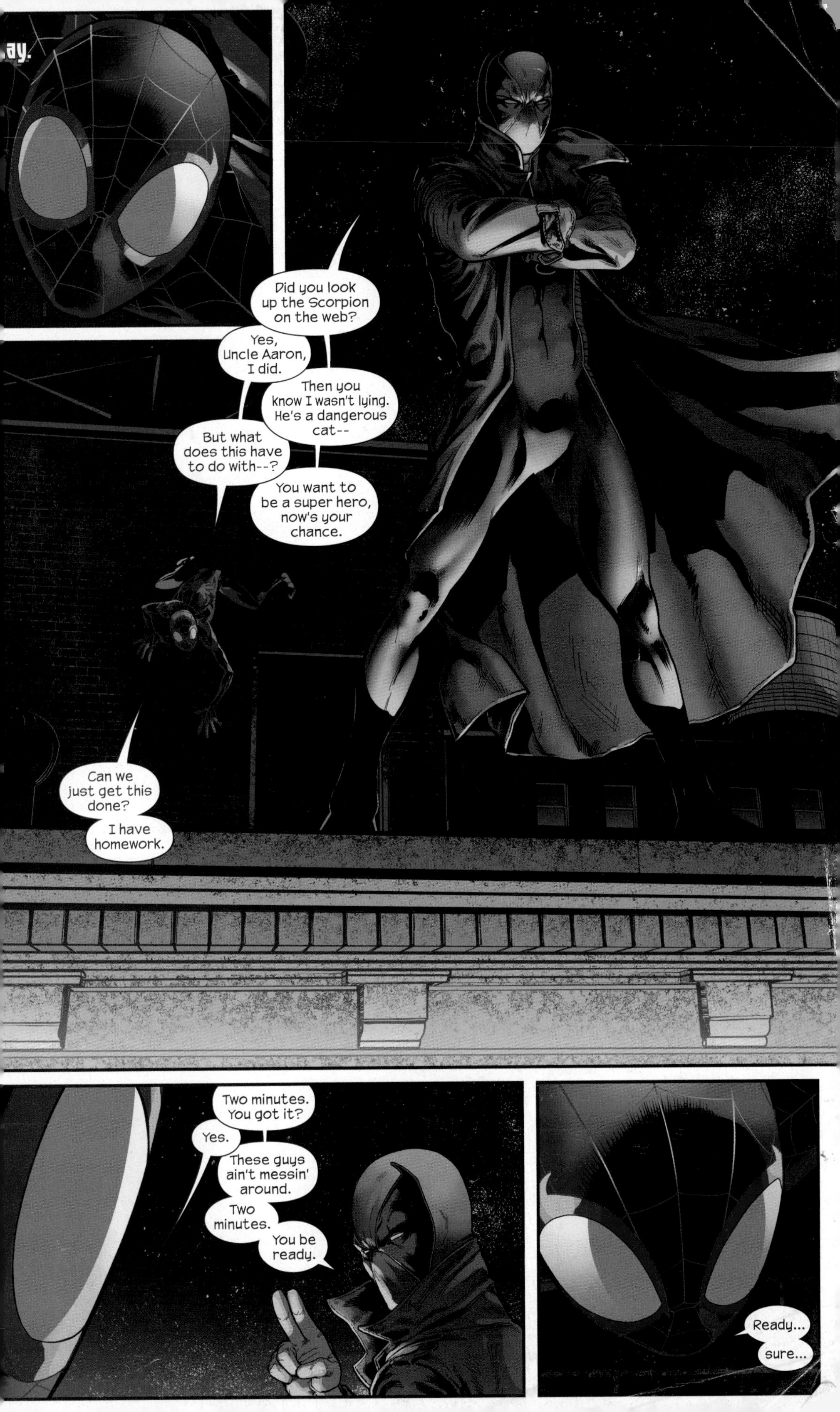
ay.
Did you look up the Scorpion on the web?
Yes, Uncle Aaron, I did.
Then you know I wasn't lying. He's a dangerous cat--
But what does this have to do with--?
You want to be a super hero, now's your chance.
Can we just get this done?
I have homework.
Two minutes. You got it?
Yes.
These guys ain't messin' around.
Two minutes.
You be ready.
Ready...
sure...

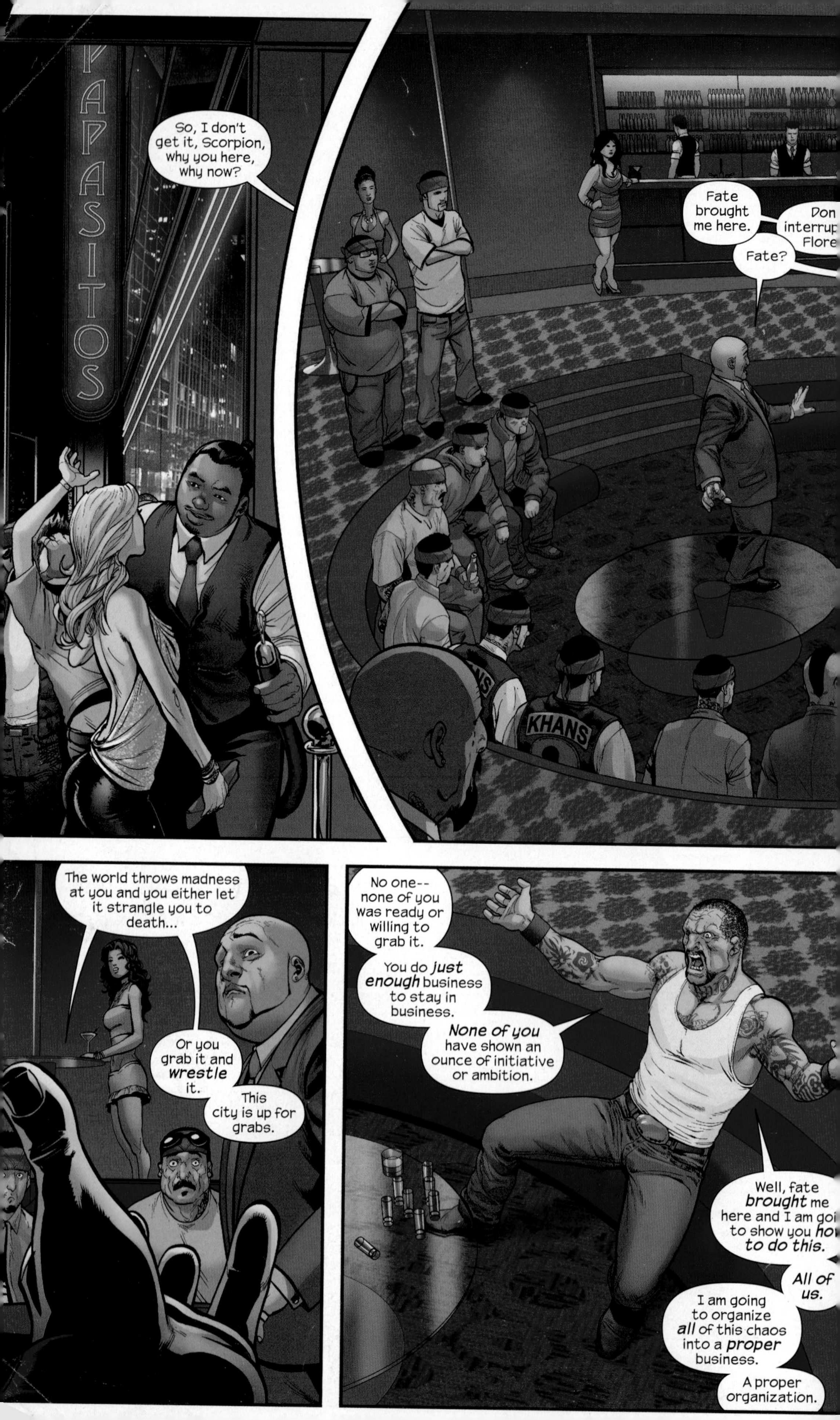
PAPASITOS
So, I don't get it, Scorpion, why you here, why now?
Fate brought me here.
Don interrup Flore
Fate?
KHANS
The world throws madness at you and you either let it strangle you to death...
Or you grab it and *wrestle* it.
This city is up for grabs.
No one-- none of you was ready or willing to grab it.
You do *just enough* business to stay in business.
None of you have shown an ounce of initiative or ambition.
Well, fate *brought* me here and I am goi to show you *ho* *to do this.*
All of us.
I am going to organize *all* of this chaos into a *proper* business.
A proper organization.

You were interrupting and questioning me.

Both things I hate.

...sn't! just--

Both things *at once* I hate even more.

Fate brought me here.

That's what brings anyone anywhere.

We pretend we're in control of the chaos of the world...but we're not.

We pretend we have a plan.

An ...anization ...respect.

An ...rganization of pride.

An ...anization ...f fear.

Fear and--

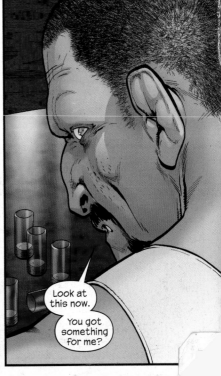

Look at this now.

You got something for me?

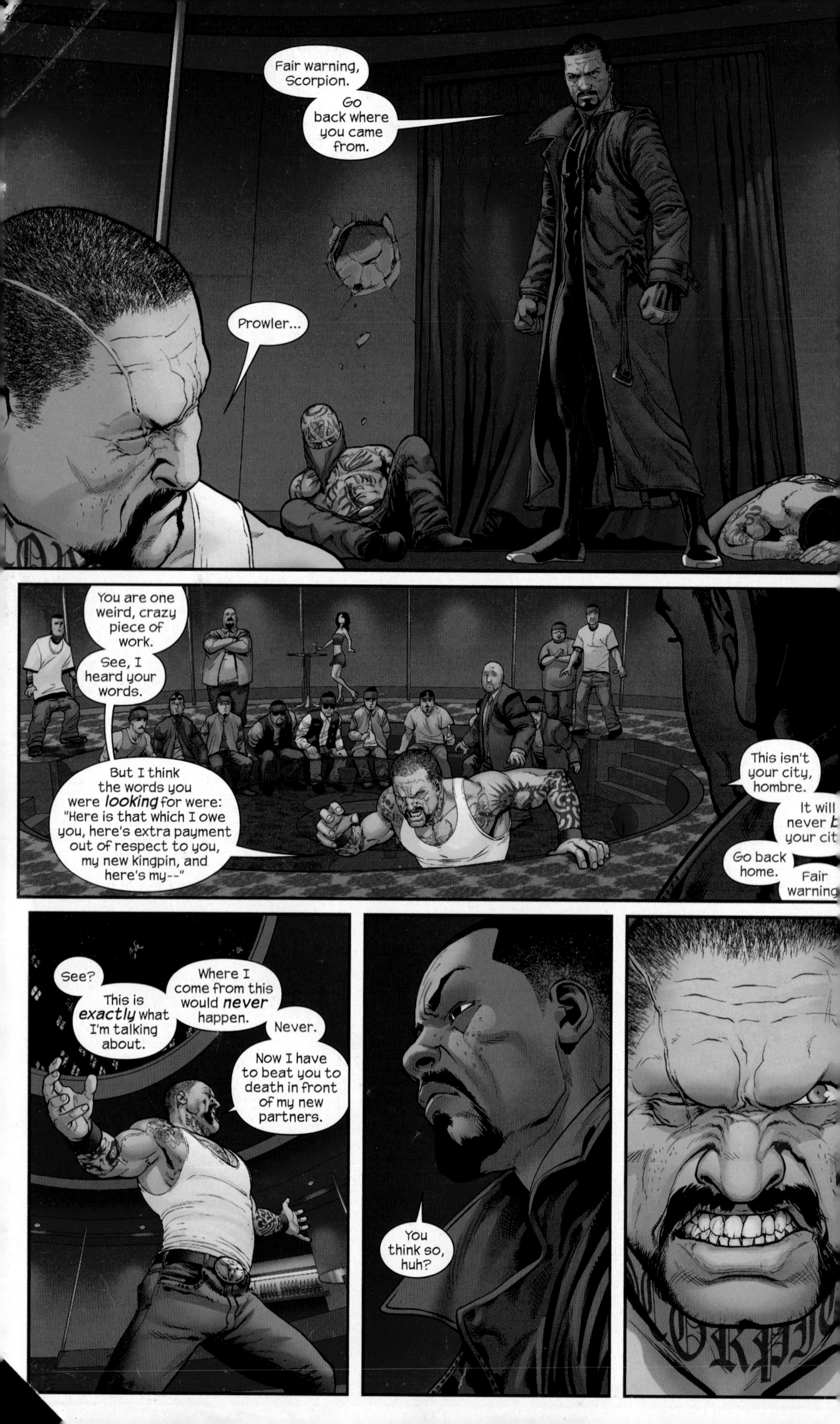
Fair warning, Scorpion.
Go back where you came from.
Prowler...
You are one weird, crazy piece of work.
See, I heard your words.
But I think the words you were *looking* for were: "Here is that which I owe you, here's extra payment out of respect to you, my new kingpin, and here's my--"
This isn't your city, hombre.
It will never
Go back home.
Fair
See?
This is *exactly* what I'm talking about.
Where I come from this would *never* happen.
Never.
Now I have to beat you to death in front of my new partners.
You think so, huh?

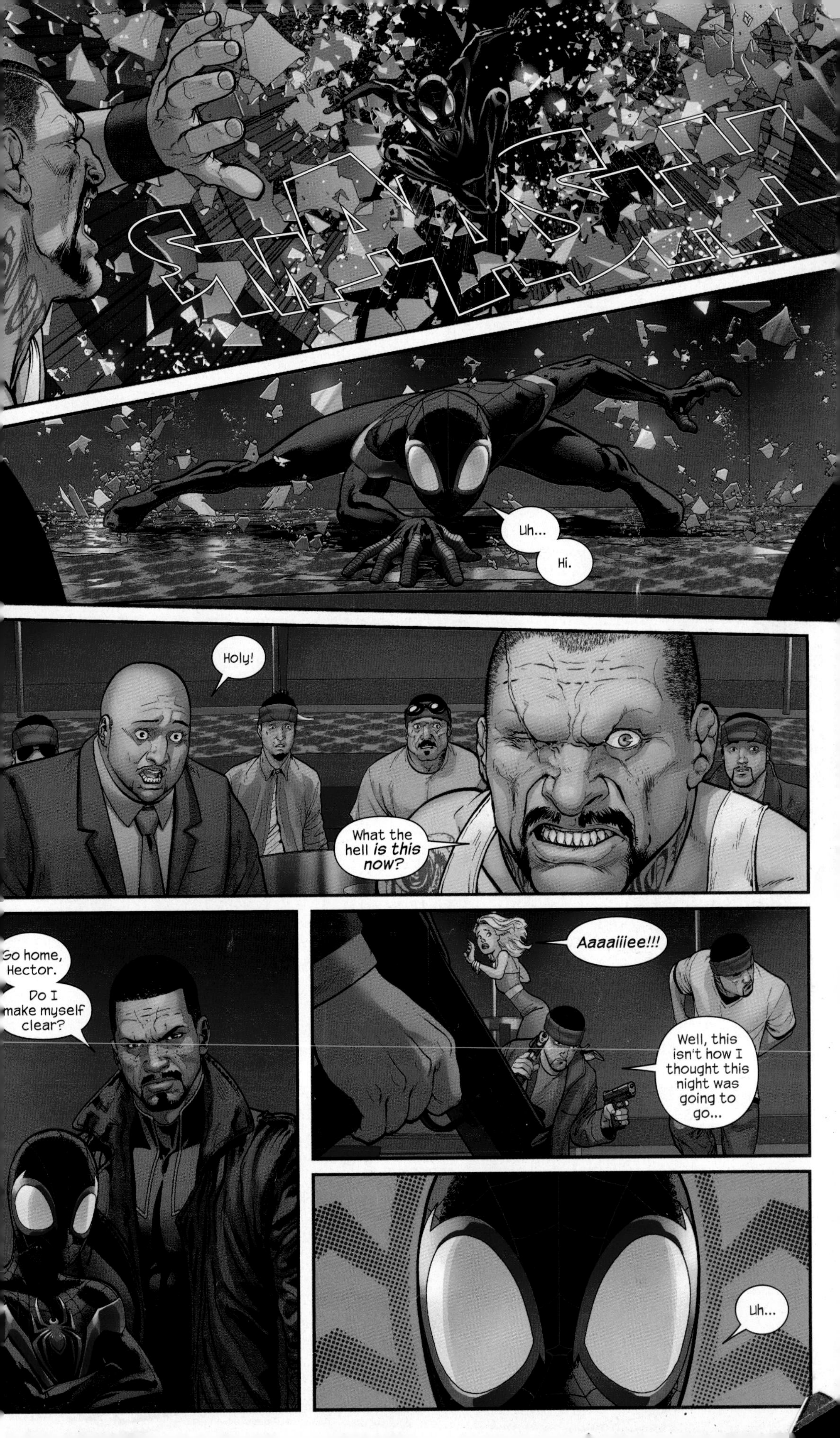

Uh...
Hi.
Holy!
What the hell is this now?
Go home, Hector.
Do I make myself clear?
Aaaaiiiee!!!
Well, this isn't how I thought this night was going to go...
Uh...

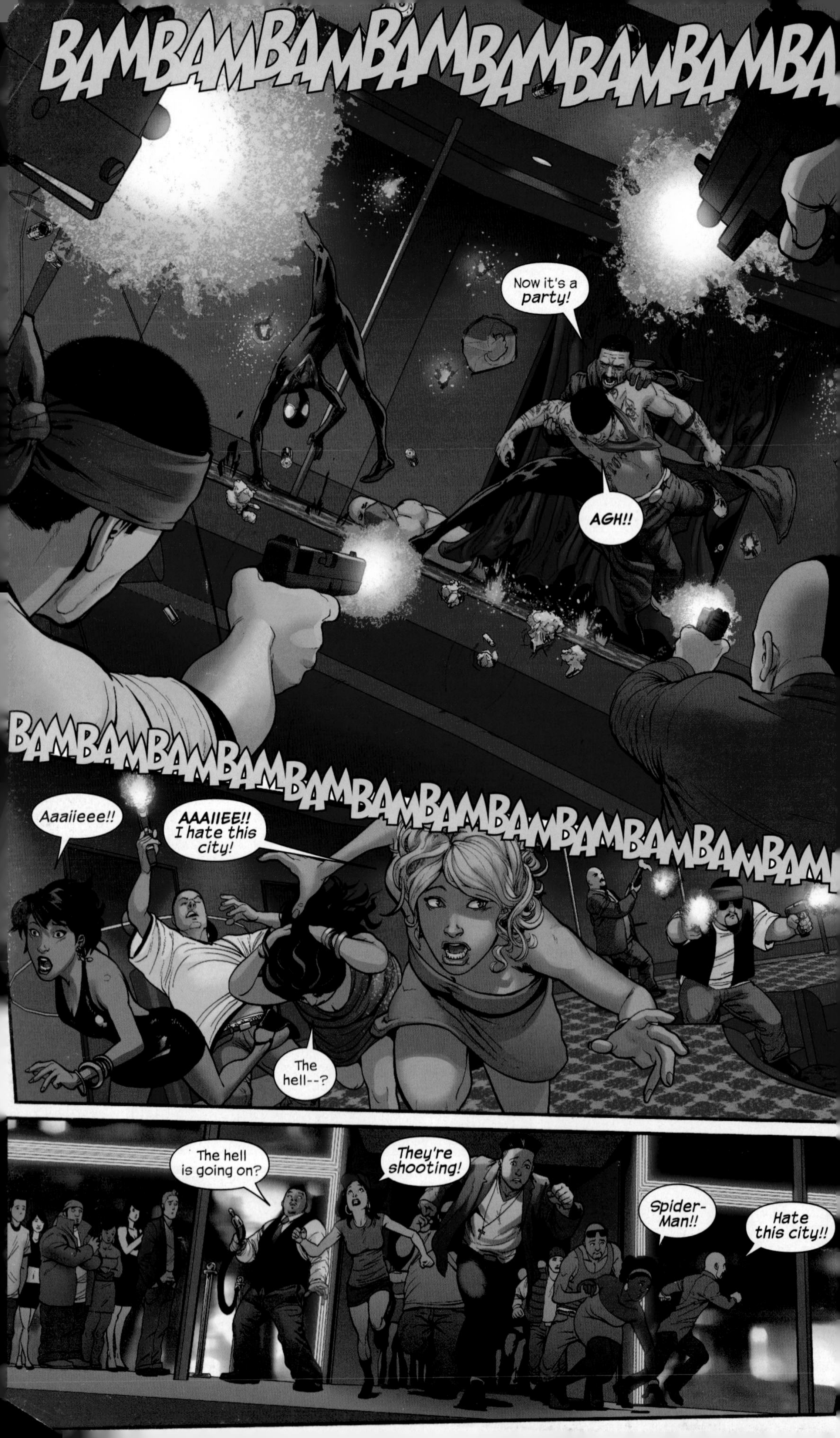
BAMBAMBAMBAMBAMBAMBAMBAMBA
Now it's a party!
AGH!!
BAMBAMBAMBAMBAMBAMBAMBAMBAMBAMBAMBAMBAMBAM
Aaaiieee!!
AAAIIEE!! I hate this city!
The hell--?
The hell is going on?
They're shooting!
Spider-Man!!
Hate this city!!

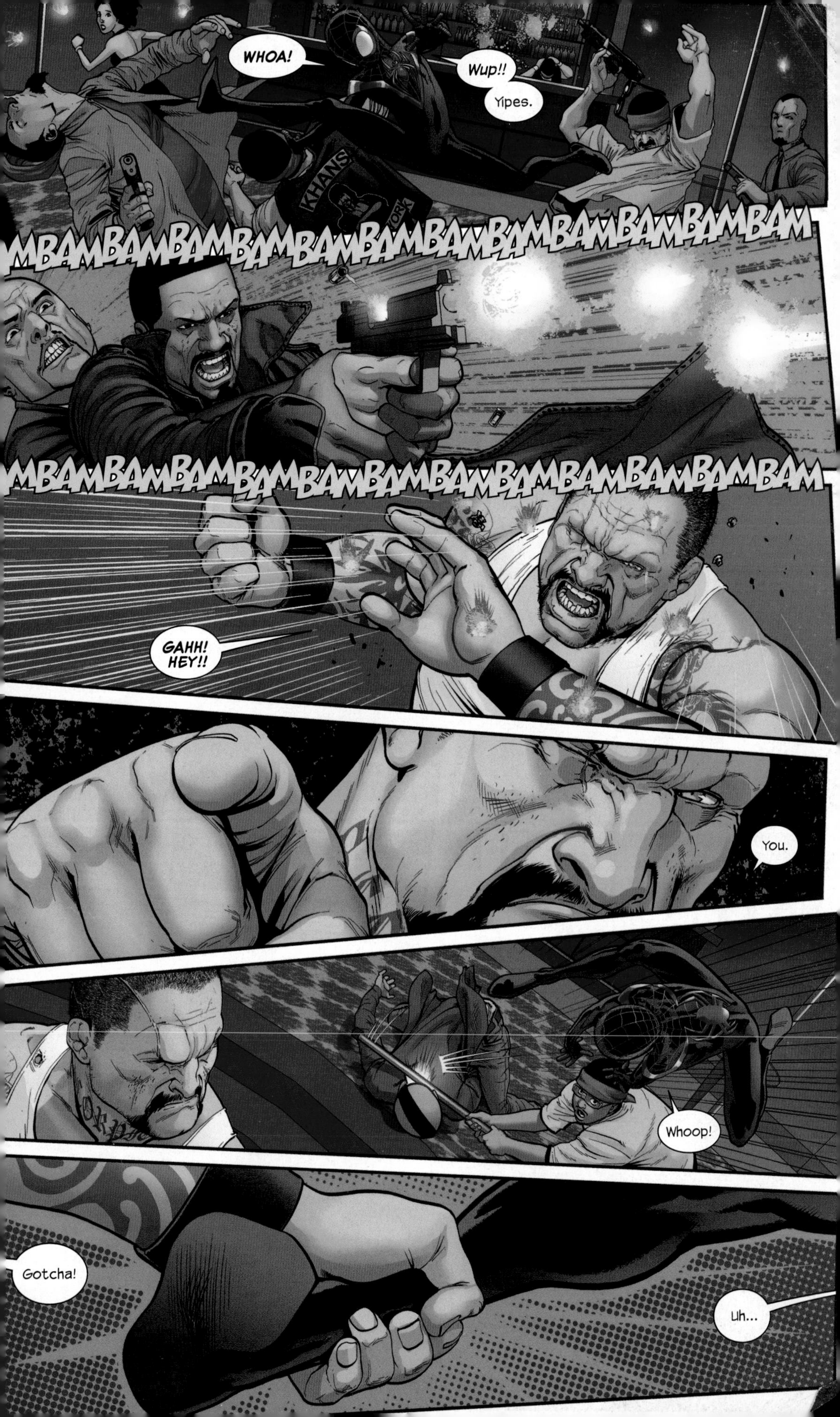
WHOA!
Wup!!
Yipes.
MBAMBAMBAMBAMBAMBAMBAMBAMBAMBAMBAMBAMBAM
MBAMBAMBAMBAMBAMBAMBAMBAMBAMBAMBAMBAMBAM
GAHH! HEY!!
You.
Whoop!
Gotcha!
Uh...

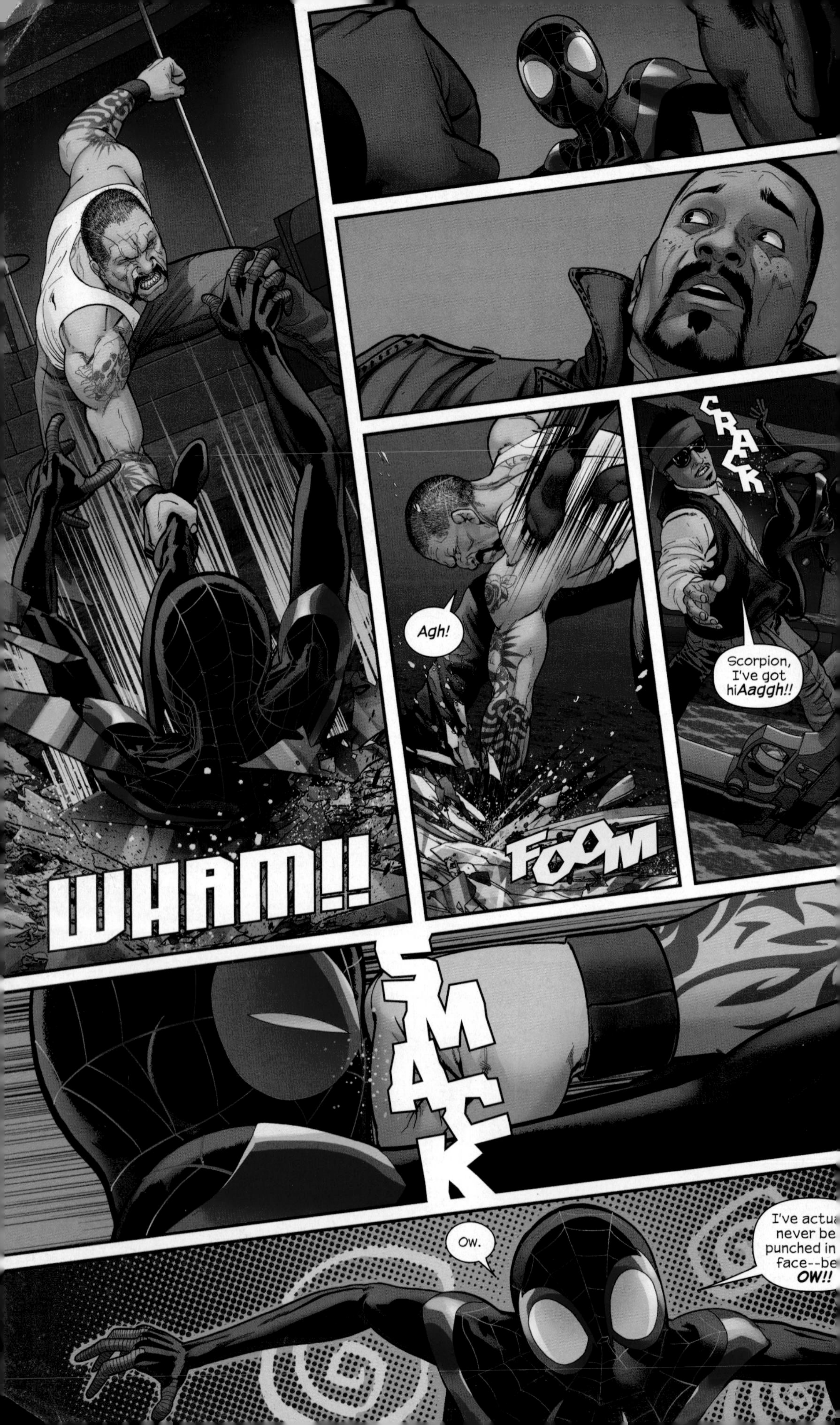
WHAM!!
Agh!
FOOM
CRACK
Scorpion, I've got hiAaggh!!
SMACK
Ow.
I've actua never be punched in face--be OW!!

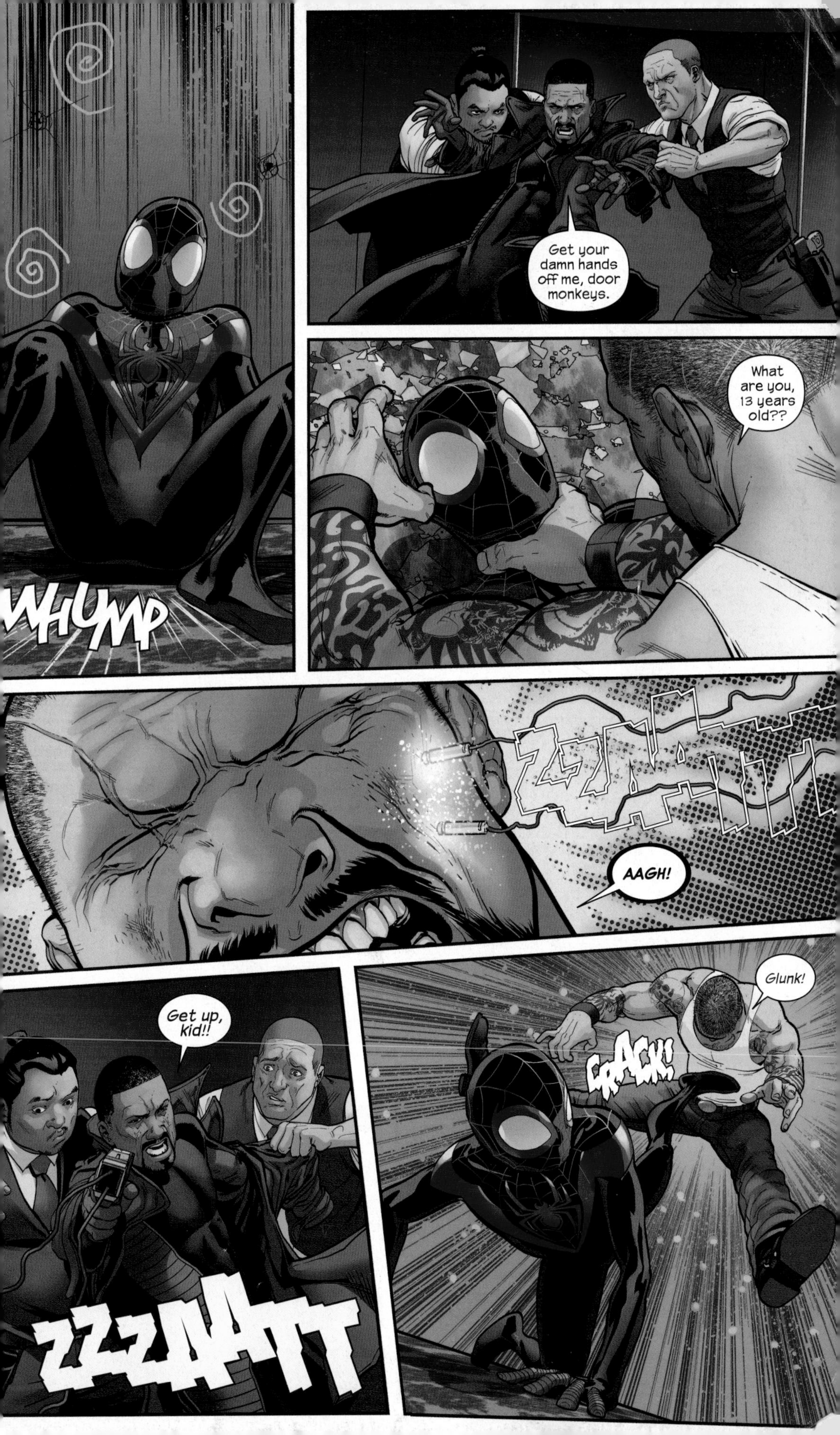

Get your damn hands off me, door monkeys.
WHUMP
What are you, 13 years old??
AAGH!
Get up, kid!!
ZZZAATT
Glunk!
CRACK!

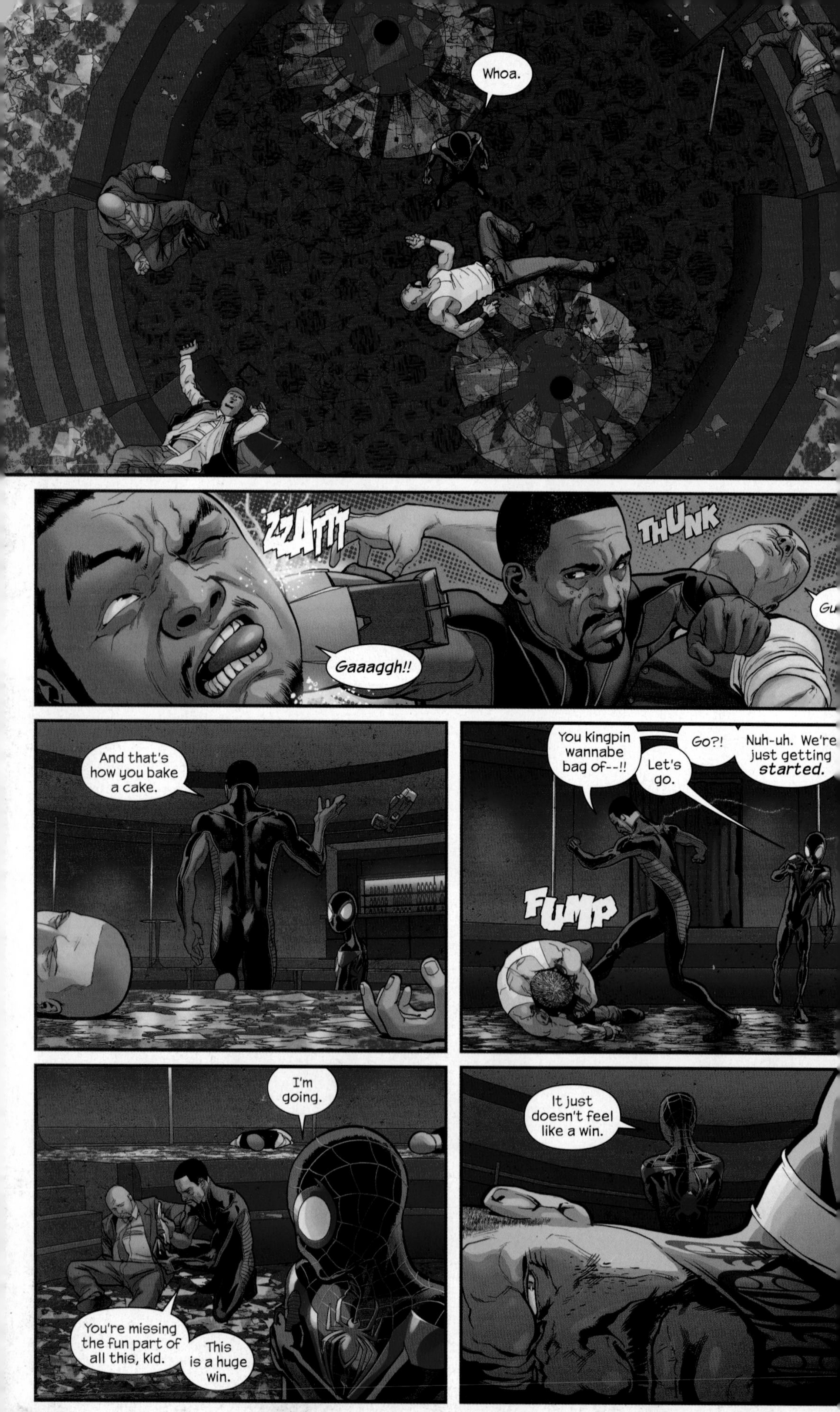
Whoa.
ZZATTT
THUNK
Gaaaggh!!
And that's how you bake a cake.
You kingpin wannabe bag of--!!
Go?!
Let's go.
Nuh-uh. We're just getting *started.*
FUMP
I'm going.
You're missing the fun part of all this, kid.
This is a huge win.
It just doesn't feel like a win.

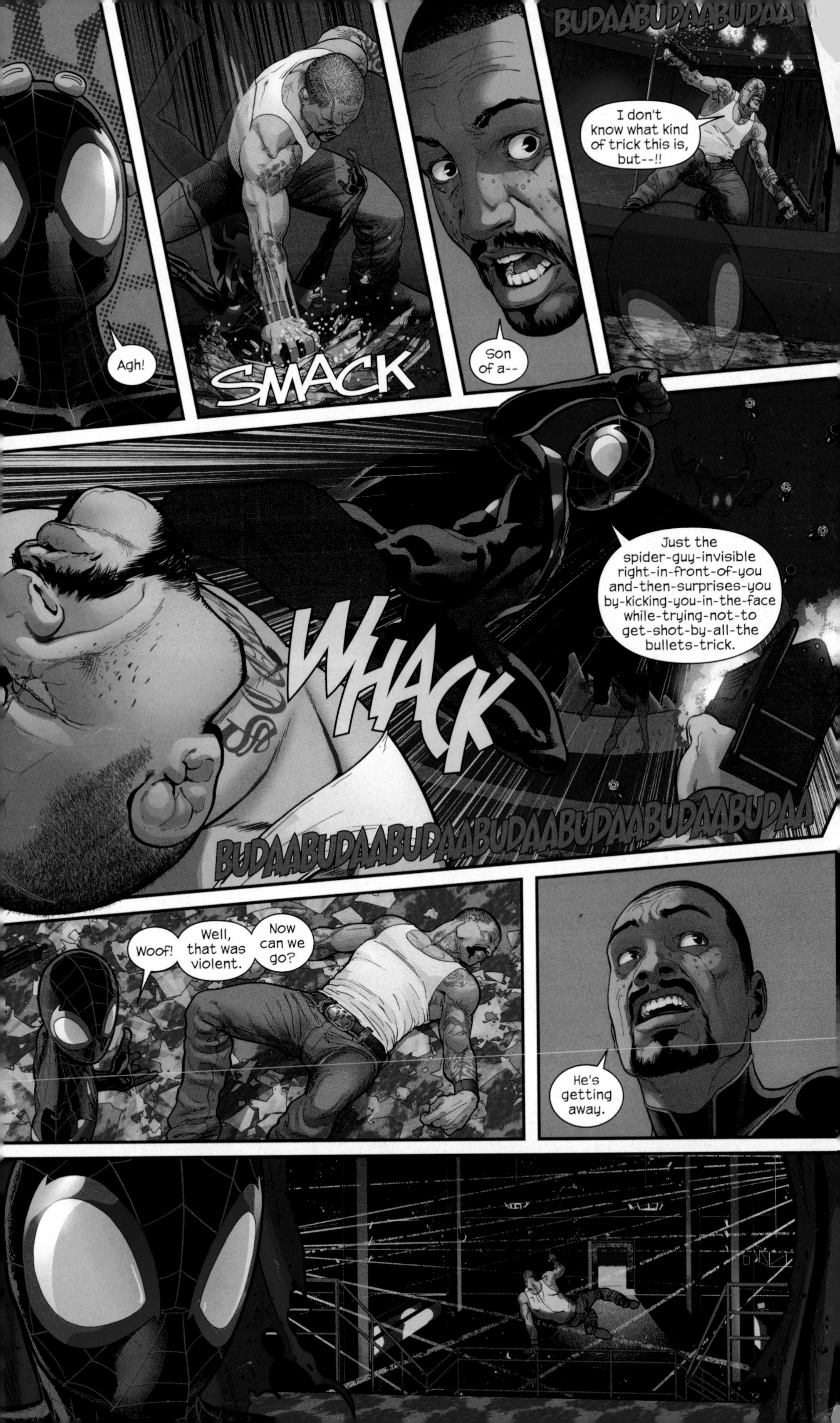
BUDAABUDAABUDAA
I don't know what kind of trick this is, but--!!
Agh!
SMACK
Son of a--
Just the spider-guy-invisible right-in-front-of-you and-then-surprises-you by-kicking-you-in-the-face while-trying-not-to get-shot-by-all-the bullets-trick.
WHACK
BUDAABUDAABUDAABUDAABUDAABUDAA
Woof!
Well, that was violent.
Now can we go?
He's getting away.

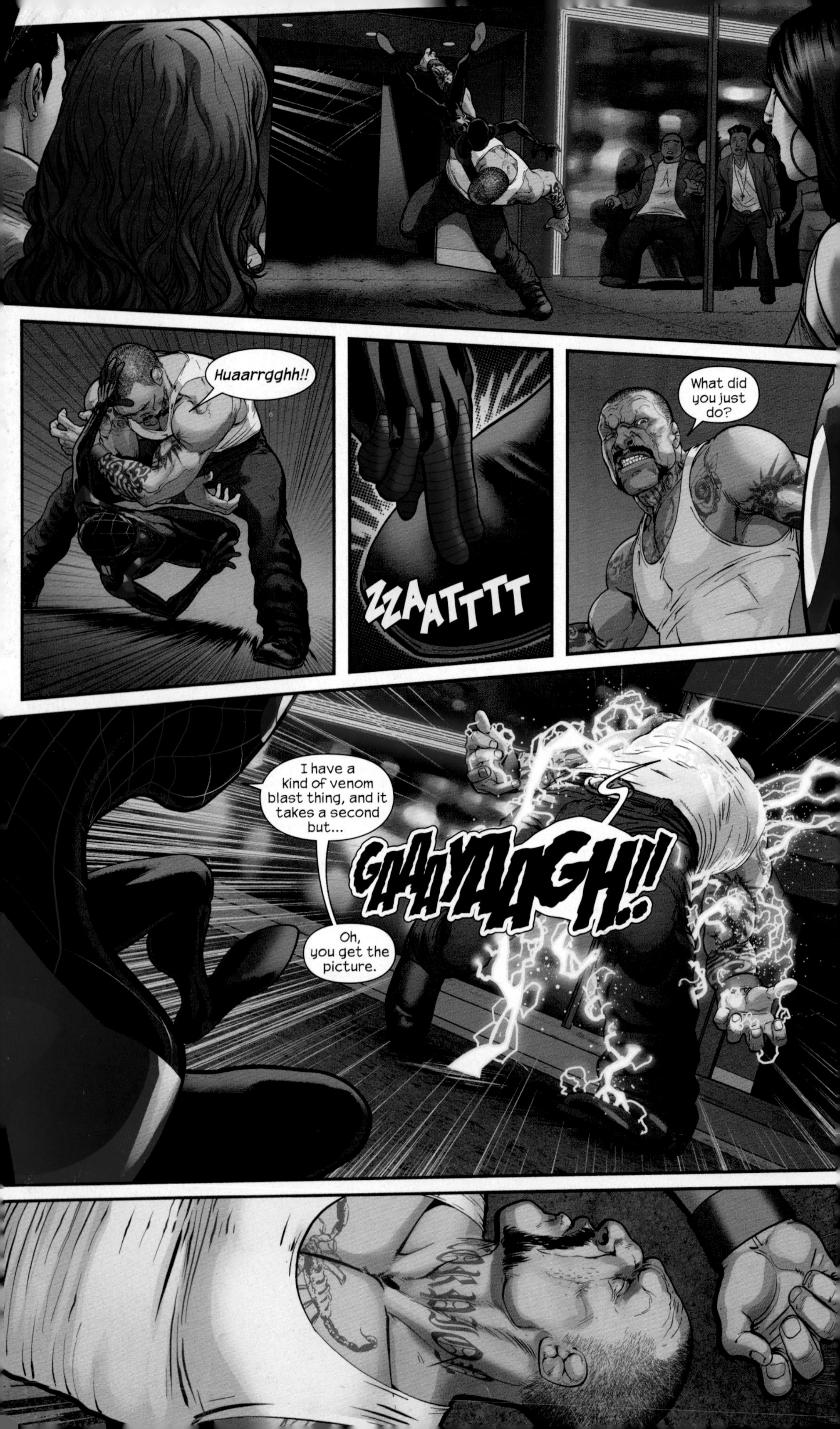
Huaarrgghh!!
ZZAATTTT
What did you just do?
I have a kind of venom blast thing, and it takes a second but...
GAAAYAAGH!!
Oh, you get the picture.

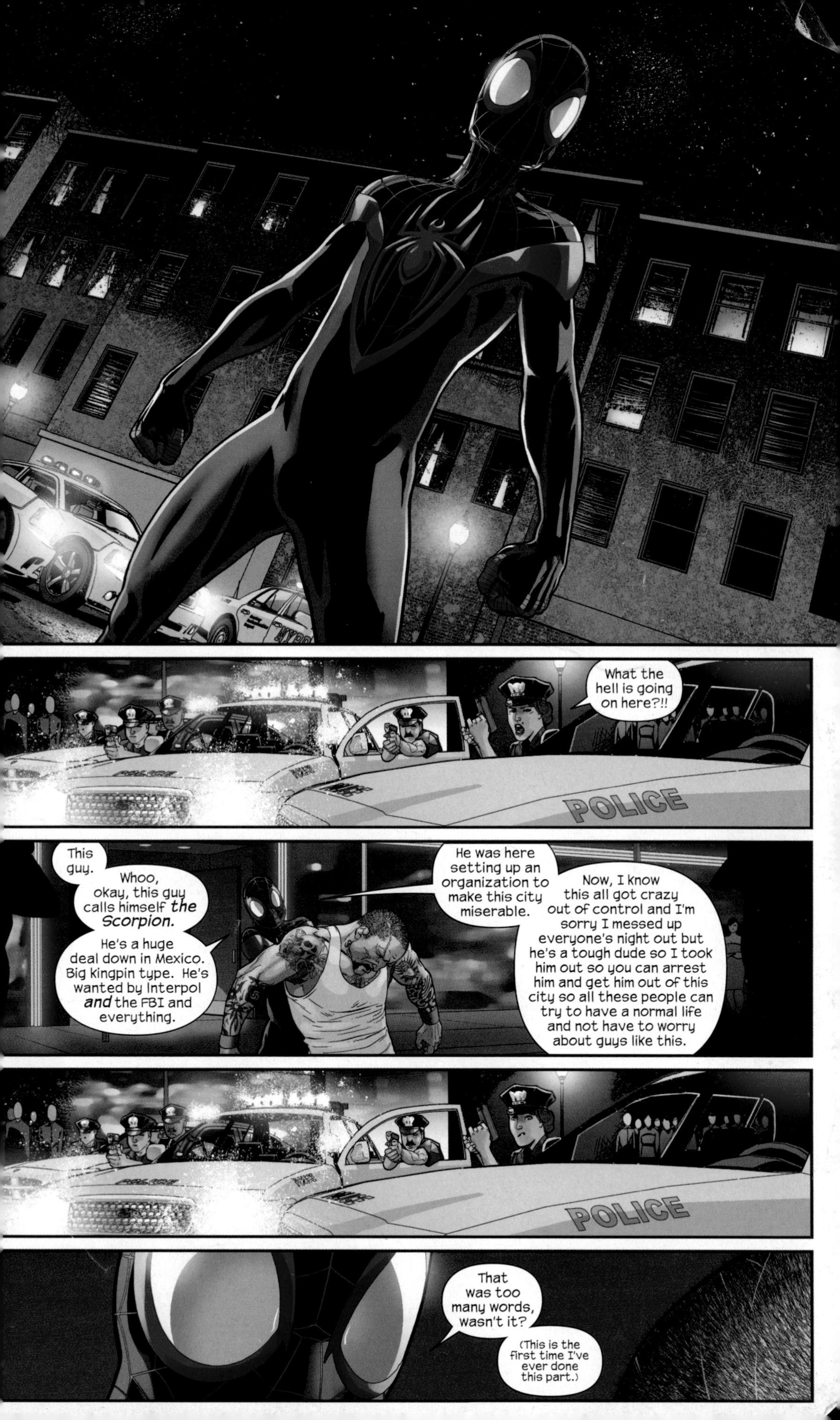

What the hell is going on here?!!
This guy.
Whoo, okay, this guy calls himself *the Scorpion.*
He's a huge deal down in Mexico. Big kingpin type. He's wanted by Interpol ***and*** the FBI and everything.
He was here setting up an organization to make this city miserable.
Now, I know this all got crazy out of control and I'm sorry I messed up everyone's night out but he's a tough dude so I took him out so you can arrest him and get him out of this city so all these people can try to have a normal life and not have to worry about guys like this.
That was too many words, wasn't it?
(This is the first time I've ever done this part.)

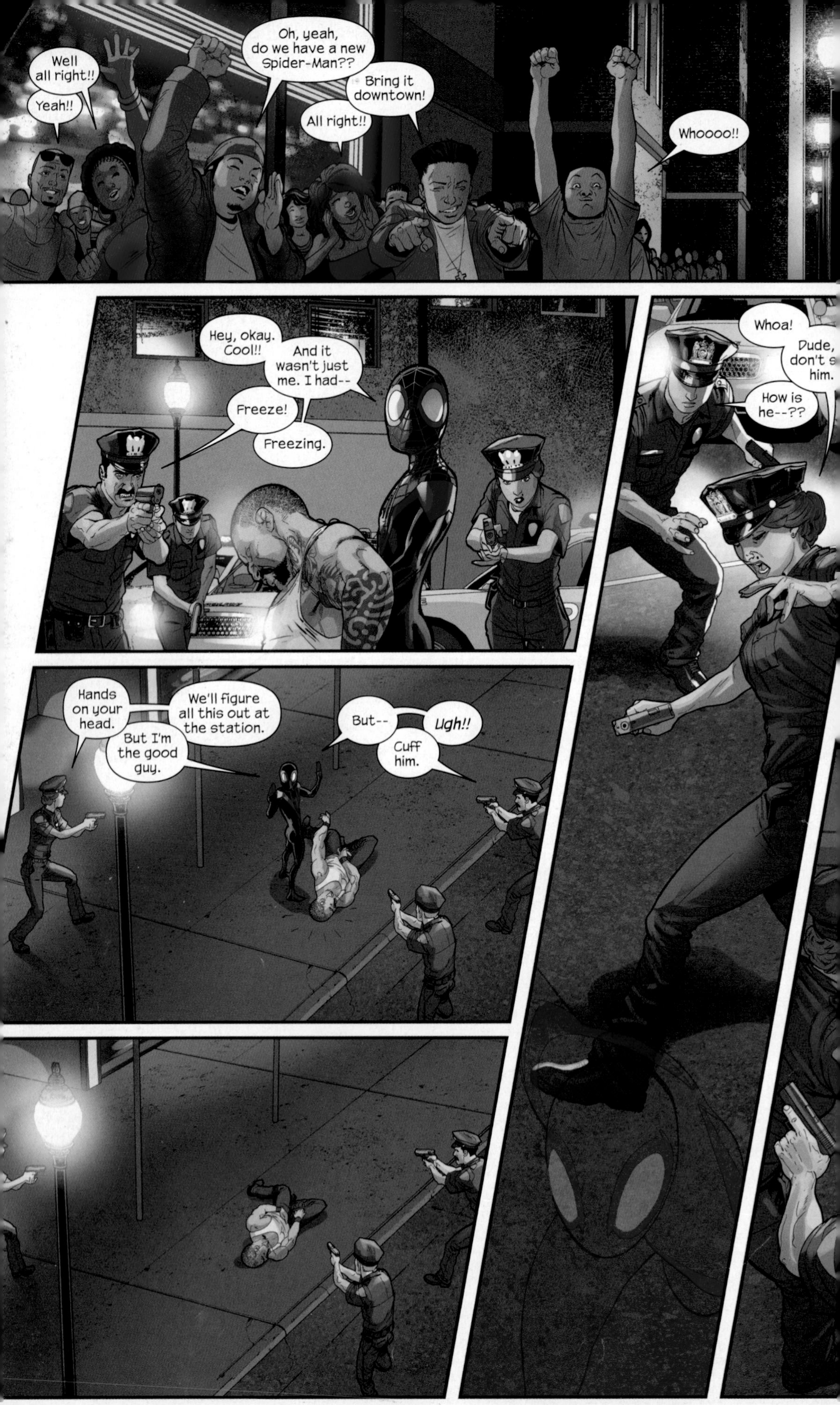
Well all right!!
Yeah!!
Oh, yeah, do we have a new Spider-Man??
All right!!
Bring it downtown!
Whoooo!!
Hey, okay. Cool!!
And it wasn't just me. I had--
Freeze!
Freezing.
Whoa!
How is he--??
Hands on your head.
We'll figure all this out at the station.
But I'm the good guy.
But--
Ugh!!
Cuff him.

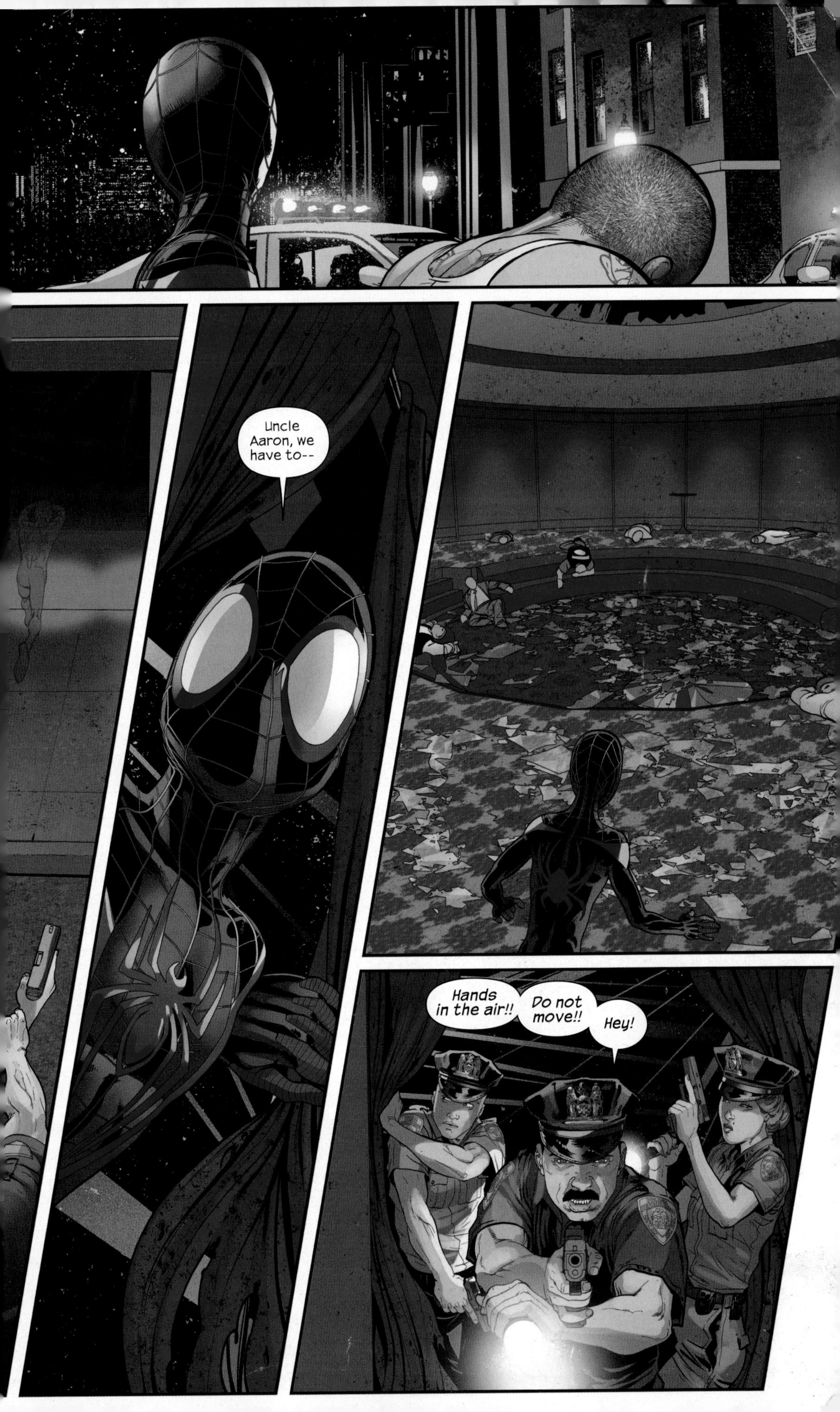
Uncle Aaron, we have to--
Hands in the air!!
Do not move!!
Hey!

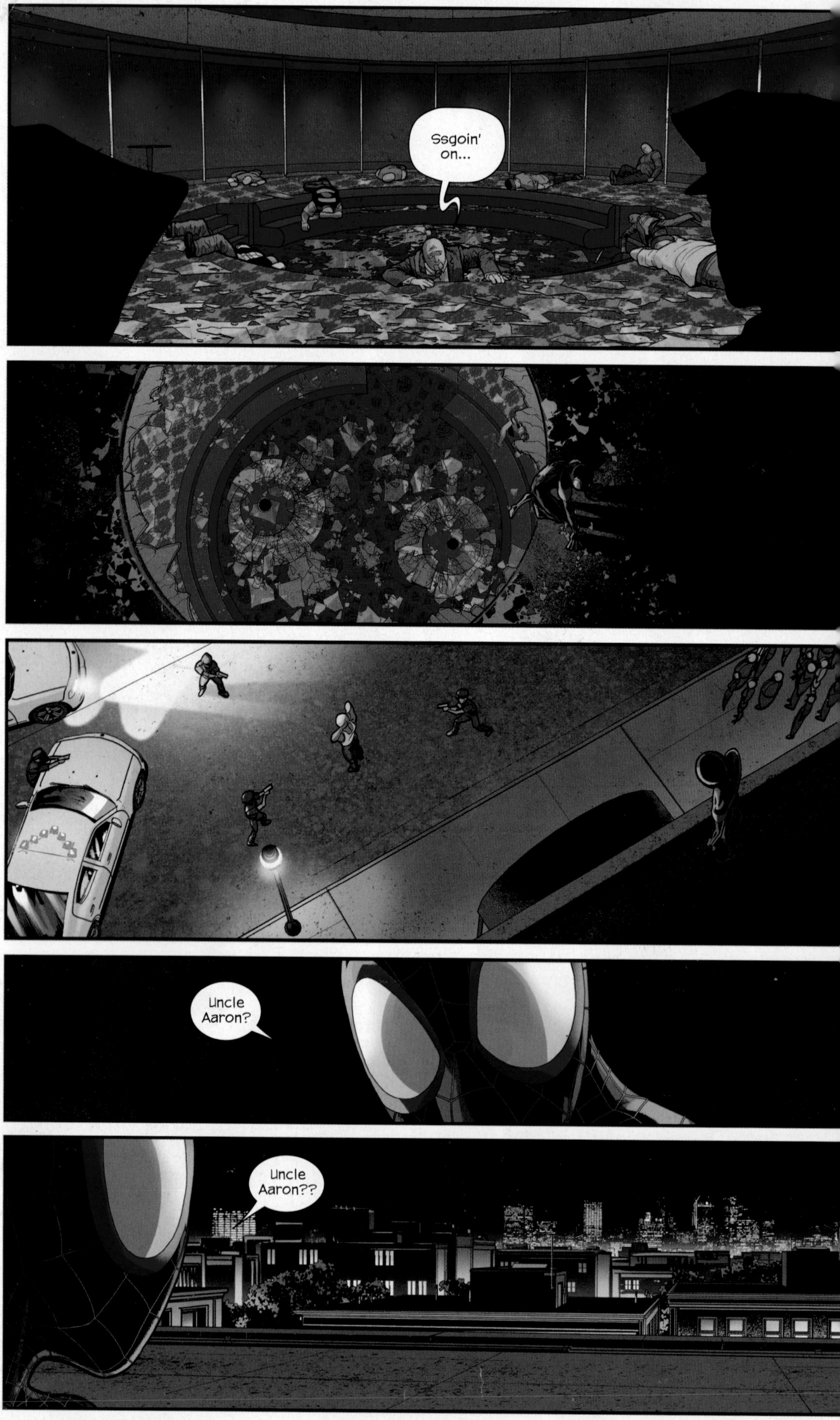
Ssgoin' on...
Uncle Aaron?
Uncle Aaron??

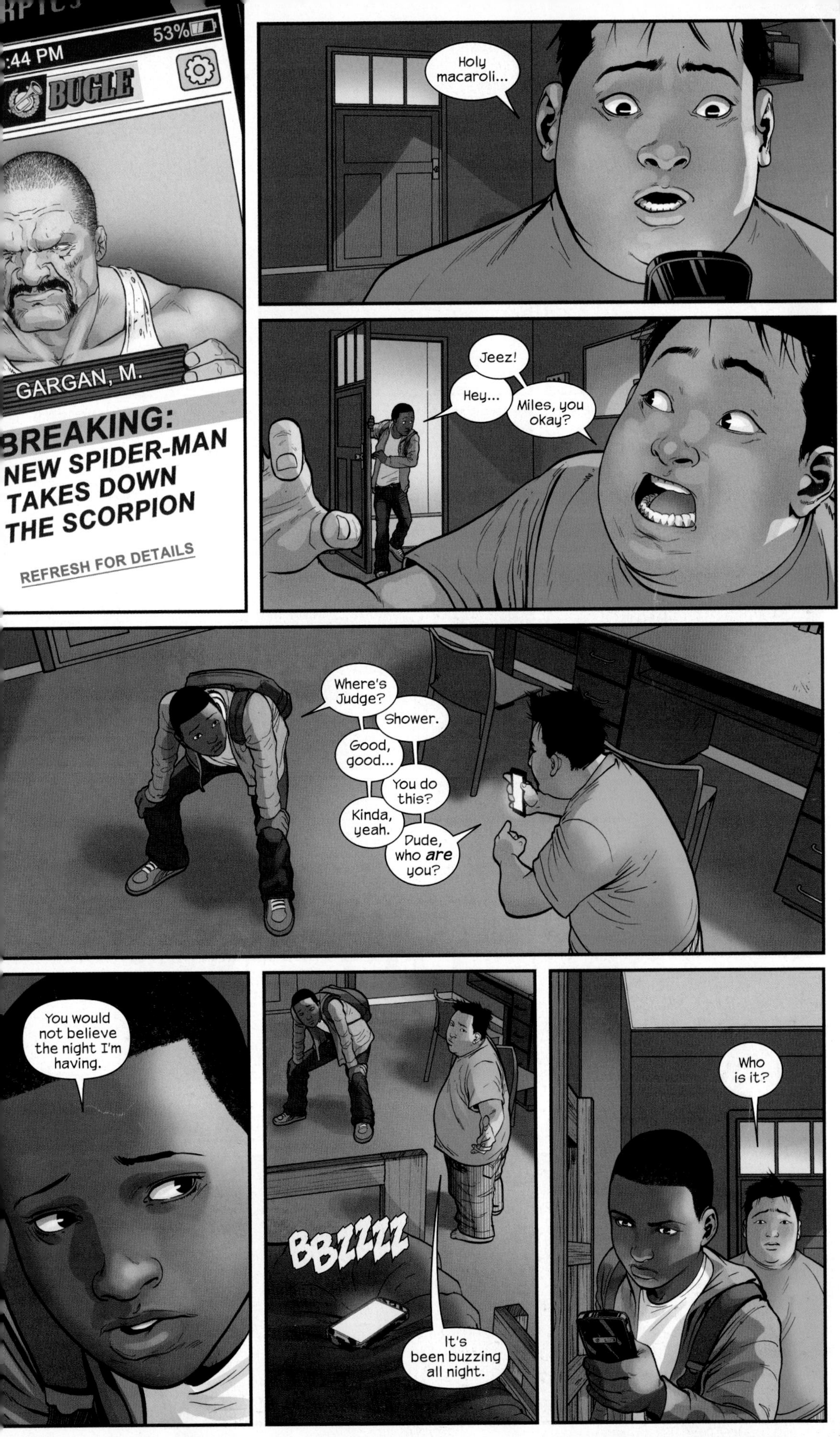
53%
:44 PM
BUGLE
GARGAN, M.
BREAKING:
NEW SPIDER-MAN TAKES DOWN THE SCORPION
REFRESH FOR DETAILS
Holy macaroli...
Jeez!
Hey...
Miles, you okay?
Where's Judge?
Shower.
Good, good...
You do this?
Kinda, yeah.
Dude, who *are* you?
You would not believe the night I'm having.
BBZZZZ
It's been buzzing all night.
Who is it?

UNCLE AARON
today, 8:15 pm

hey, little man. you in one piece?

SIR MILES
today, 9:47 pm

Where'd you go?

UNCLE AARON
today, 9:48 pm

Get some rest. We're just getting started.

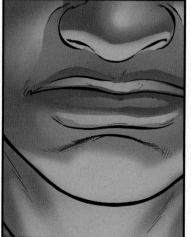

SIR MI
today,

no.

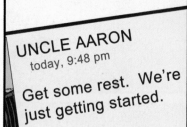

NCLE A
today, 9:49

no?

today,

no.

UNCLE AARON
today, 9:50 pm

Then maybe I should call you dad?

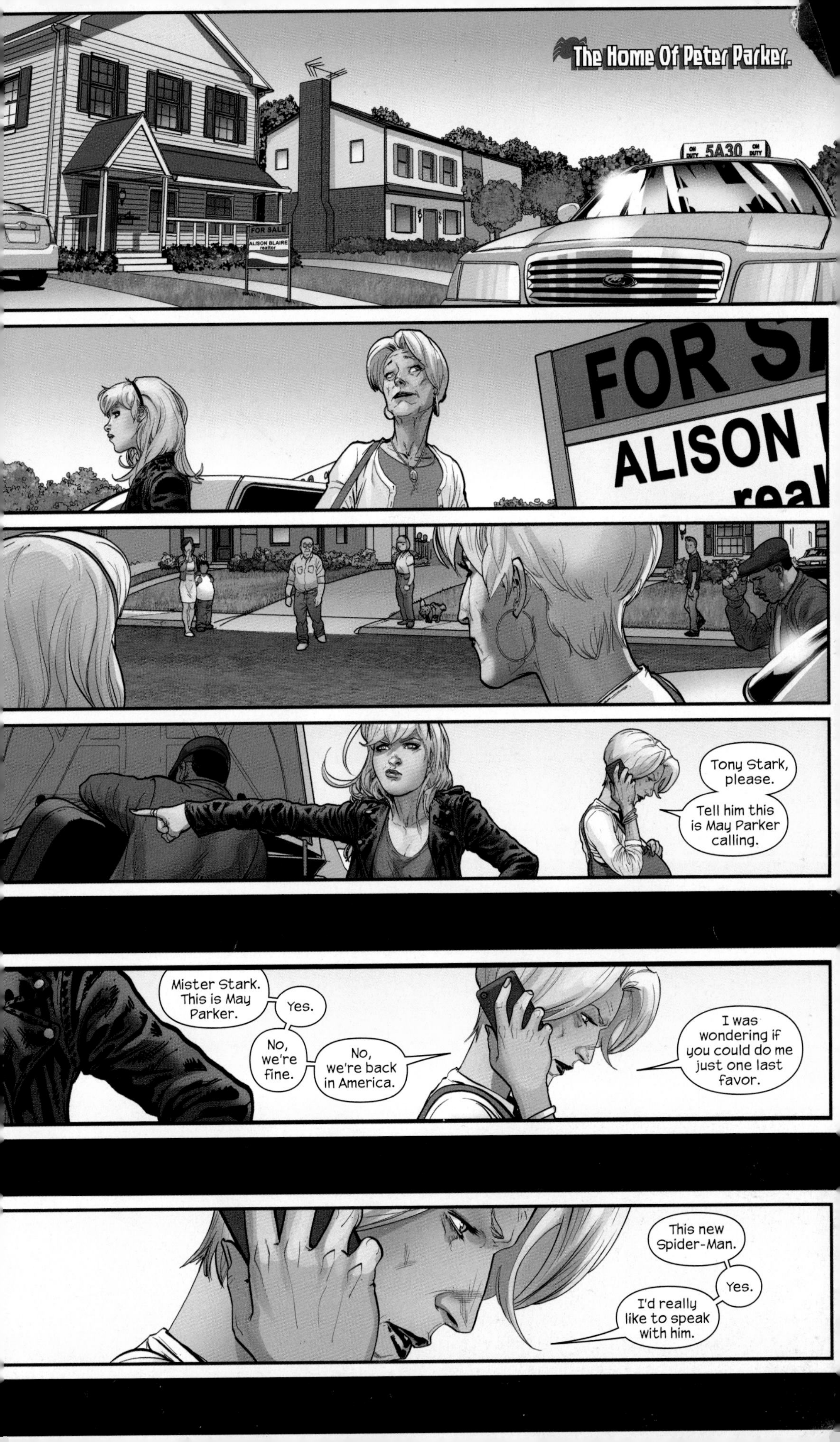
The Home Of Peter Parker.
5A30
FOR SALE
ALISON BLAIRE realtor
Tony Stark, please.
Tell him this is May Parker calling.
Mister Stark. This is May Parker.
Yes.
No, we're fine.
No, we're back in America.
I was wondering if you could do me just one last favor.
This new Spider-Man.
Yes.
I'd really like to speak with him.

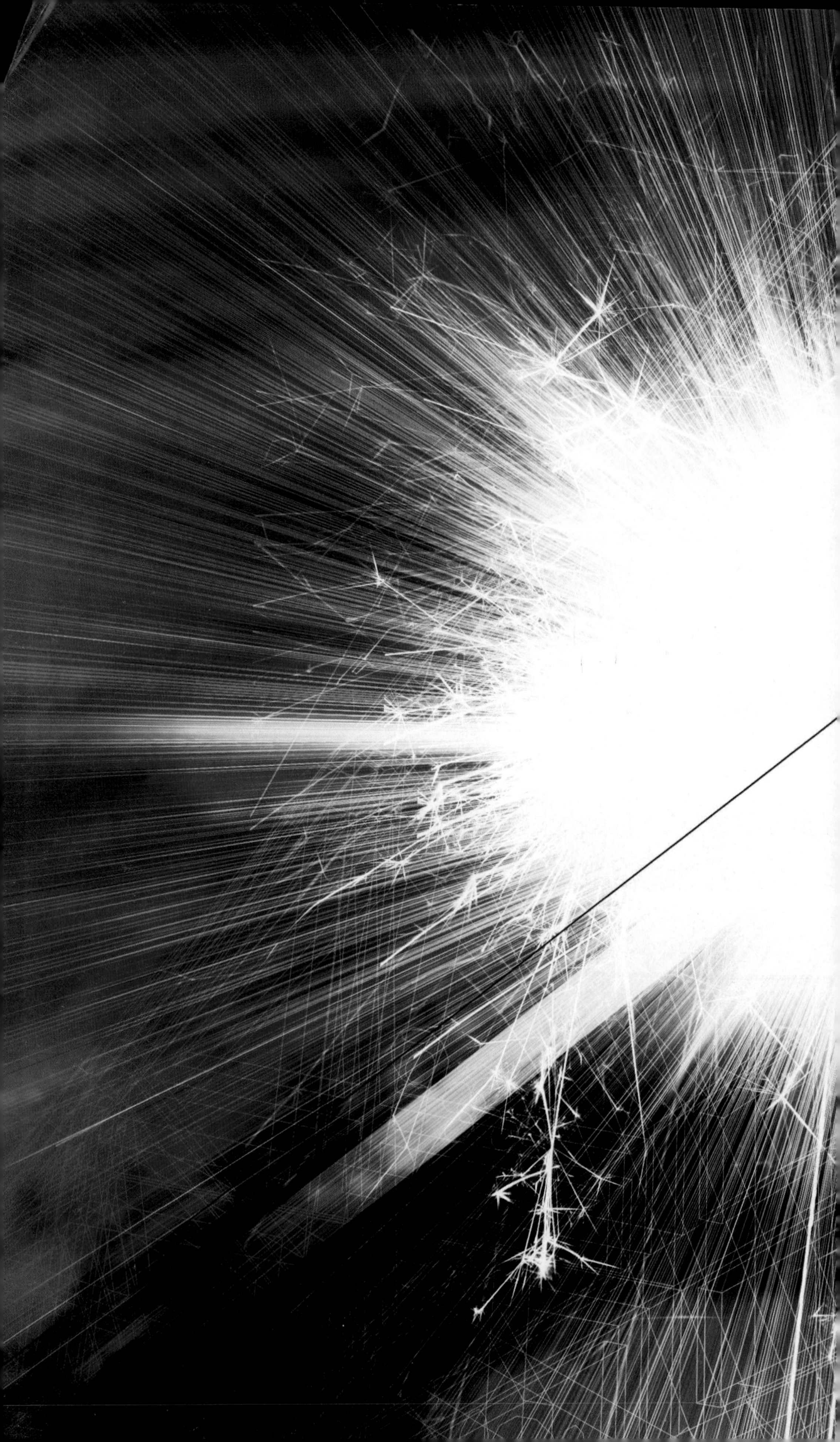

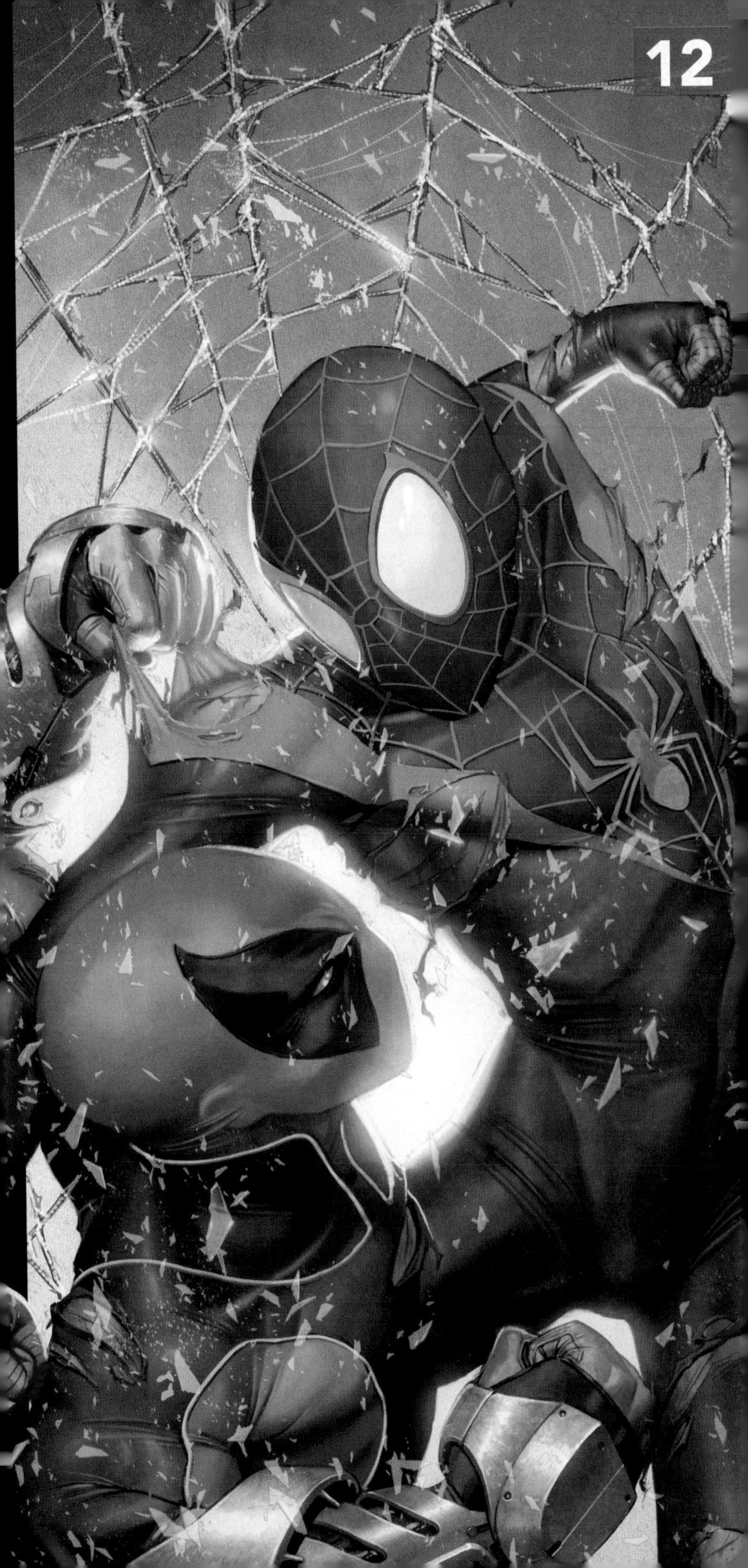
12

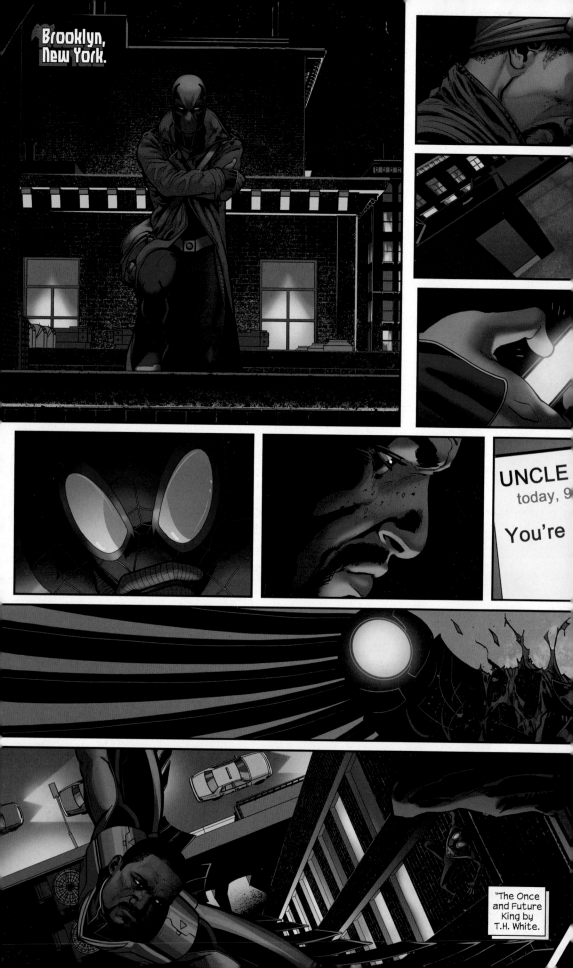

Brooklyn, New York.

UNCLE
today, 9

You're

"The Once and Future King by T.H. White.

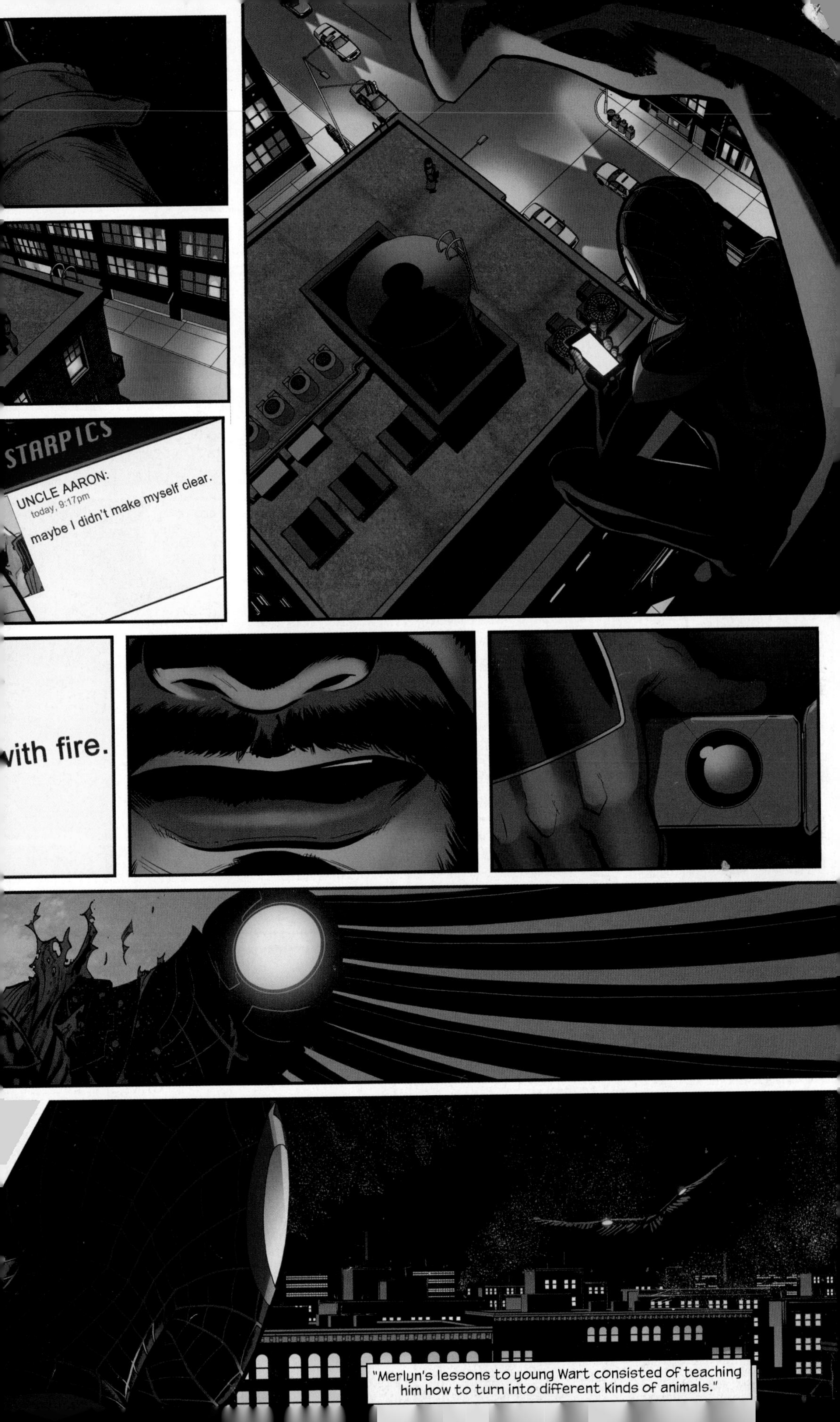
STARPICS
UNCLE AARON:
today, 9:17pm
maybe I didn't make myself clear.
vith fire.
"Merlyn's lessons to young Wart consisted of teaching him how to turn into different kinds of animals."

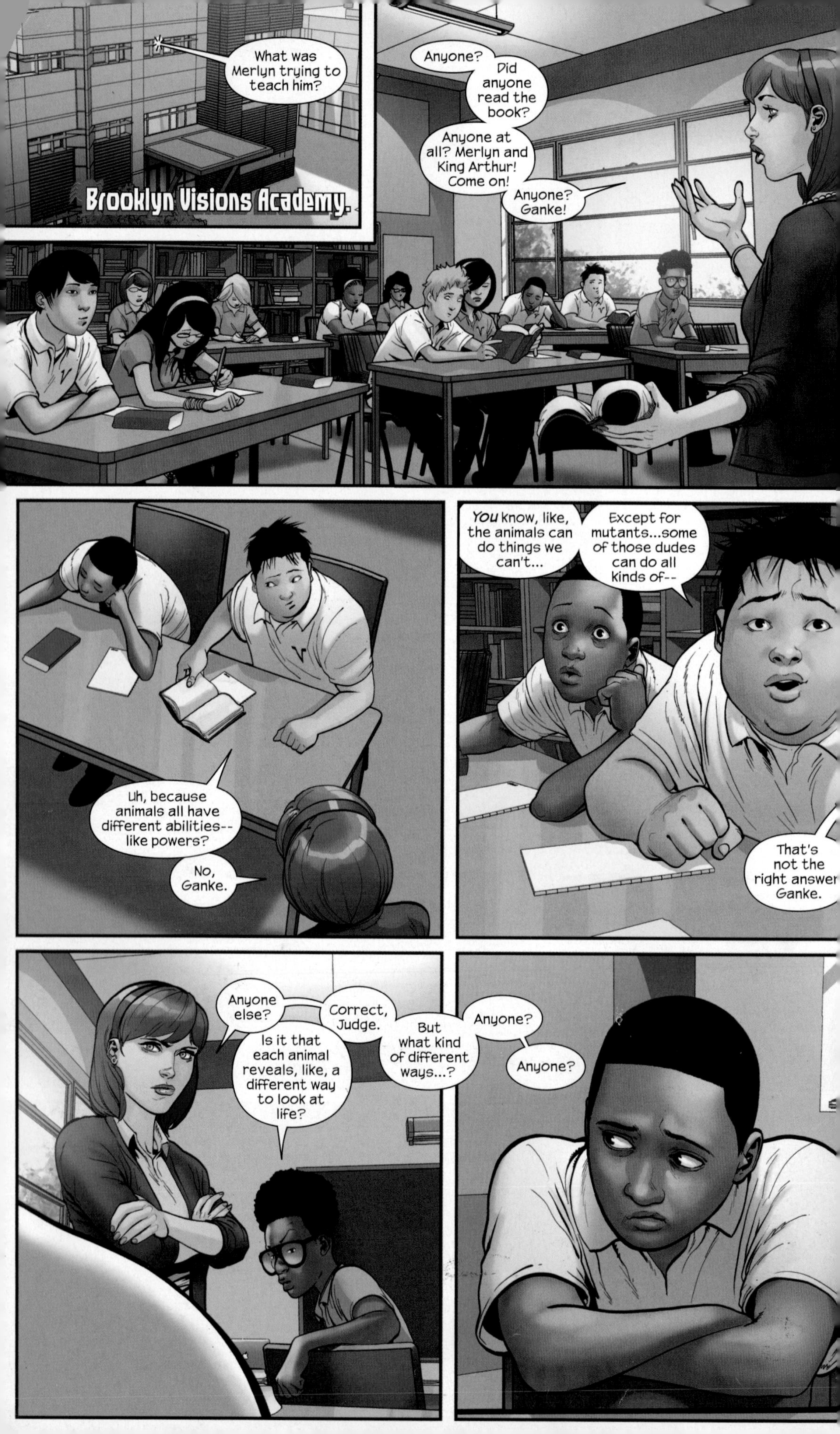
What was Merlyn trying to teach him?
Brooklyn Visions Academy.
Anyone?
Did anyone read the book?
Anyone at all? Merlyn and King Arthur! Come on!
Anyone? Ganke!
Uh, because animals all have different abilities-- like powers?
No, Ganke.
YOU know, like, the animals can do things we can't...
Except for mutants...some of those dudes can do all kinds of--
That's not the right answer Ganke.
Anyone else?
Is it that each animal reveals, like, a different way to look at life?
Correct, Judge.
But what kind of different ways...?
Anyone?
Anyone?

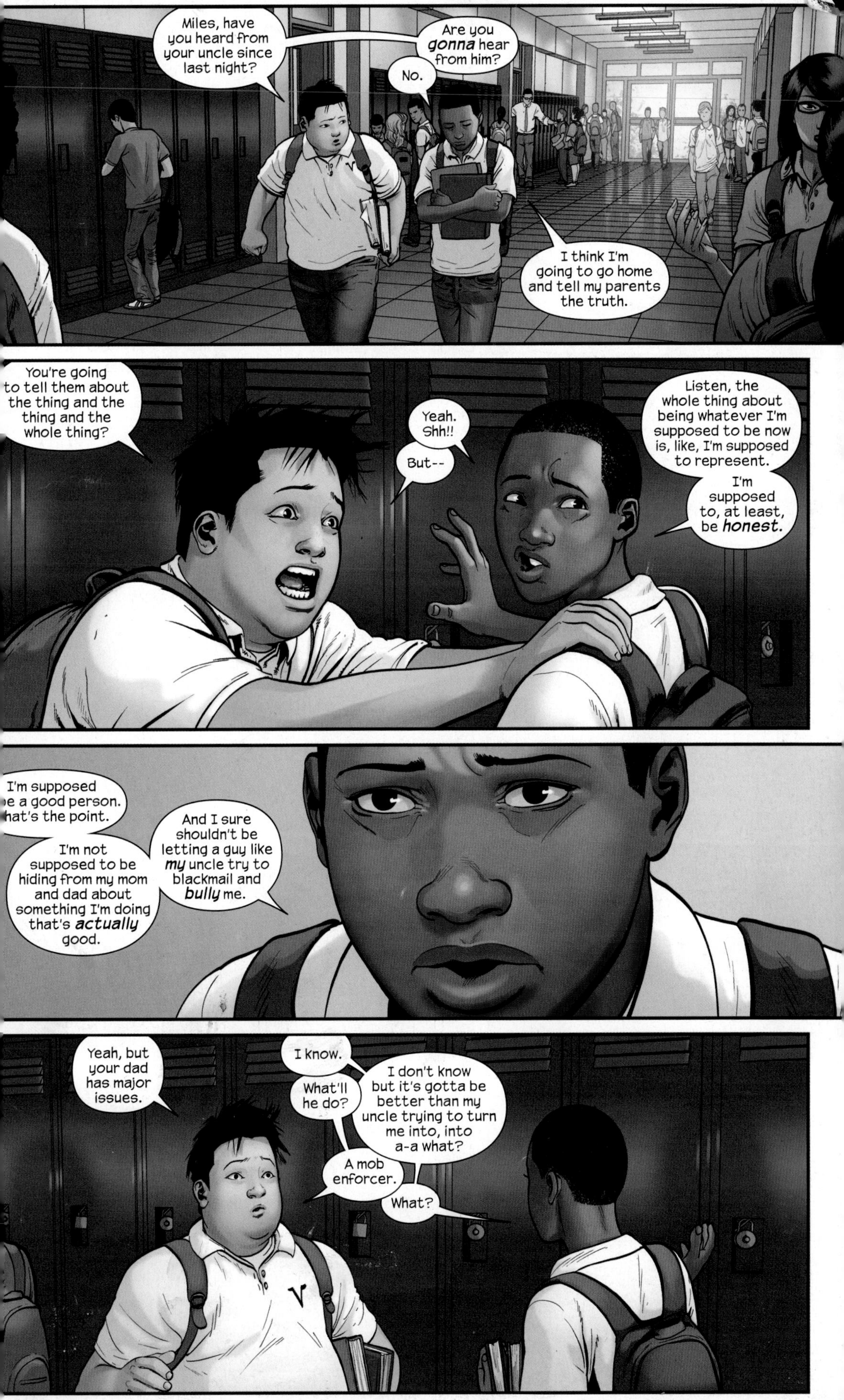
Miles, have you heard from your uncle since last night?
No.
Are you *gonna* hear from him?
I think I'm going to go home and tell my parents the truth.
You're going to tell them about the thing and the thing and the whole thing?
Yeah. Shh!!
But--
Listen, the whole thing about being whatever I'm supposed to be now is, like, I'm supposed to represent.
I'm supposed to, at least, be *honest*.
I'm supposed e a good person. hat's the point.
I'm not supposed to be hiding from my mom and dad about something I'm doing that's *actually* good.
And I sure shouldn't be letting a guy like *my* uncle try to blackmail and *bully* me.
Yeah, but your dad has major issues.
I know.
What'll he do?
I don't know but it's gotta be better than my uncle trying to turn me into, into a-a what?
A mob enforcer.
What?

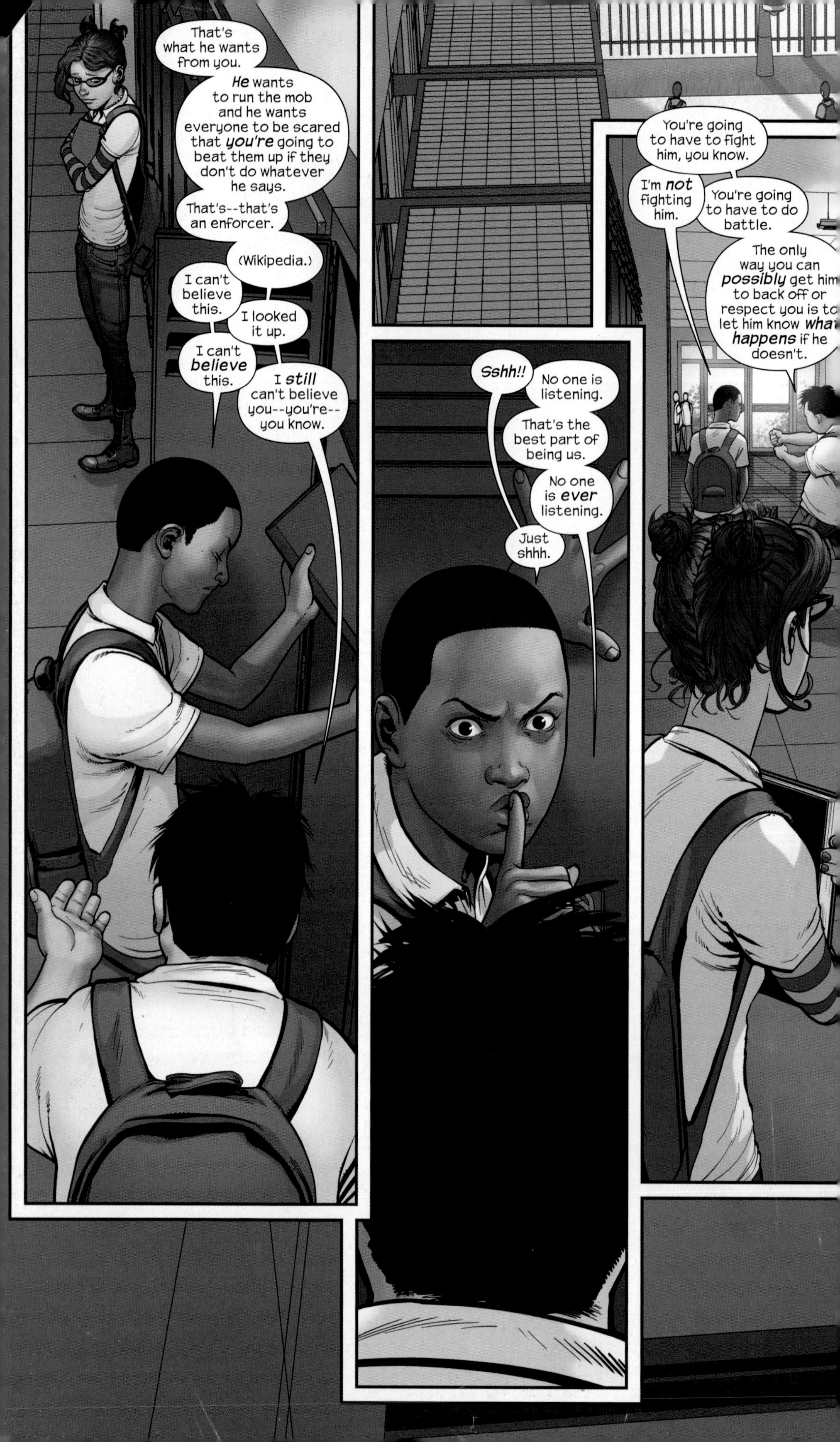
That's what he wants from you.
He wants to run the mob and he wants everyone to be scared that *you're* going to beat them up if they don't do whatever he says.
That's--that's an enforcer.
(Wikipedia.)
I can't believe this.
I looked it up.
I can't *believe* this.
I *still* can't believe you--you're--you know.
Sshh!!
No one is listening.
That's the best part of being us.
No one is *ever* listening.
Just shhh.
You're going to have to fight him, you know.
I'm *not* fighting him.
You're going to have to do battle.
The only way you can *possibly* get him to back off or respect you is to let him know *what happens* if he doesn't.

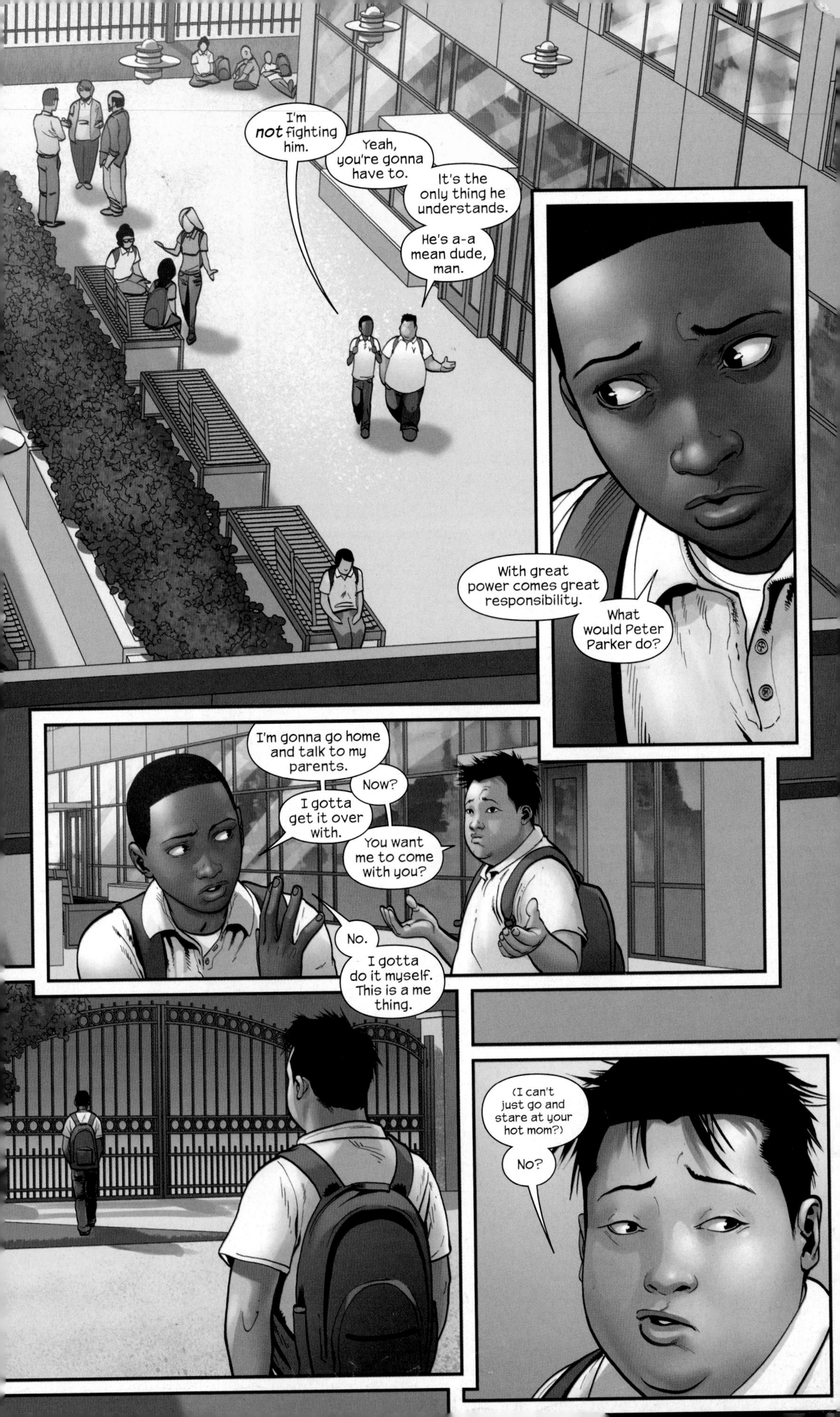
I'm *not* fighting him.
Yeah, you're gonna have to.
It's the only thing he understands.
He's a-a mean dude, man.
With great power comes great responsibility.
What would Peter Parker do?
I'm gonna go home and talk to my parents.
Now?
I gotta get it over with.
You want me to come with you?
No.
I gotta do it myself. This is a me thing.
(I can't just go and stare at your hot mom?)
No?

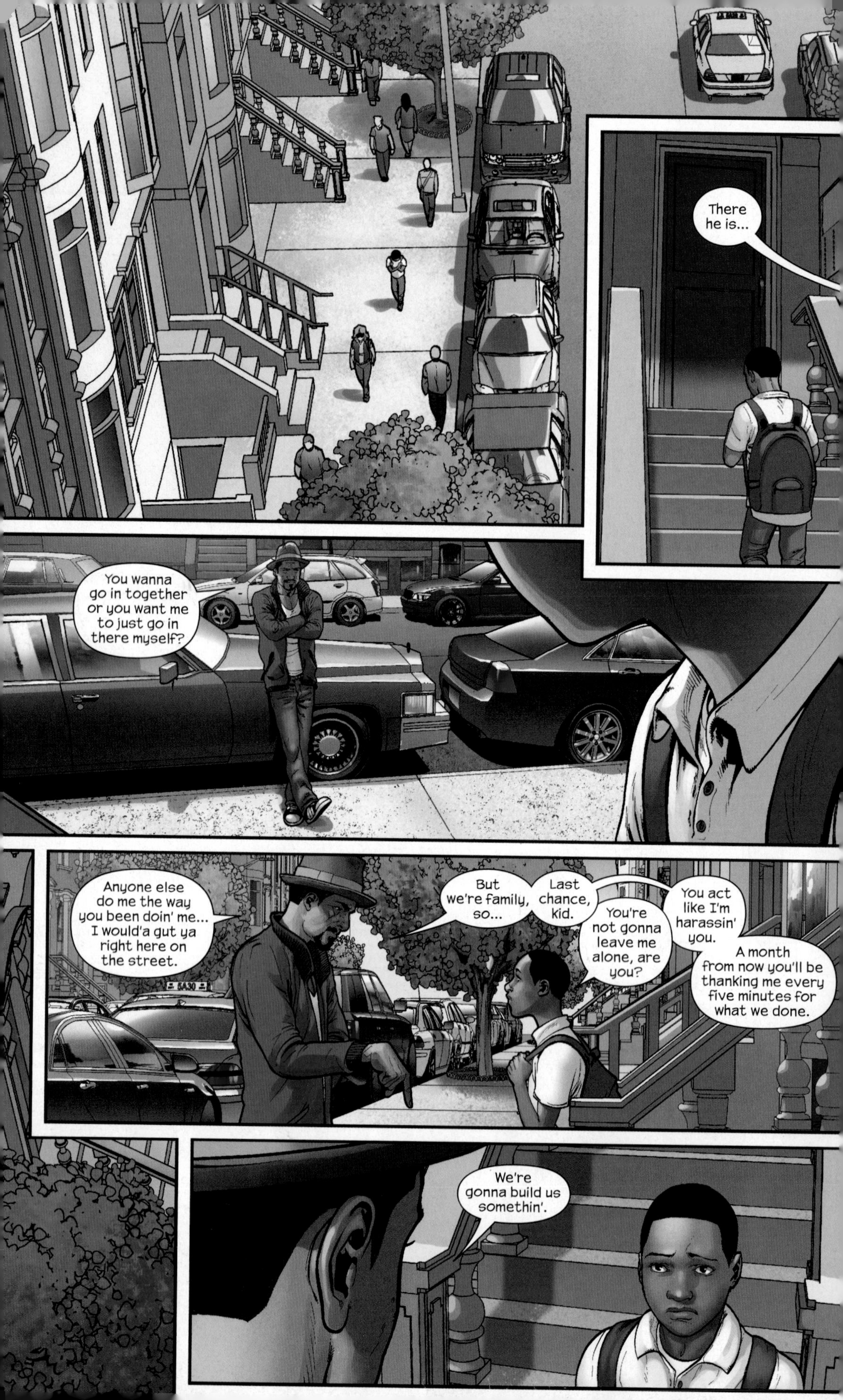
There he is...
You wanna go in together or you want me to just go in there myself?
Anyone else do me the way you been doin' me... I would'a gut ya right here on the street.
But we're family, so...
Last chance, kid.
You're not gonna leave me alone, are you?
You act like I'm harassin' you.
A month from now you'll be thanking me every five minutes for what we done.
We're gonna build us somethin'.

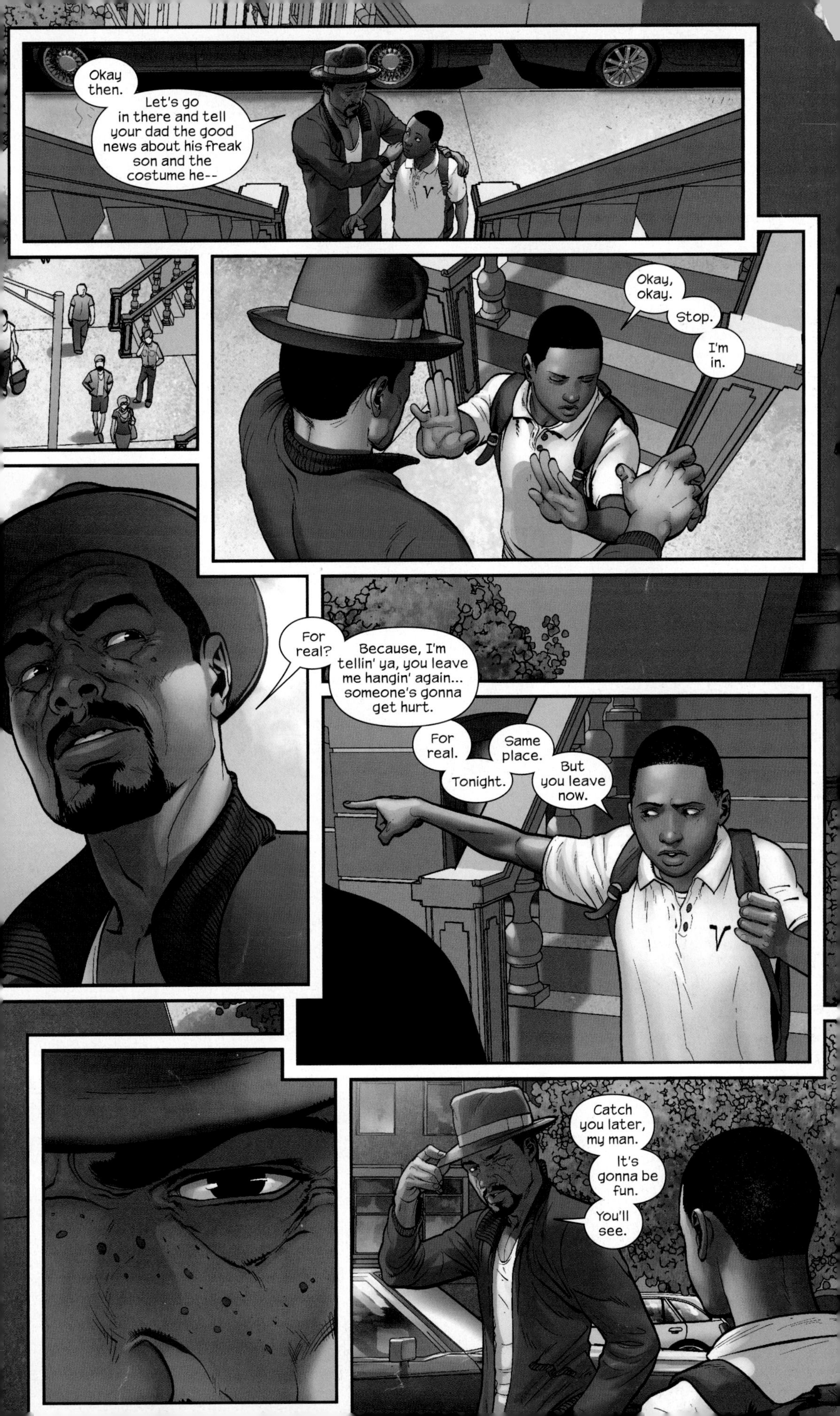
Okay then.
Let's go in there and tell your dad the good news about his freak son and the costume he--
Okay, okay.
Stop.
I'm in.
For real?
Because, I'm tellin' ya, you leave me hangin' again... someone's gonna get hurt.
For real.
Tonight.
Same place.
But you leave now.
Catch you later, my man.
It's gonna be fun.
You'll see.

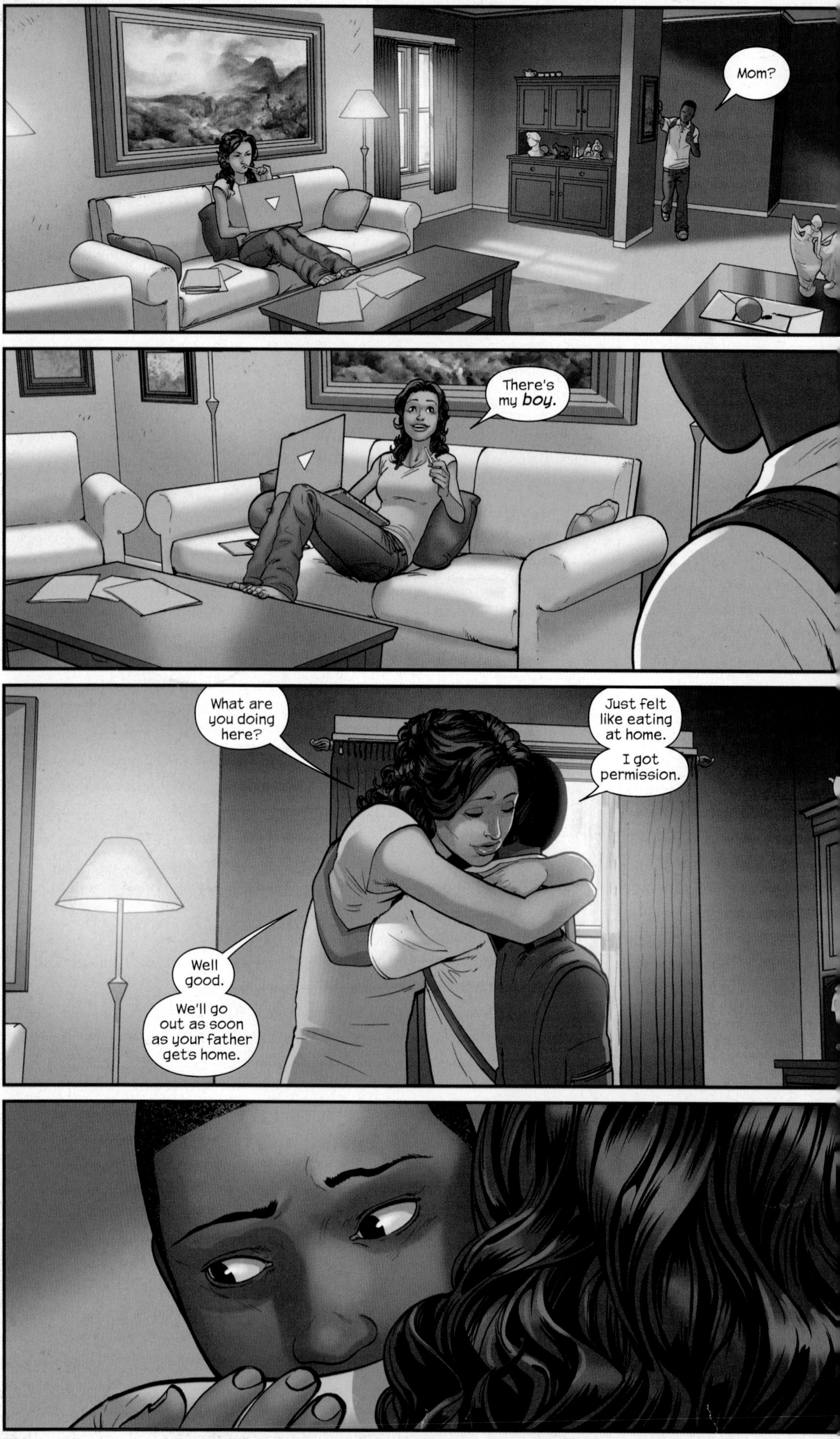
Mom?
There's my *boy.*
What are you doing here?
Just felt like eating at home.
I got permission.
Well good.
We'll go out as soon as your father gets home.

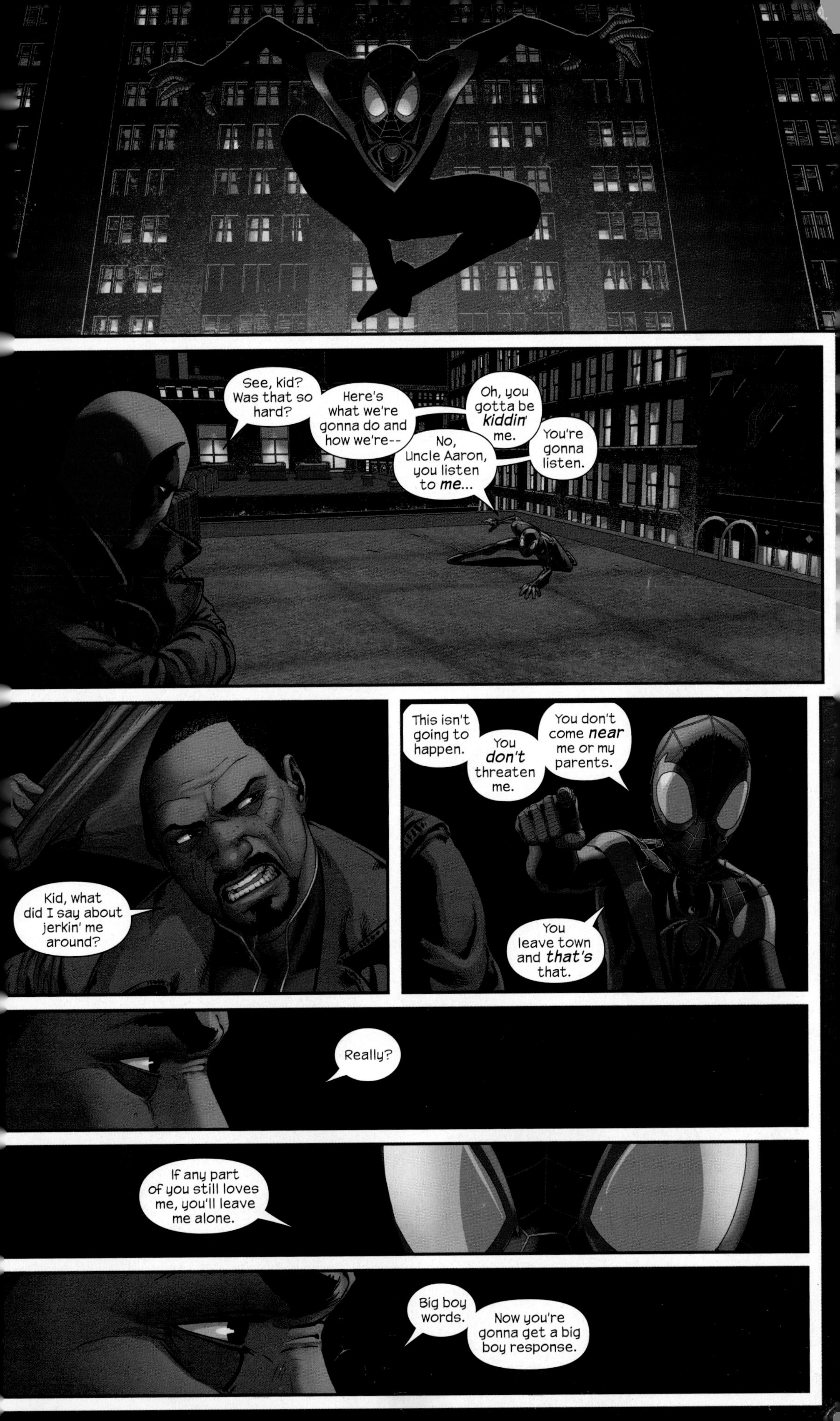
See, kid? Was that so hard?
Here's what we're gonna do and how we're--
Oh, you gotta be kiddin' me.
No, Uncle Aaron, you listen to me...
You're gonna listen.
Kid, what did I say about jerkin' me around?
This isn't going to happen.
You don't threaten me.
You don't come near me or my parents.
You leave town and that's that.
Really?
If any part of you still loves me, you'll leave me alone.
Big boy words.
Now you're gonna get a big boy response.

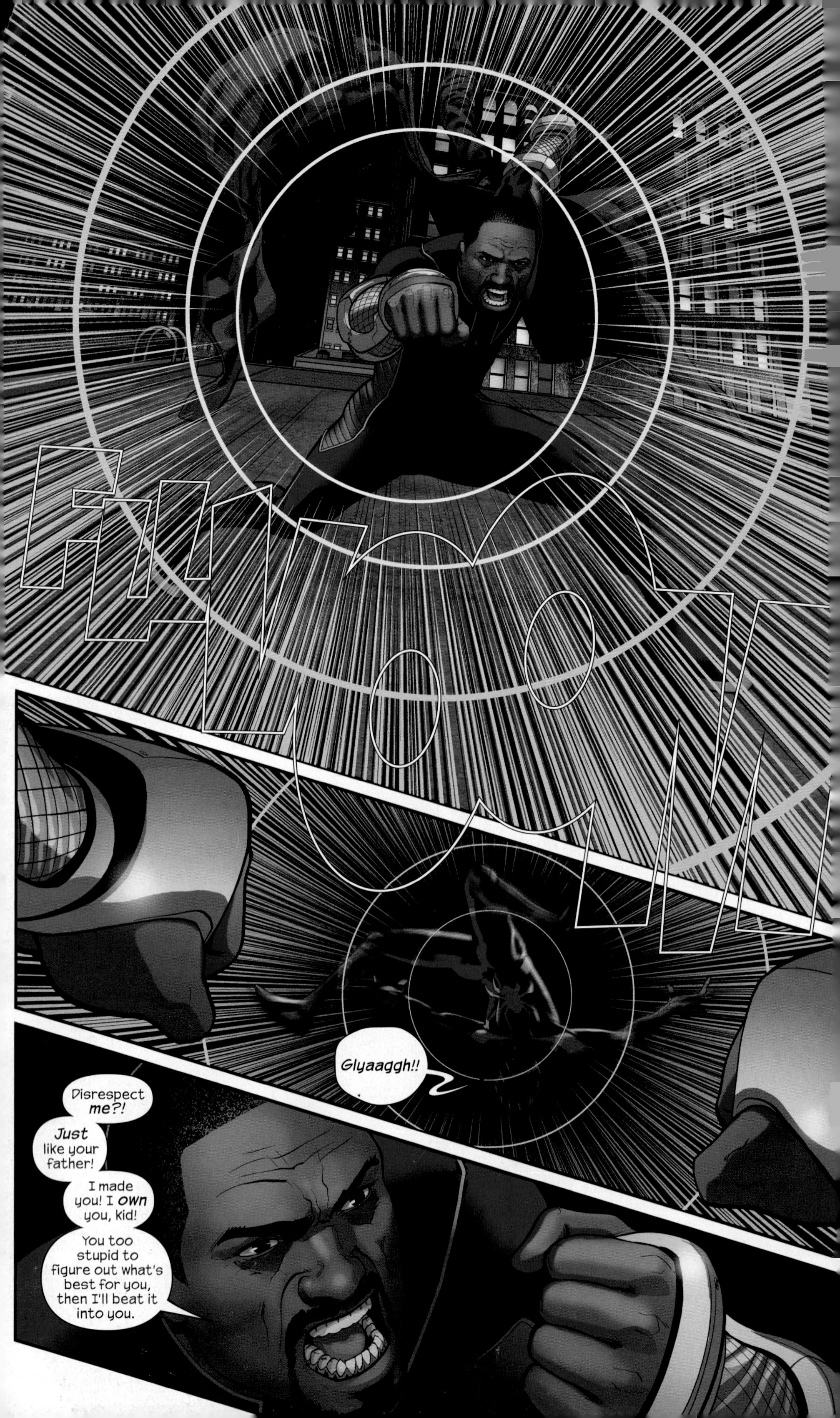
Glyaaggh!!
Disrespect *me*?!
Just like your father!
I made you! I *own* you, kid!
You too stupid to figure out what's best for you, then I'll beat it into you.

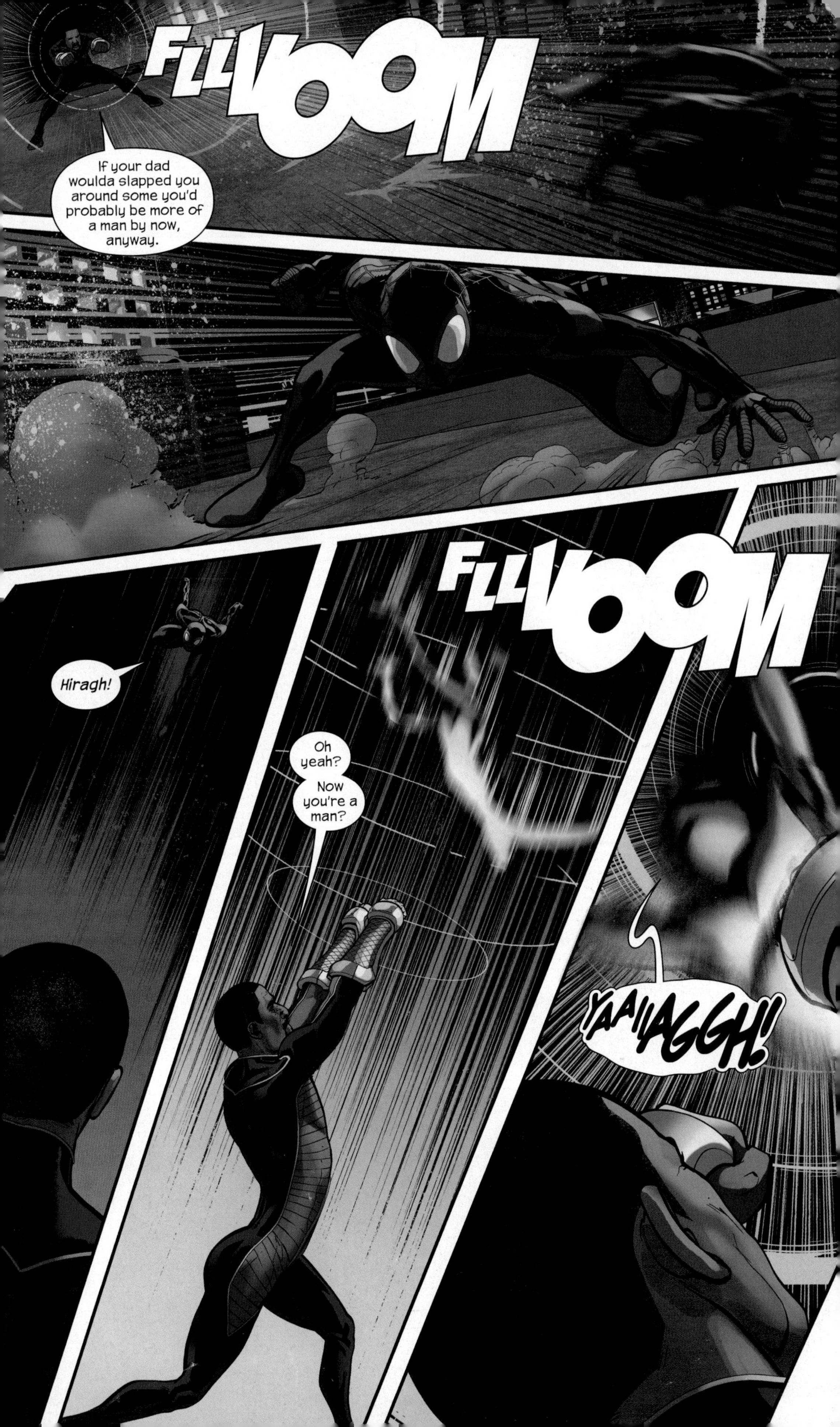
FLLVOOM
If your dad woulda slapped you around some you'd probably be more of a man by now, anyway.
Hiragh!
FLLVOOM
Oh yeah?
Now you're a man?
YAAAAGGH!

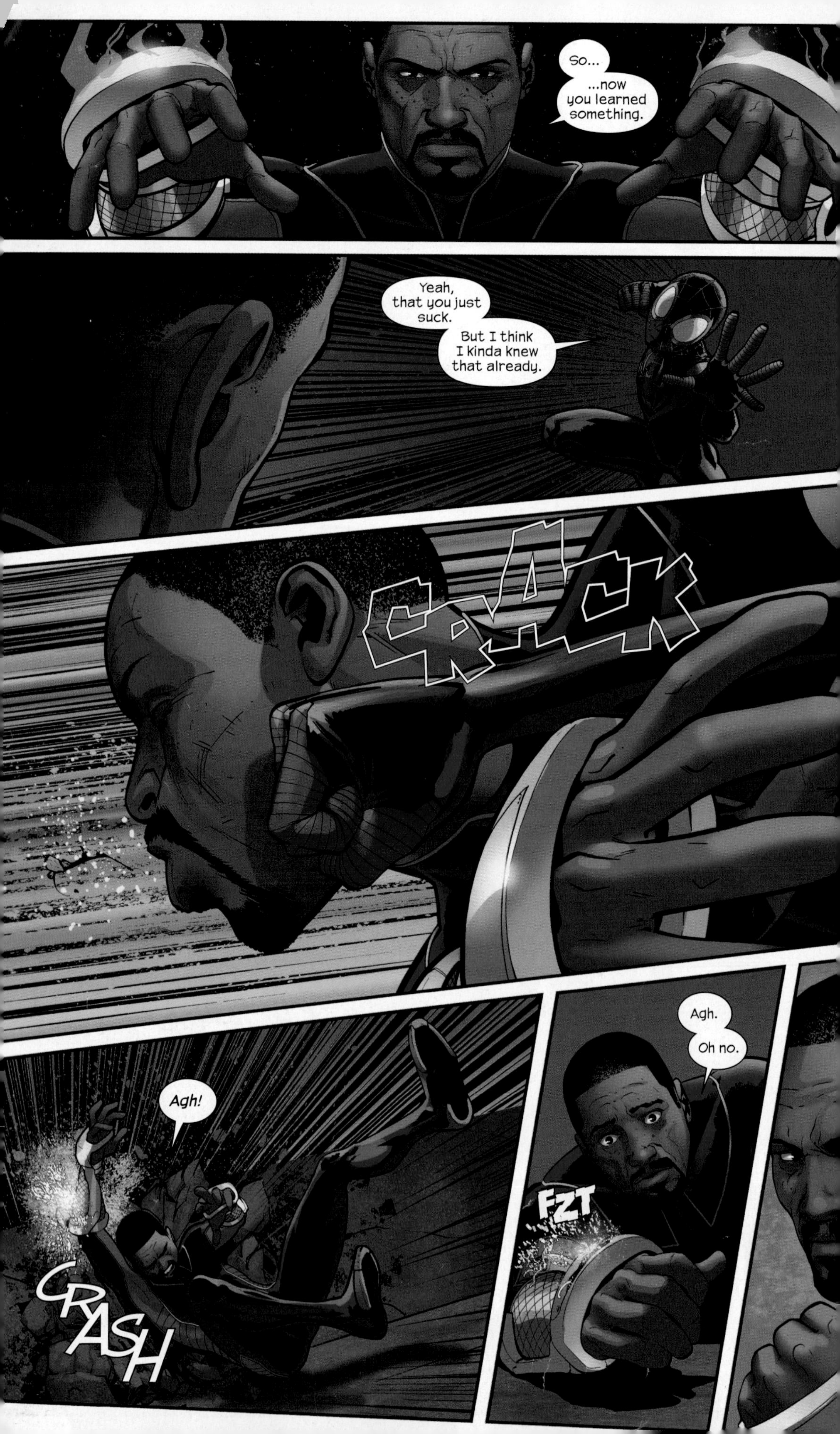
So...
...now you learned something.
Yeah, that you just suck.
But I think I kinda knew that already.
CRACK
Agh!
CRASH
Agh.
Oh no.
FZT

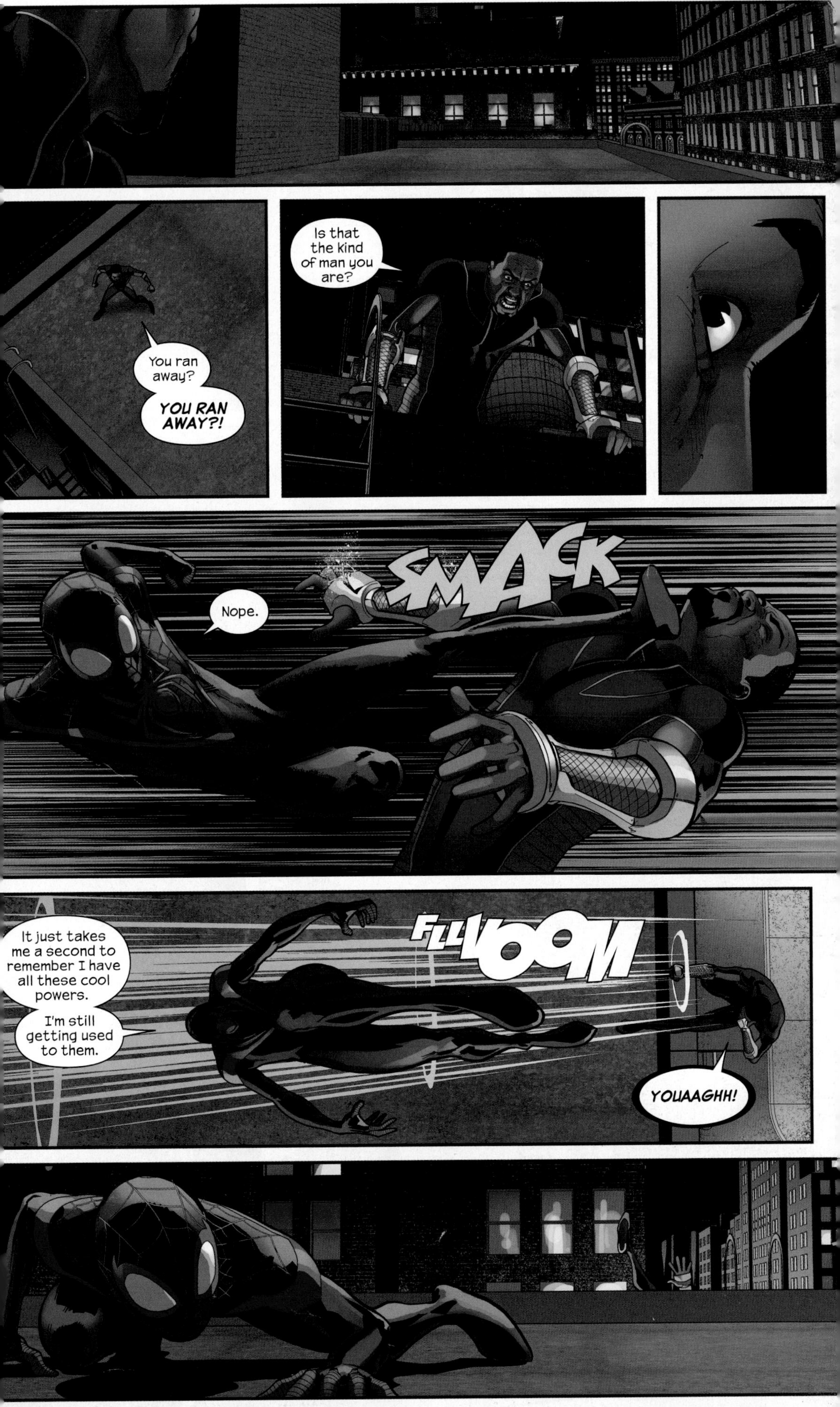
You ran away?
YOU RAN AWAY?!
Is that the kind of man you are?
Nope.
SMACK
It just takes me a second to remember I have all these cool powers.
I'm still getting used to them.
FLLUOOM
YOUAAGHH!

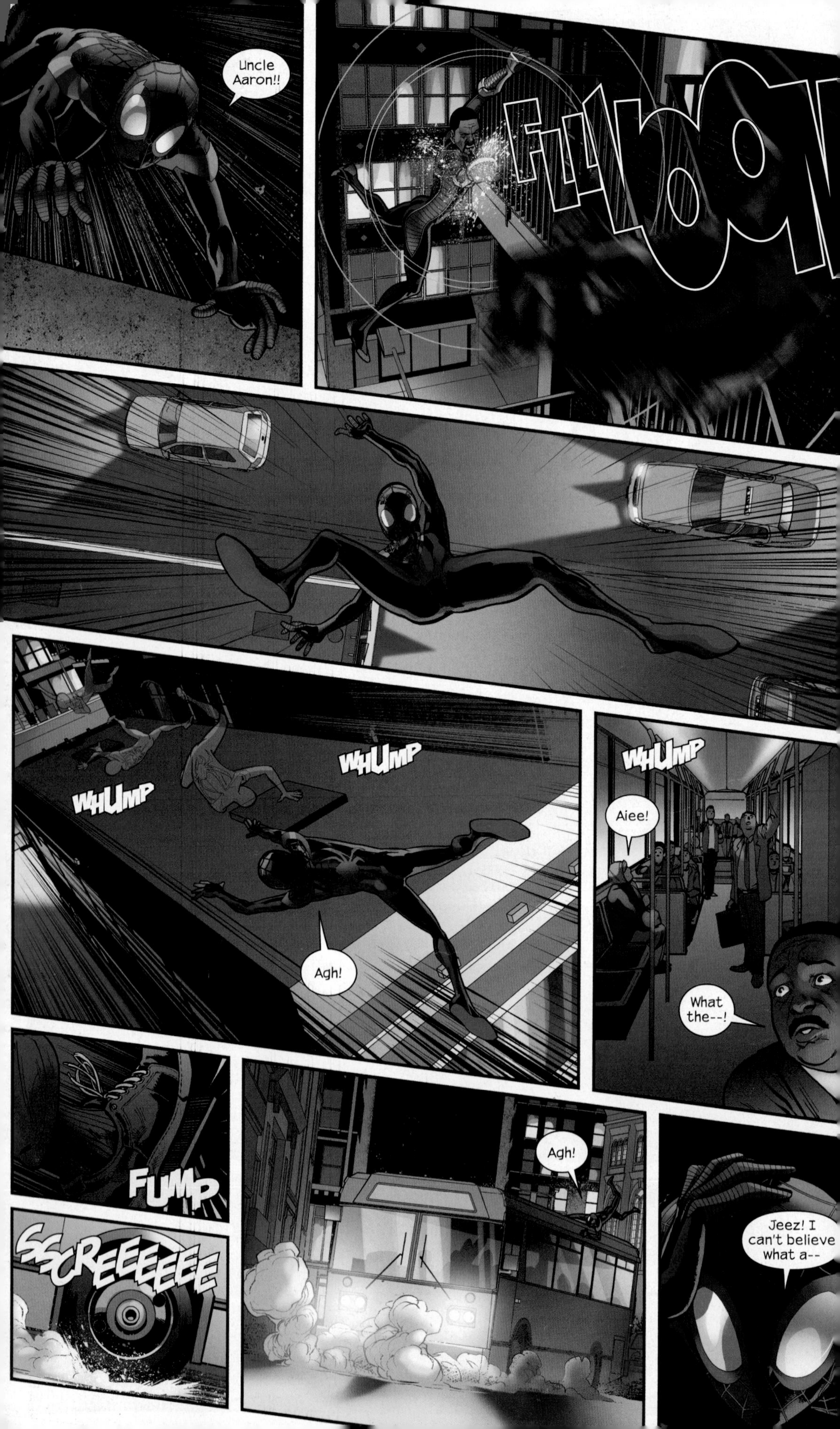
Uncle Aaron!!
FZZAKOOM
WHUMP
WHUMP
Agh!
WHUMP
Aiee!
What the--!
FUMP
SSCREEEEEEE
Agh!
Jeez! I can't believe what a--

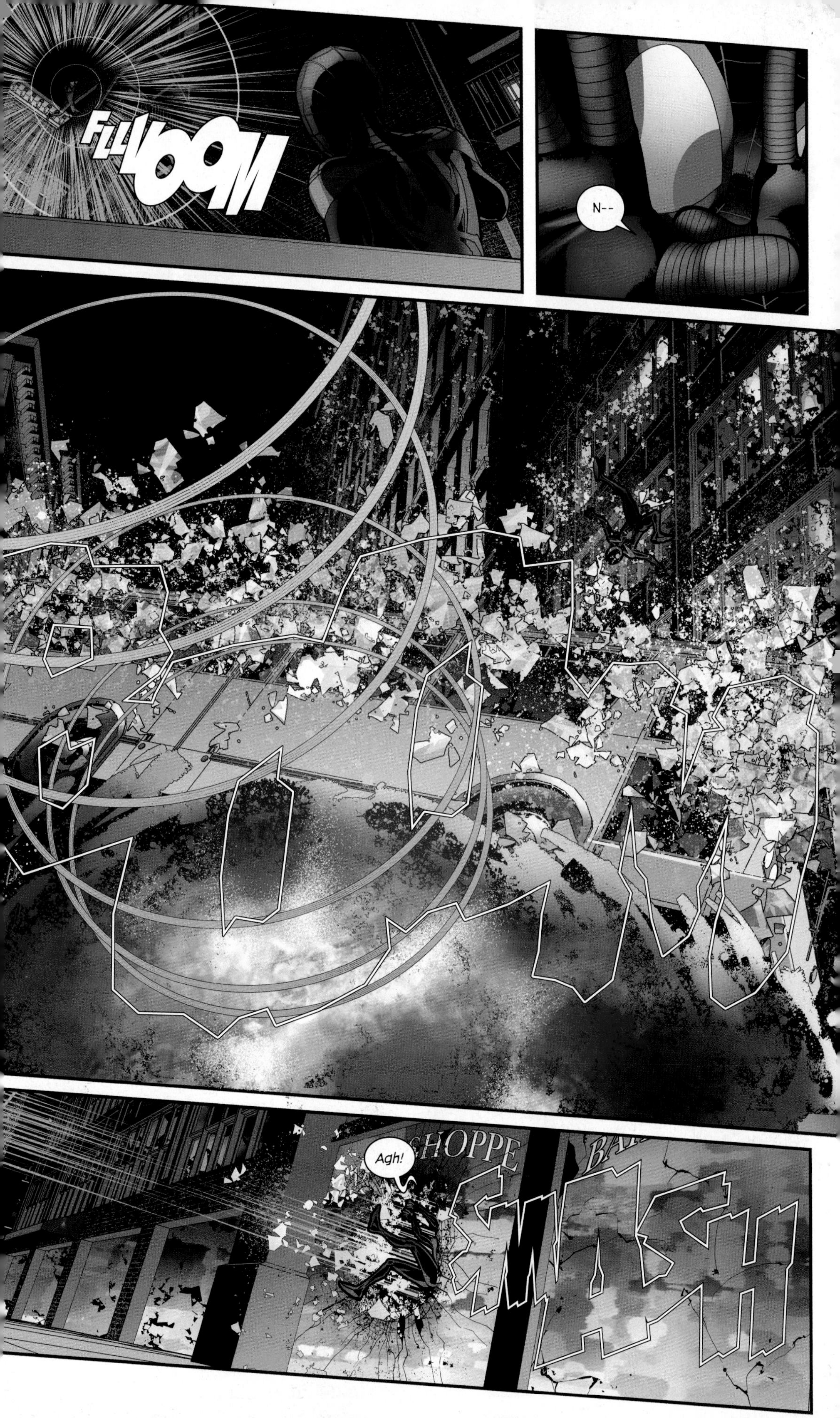
FLLLOOOM
N--
Agh!
SHOPPE
SMASH

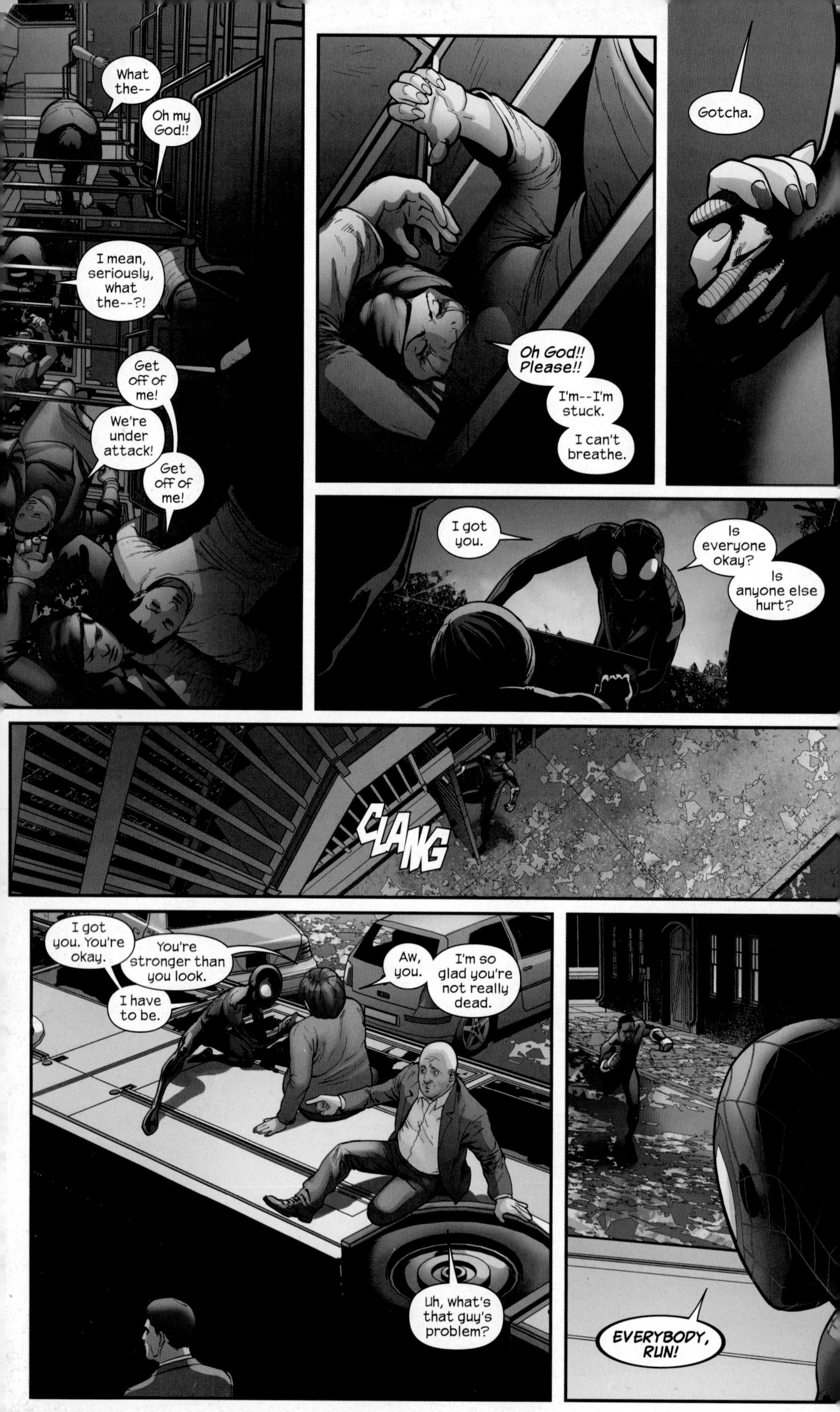
What the--
Oh my God!!
I mean, seriously, what the--?!
Get off of me!
We're under attack!
Get off of me!
Oh God!! Please!!
I'm--I'm stuck.
I can't breathe.
Gotcha.
I got you.
Is everyone okay?
Is anyone else hurt?
CLANG
I got you. You're okay.
You're stronger than you look.
I have to be.
Aw, you.
I'm so glad you're not really dead.
Uh, what's that guy's problem?
EVERYBODY, RUN!

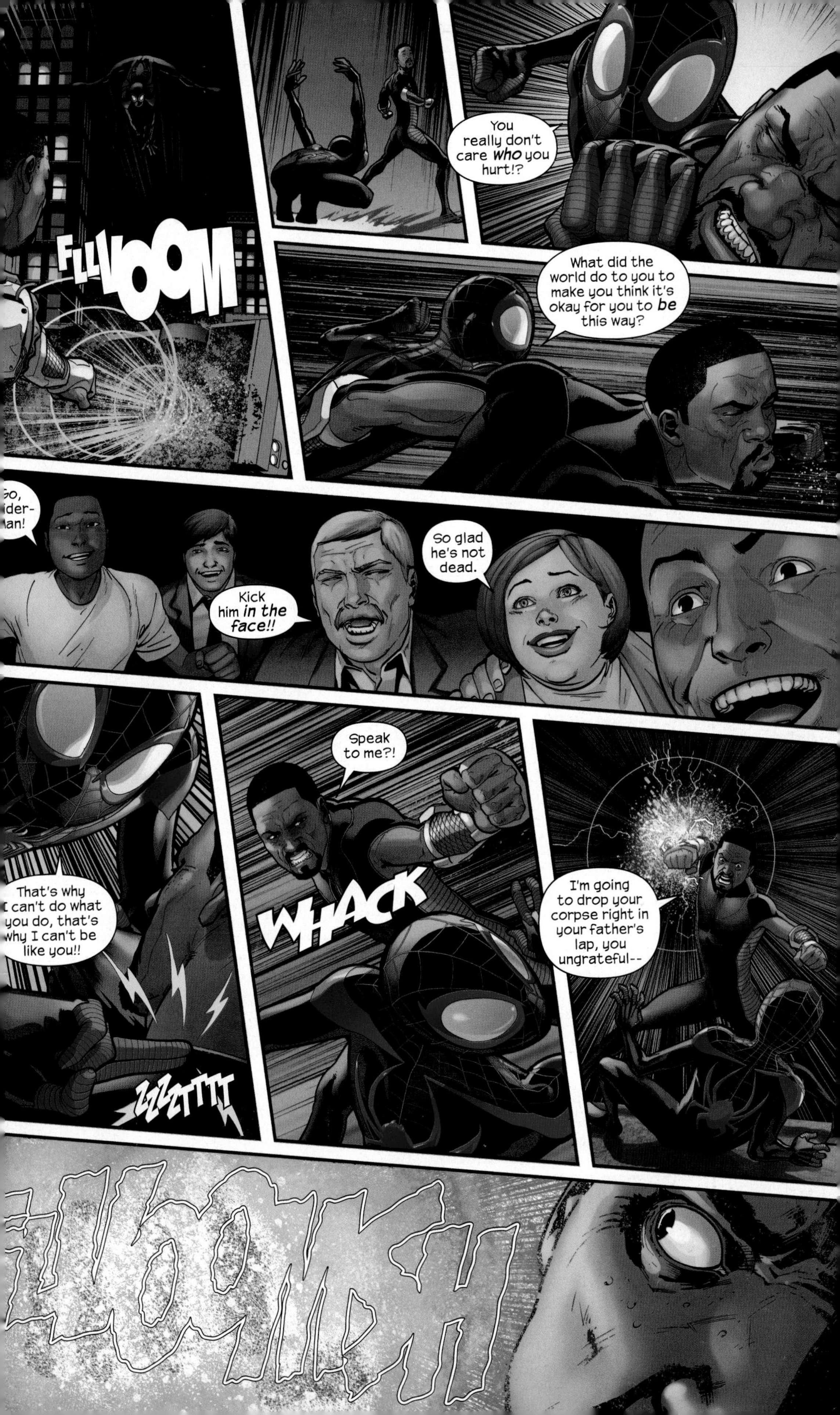
FLLVOOM
You really don't care *who* you hurt!?
What did the world do to you to make you think it's okay for you to *be* this way?
Go, Spider-Man!
Kick him *in the face!!*
So glad he's not dead.
That's why I can't do what you do, that's why I can't be like you!!
ZZZZTTTT
Speak to me?!
WHACK
I'm going to drop your corpse right in your father's lap, you ungrateful--

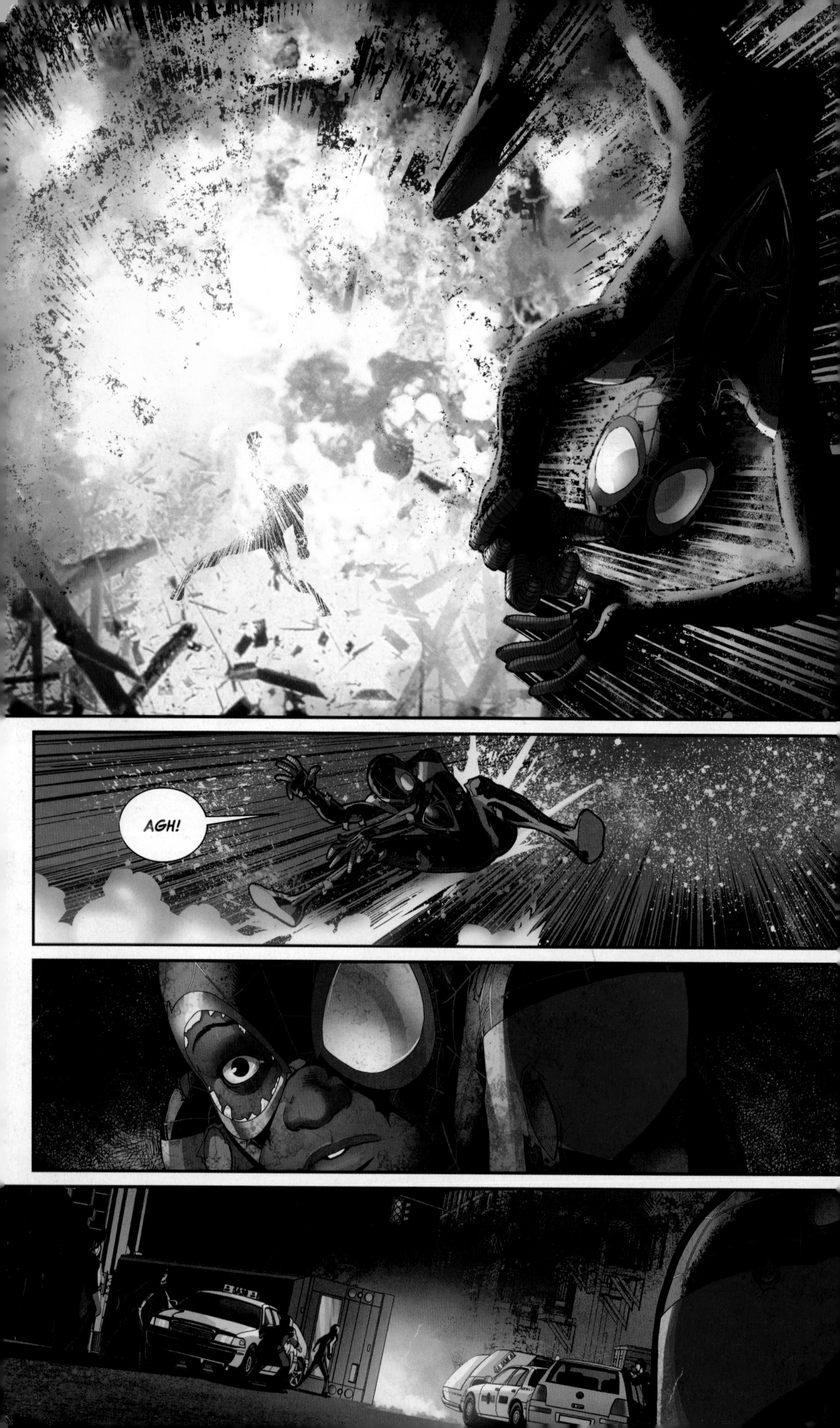
AGH!

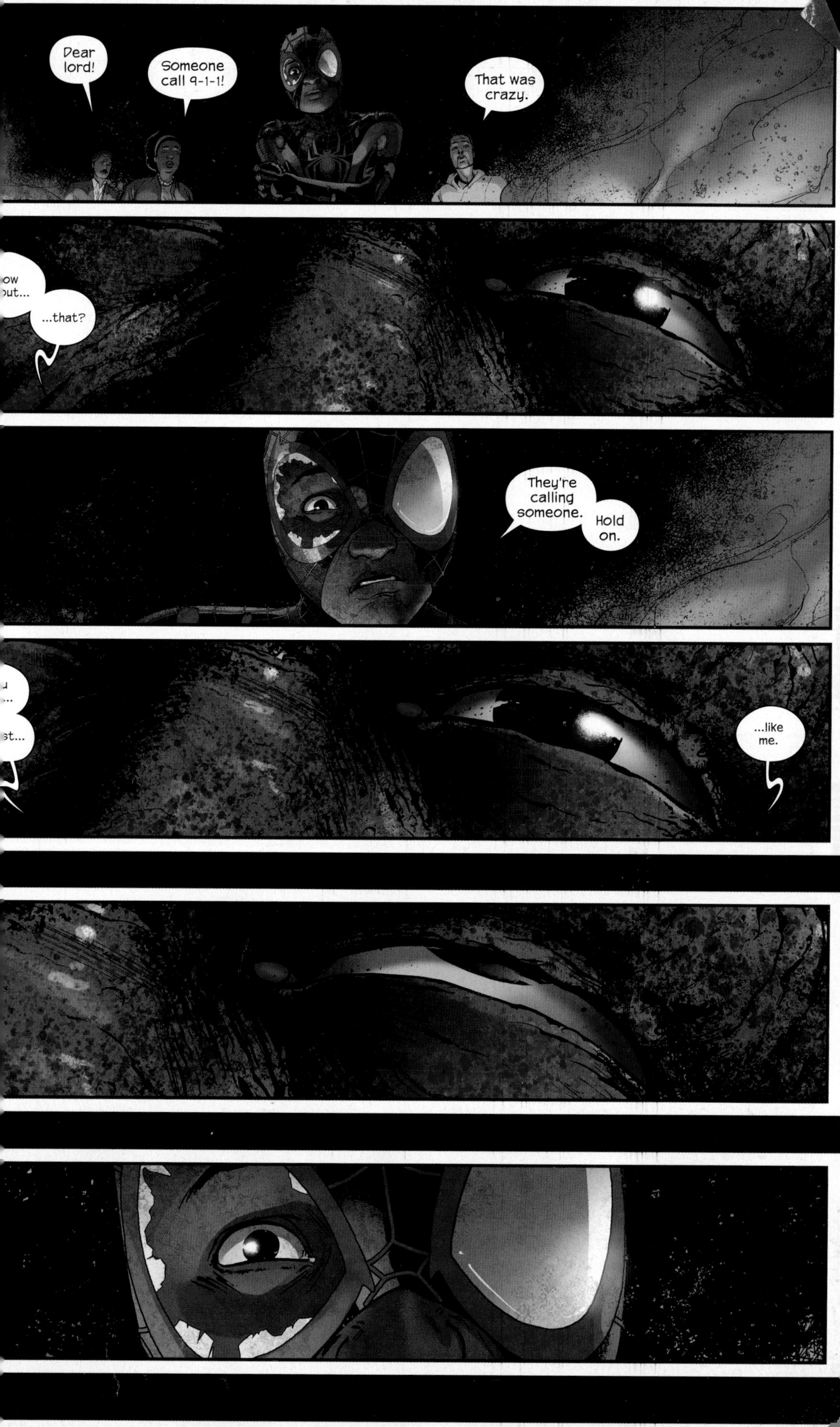
Dear lord!
Someone call 9-1-1!
That was crazy.
...that?
They're calling someone.
Hold on.
...like me.

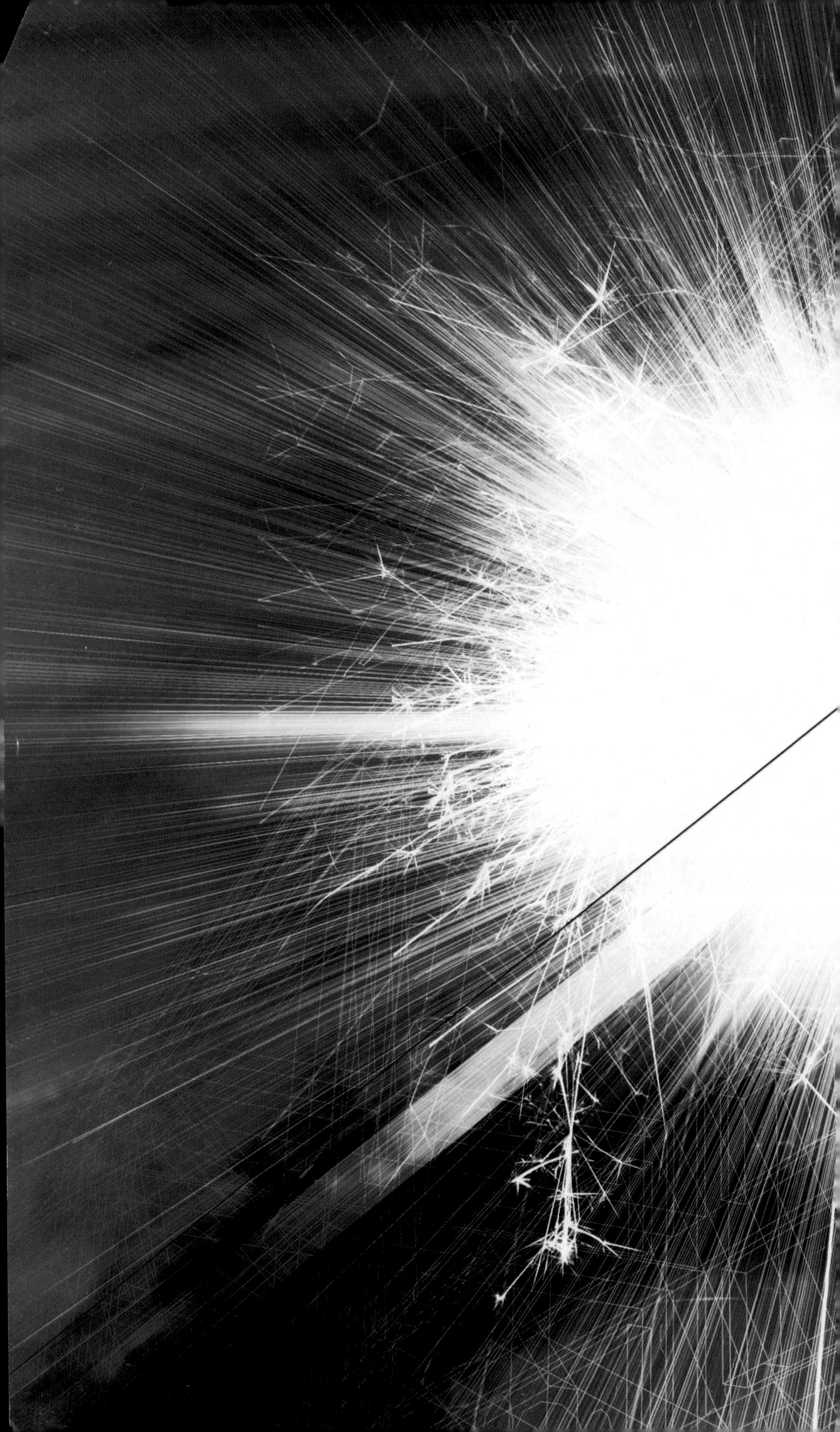

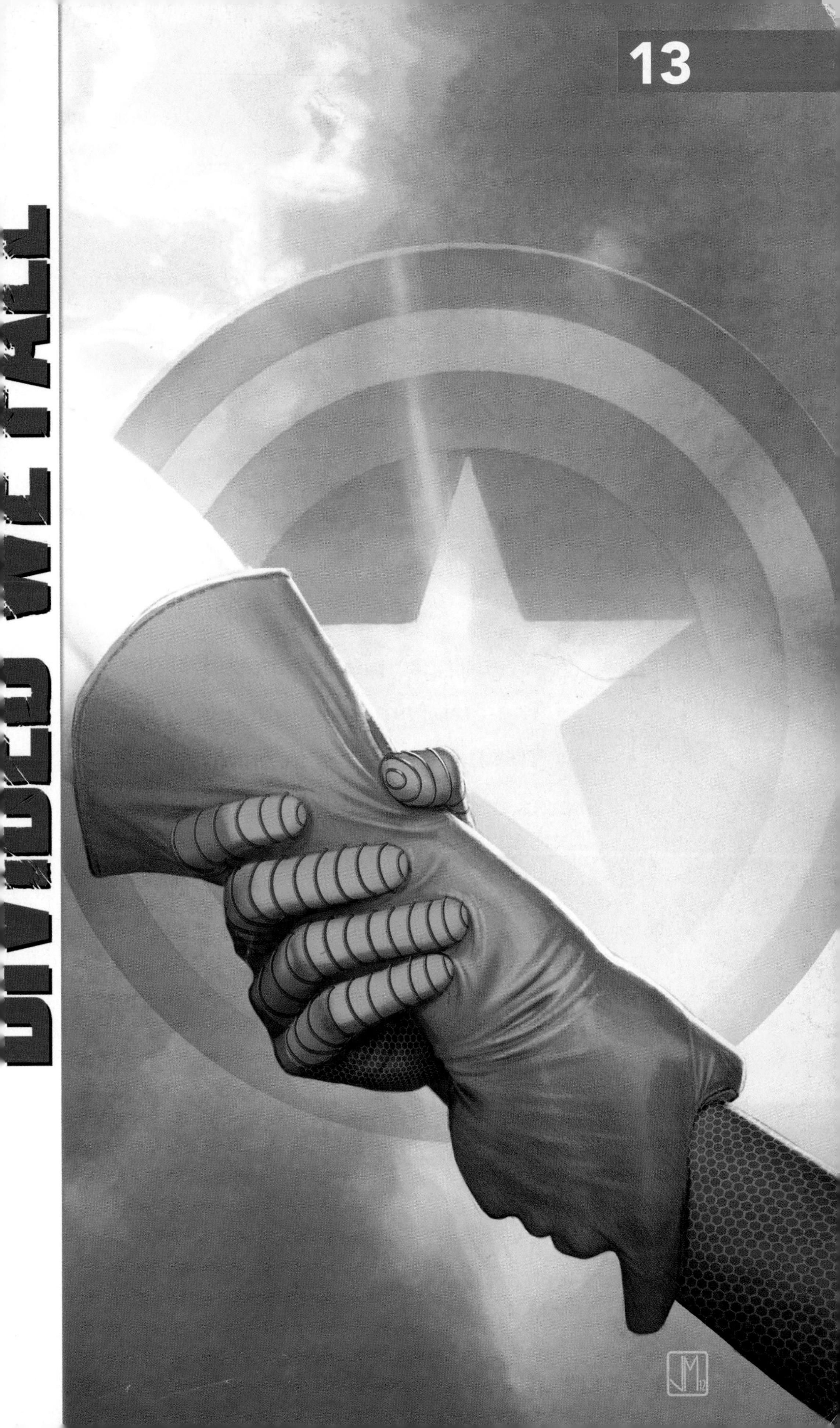
DIVIDED WE FALL
13

MONTHS BEFORE PETER PARKER WAS SHOT AND KILLED, GRADE-SCHOOLER MILES MORALES WAS ABOUT TO START A NEW CHAPTER IN HIS LIFE AT A NEW SCHOOL--WHEN HE WAS SUDDENLY BITTEN BY A STOLEN, GENETICALLY ALTERED SPIDER THAT GAVE HIM INCREDIBLE ARACHNID-LIKE POWERS.

ULTIMATE COM
ALL NEW SPIDER-M

SPIDER-MAN

GANKE

CAPTAI
AMERIC

IRON M

Washington is decimated.

The government is a mess.

The Southwest is in chaos.

States are seceding from the union.

America is falling apart.

Spider-Man commits murder?

DIVIDED WE FALL

.H.I.E.L.D. SITUATION MAP:

[...ti-government militia hot spots]

ntana, N. Dakota
Dakota, Wyoming
izona, New Mexico
Carolina, S. Carolina,
orgia

[Eastern seaboard control zone]

New England,
New York,
New Jersey,
Delaware,
Washington, D.C.,
Maryland,
Virginia

secured by
National Guard
under emergency
powers
committee

[...e West Coast]

lifornia, Oregon
shington

atus unknown

[Great Lakes states]

Minnesota,
Wisconsin,
Michigan,
Illinois,
Indiana, Ohio

status unknown

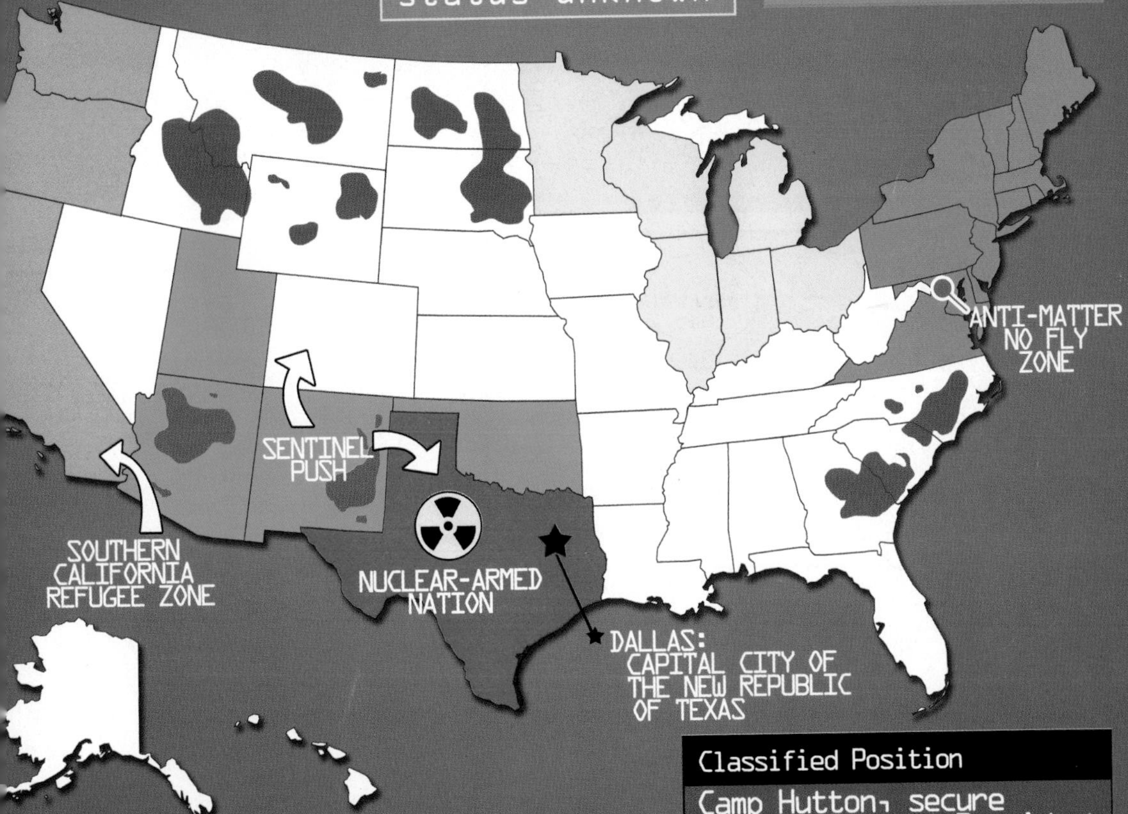

ANTI-MATTER
NO FLY
ZONE
SENTINEL
PUSH
SOUTHERN
CALIFORNIA
REFUGEE ZONE
NUCLEAR-ARMED
NATION
DALLAS:
CAPITAL CITY OF
THE NEW REPUBLIC
OF TEXAS

Classified Position

Camp Hutton, secure location of the President of the United States

[...entinel-controlled no-man's-land]

ew Mexico, Arizona
tah, Oklahoma

bandoned by the
.S. government

[The New Republic of Texas]

Texas

declared state
independence

ALL STATES
SHOWN IN WHITE
ARE U.S. GOVERNMENT-
CONTROLLED ZONES

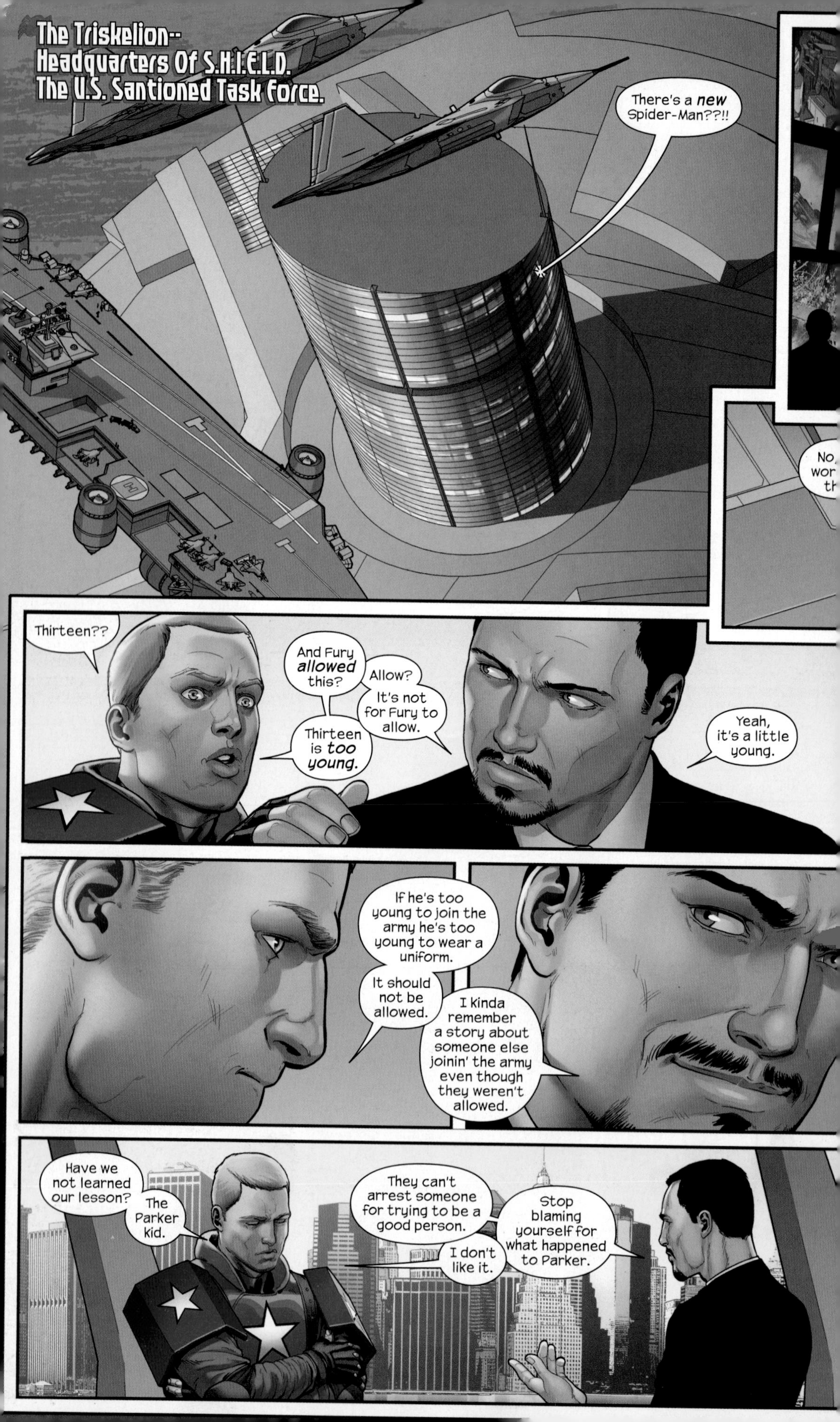
The Triskelion-- Headquarters Of S.H.I.E.L.D. The U.S. Santioned Task Force.
There's a new Spider-Man??!!
Thirteen??
And Fury allowed this?
Allow? It's not for Fury to allow.
Thirteen is too young.
Yeah, it's a little young.
If he's too young to join the army he's too young to wear a uniform.
It should not be allowed.
I kinda remember a story about someone else joinin' the army even though they weren't allowed.
Have we not learned our lesson?
The Parker kid.
They can't arrest someone for trying to be a good person.
I don't like it.
Stop blaming yourself for what happened to Parker.

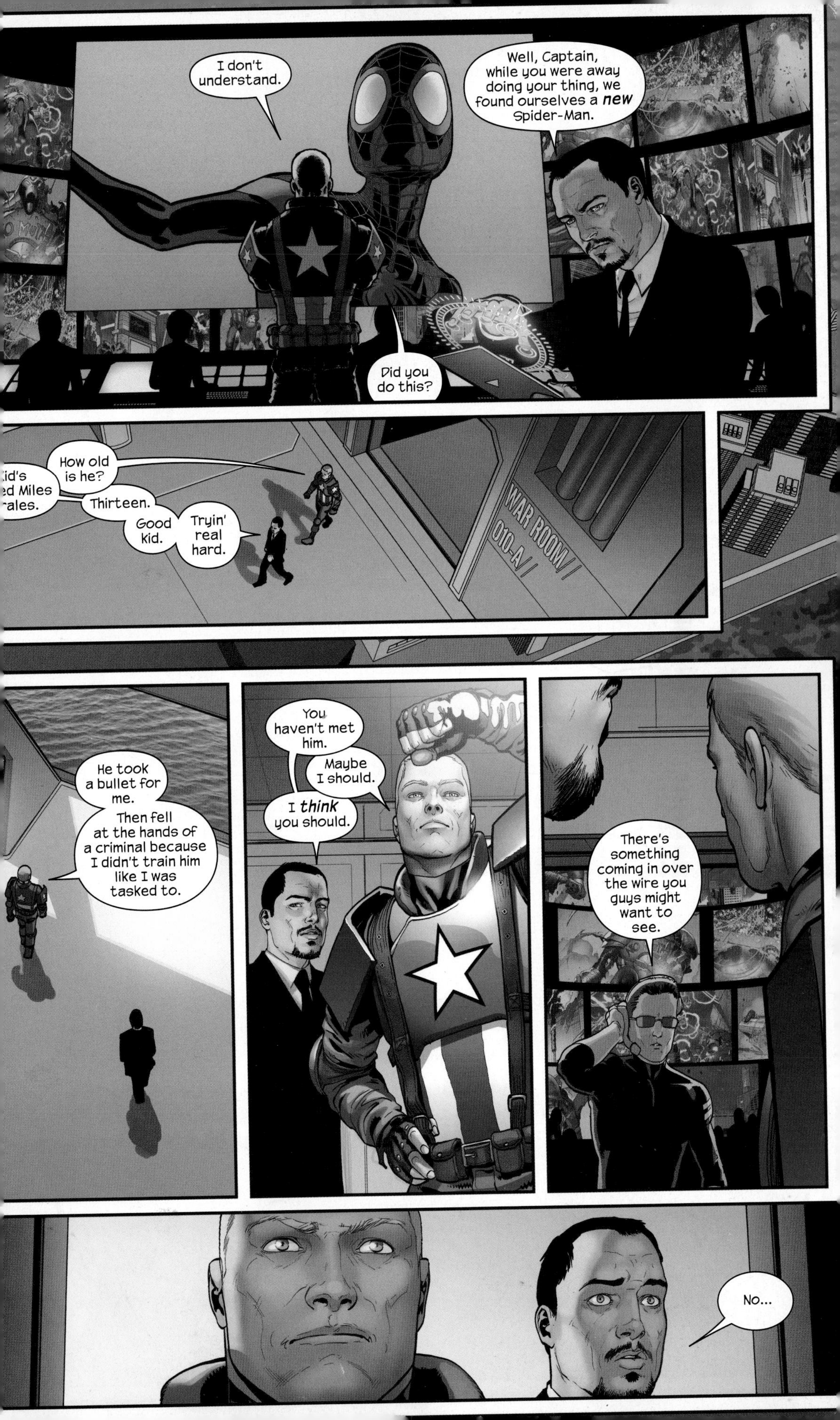
I don't understand.
Well, Captain, while you were away doing your thing, we found ourselves a *new* Spider-Man.
Did you do this?
How old is he?
Kid's ...ed Miles ...rales.
Thirteen.
Good kid.
Tryin' real hard.
WAR ROOM// 010-A//
He took a bullet for me.
Then fell at the hands of a criminal because I didn't train him like I was tasked to.
You haven't met him.
Maybe I should.
I *think* you should.
There's something coming in over the wire you guys might want to see.
No...

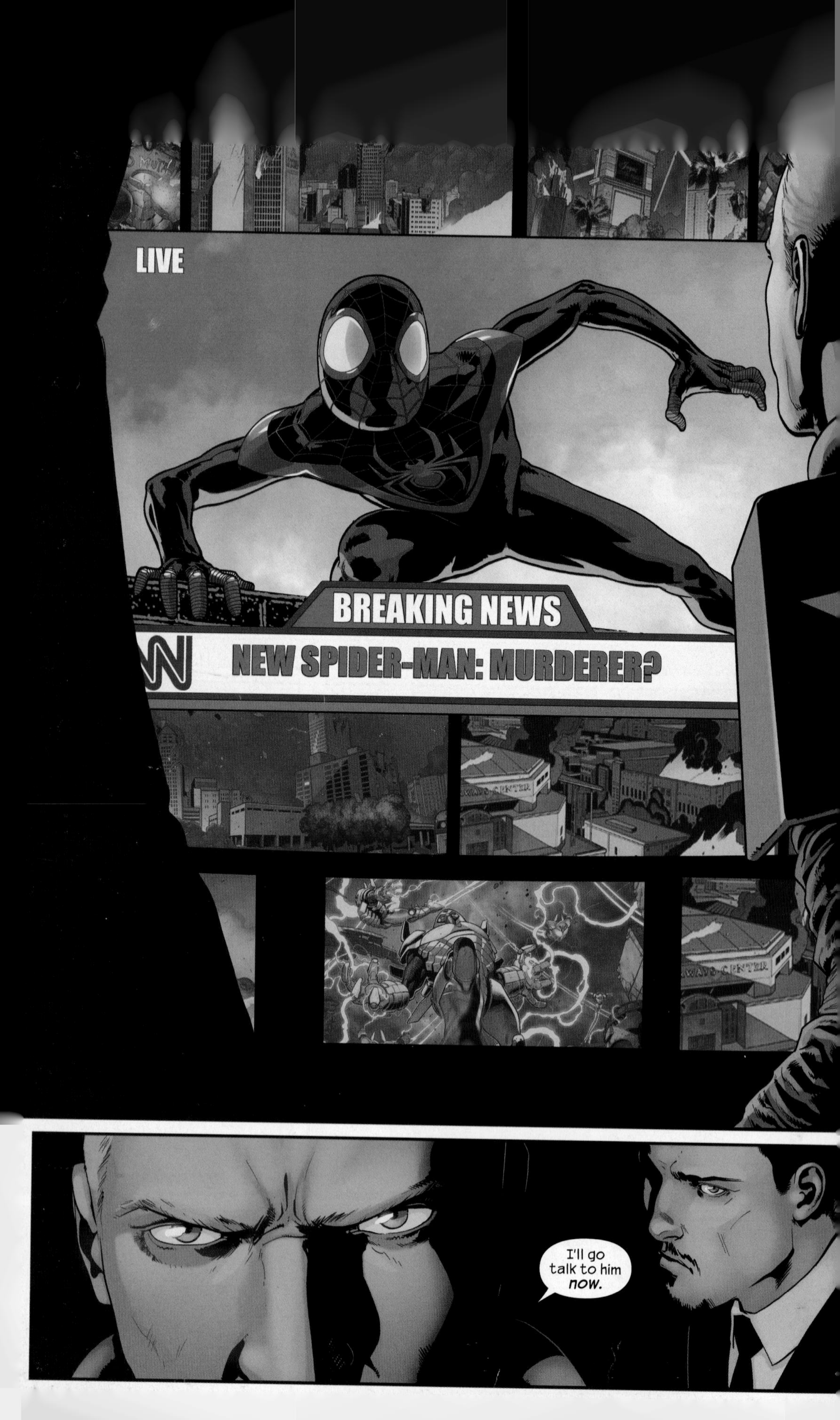
LIVE
BREAKING NEWS
NEW SPIDER-MAN: MURDERER?
I'll go talk to him *now*.

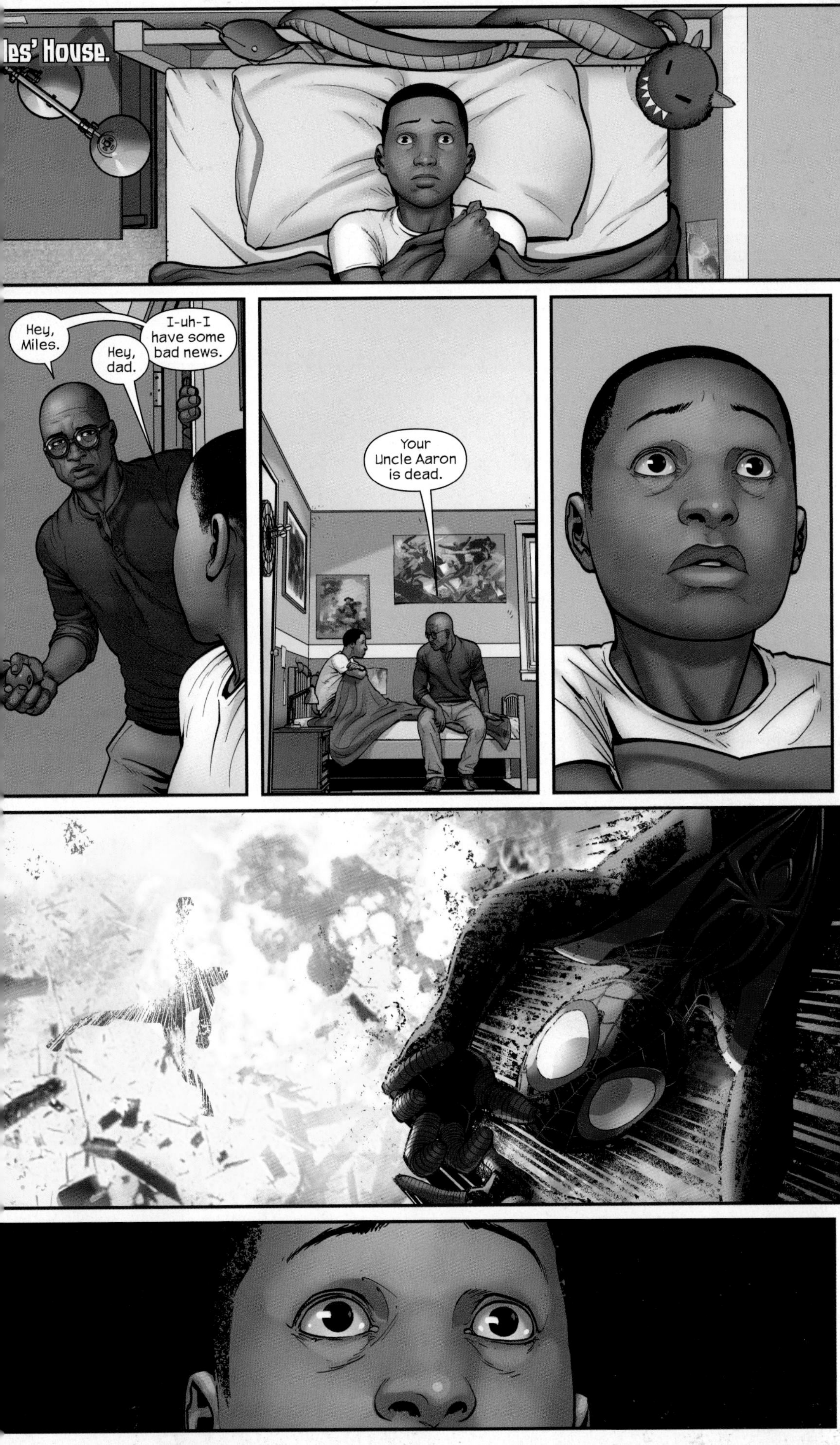
iles' House.
Hey, Miles.
Hey, dad.
I-uh-I have some bad news.
Your Uncle Aaron is dead.

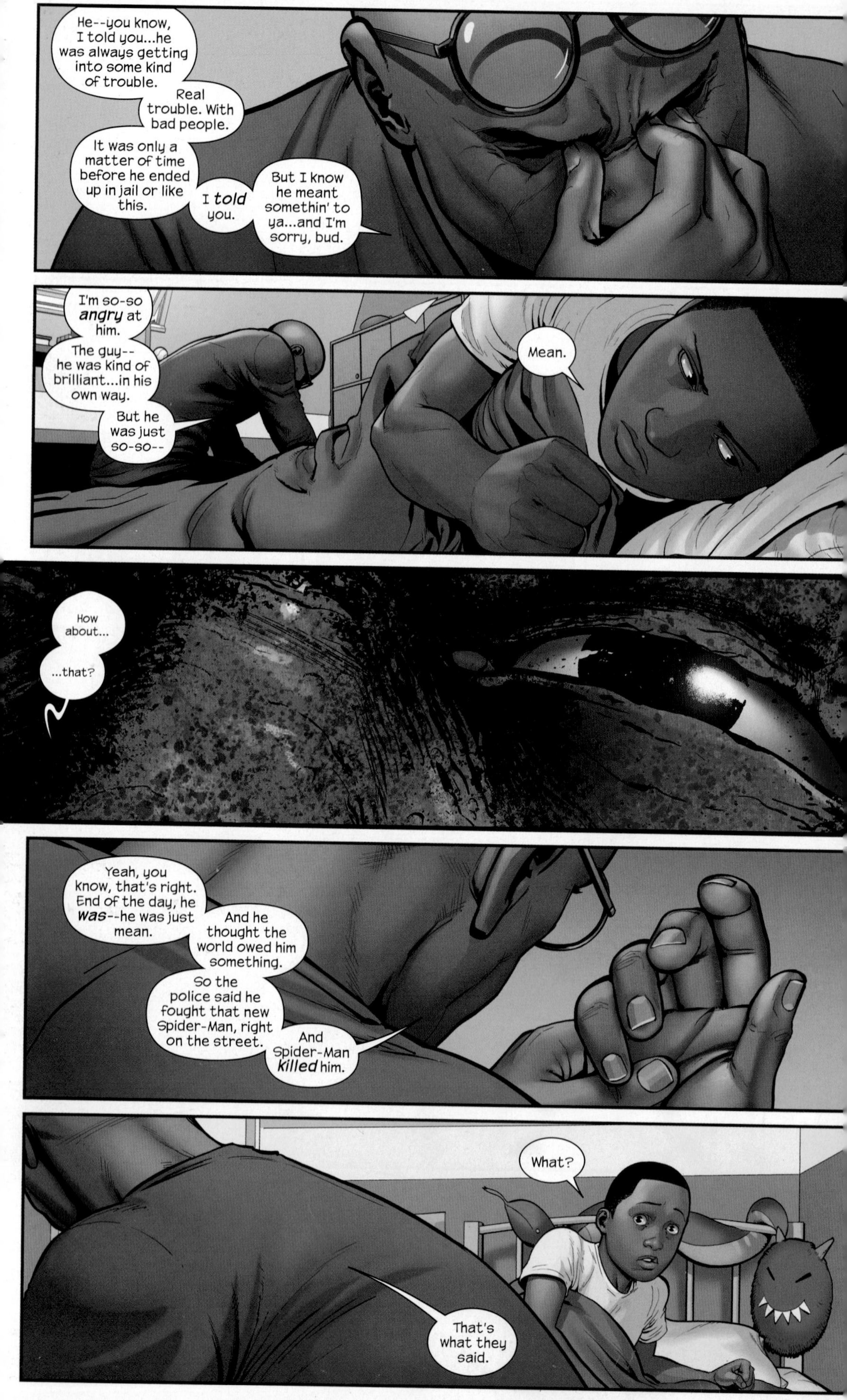
He--you know, I told you...he was always getting into some kind of trouble.
Real trouble. With bad people.
It was only a matter of time before he ended up in jail or like this.
I *told* you.
But I know he meant somethin' to ya...and I'm sorry, bud.
I'm so-so ***angry*** at him.
The guy--he was kind of brilliant...in his own way.
But he was just so-so--
Mean.
How about...
...that?
Yeah, you know, that's right. End of the day, he ***was***--he was just mean.
And he thought the world owed him something.
So the police said he fought that new Spider-Man, right on the street.
And Spider-Man *killed* him.
What?
That's what they said.

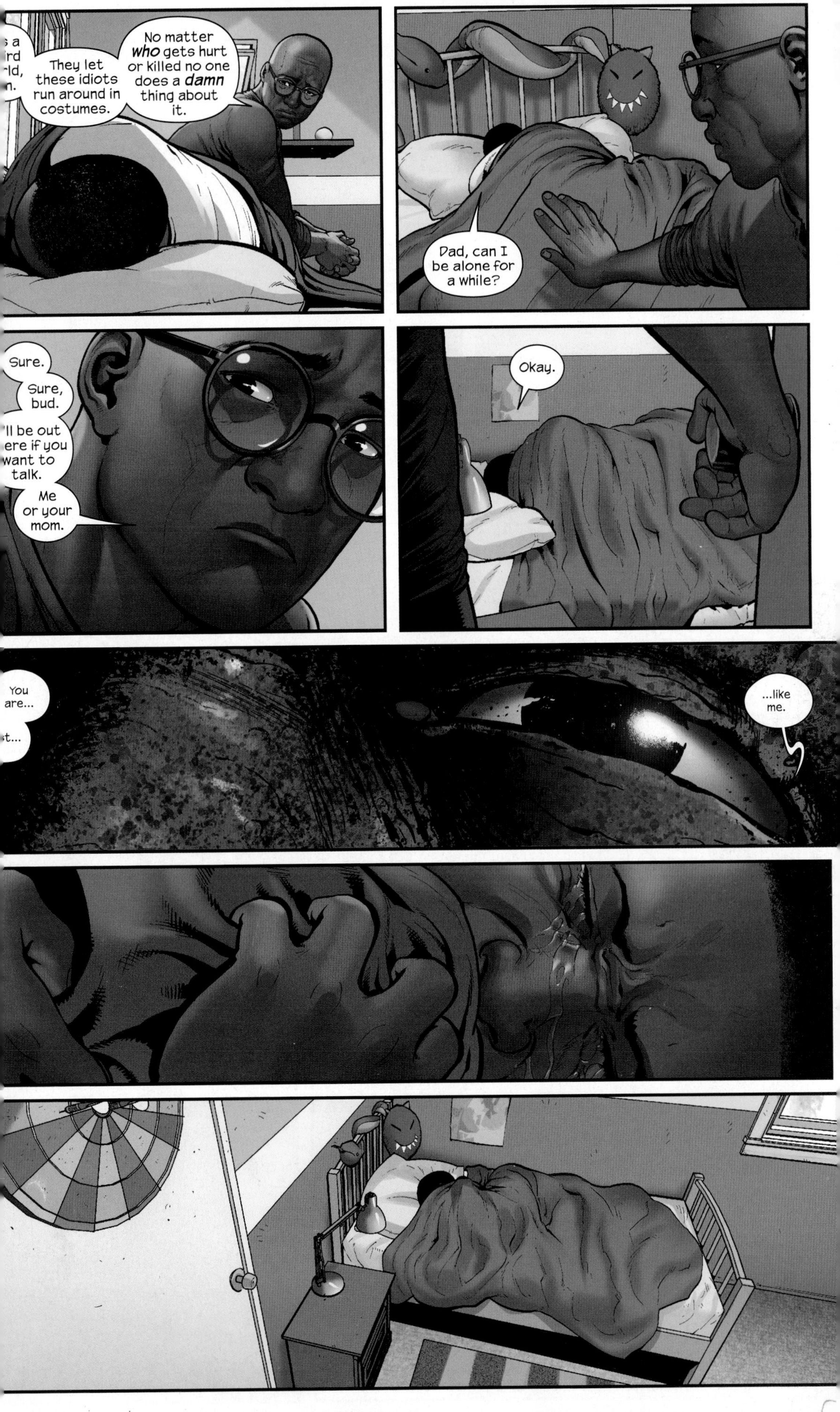
They let these idiots run around in costumes.
No matter who gets hurt or killed no one does a damn thing about it.
Dad, can I be alone for a while?
Sure.
Sure, bud.
'll be out ere if you want to talk.
Me or your mom.
Okay.
You are...
...like me.

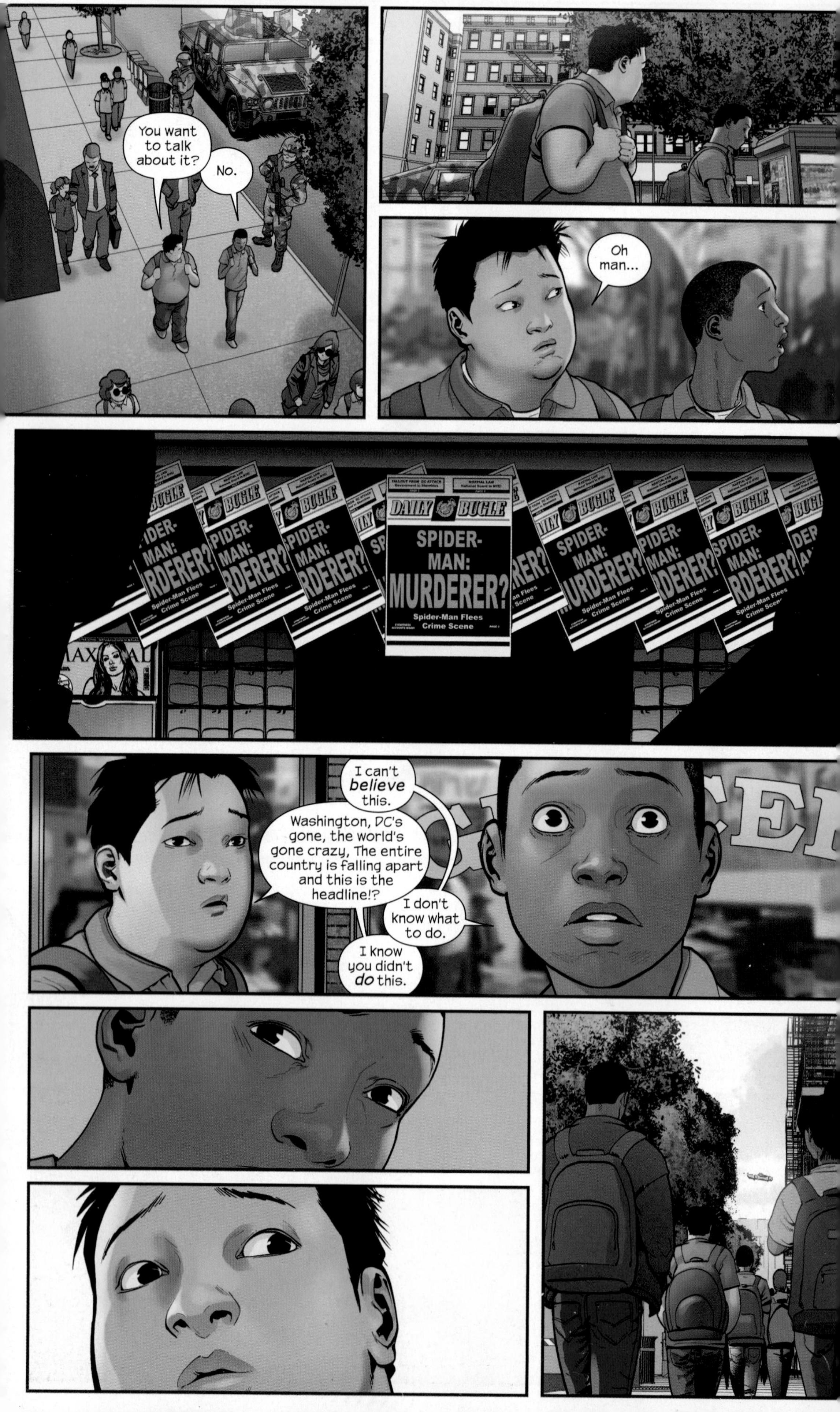

You want to talk about it?
No.
Oh man...
DAILY BUGLE
SPIDER-MAN: MURDERER?
Spider-Man Flees Crime Scene
I can't *believe* this.
Washington, DC's gone, the world's gone crazy, The entire country is falling apart and this is the headline!?
I don't know what to do.
I know you didn't *do* this.

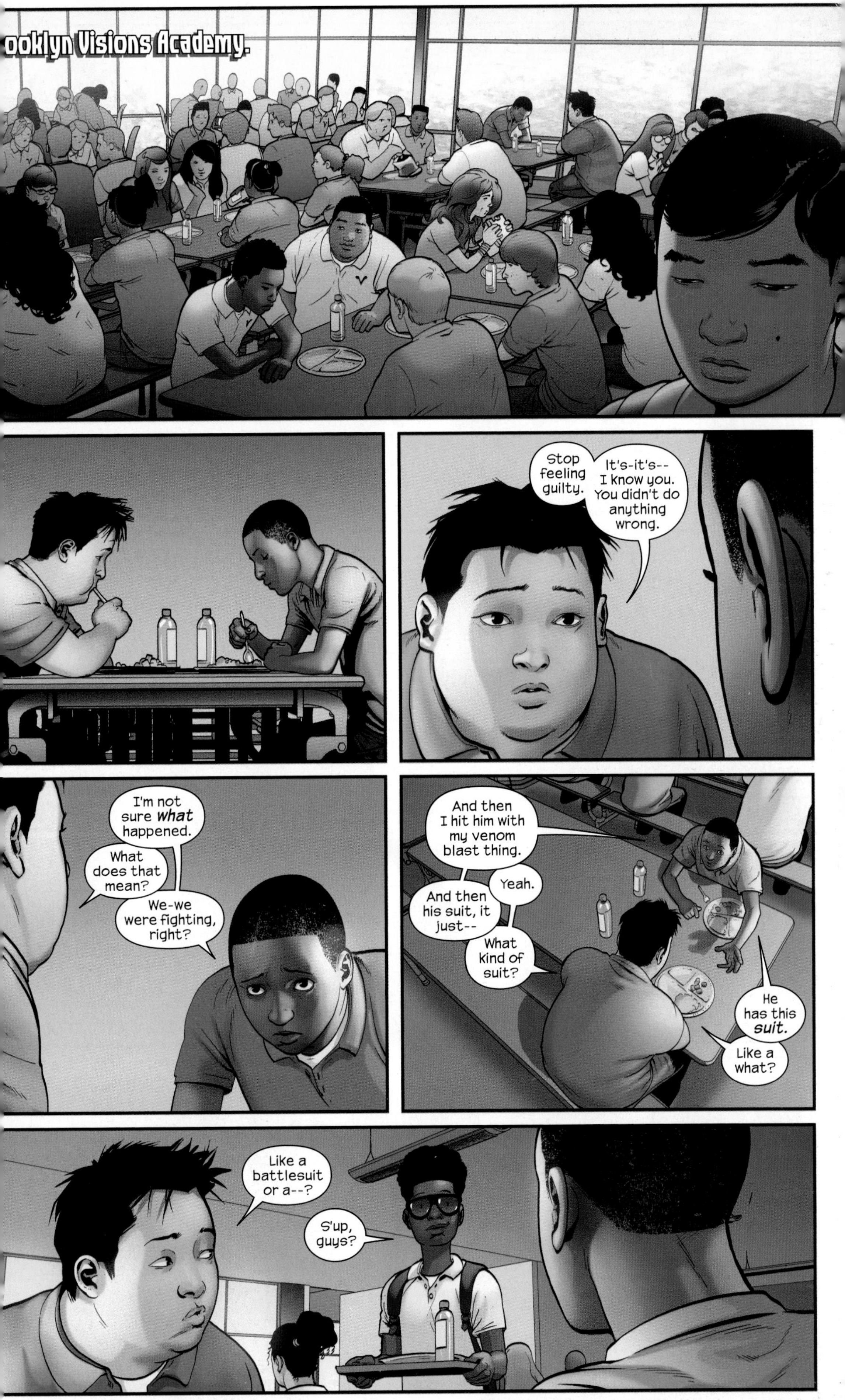
ooklyn Visions Academy.
Stop feeling guilty.
It's-it's-- I know you. You didn't do anything wrong.
I'm not sure what happened.
What does that mean?
We-we were fighting, right?
And then I hit him with my venom blast thing.
And then his suit, it just--
Yeah.
What kind of suit?
He has this suit.
Like a what?
Like a battlesuit or a--?
S'up, guys?

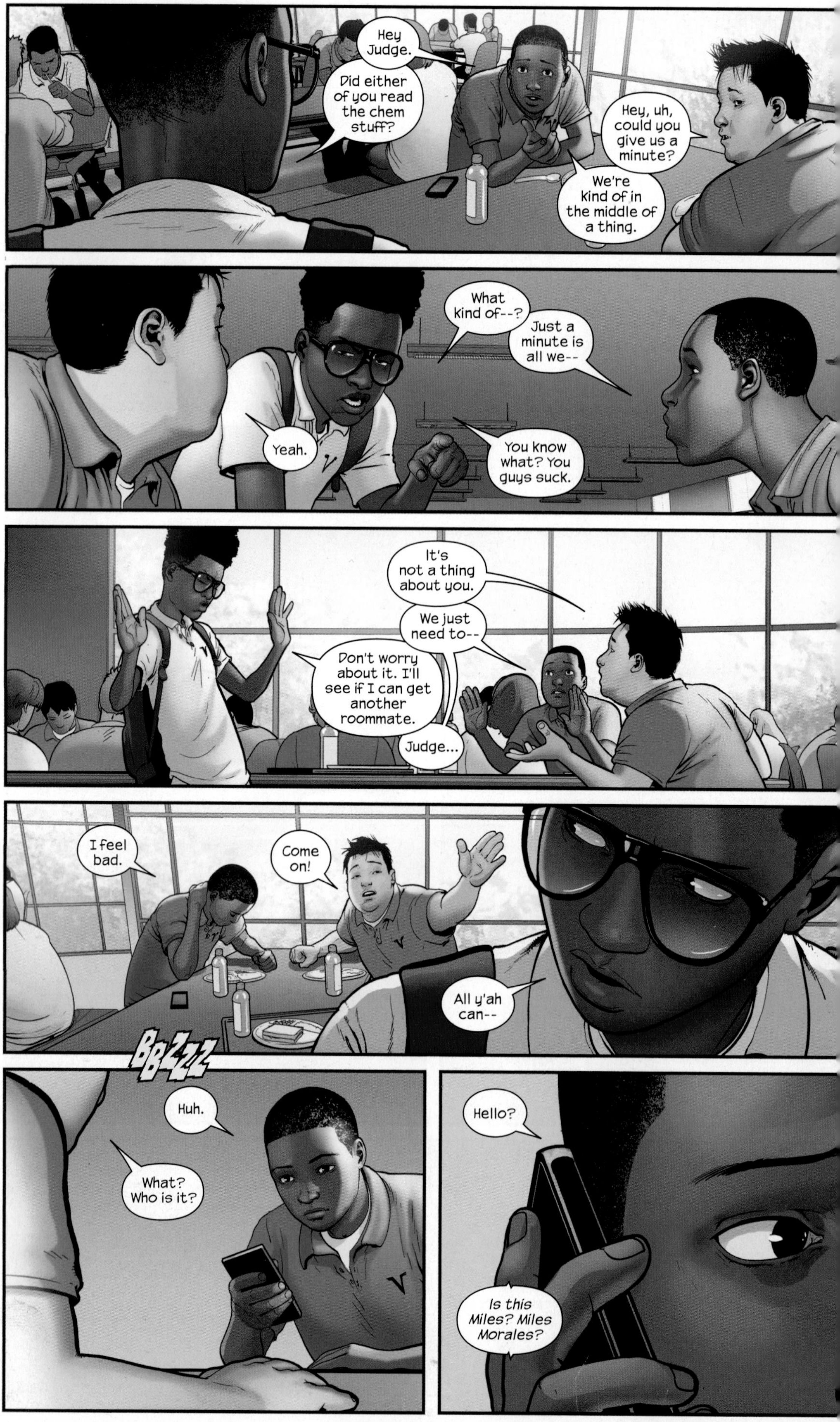
Hey Judge.
Did either of you read the chem stuff?
Hey, uh, could you give us a minute?
We're kind of in the middle of a thing.
What kind of--?
Just a minute is all we--
Yeah.
You know what? You guys suck.
It's not a thing about you.
We just need to--
Don't worry about it. I'll see if I can get another roommate.
Judge...
I feel bad.
Come on!
All y'ah can--
BBZZZ
Huh.
What? Who is it?
Hello?
Is this Miles? Miles Morales?

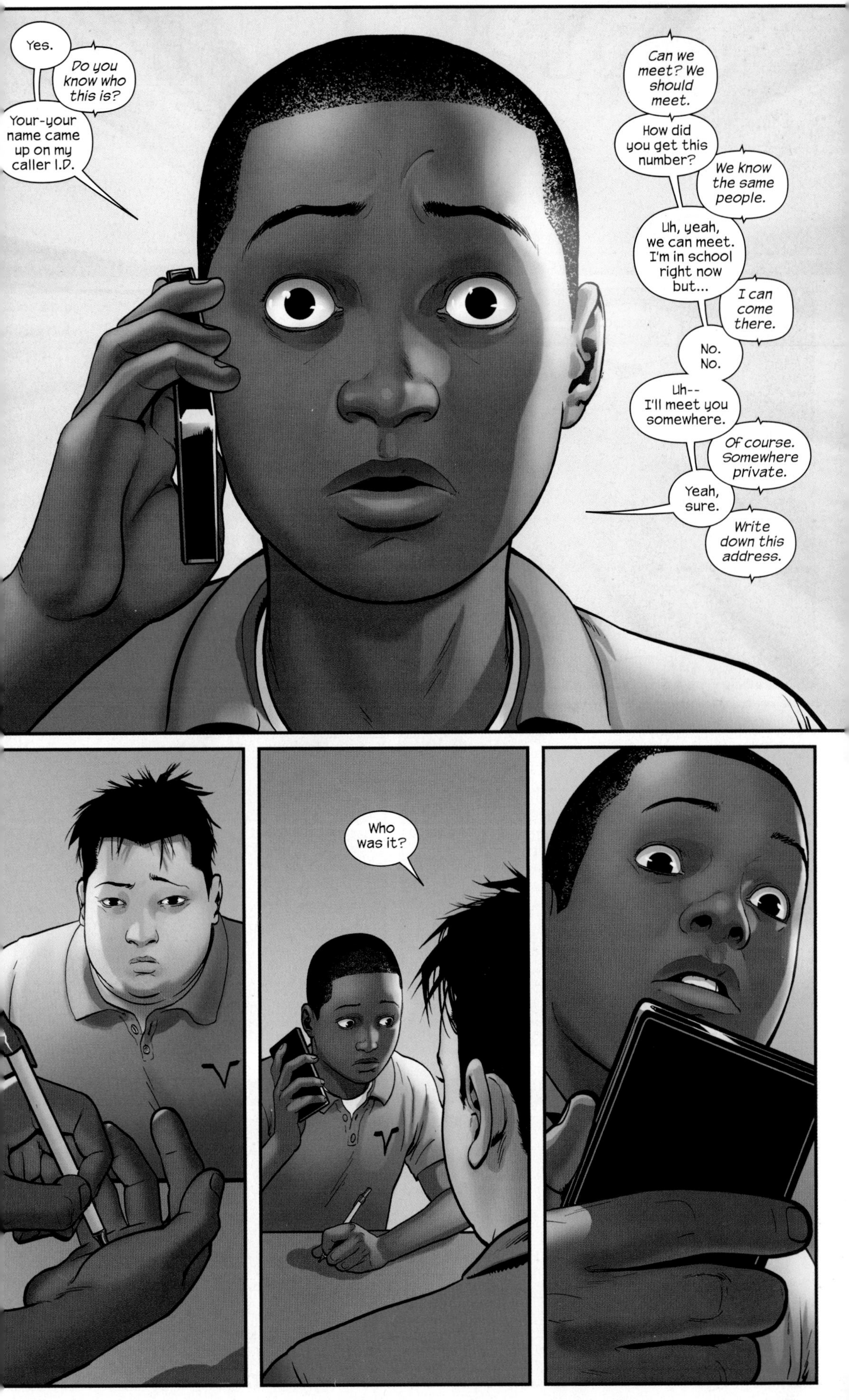
Yes.
Do you know who this is?
Your-your name came up on my caller I.D.
Can we meet? We should meet.
How did you get this number?
We know the same people.
Uh, yeah, we can meet. I'm in school right now but...
I can come there.
No. No.
Uh-- I'll meet you somewhere.
Of course. Somewhere private.
Yeah, sure.
Write down this address.
Who was it?

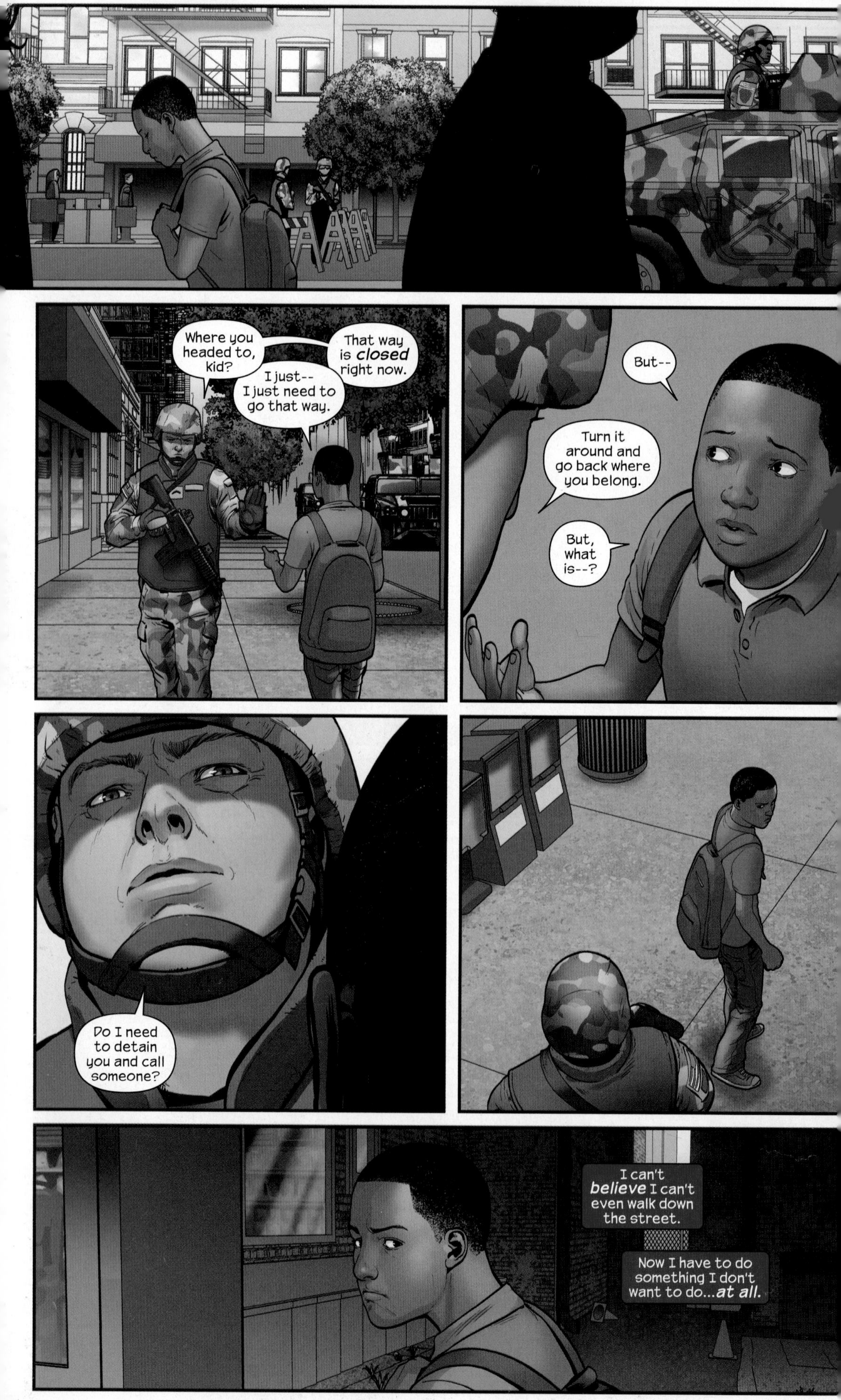

Where you headed to, kid?
That way is *closed* right now.
I just-- I just need to go that way.
But--
Turn it around and go back where you belong.
But, what is--?
Do I need to detain you and call someone?
I can't *believe* I can't even walk down the street.
Now I have to do something I don't want to do...*at all.*

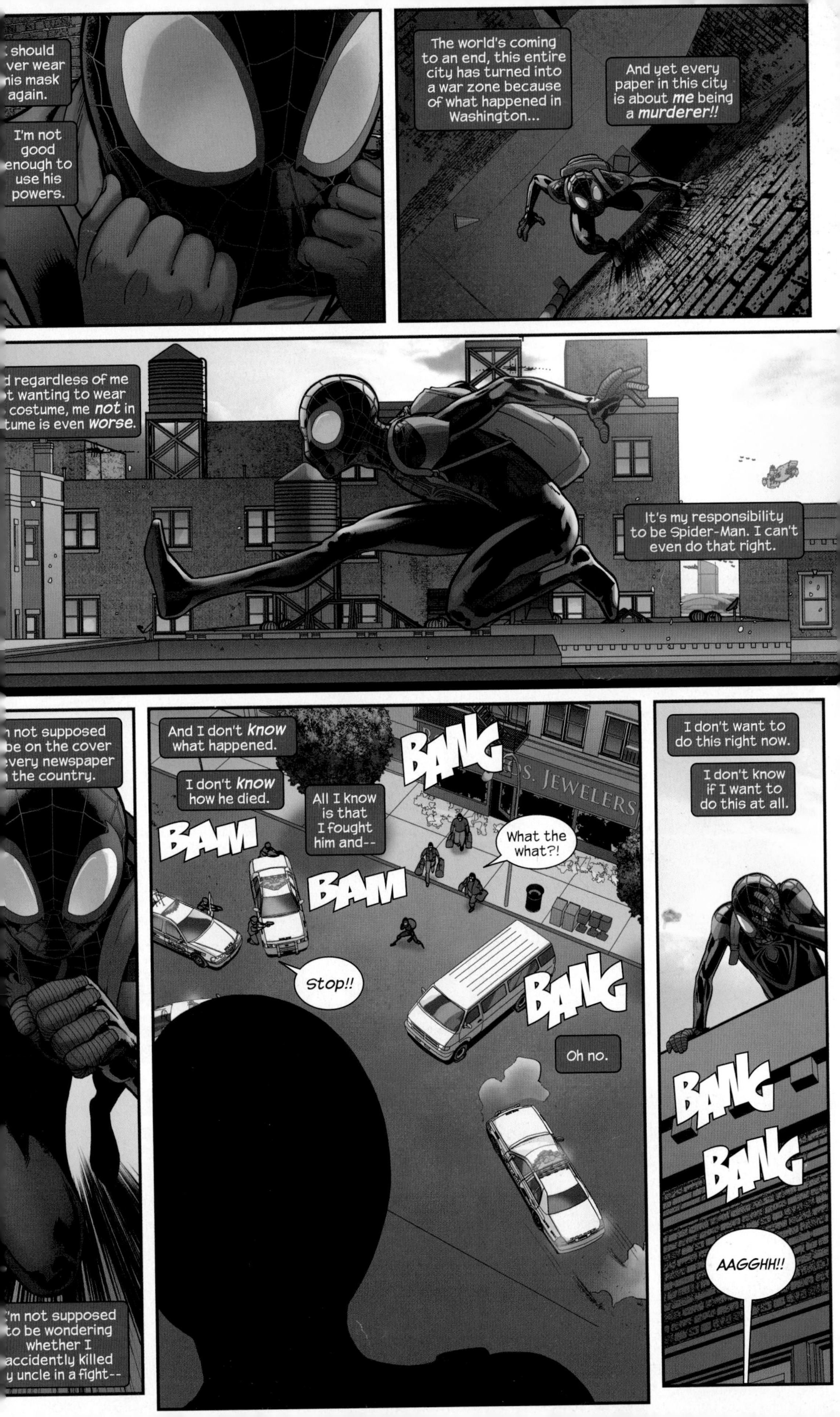

should
ver wear
is mask
again.
I'm not
good
enough to
use his
powers.
The world's coming to an end, this entire city has turned into a war zone because of what happened in Washington...
And yet every paper in this city is about *me* being a *murderer!!*
d regardless of me
t wanting to wear
costume, me *not* in
tume is even *worse*.
It's my responsibility to be Spider-Man. I can't even do that right.
n not supposed
be on the cover
every newspaper
the country.
'm not supposed
to be wondering
whether I
accidently killed
y uncle in a fight--
And I don't *know* what happened.
I don't *know* how he died.
All I know is that I fought him and--
BANG
S. JEWELERS
BAM
BAM
What the what?!
Stop!!
BANG
Oh no.
I don't want to do this right now.
I don't know if I want to do this at all.
BANG
BANG
AAGGHH!!

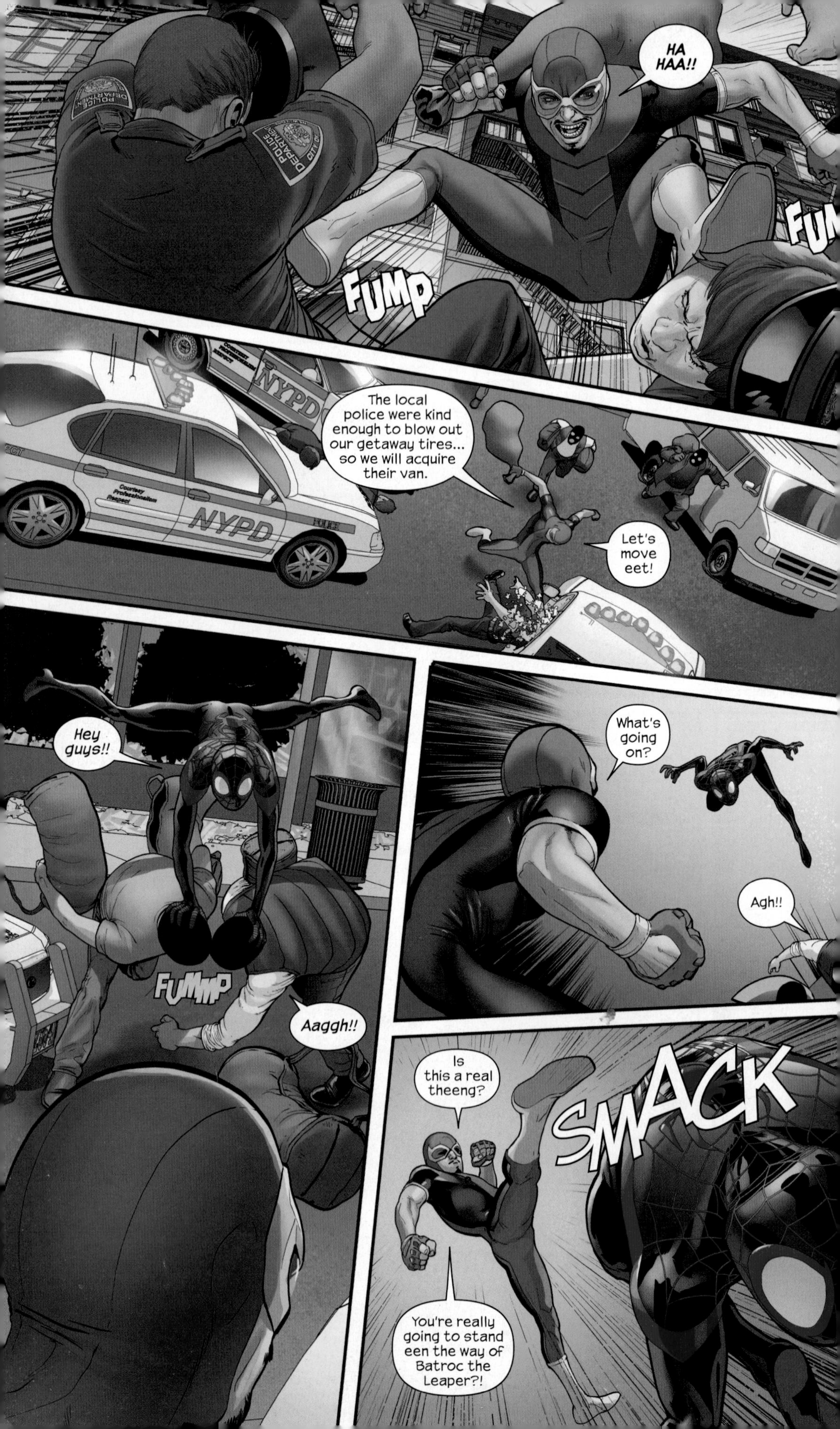

HA HAA!!
FUMP
FUM
The local police were kind enough to blow out our getaway tires... so we will acquire their van.
Let's move eet!
NYPD
Hey guys!!
FUMMP
Aaggh!!
What's going on?
Agh!!
Is this a real theeng?
SMACK
You're really going to stand een the way of Batroc the Leaper?!

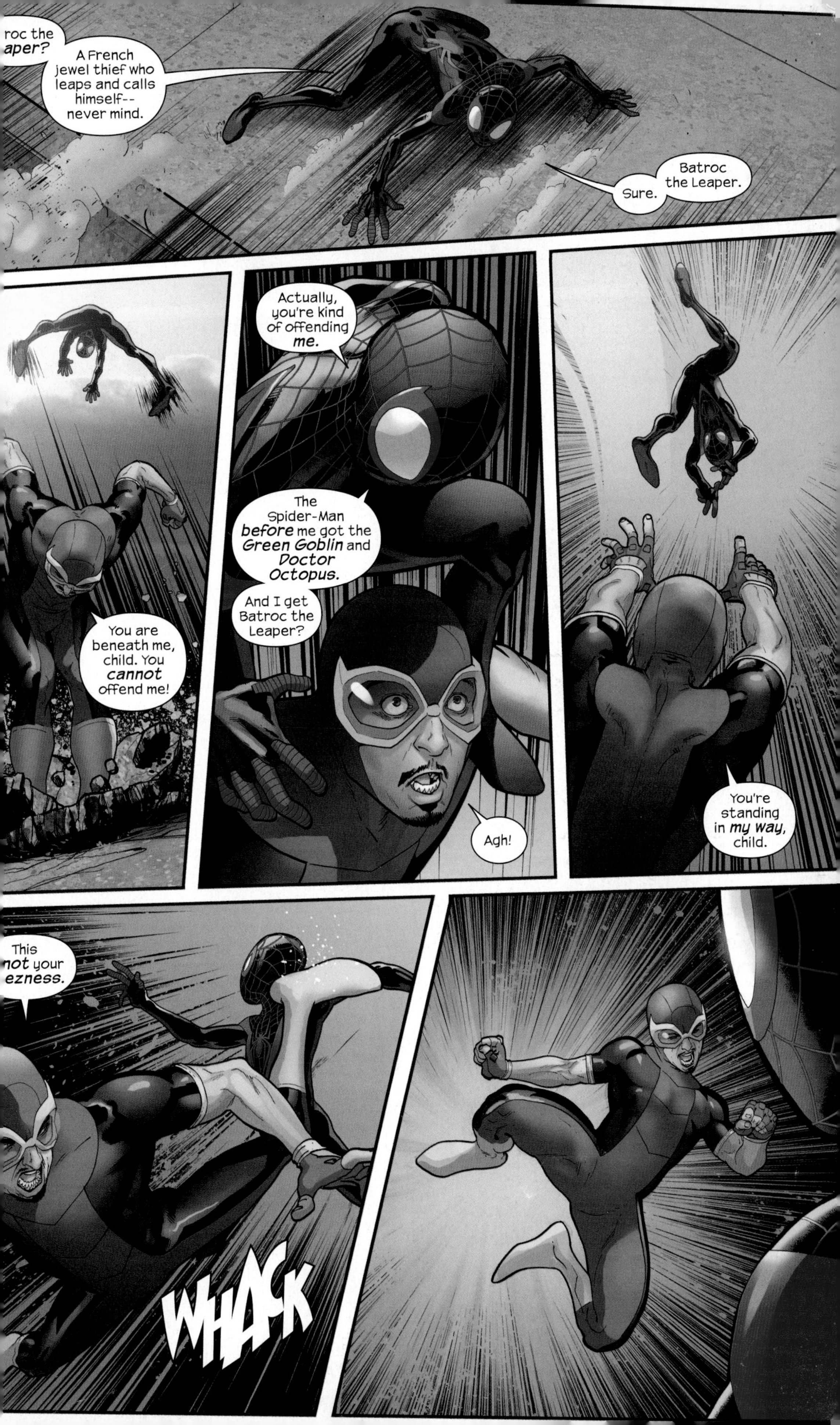
roc the
aper?
A French jewel thief who leaps and calls himself-- never mind.
Sure.
Batroc the Leaper.
Actually, you're kind of offending *me.*
You are beneath me, child. You *cannot* offend me!
The Spider-Man *before* me got the *Green Goblin* and *Doctor Octopus.*
And I get Batroc the Leaper?
Agh!
You're standing in *my way*, child.
This
not your
ezness.
WHACK

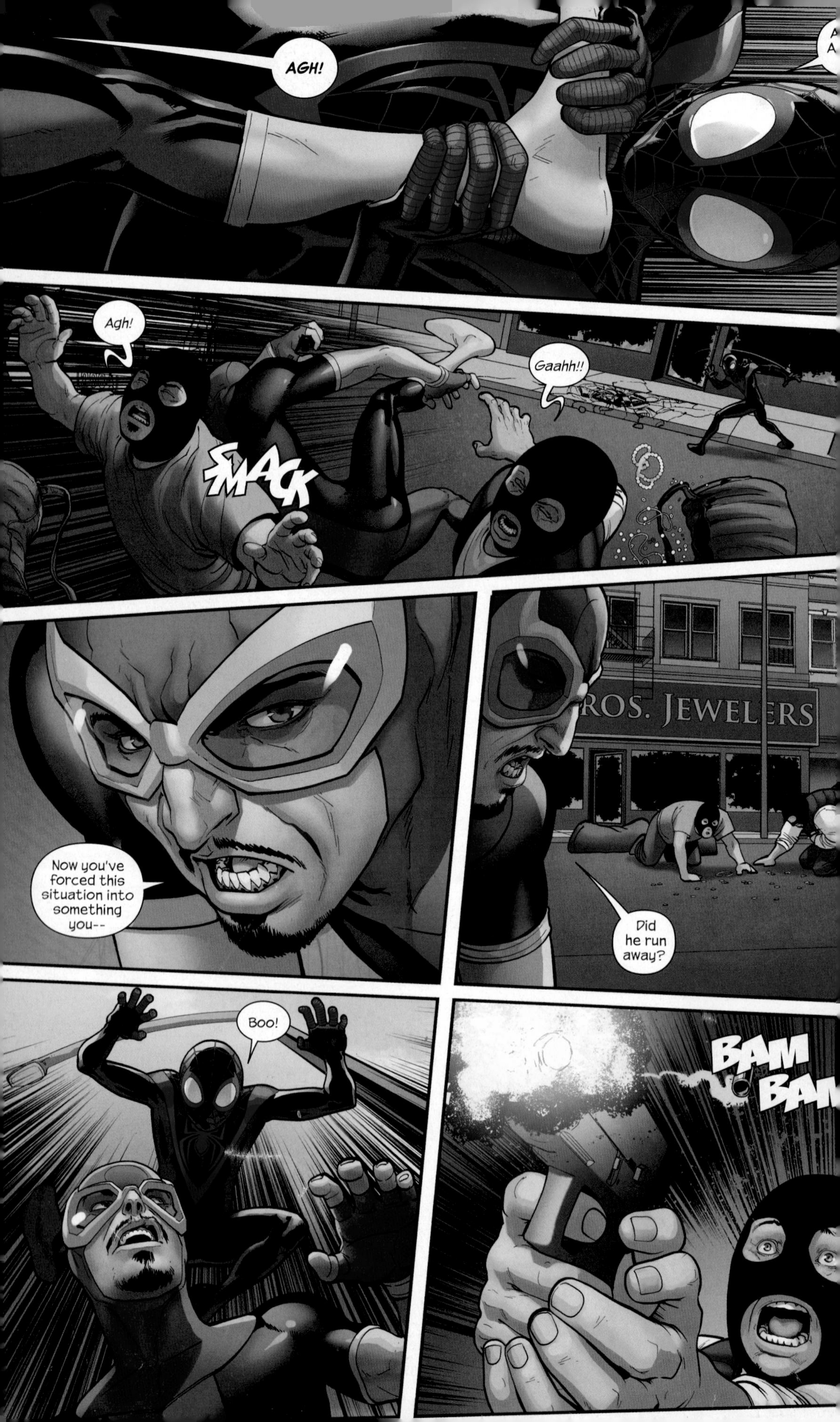
AGH!
Agh!
Gaahh!!
SMACK
Now you've forced this situation into something you--
ROS. JEWELERS
Did he run away?
Boo!
BAM
BAM

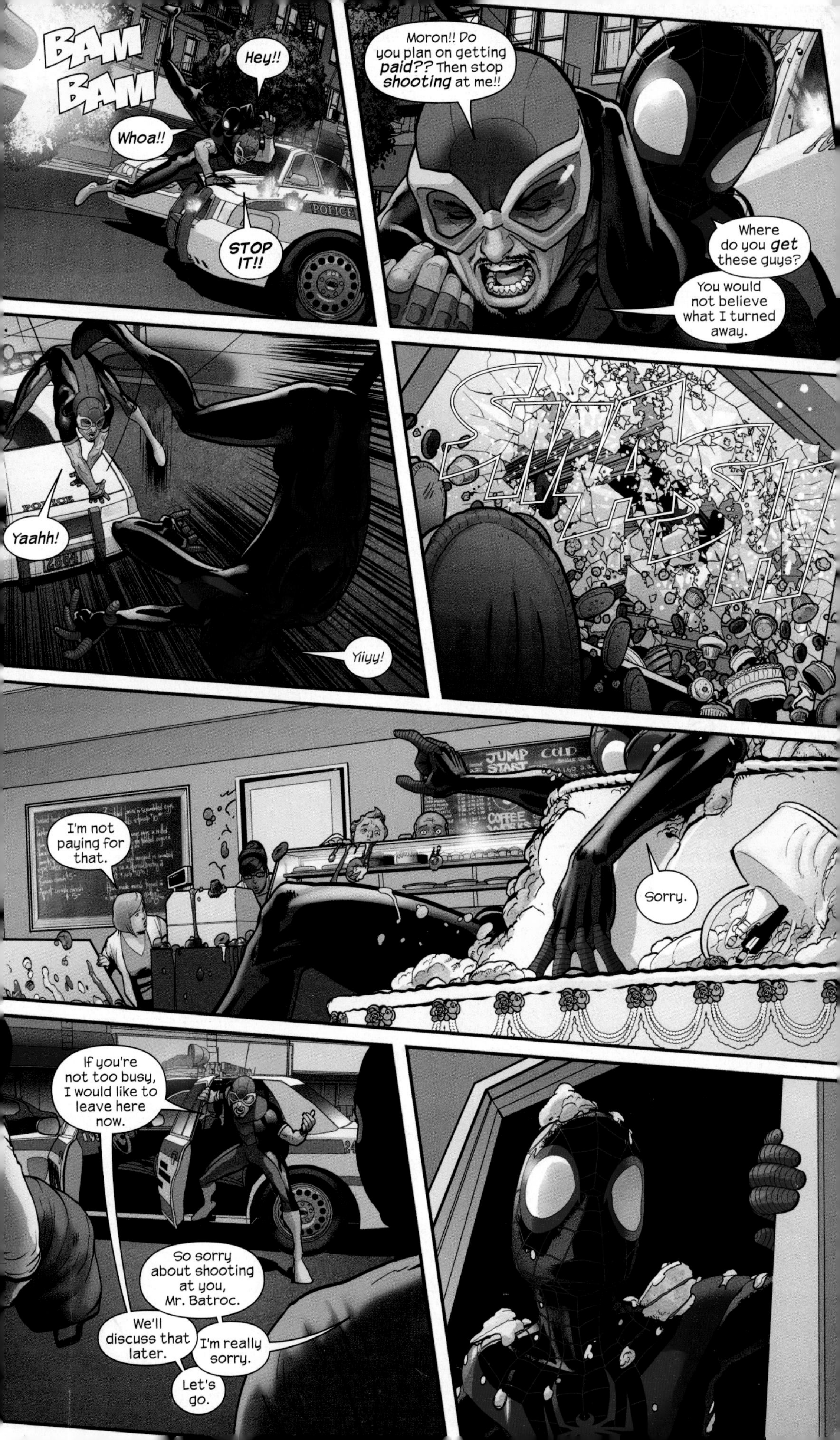
BAM BAM
Hey!!
Whoa!!
STOP IT!!
POLICE
Moron!! Do you plan on getting *paid??* Then stop *shooting* at me!!
Where do you *get* these guys?
You would not believe what I turned away.
Yaahh!
Yiiyy!
I'm not paying for that.
JUMP START
COLD
Sorry.
If you're not too busy, I would like to leave here now.
So sorry about shooting at you, Mr. Batroc.
We'll discuss that later.
I'm really sorry.
Let's go.

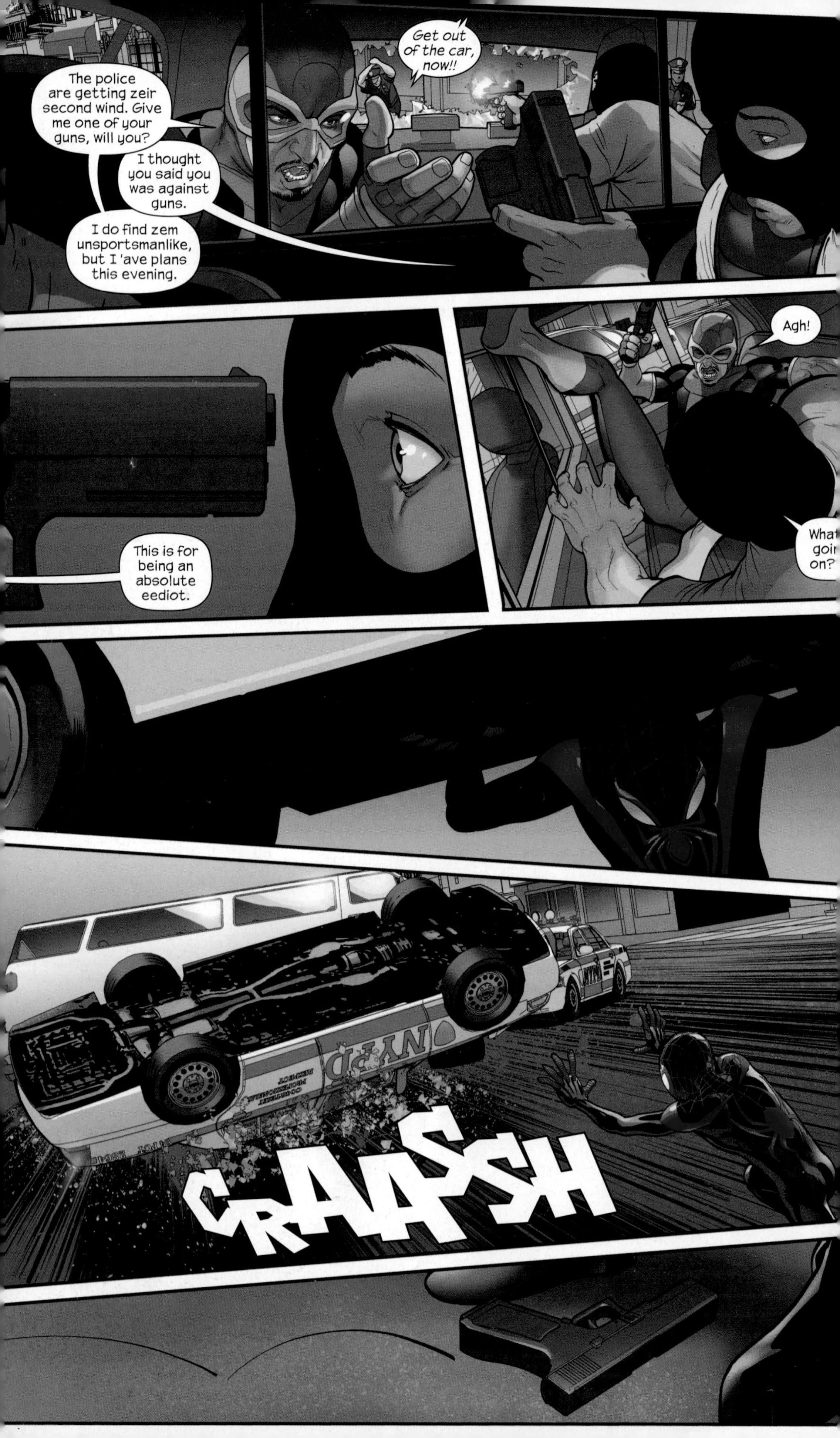
The police are getting zeir second wind. Give me one of your guns, will you?
Get out of the car, now!!
I thought you said you was against guns.
I do find zem unsportsmanlike, but I 'ave plans this evening.
This is for being an absolute eediot.
Agh!
Wha goi on?
CRAAASH

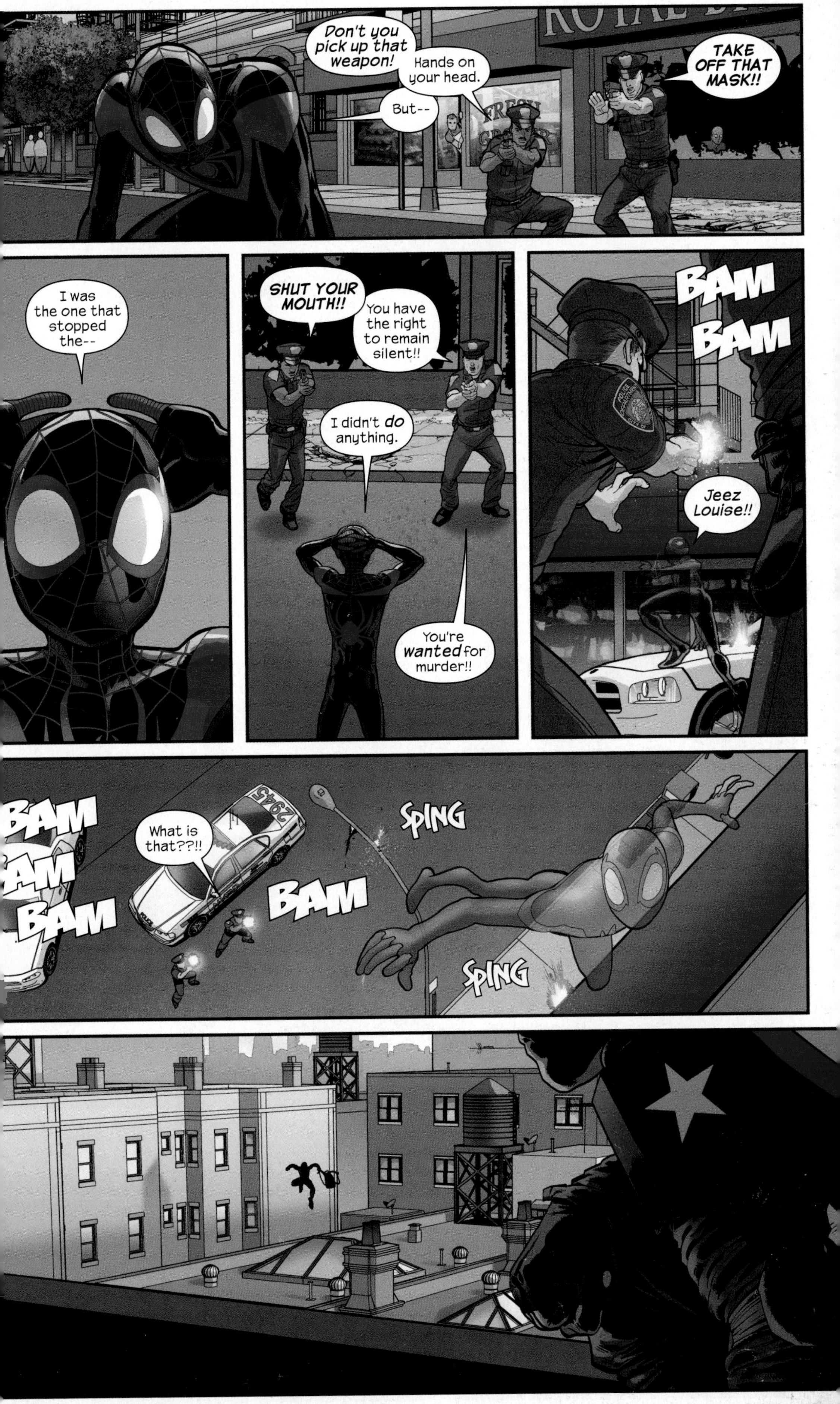
Don't you pick up that weapon!
Hands on your head.
But--
TAKE OFF THAT MASK!!
I was the one that stopped the--
SHUT YOUR MOUTH!!
You have the right to remain silent!!
I didn't do anything.
You're wanted for murder!!
BAM
BAM
Jeez Louise!!
BAM
AM
BAM
What is that??!!
2945
SPING
BAM
SPING

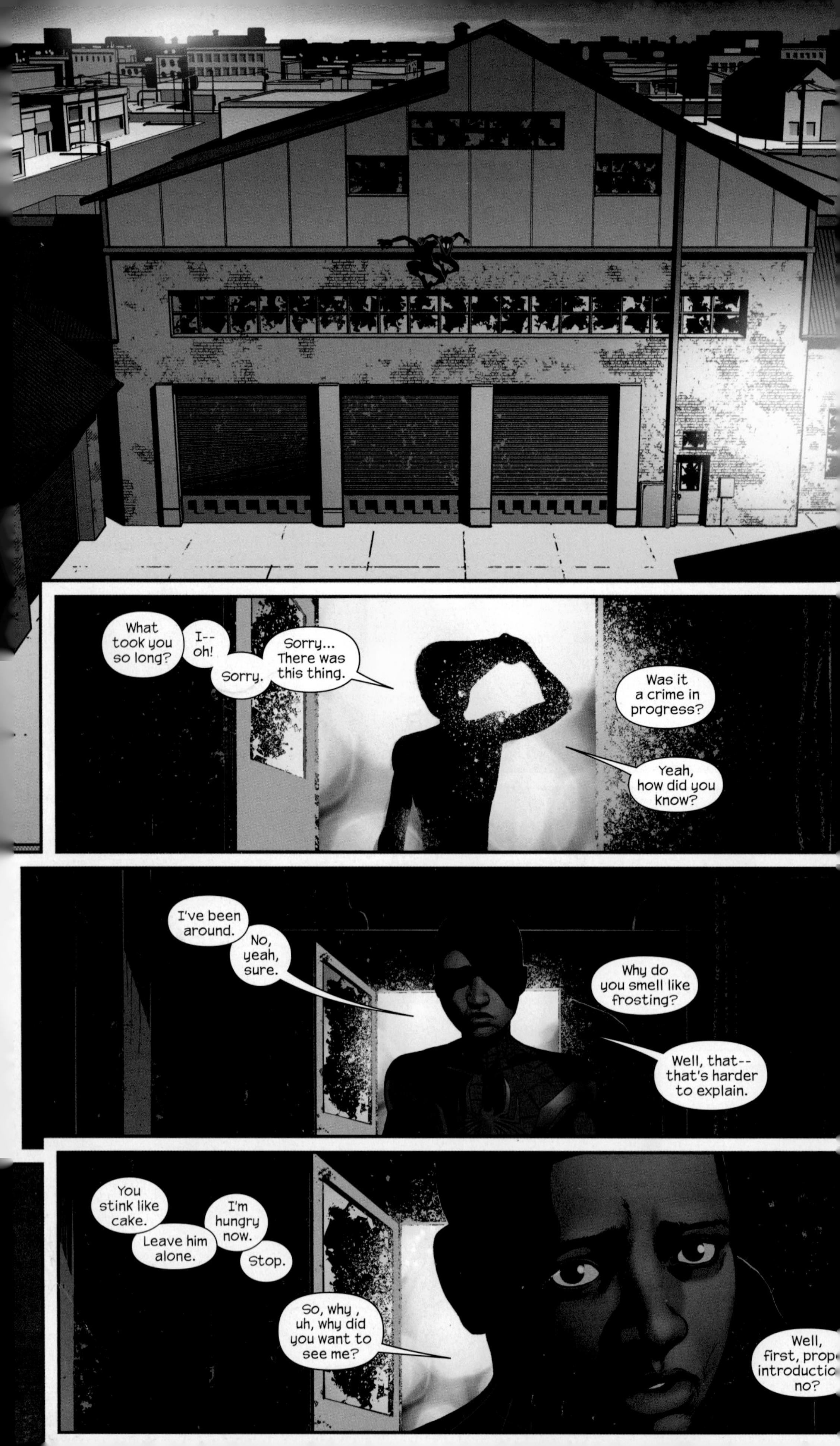
What took you so long?
I-- oh!
Sorry.
Sorry... There was this thing.
Was it a crime in progress?
Yeah, how did you know?
I've been around.
No, yeah, sure.
Why do you smell like frosting?
Well, that-- that's harder to explain.
You stink like cake.
Leave him alone.
I'm hungry now.
Stop.
So, why , uh, why did you want to see me?
Well, first, prop introductio no?

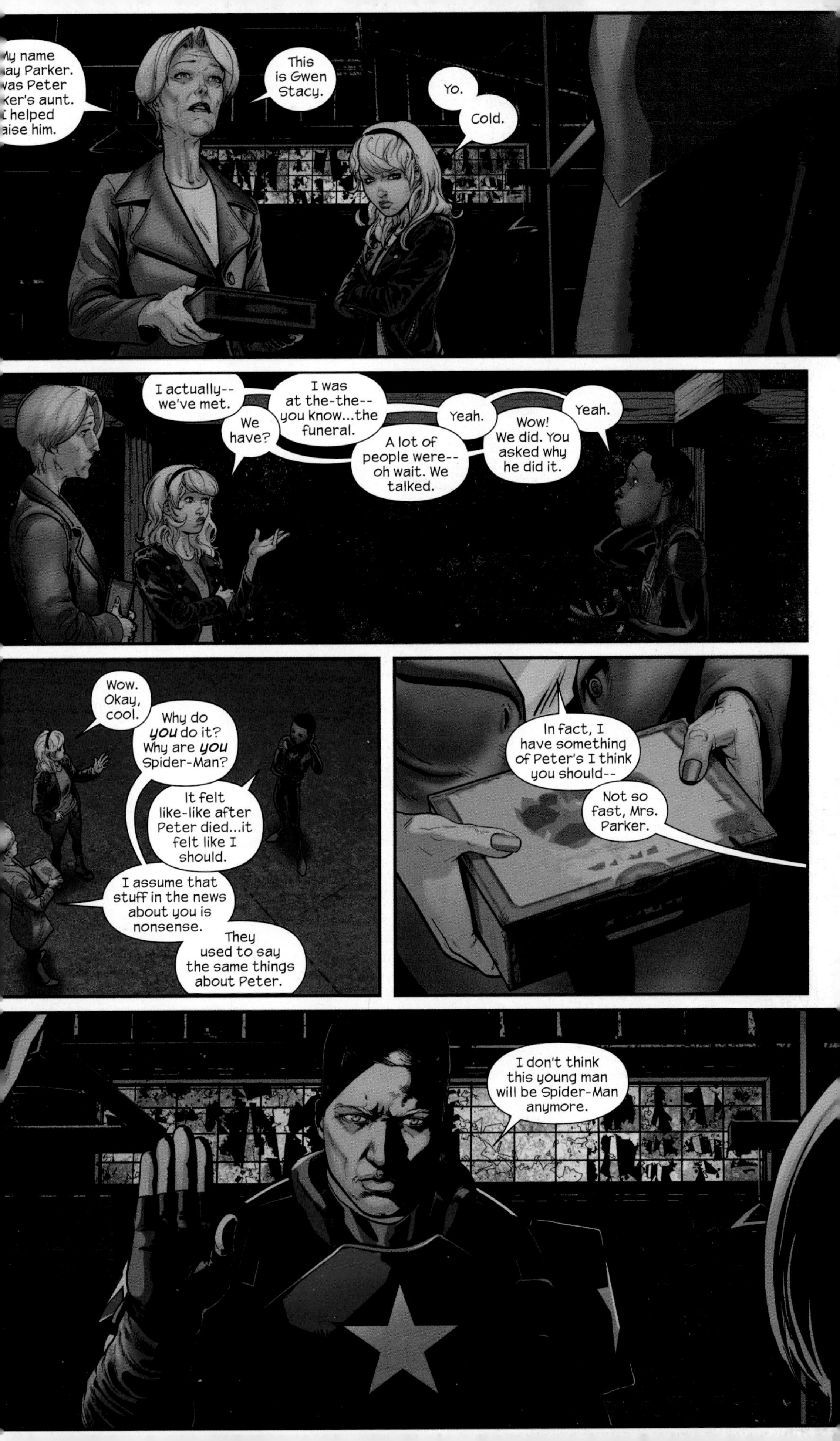

ly name ay Parker. vas Peter ker's aunt. I helped aise him.
This is Gwen Stacy.
Yo.
Cold.
I actually-- we've met.
We have?
I was at the-the-- you know...the funeral.
A lot of people were-- oh wait. We talked.
Yeah.
Wow! We did. You asked why he did it.
Yeah.
Wow. Okay, cool.
Why do *you* do it? Why are *you* Spider-Man?
It felt like-like after Peter died...it felt like I should.
I assume that stuff in the news about you is nonsense.
They used to say the same things about Peter.
In fact, I have something of Peter's I think you should--
Not so fast, Mrs. Parker.
I don't think this young man will be Spider-Man anymore.

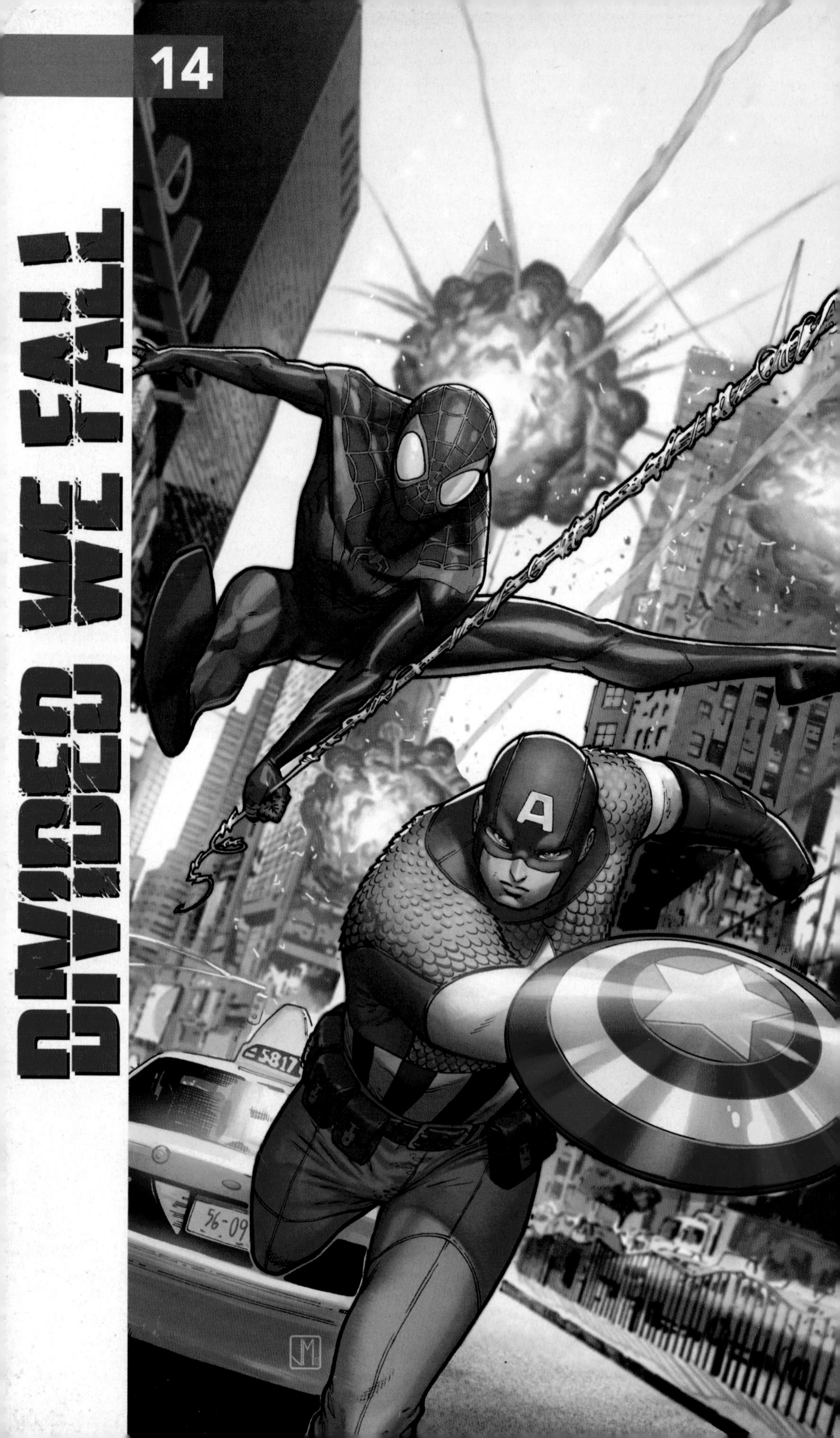
14
DIVIDED WE FALL
5817
56-09

.H.I.E.L.D. SITUATION MAP:

[ti-government militia hot spots]

ntana, N. Dakota,
Dakota, Wyoming,
izona, New Mexico,
Carolina, S. Carolina,
orgia

[Eastern seaboard control zone]

New England,
New York,
New Jersey,
Delaware,
Washington D.C.,
Maryland,
Virginia

secured by National Guard under emergency powers committee

[Great Lakes states]

Minnesota,
Wisconsin,
Michigan,
Illinois,
Indiana, Ohio

status unknown

e West Coast]

lifornia, Oregon,
shington

tatus unknown

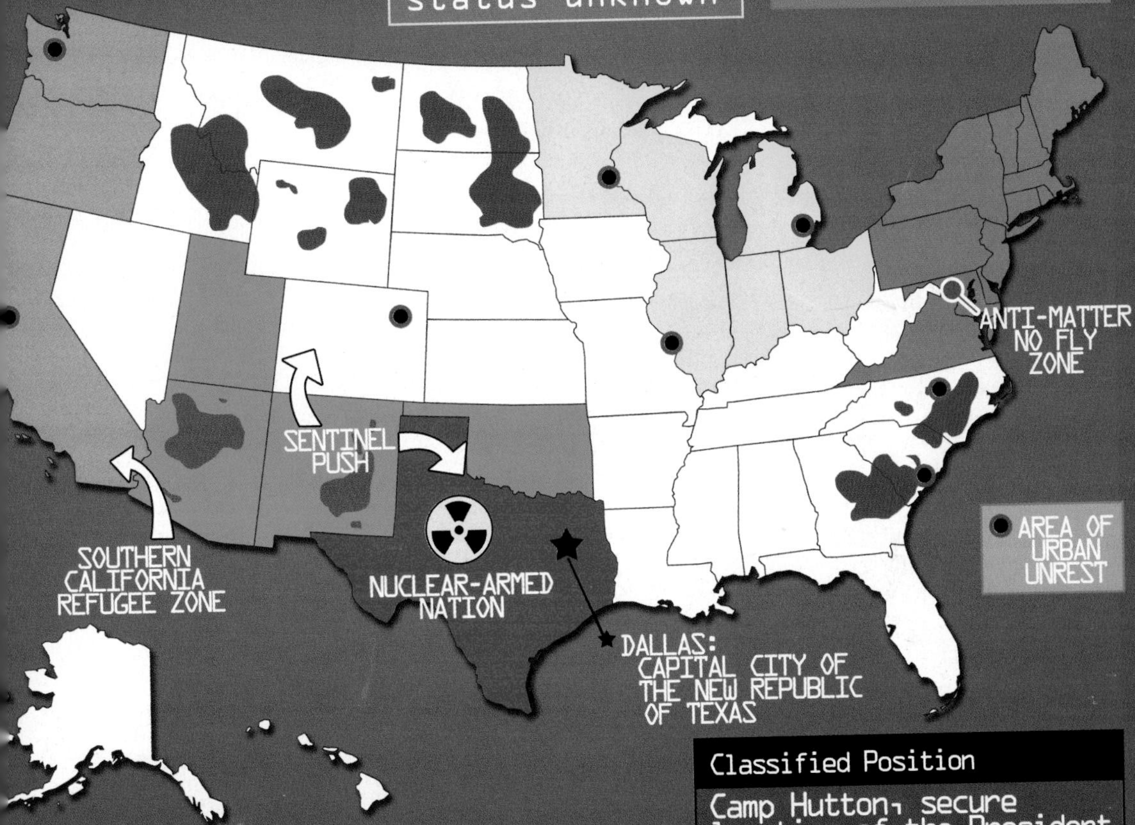

ANTI-MATTER NO FLY ZONE
SENTINEL PUSH
AREA OF URBAN UNREST
SOUTHERN CALIFORNIA REFUGEE ZONE
NUCLEAR-ARMED NATION
DALLAS: CAPITAL CITY OF THE NEW REPUBLIC OF TEXAS

Classified Position

Camp Hutton, secure location of the President of the United States

Sentinel-controlled no-man's-land]

ew Mexico, Arizona,
tah, Oklahoma

abandoned by the
J.S. government

[The New Republic of Texas]

Texas

declared state independence

ALL STATES SHOWN IN WHITE ARE U.S. GOVERNMENT-CONTROLLED ZONES

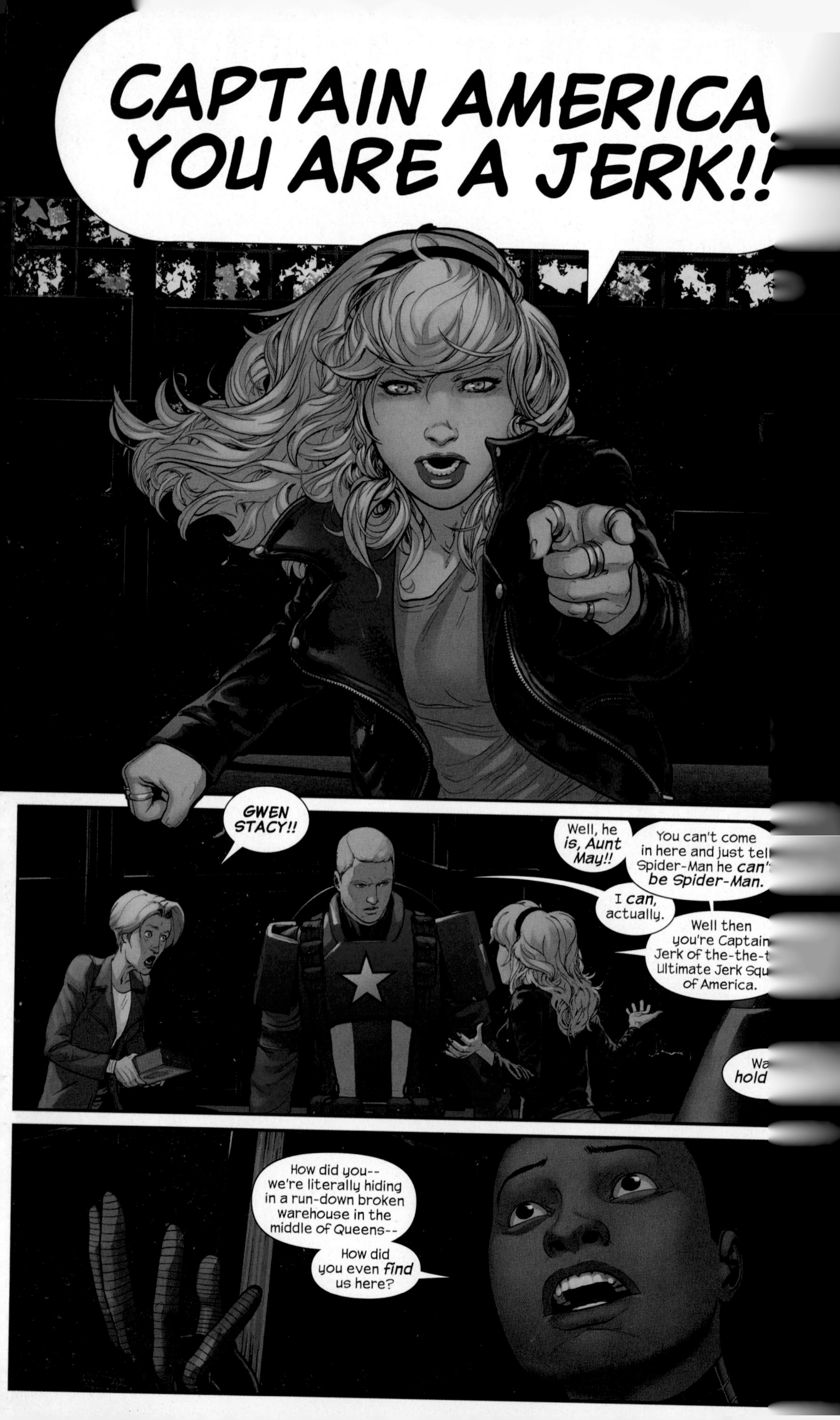
CAPTAIN AMERICA YOU ARE A JERK!!
GWEN STACY!!
Well, he is, Aunt May!!
You can't come in here and just tel
Spider-Man he can'
be Spider-Man.
I can, actually.
Well then you're Captain Jerk of the-the-t
Ultimate Jerk Squ
of America.
Wa
hold
How did you-- we're literally hiding in a run-down broken warehouse in the middle of Queens--
How did you even find us here?

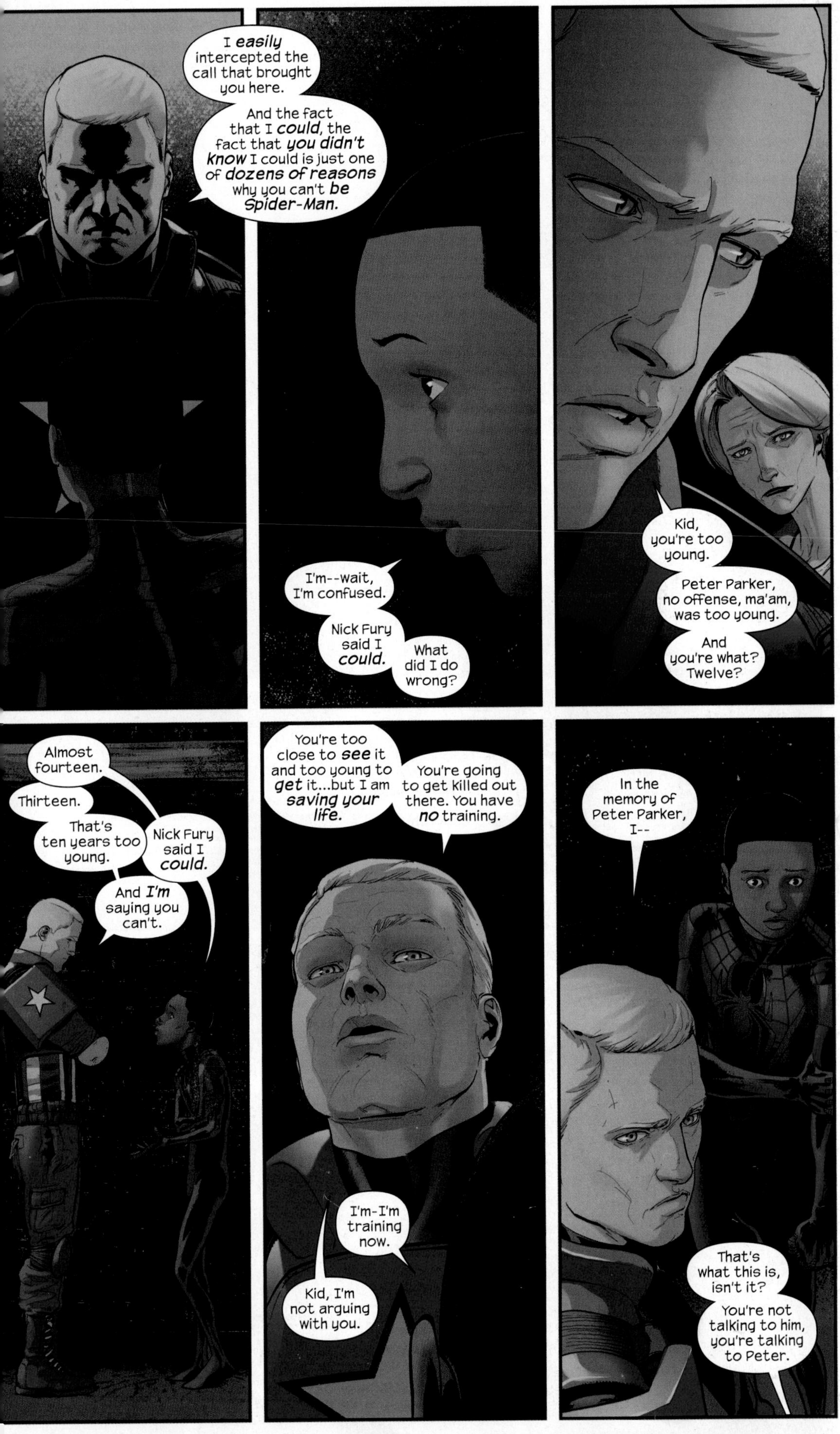
I easily intercepted the call that brought you here.
And the fact that I could, the fact that you didn't know I could is just one of dozens of reasons why you can't be Spider-Man.
I'm--wait, I'm confused.
Nick Fury said I could.
What did I do wrong?
Kid, you're too young.
Peter Parker, no offense, ma'am, was too young.
And you're what? Twelve?
Almost fourteen.
Thirteen.
That's ten years too young.
Nick Fury said I could.
And I'm saying you can't.
You're too close to see it and too young to get it...but I am saving your life.
You're going to get killed out there. You have no training.
I'm-I'm training now.
Kid, I'm not arguing with you.
In the memory of Peter Parker, I--
That's what this is, isn't it?
You're not talking to him, you're talking to Peter.

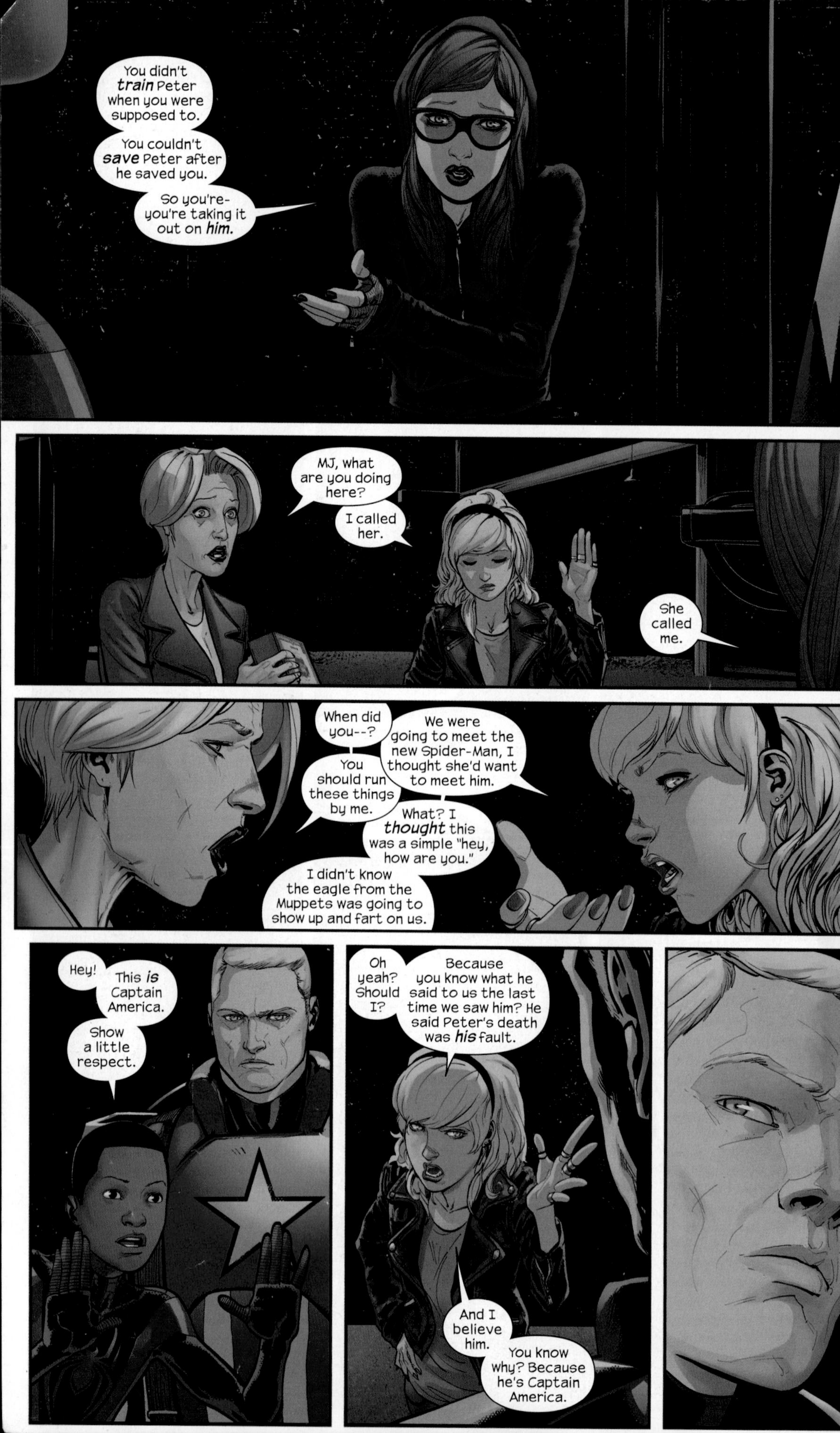
You didn't *train* Peter when you were supposed to.
You couldn't *save* Peter after he saved you.
So you're- you're taking it out on *him.*
MJ, what are you doing here?
I called her.
She called me.
When did you--?
We were going to meet the new Spider-Man, I thought she'd want to meet him.
You should run these things by me.
What? I *thought* this was a simple "hey, how are you."
I didn't know the eagle from the Muppets was going to show up and fart on us.
Hey!
This *is* Captain America.
Show a little respect.
Oh yeah? Should I?
Because you know what he said to us the last time we saw him? He said Peter's death was *his* fault.
And I believe him.
You know why? Because he's Captain America.

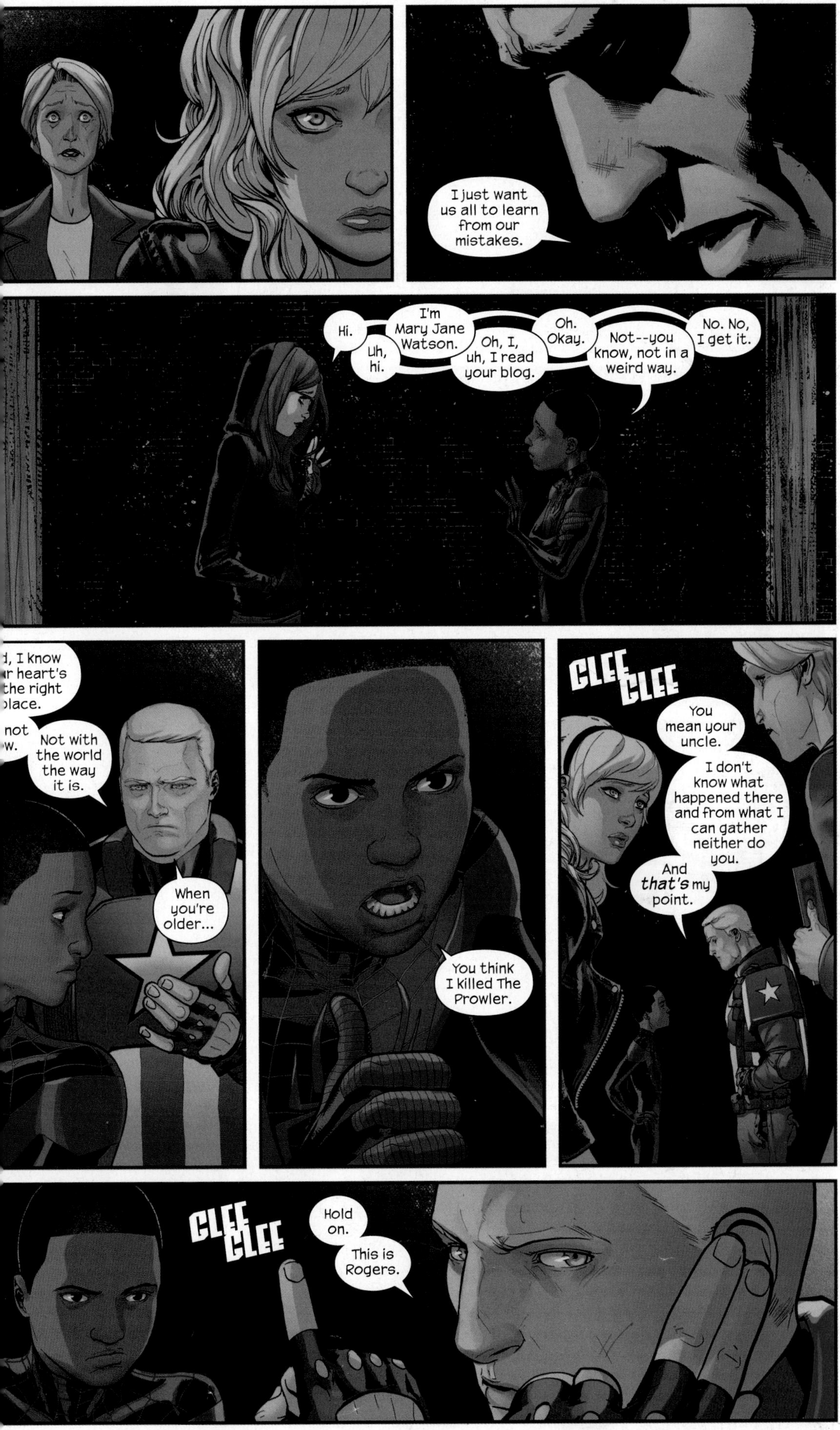
I just want us all to learn from our mistakes.
Hi.
Uh, hi.
I'm Mary Jane Watson.
Oh, I, uh, I read your blog.
Oh. Okay.
Not--you know, not in a weird way.
No. No, I get it.
d, I know r heart's the right place.
not w.
Not with the world the way it is.
When you're older...
You think I killed The Prowler.
CLEE CLEE
You mean your uncle.
I don't know what happened there and from what I can gather neither do you.
And that's my point.
CLEE CLEE
Hold on.
This is Rogers.

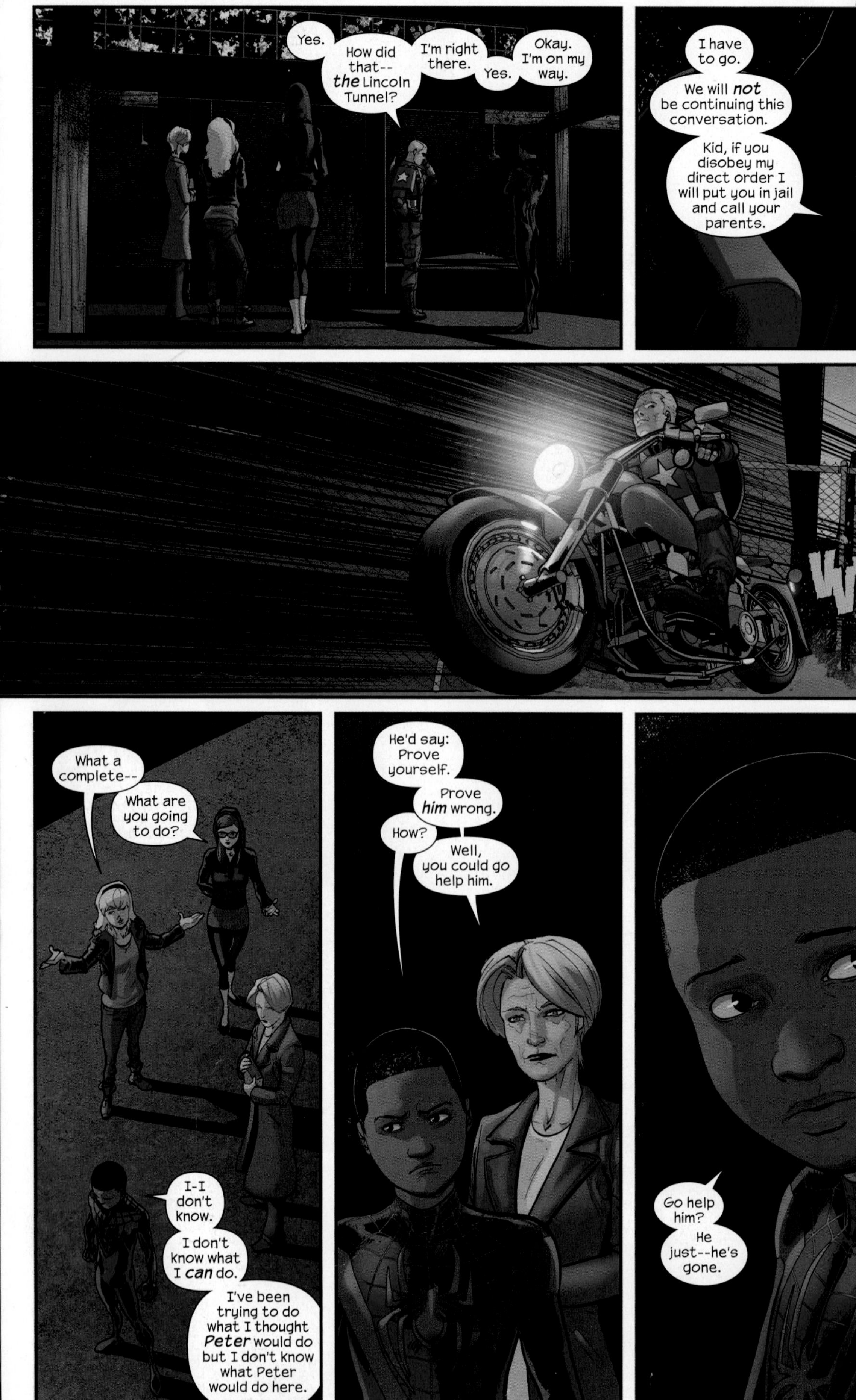
Yes.
How did that-- *the* Lincoln Tunnel?
I'm right there.
Yes.
Okay. I'm on my way.
I have to go.
We will *not* be continuing this conversation.
Kid, if you disobey my direct order I will put you in jail and call your parents.
What a complete--
What are you going to do?
I-I don't know.
I don't know what I *can* do.
I've been trying to do what I thought *Peter* would do but I don't know what Peter would do here.
He'd say: Prove yourself.
Prove *him* wrong.
How?
Well, you could go help him.
Go help him?
He just--he's gone.

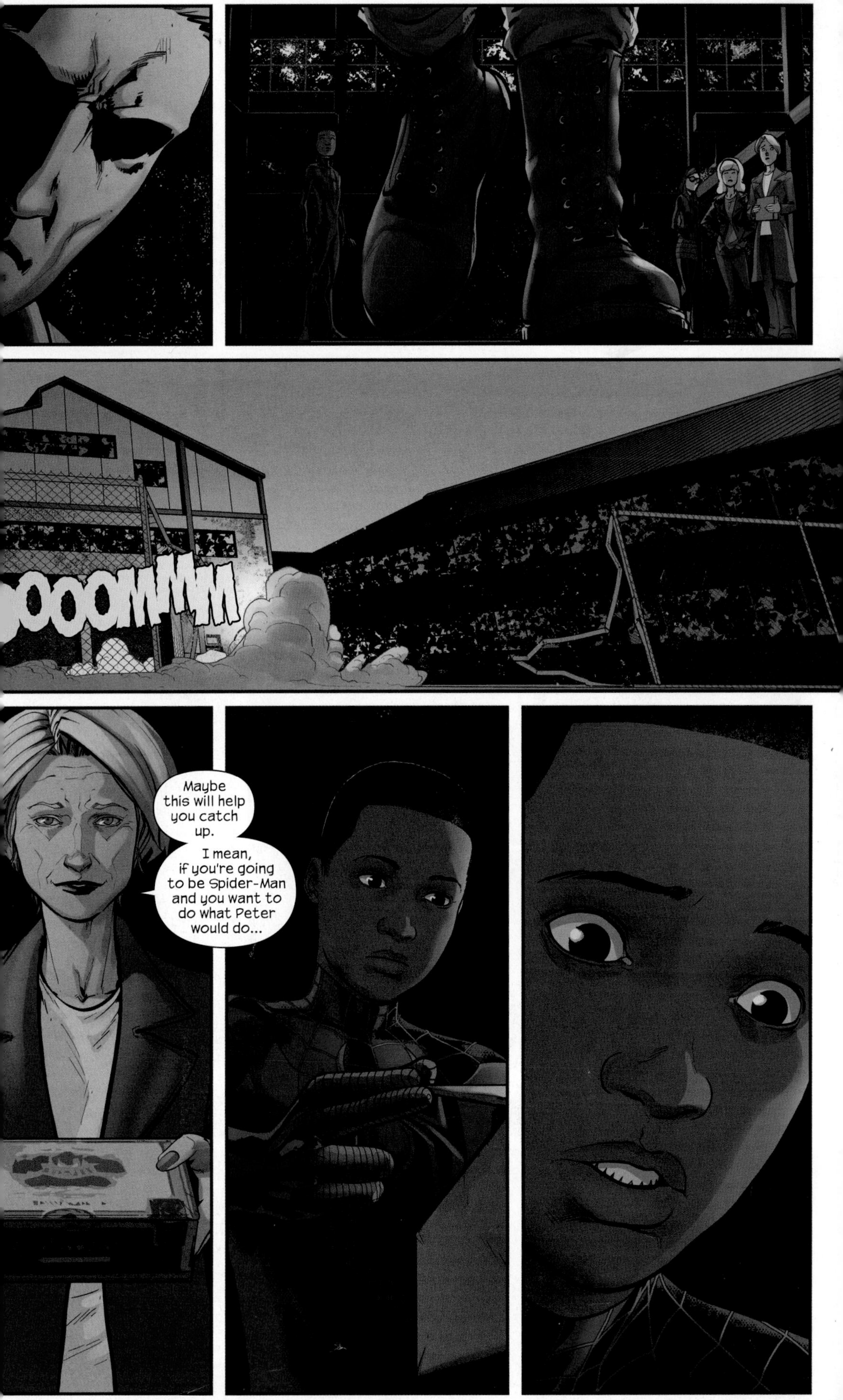
OOOMMMM
Maybe this will help you catch up.
I mean, if you're going to be Spider-Man and you want to do what Peter would do...

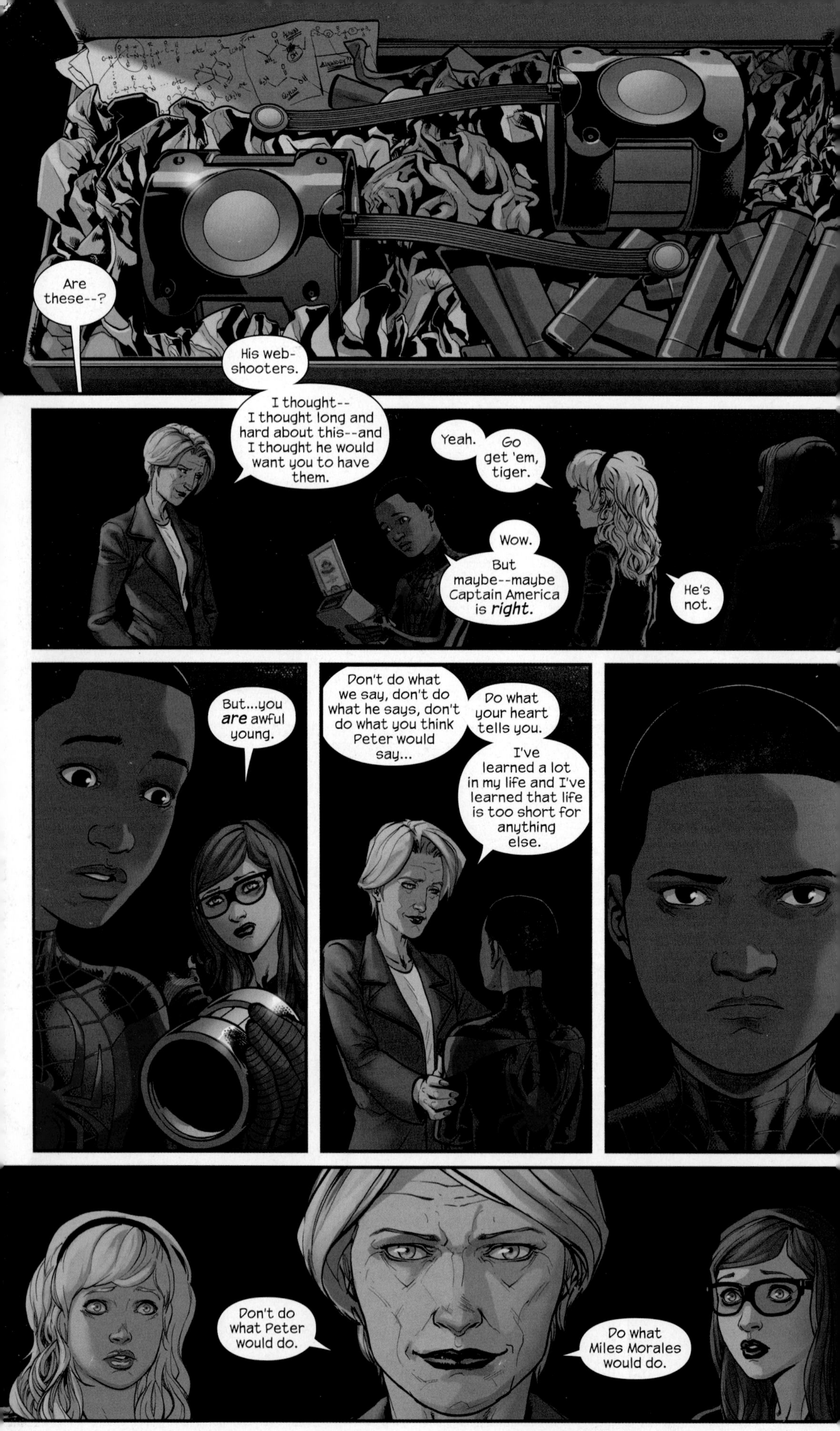
Are these--?
His web-shooters.
I thought-- I thought long and hard about this--and I thought he would want you to have them.
Yeah.
Go get 'em, tiger.
Wow.
But maybe--maybe Captain America is *right.*
He's not.
But...you *are* awful young.
Don't do what we say, don't do what he says, don't do what you think Peter would say...
Do what your heart tells you.
I've learned a lot in my life and I've learned that life is too short for anything else.
Don't do what Peter would do.
Do what Miles Morales would do.

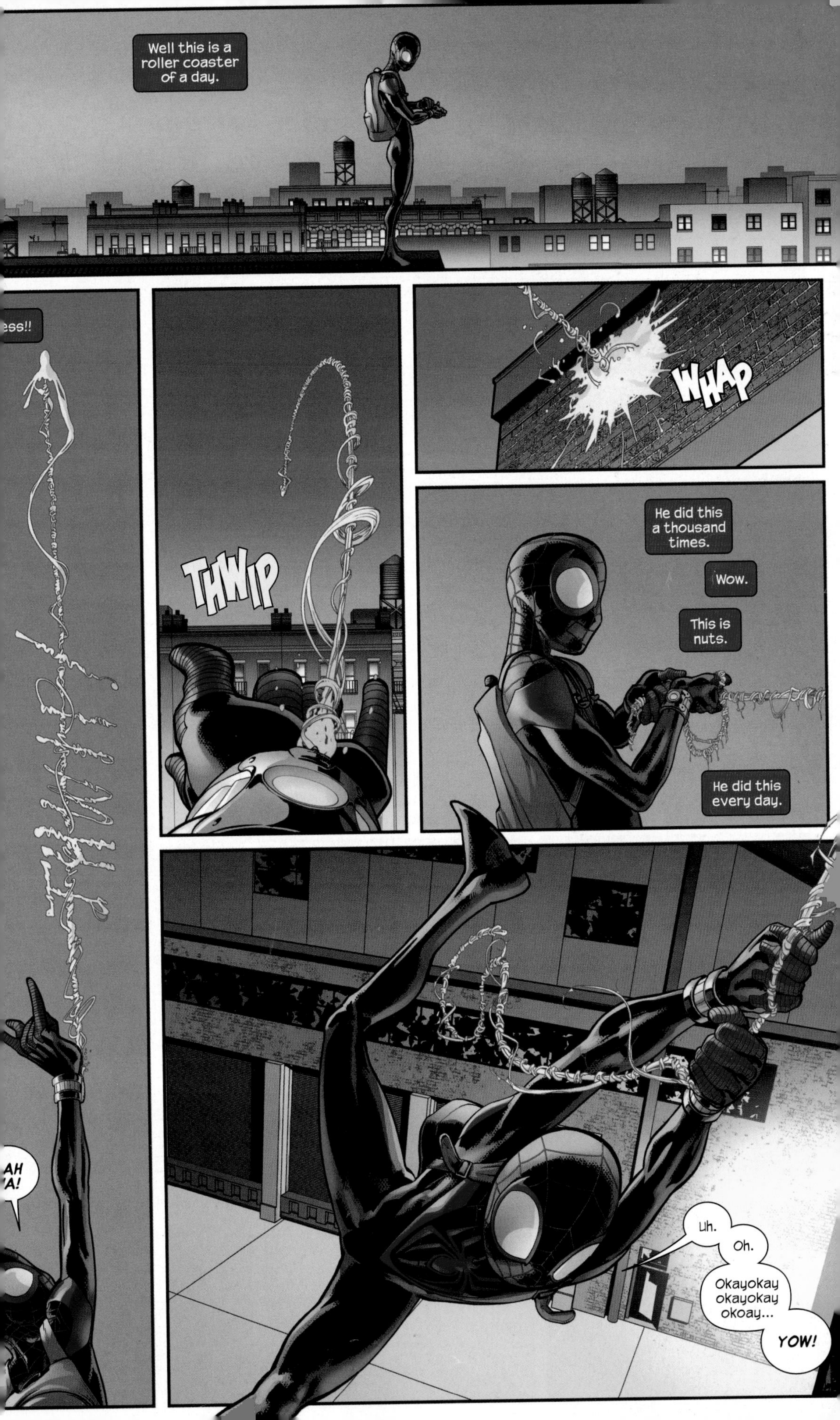

Well this is a roller coaster of a day.
ess!!
THWIP
WHAP
He did this a thousand times.
Wow.
This is nuts.
He did this every day.
Uh.
Oh.
Okayokay okayokay okoay...
YOW!

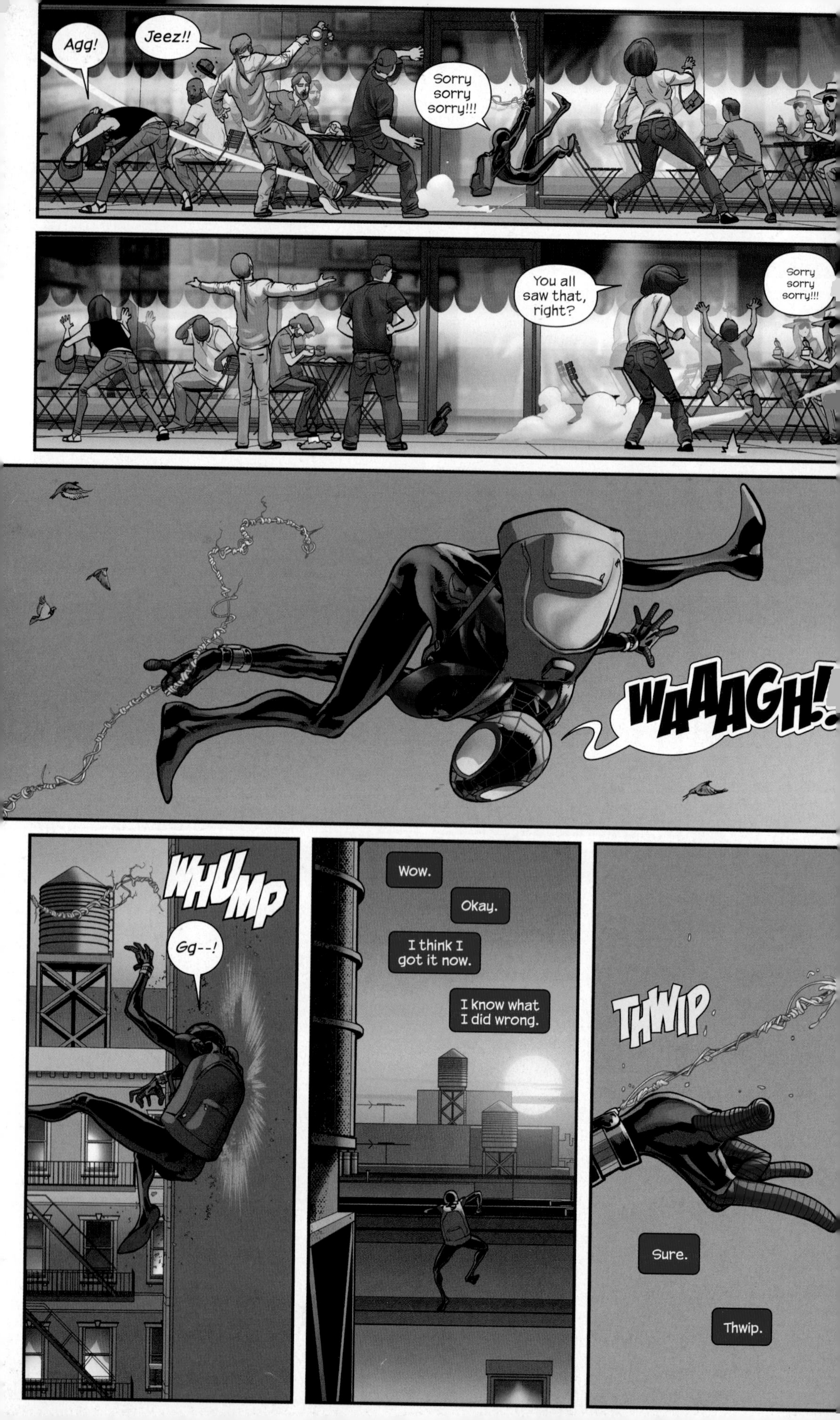
Agg!
Jeez!!
Sorry sorry sorry!!!
You all saw that, right?
Sorry sorry sorry!!!
WAAAGH!
WHUMP
Gg--!
Wow.
Okay.
I think I got it now.
I know what I did wrong.
THWIP
Sure.
Thwip.

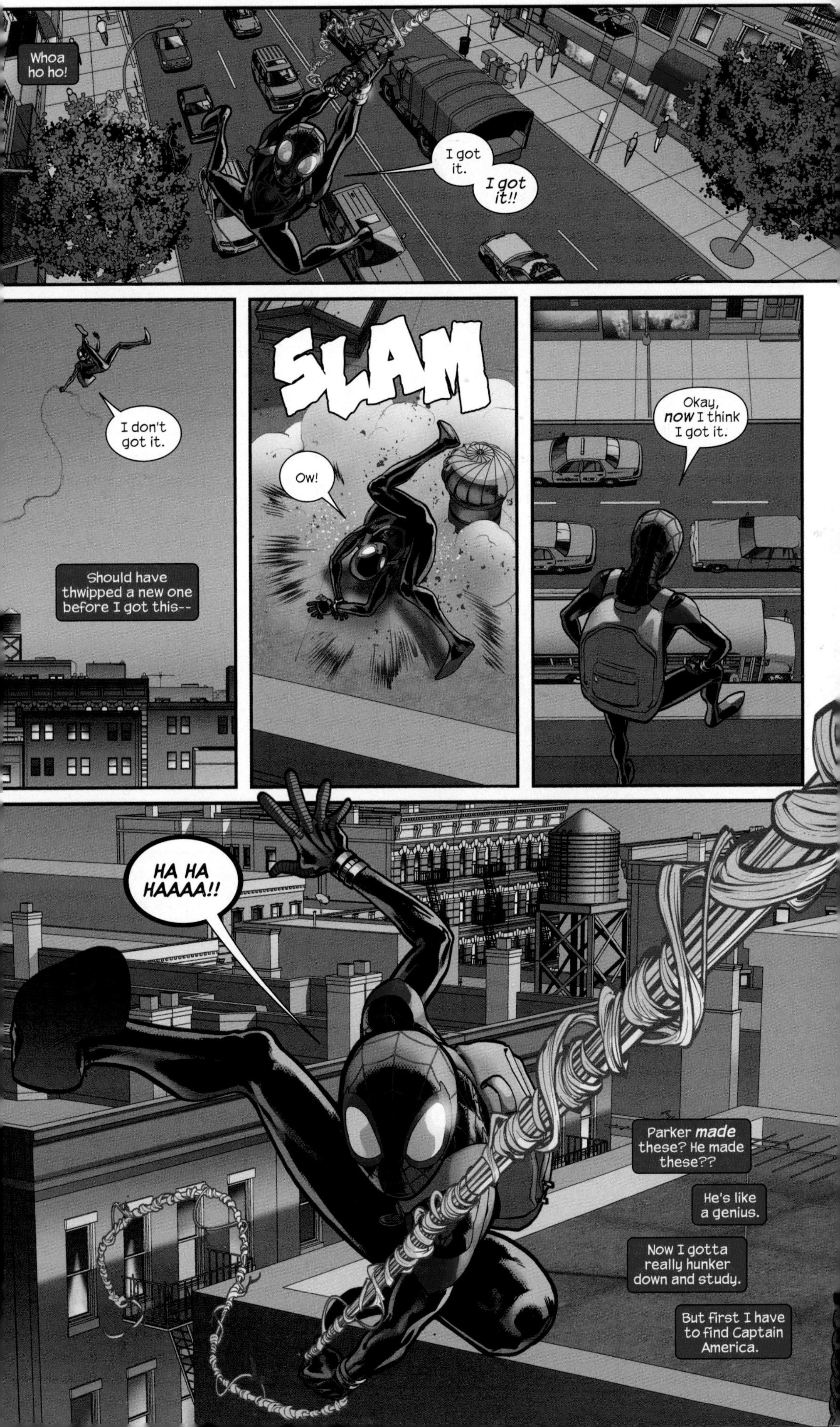
Whoa ho ho!
I got it.
I got it!!
I don't got it.
Should have thwipped a new one before I got this--
SLAM
Ow!
Okay, now I think I got it.
HA HA HAAAA!!
Parker made these? He made these??
He's like a genius.
Now I gotta really hunker down and study.
But first I have to find Captain America.

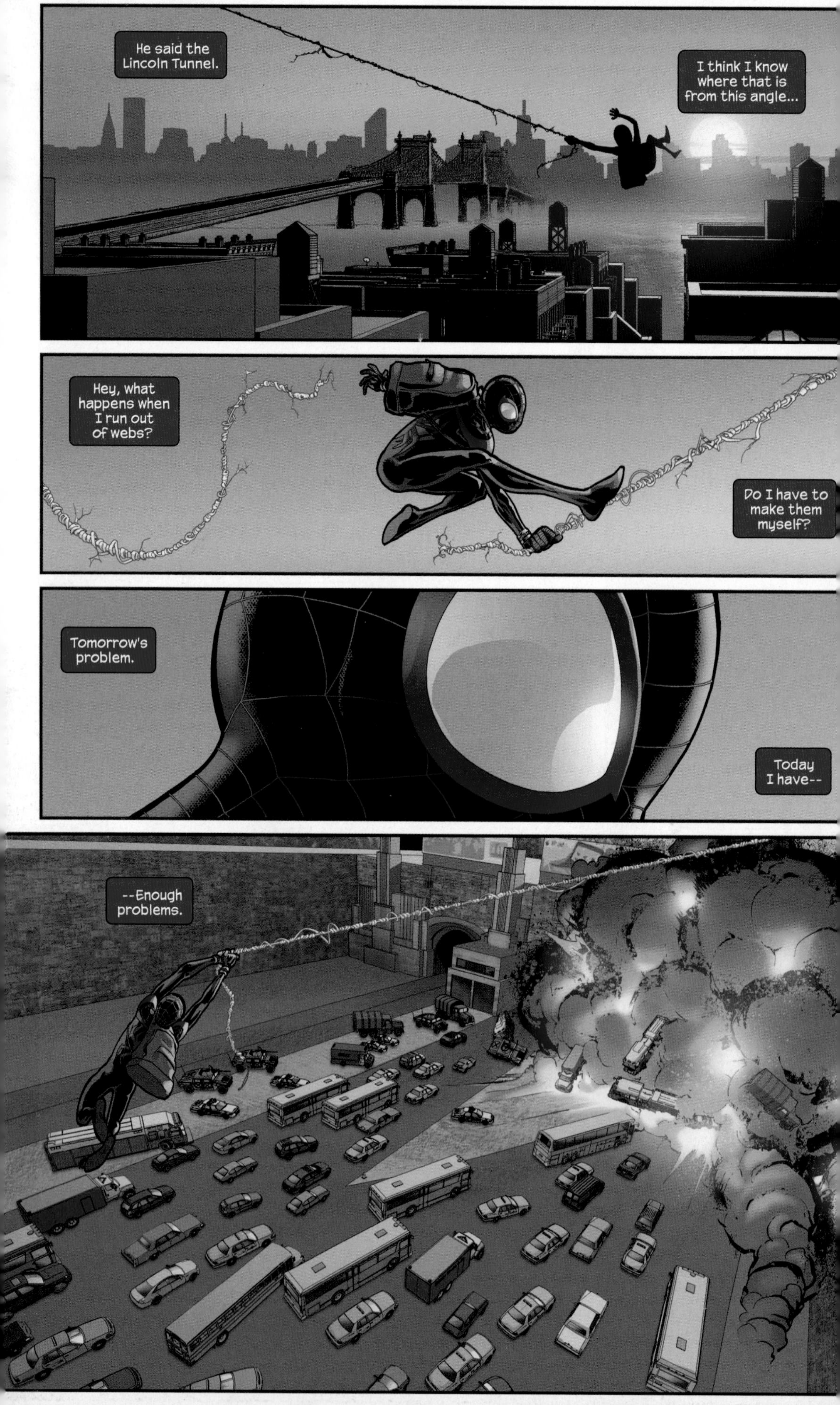
He said the Lincoln Tunnel.
I think I know where that is from this angle...
Hey, what happens when I run out of webs?
Do I have to make them myself?
Tomorrow's problem.
Today I have--
--Enough problems.

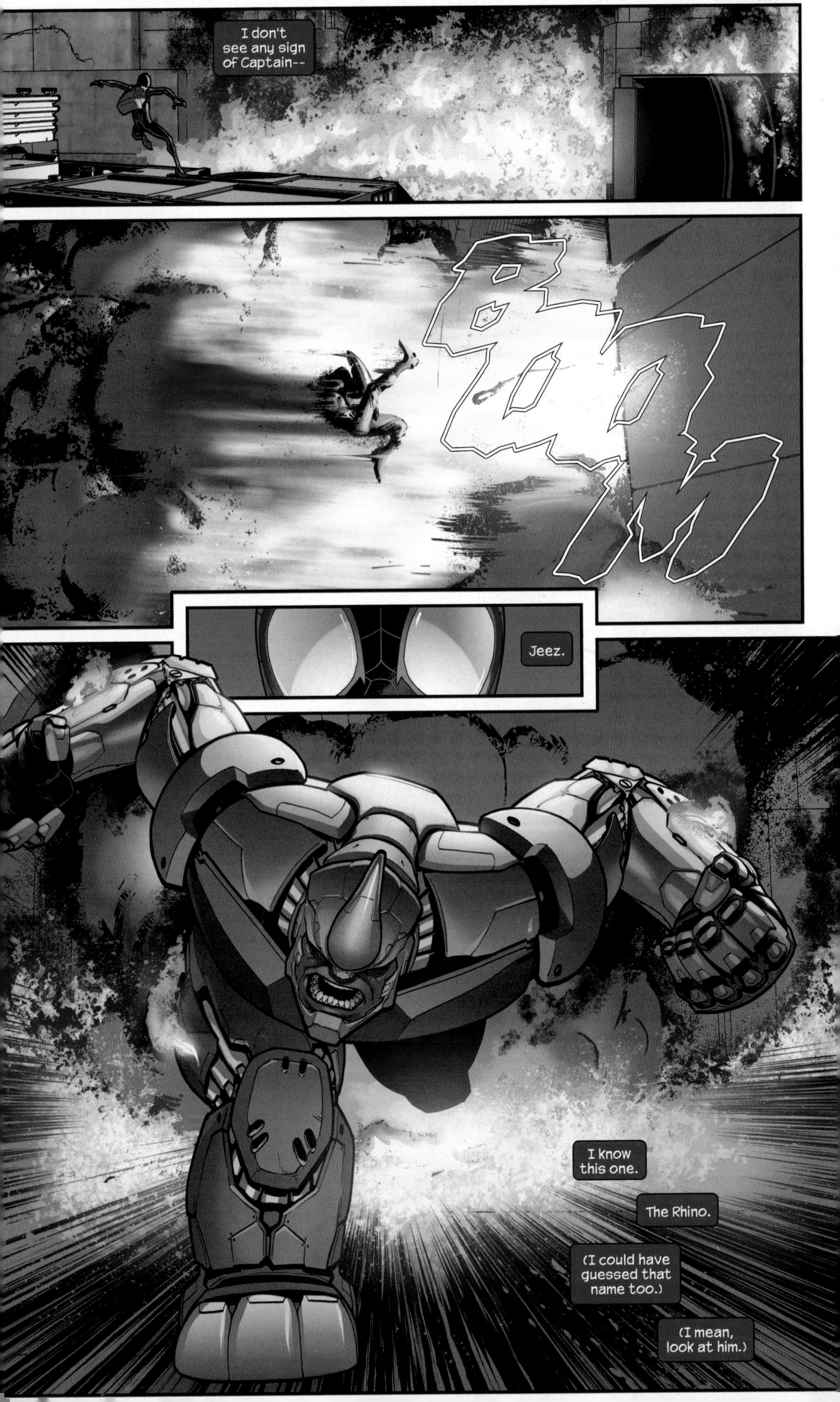
I don't see any sign of Captain--
BOOM
Jeez.
I know this one.
The Rhino.
(I could have guessed that name too.)
(I mean, look at him.)

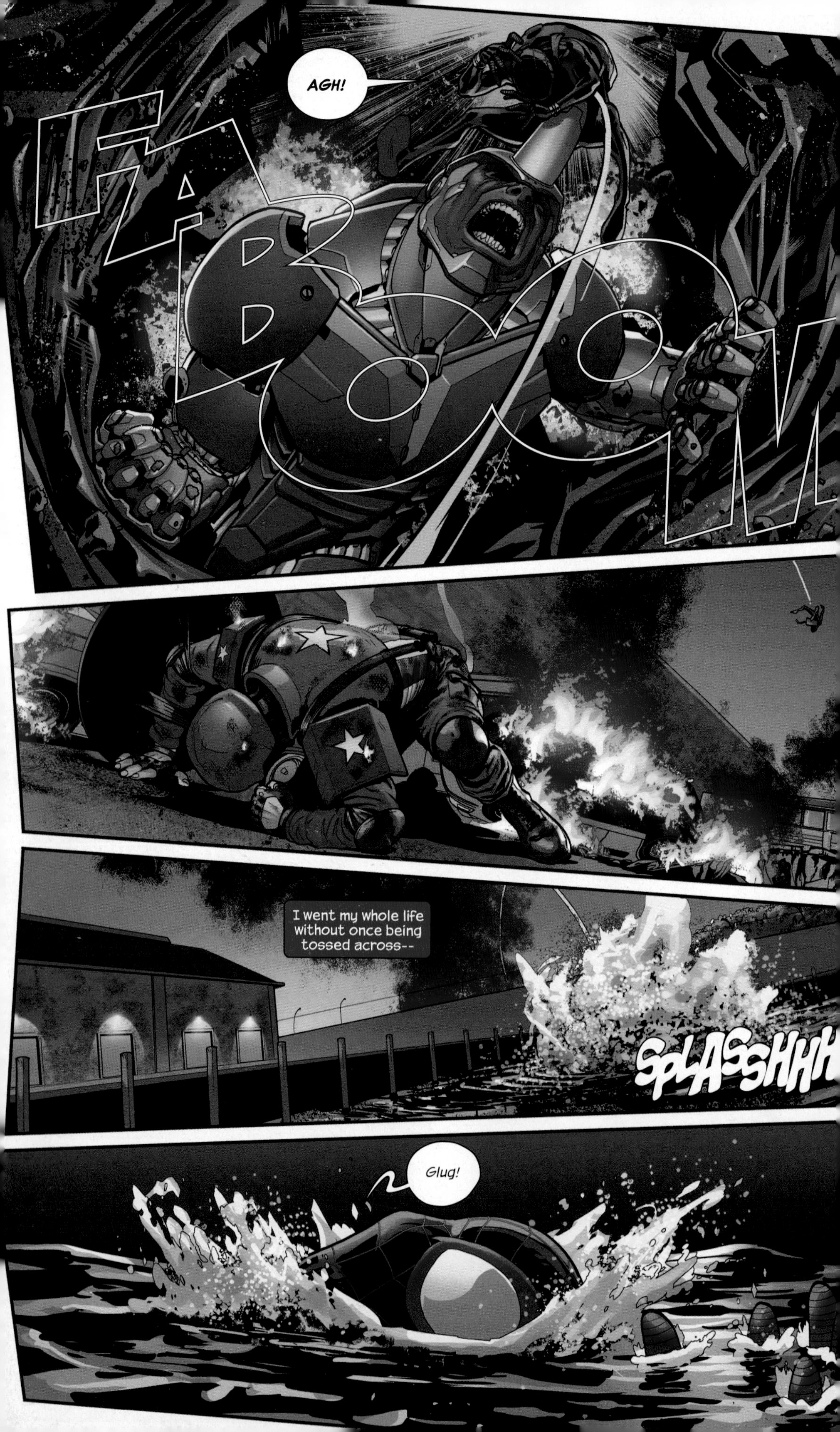
AGH!
KA-BOOM
I went my whole life without once being tossed across--
SPLASSHHH
Glug!

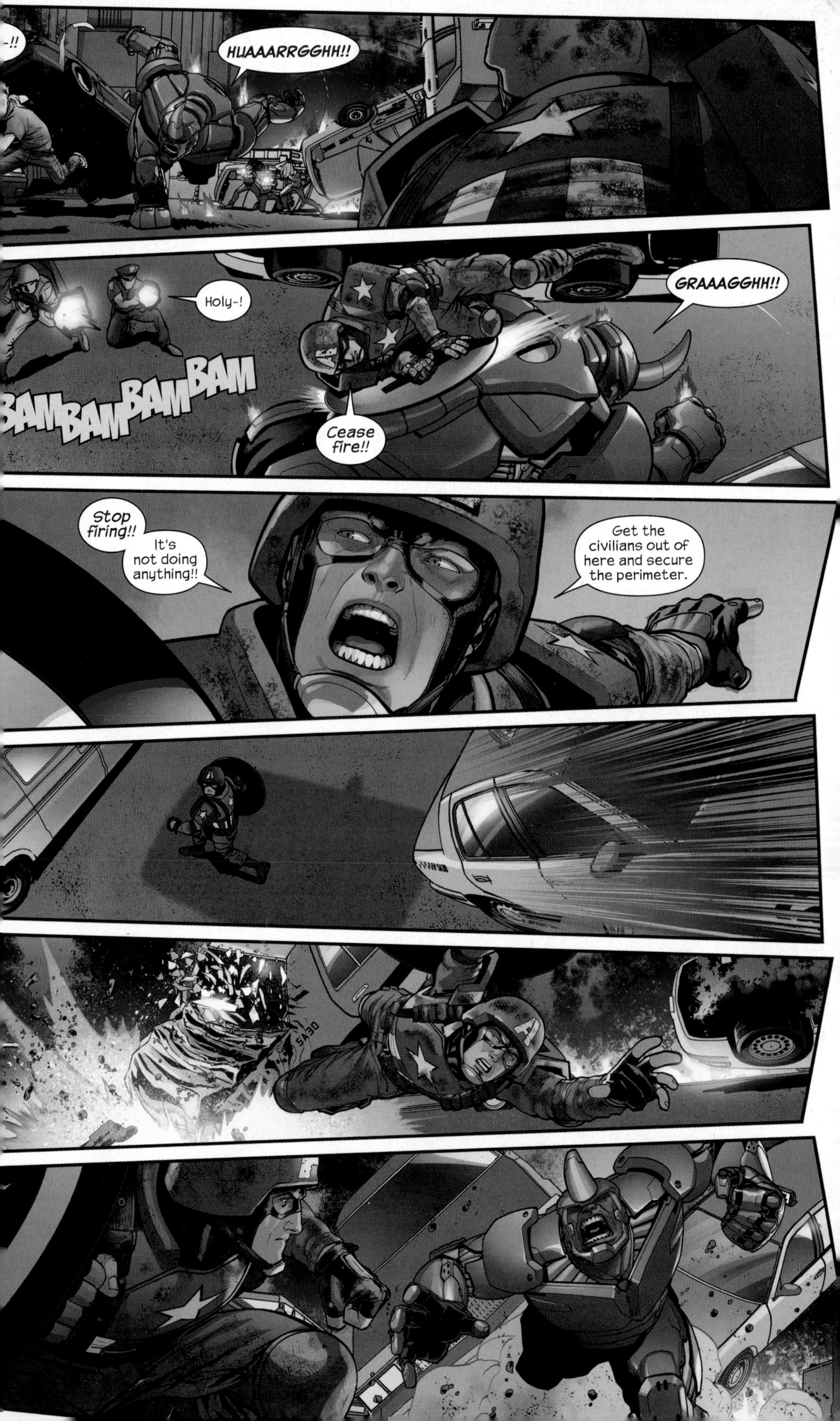

-!!
HUAAARRGGHH!!
Holy-!
GRAAAGGHH!!
BAMBAMBAMBAM
Cease fire!!
Stop firing!!
It's not doing anything!!
Get the civilians out of here and secure the perimeter.

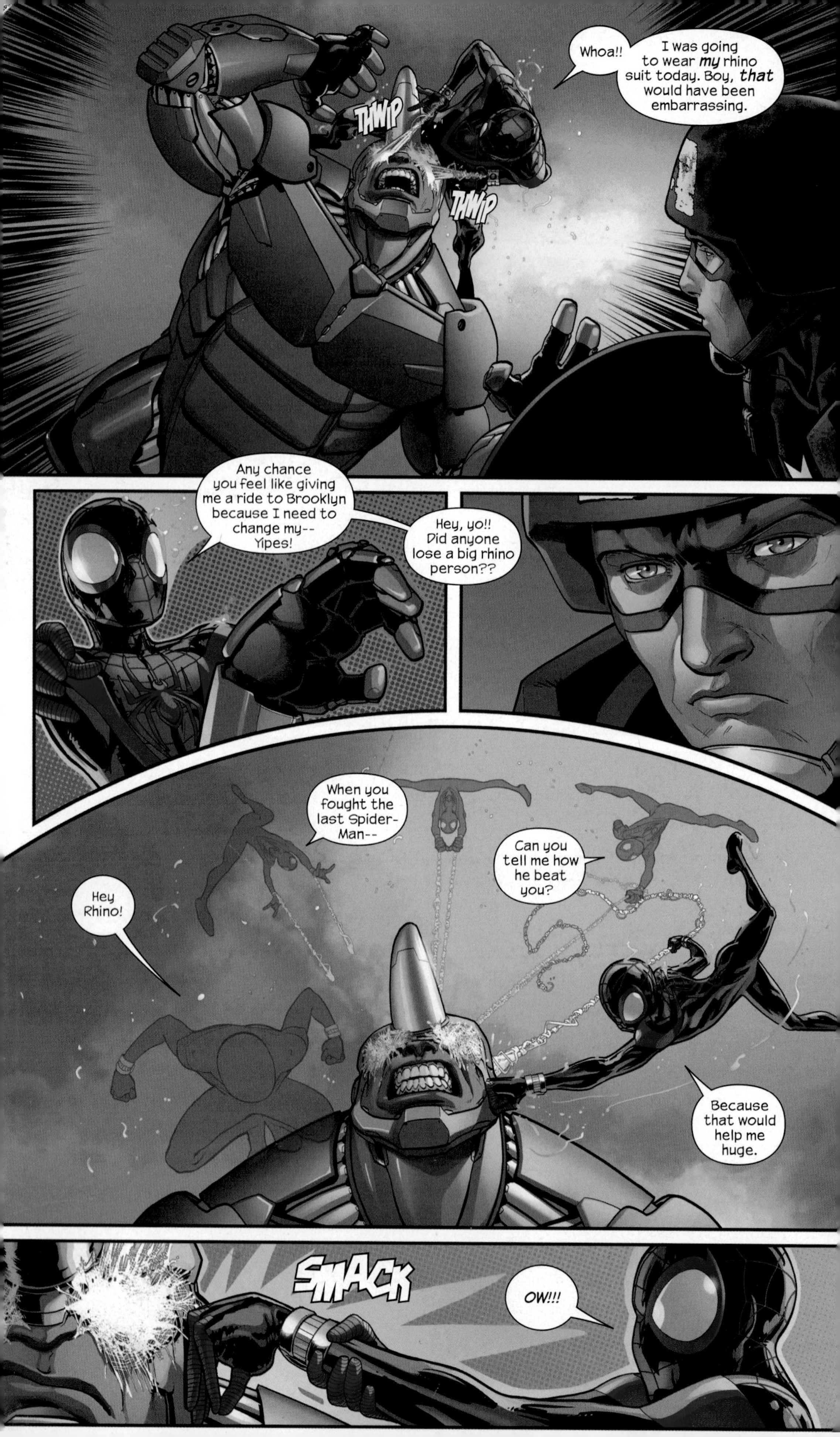

THWIP
THWIP
Whoa!!
I was going to wear *my* rhino suit today. Boy, *that* would have been embarrassing.
Any chance you feel like giving me a ride to Brooklyn because I need to change my-- Yipes!
Hey, yo!! Did anyone lose a big rhino person??
Hey Rhino!
When you fought the last Spider-Man--
Can you tell me how he beat you?
Because that would help me huge.
SMACK
OW!!!

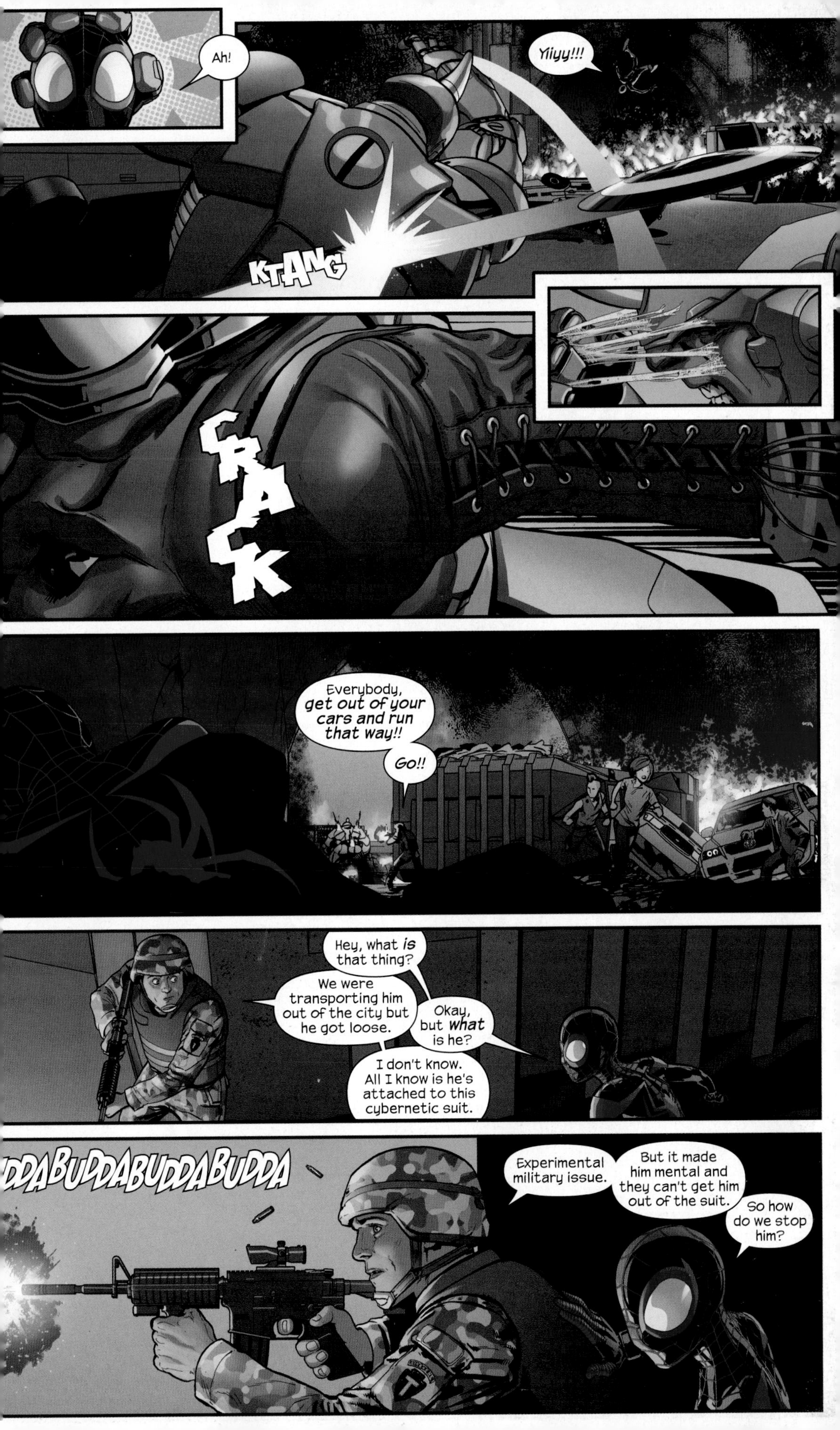
Ah!
Yiiyy!!!
KTANG
CRACK
Everybody, get out of your cars and run that way!!
Go!!
Hey, what is that thing?
We were transporting him out of the city but he got loose.
Okay, but what is he?
I don't know. All I know is he's attached to this cybernetic suit.
DDABUDDABUDDABUDDA
Experimental military issue.
But it made him mental and they can't get him out of the suit.
So how do we stop him?

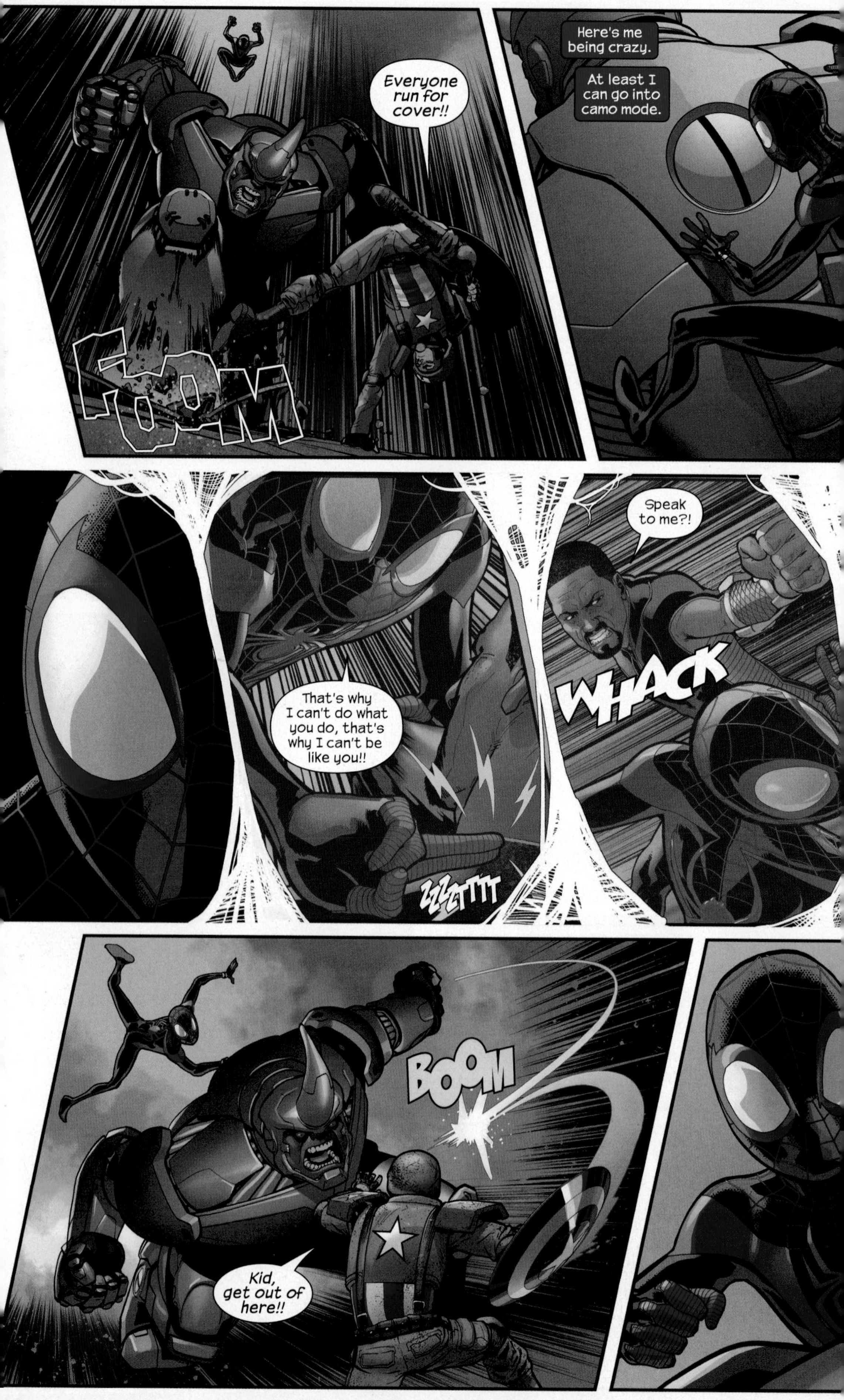
Everyone run for cover!!
FOOM
Here's me being crazy.
At least I can go into camo mode.
That's why I can't do what you do, that's why I can't be like you!!
ZZZZTTTT
Speak to me?!
WHACK
BOOM
Kid, get out of here!!

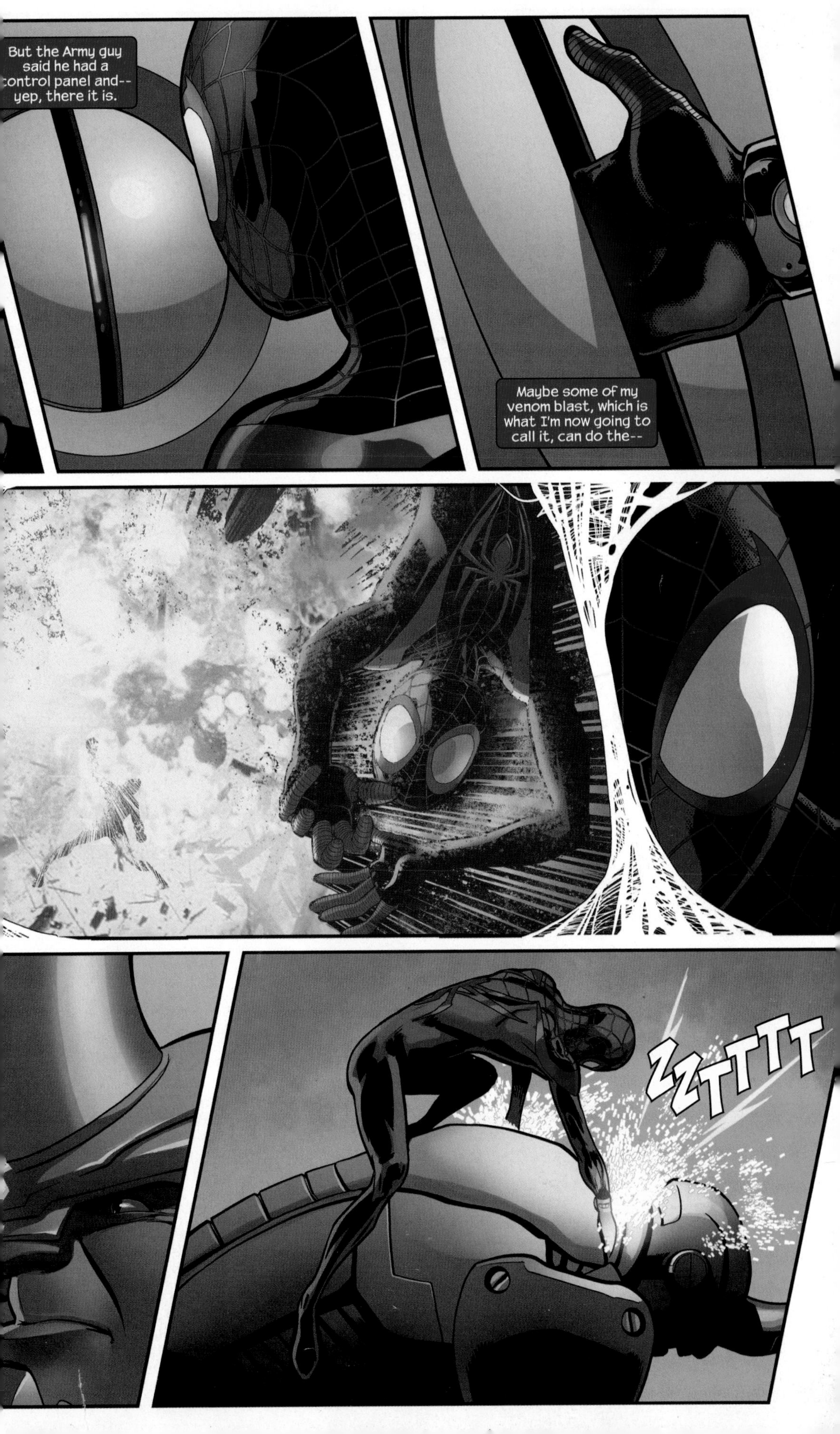
But the Army guy said he had a control panel and-- yep, there it is.
Maybe some of my venom blast, which is what I'm now going to call it, can do the--
ZZTTTT

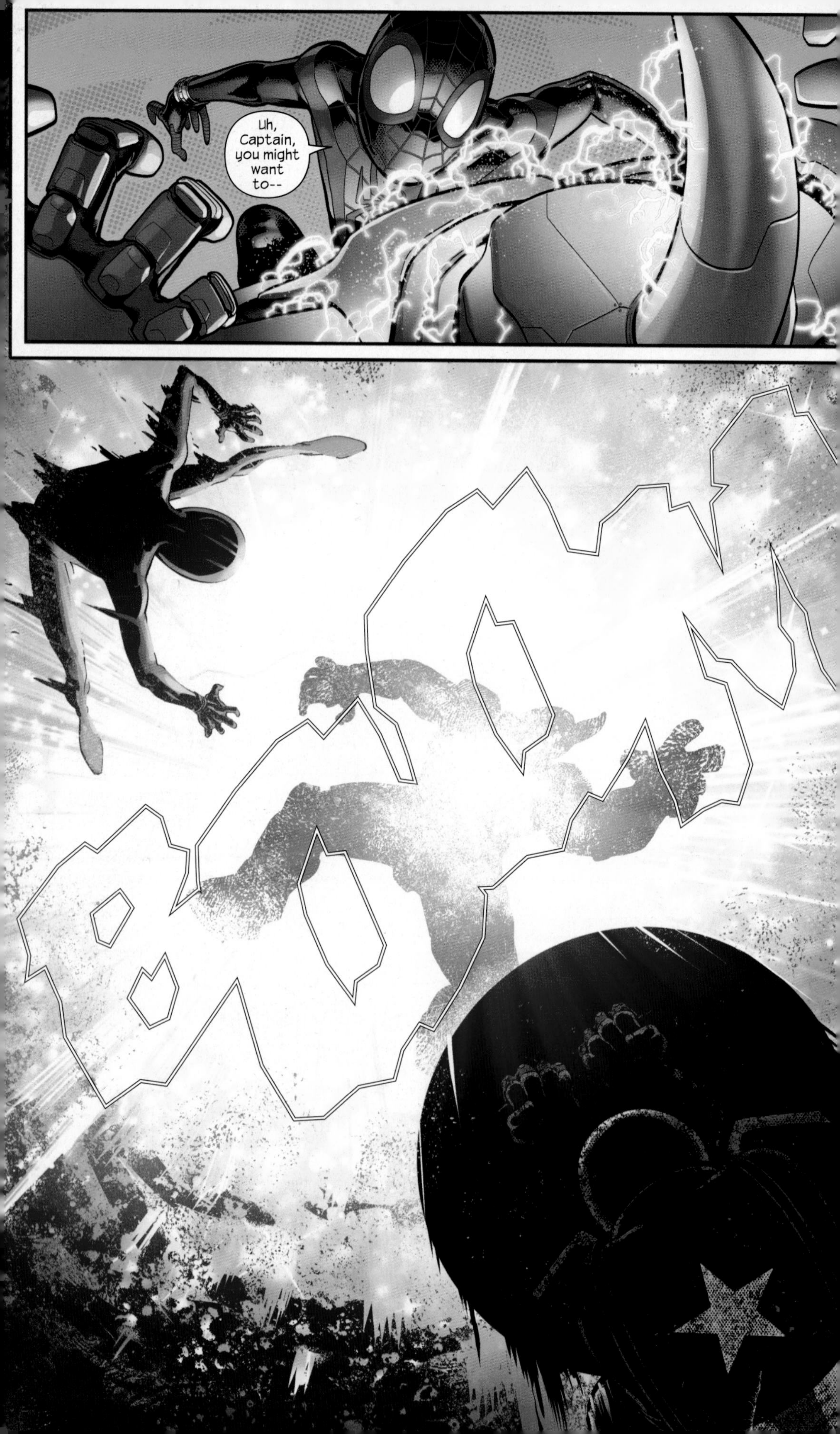
Uh, Captain, you might want to--
BOOM

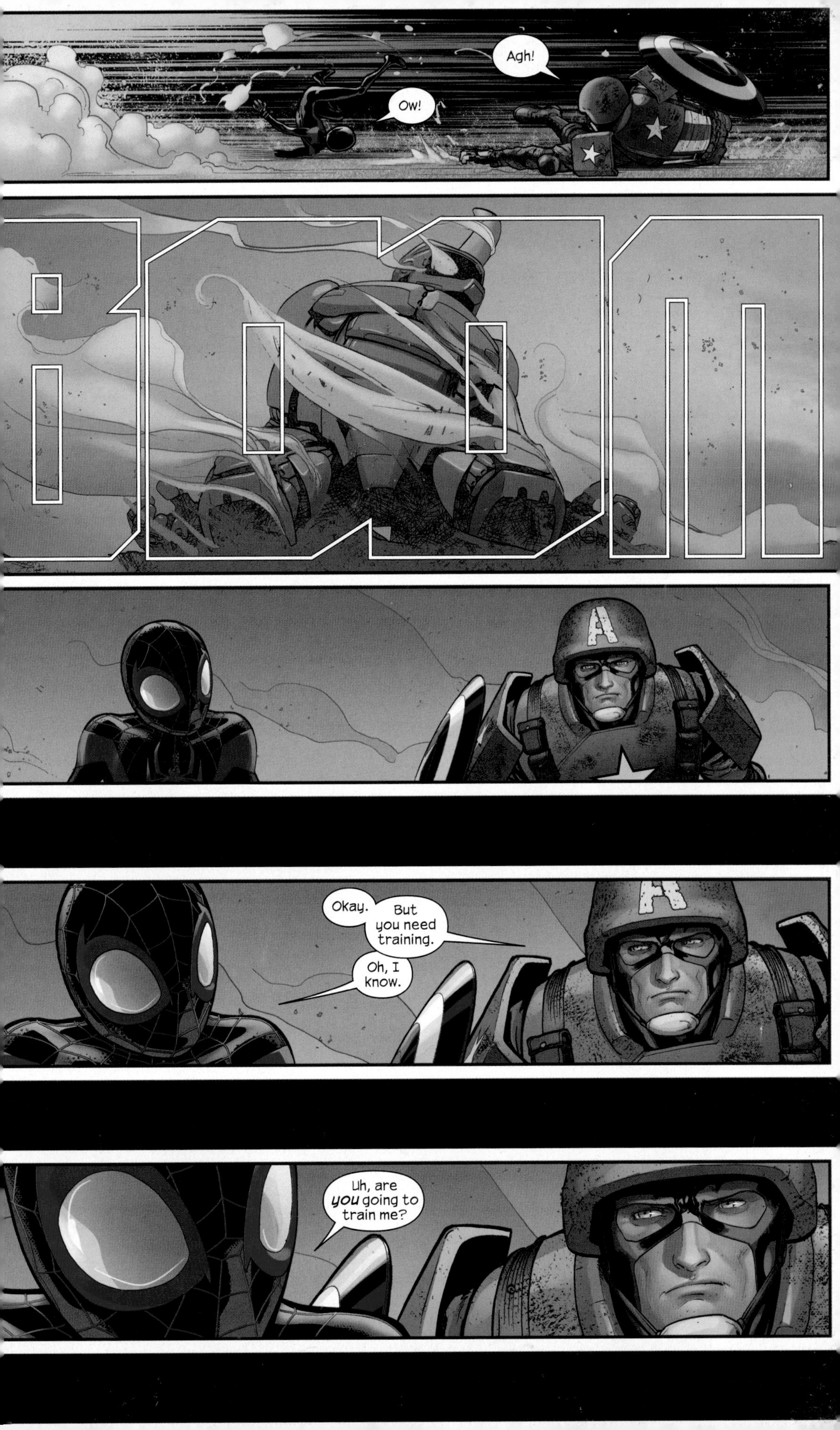
Agh!
Ow!
Okay.
But you need training.
Oh, I know.
Uh, are *you* going to train me?

15

UNITED WE STAND

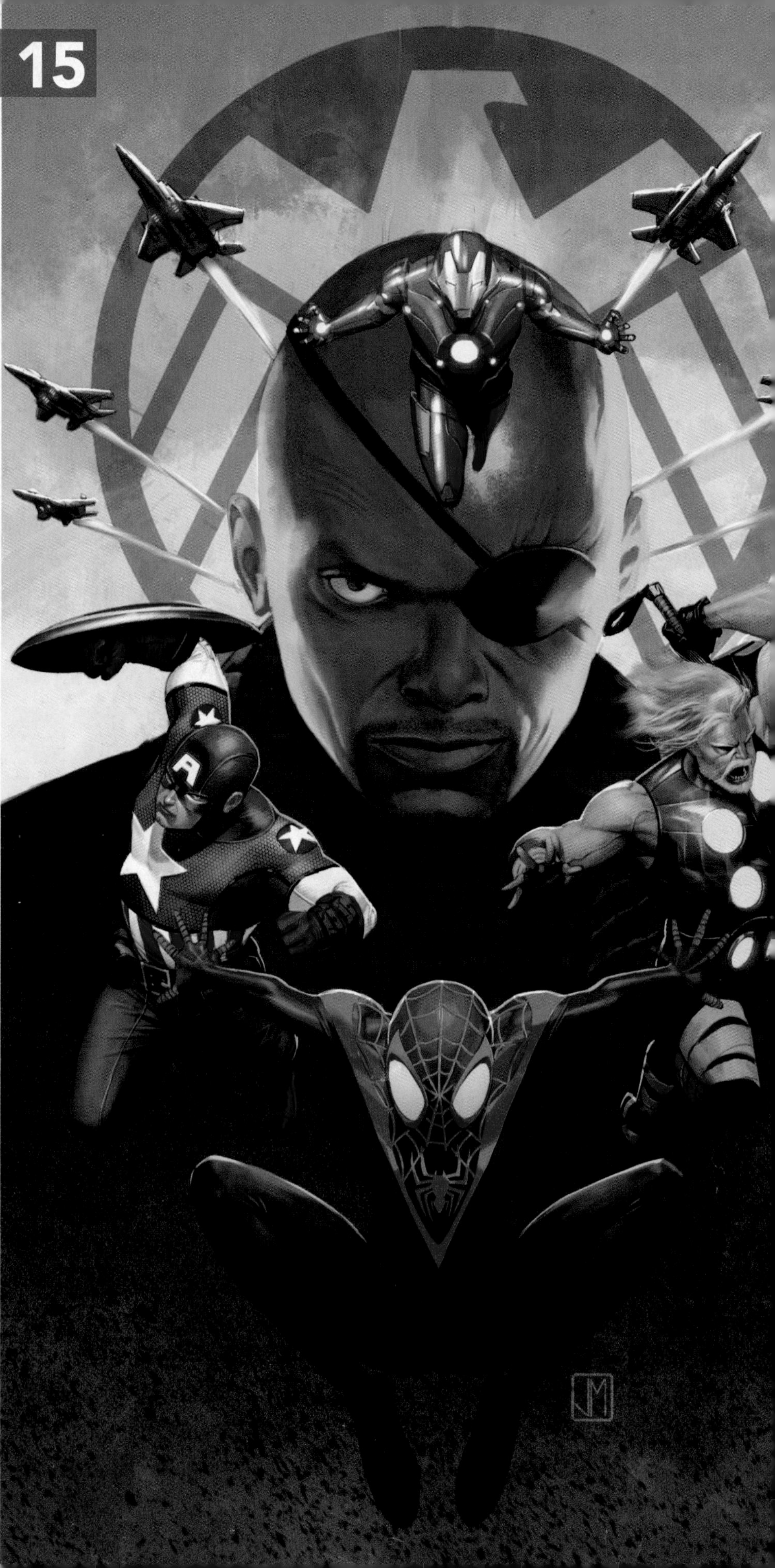

.H.I.E.L.D. SITUATION MAP:

[ti-government militia hot spots]

ntana, N. Dakota,
Dakota, Wyoming,
izona, New Mexico,
Carolina, S. Carolina,
orgia, Idaho

[Eastern seaboard control zone]

New England,
New York,
New Jersey,
Delaware,
Washington D.C.,
Maryland,
Virginia,
Pennsylvania

secured by
National Guard
under emergency
powers
committee

[e West Coast]

lifornia, Oregon,
shington

tatus unknown

[Great Lakes states]

Minnesota,
Wisconsin,
Michigan,
Illinois,
Indiana, Ohio

status unknown

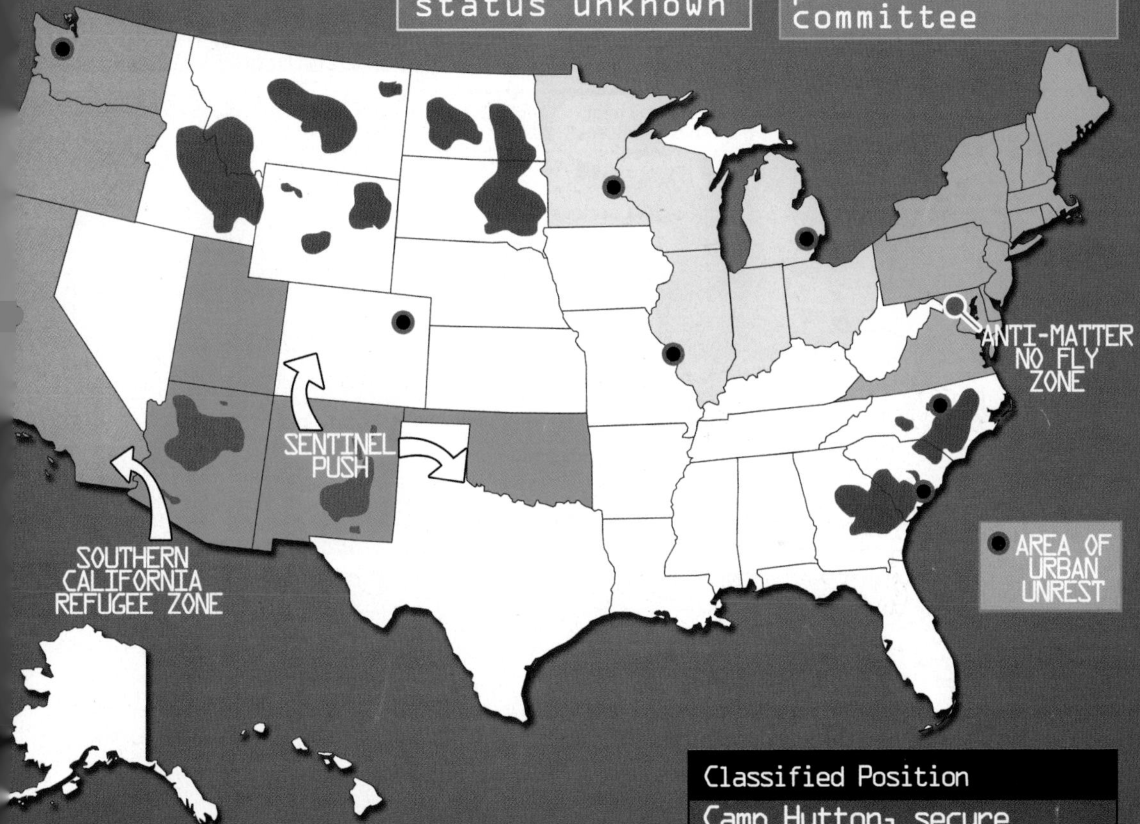

ANTI-MATTER NO FLY ZONE
SENTINEL PUSH
SOUTHERN CALIFORNIA REFUGEE ZONE
AREA OF URBAN UNREST

Classified Position

Camp Hutton, secure
location of the President
of the United States

[entinel-controlled no-man's-land]

ew Mexico, Arizona,
tah, Oklahoma

abandoned by the
J.S. government

ALL STATES
SHOWN IN WHITE
ARE U.S. GOVERNMENT-
CONTROLLED ZONES

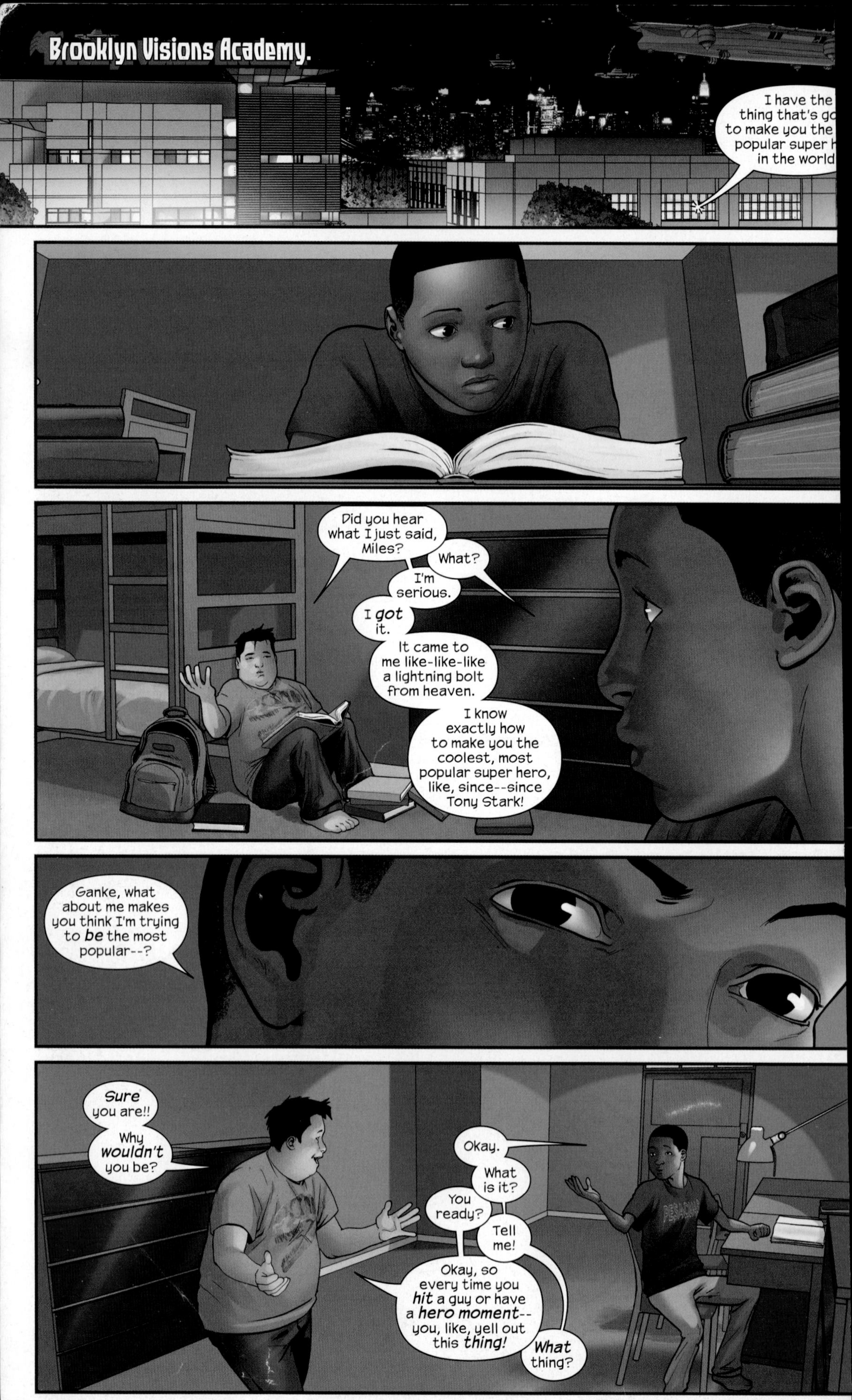
Brooklyn Visions Academy.
I have the thing that's go to make you the popular super h in the world
Did you hear what I just said, Miles?
What?
I'm serious.
I *got* it.
It came to me like-like-like a lightning bolt from heaven.
I know exactly how to make you the coolest, most popular super hero, like, since--since Tony Stark!
Ganke, what about me makes you think I'm trying to *be* the most popular--?
Sure you are!!
Why *wouldn't* you be?
Okay.
What is it?
You ready?
Tell me!
Okay, so every time you *hit* a guy or have a *hero moment*-- you, like, yell out this *thing!*
What thing?

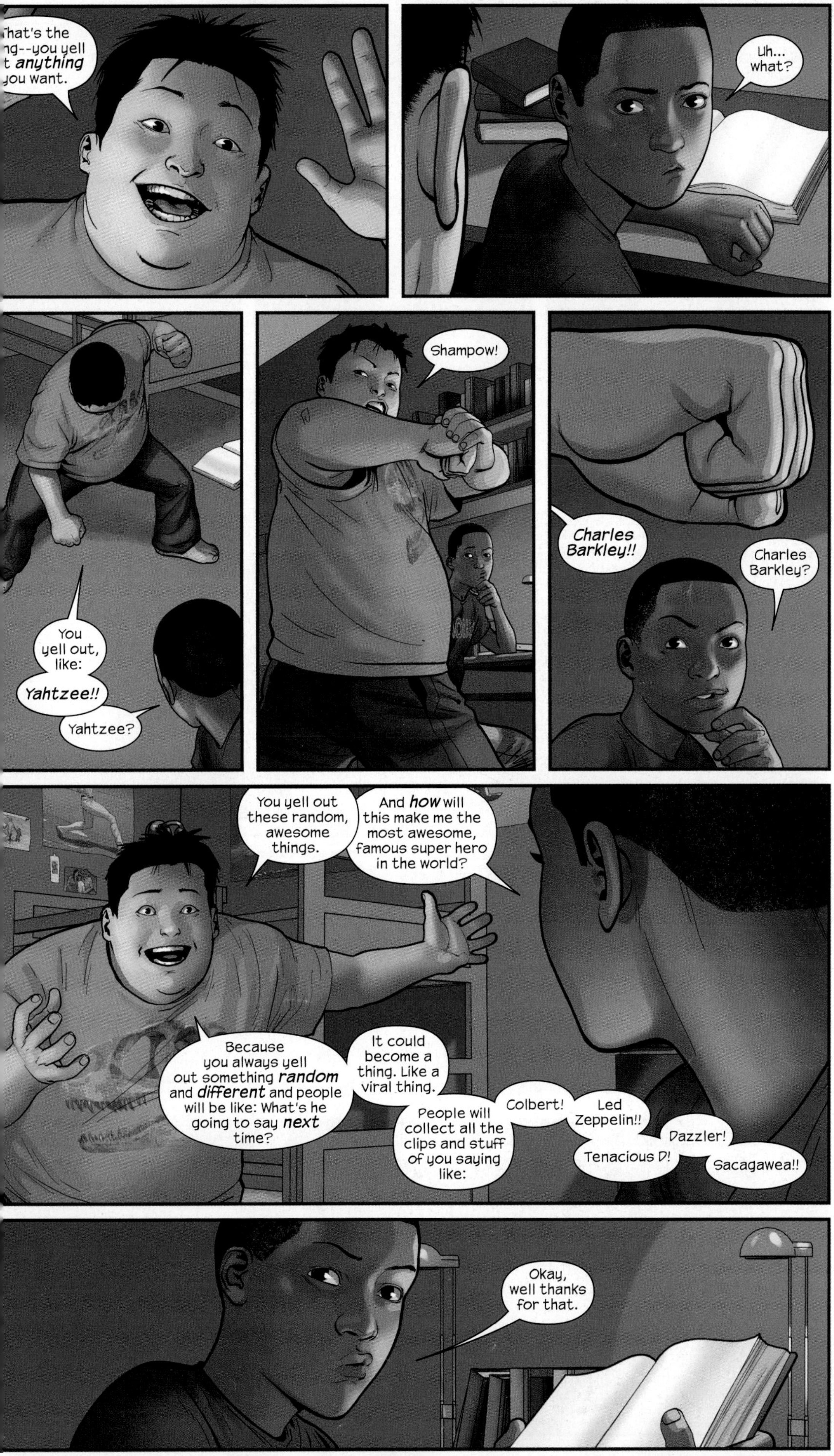
hat's the
ng--you yell
t *anything*
you want.
Uh... what?
You yell out, like:
Yahtzee!!
Yahtzee?
Shampow!
Charles Barkley!!
Charles Barkley?
You yell out these random, awesome things.
And *how* will this make me the most awesome, famous super hero in the world?
Because you always yell out something *random* and *different* and people will be like: What's he going to say *next* time?
It could become a thing. Like a viral thing.
People will collect all the clips and stuff of you saying like:
Colbert!
Led Zeppelin!!
Tenacious D!
Dazzler!
Sacagawea!!
Okay, well thanks for that.

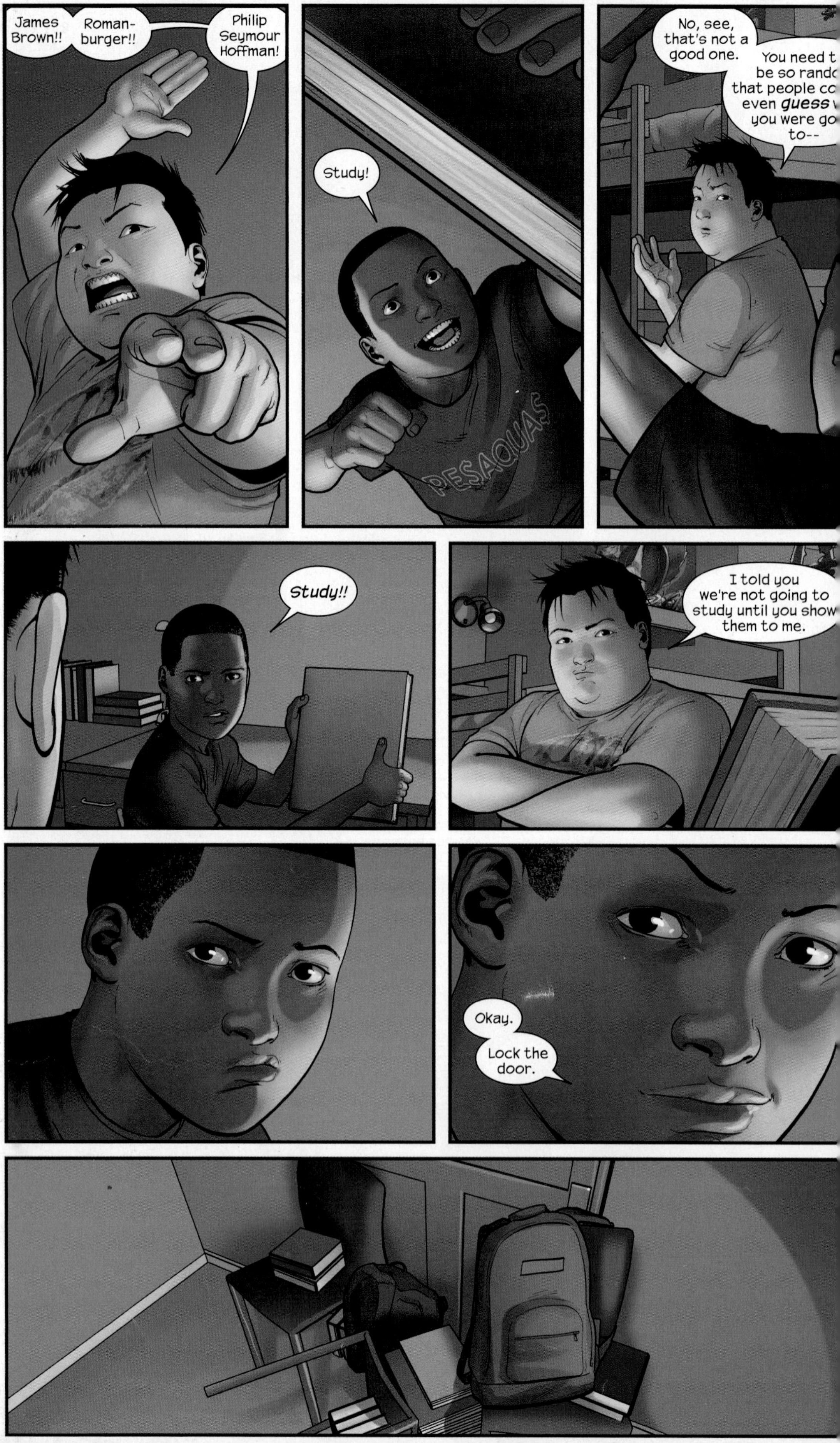
James Brown!!
Roman-burger!!
Philip Seymour Hoffman!
Study!
No, see, that's not a good one.
You need t be so rando that people co even guess you were go to--
Study!!
I told you we're not going to study until you show them to me.
Okay.
Lock the door.
PESAQUAS

Now. *The* web shooters. Right?

And his aunt just *gave* them to you?

Yup.

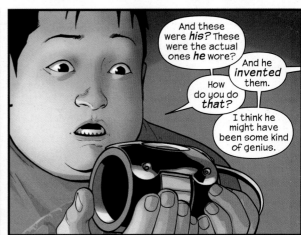

And these were *his*? These were the actual ones *he* wore?

And he *invented* them.

How do you do *that*?

I think he might have been some kind of genius.

And what's this?

...e secret ...eb fluid formula.

So we have to make more?

When this runs...

Uh-oh.

I was hoping that's where you would come in.

Me?

You're the smart one.

THWIP

I mean, I--I don't-- I can't!

If you can ...ake a Death Star ...ut of Legos using your own designs...

Yeah. But-but-but chemistry.

Oops.

THWIP

Hey!

Hey, why won't this door open?!

*

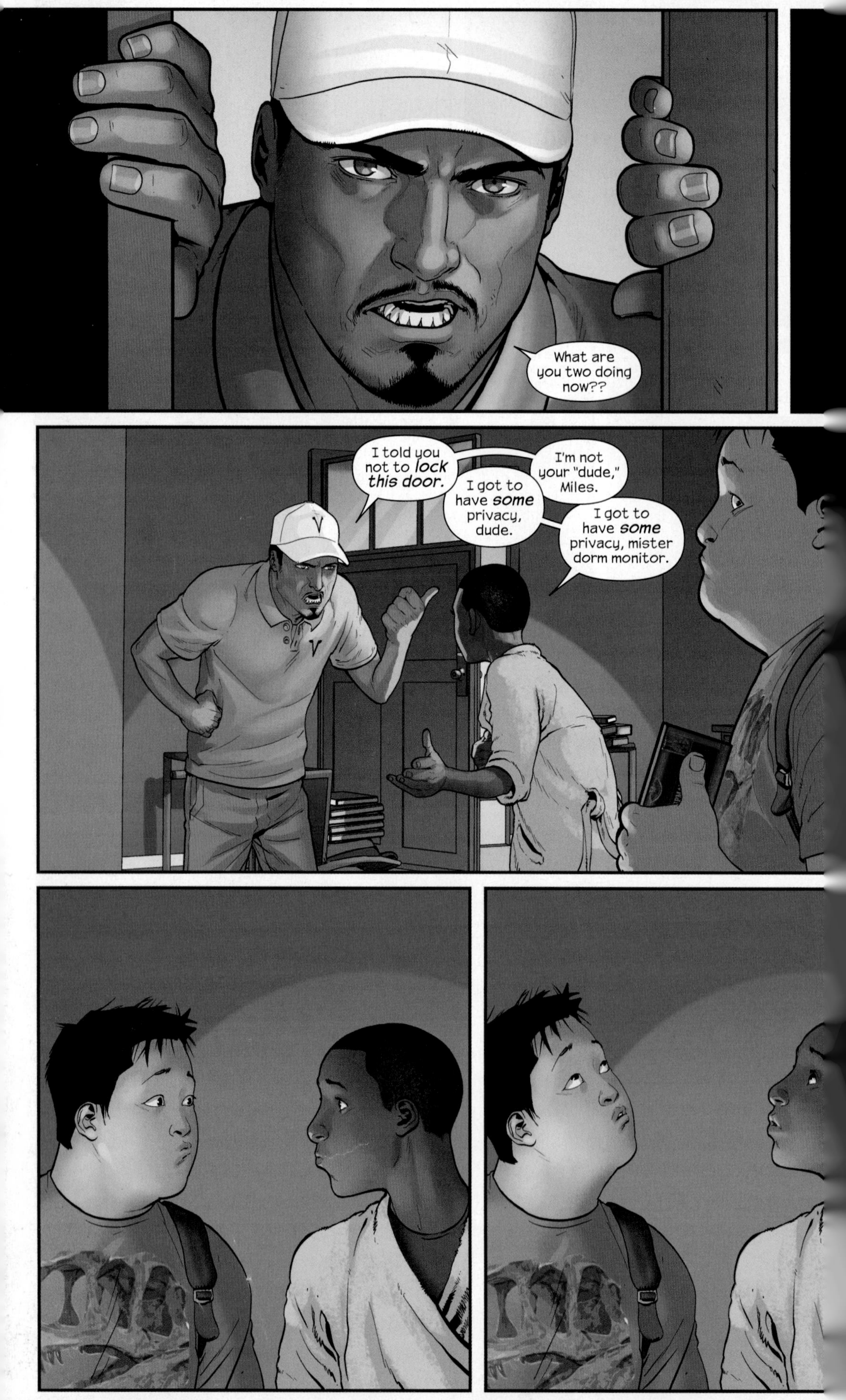
What are you two doing now??
I told you not to lock this door.
I got to have some privacy, dude.
I'm not your "dude," Miles.
I got to have some privacy, mister dorm monitor.

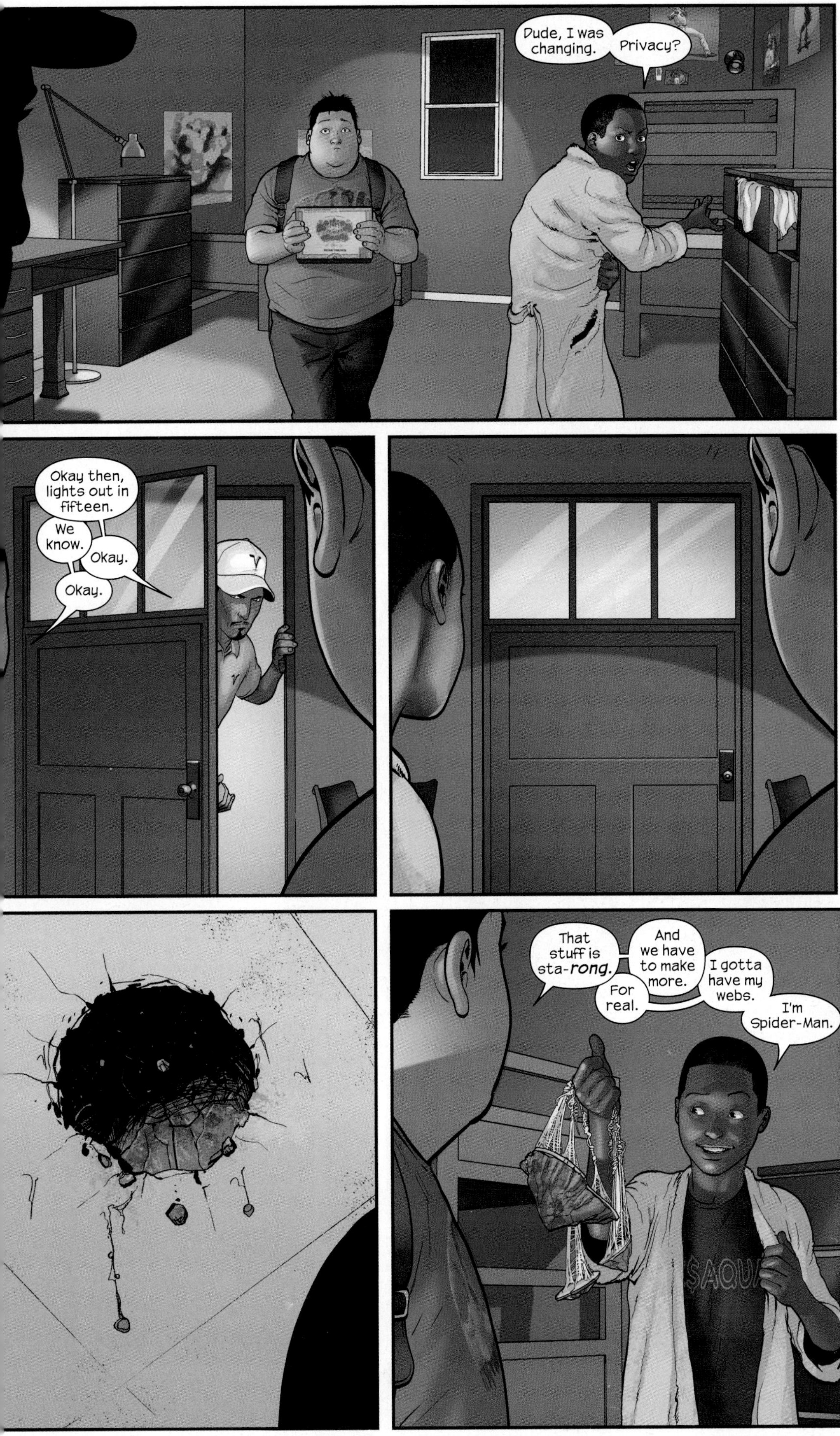
Dude, I was changing.
Privacy?
Okay then, lights out in fifteen.
We know.
Okay.
Okay.
That stuff is sta-*rong*.
For real.
And we have to make more.
I gotta have my webs.
I'm Spider-Man.

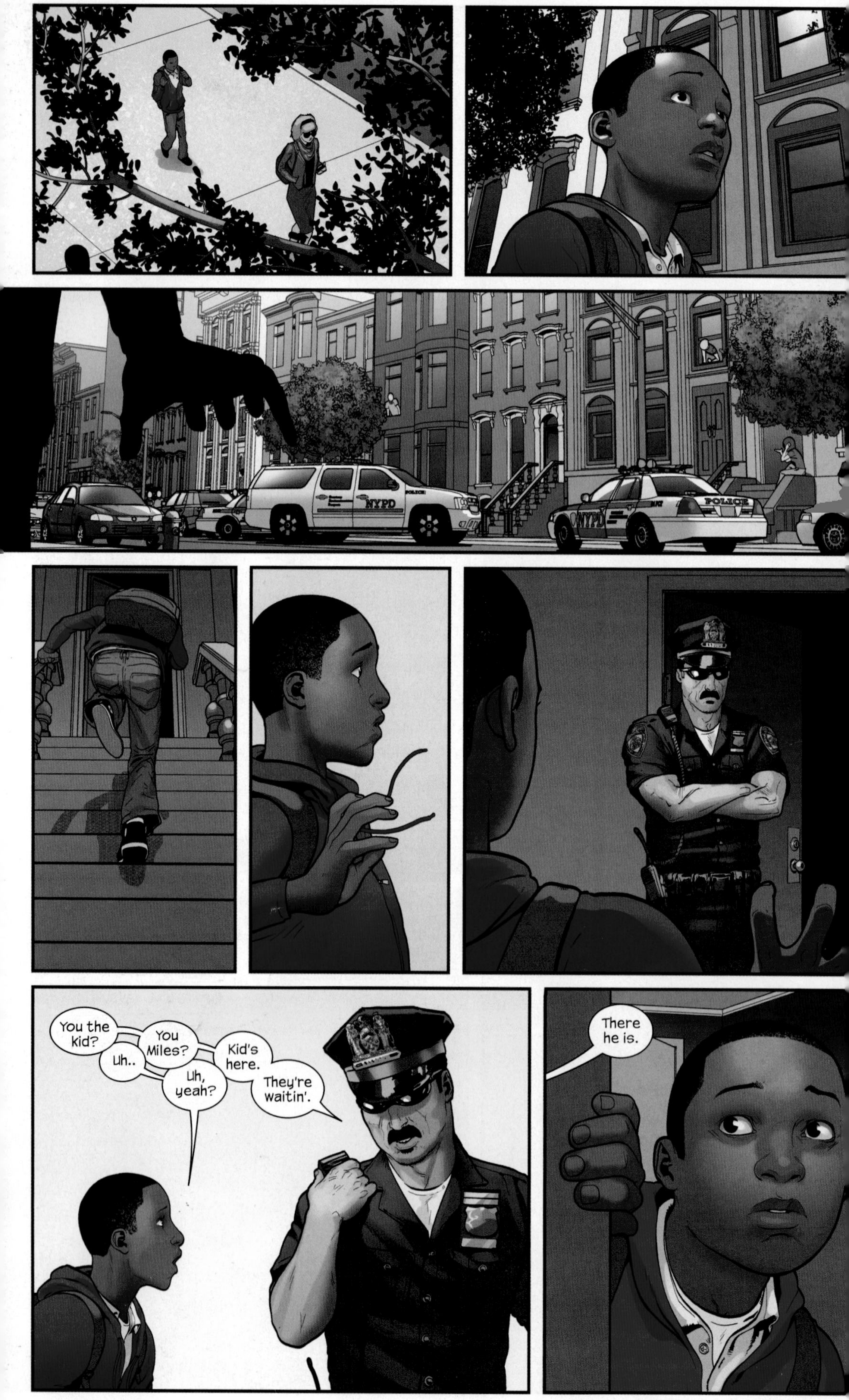
You the kid?
Uh..
You Miles?
Uh, yeah?
Kid's here.
They're waitin'.
There he is.

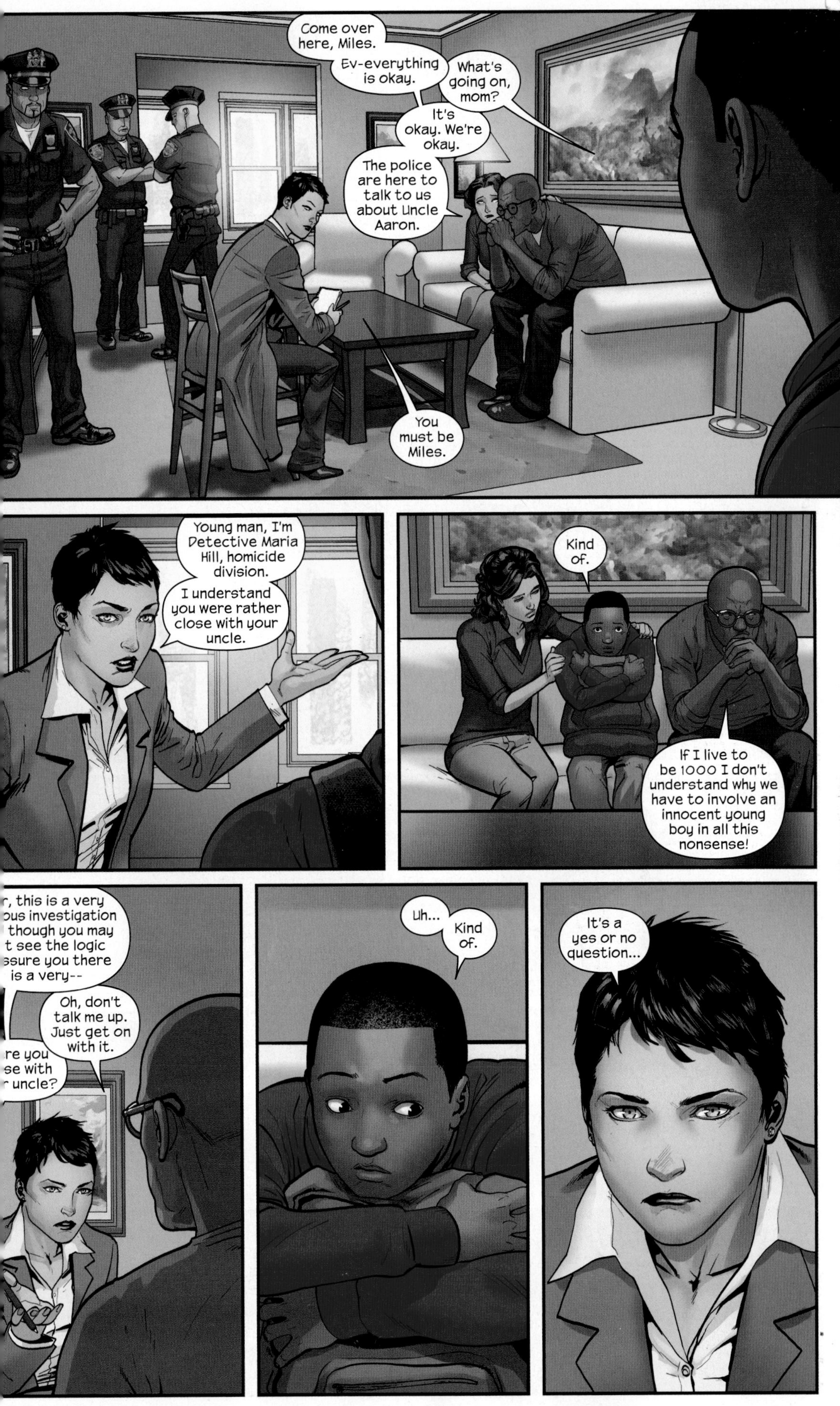

Come over here, Miles.
Ev-everything is okay.
What's going on, mom?
It's okay. We're okay.
The police are here to talk to us about Uncle Aaron.
You must be Miles.
Young man, I'm Detective Maria Hill, homicide division.
I understand you were rather close with your uncle.
Kind of.
If I live to be 1000 I don't understand why we have to involve an innocent young boy in all this nonsense!
r, this is a very ous investigation though you may t see the logic ssure you there is a very--
Oh, don't talk me up. Just get on with it.
re you se with r uncle?
Uh...
Kind of.
It's a yes or no question...

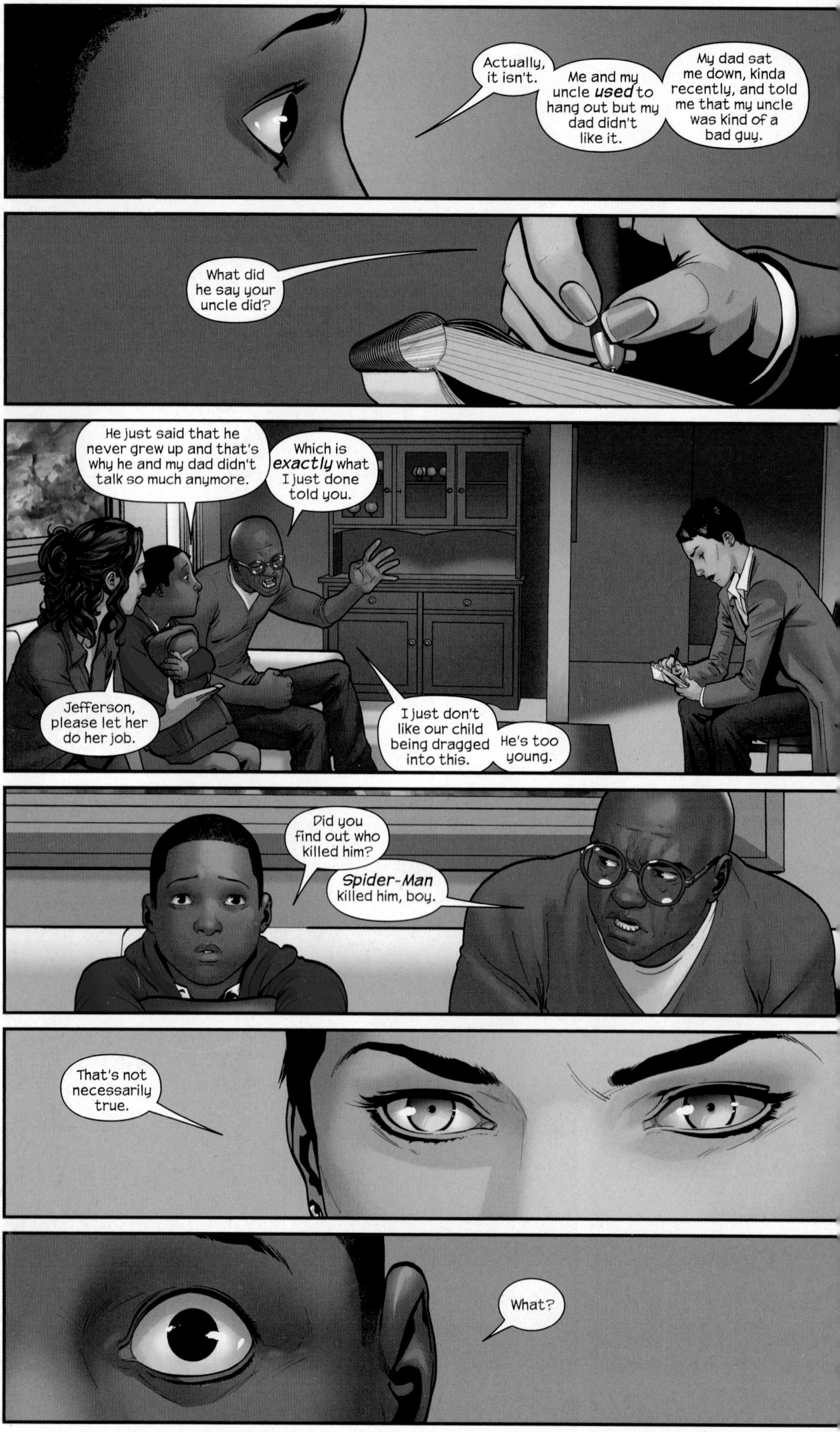
Actually, it isn't.
Me and my uncle *used* to hang out but my dad didn't like it.
My dad sat me down, kinda recently, and told me that my uncle was kind of a bad guy.
What did he say your uncle did?
He just said that he never grew up and that's why he and my dad didn't talk so much anymore.
Which is *exactly* what I just done told you.
Jefferson, please let her do her job.
I just don't like our child being dragged into this.
He's too young.
Did you find out who killed him?
Spider-Man killed him, boy.
That's not necessarily true.
What?

Your uncle had stolen some technology that he didn't know how to use...

And according to the coroner's report the tech was broken and backfired on him.

That's what killed him.

So it--it *wasn't* Spider-Man?

Uncle Aaron accidently killed *himself*?

We're still investigating.

Someone should--should, like, tell the news that it wasn't him, uh, Spider--

Well, my 13-year-old son doesn't know anything about any of this and he doesn't need to know what you're telling him.

(Filling his mind up with nonsense.)

Sir, your brother, the Prowler, was a master thief.

For years, he had a very specific agenda and a very specific modus operandi.

He knew *exactly* how far to push situations and he knew *exactly* how to dance between the raindrops of our legal system.

So for him to, all of a sudden, decide to announce his candidacy to be the *kingpin* of New York...

It just doesn't make sense.

He wasn't a "kingpin" kind of guy.

So the question is, why now?

Why all of a sudden does this master thief think himself a godfather?

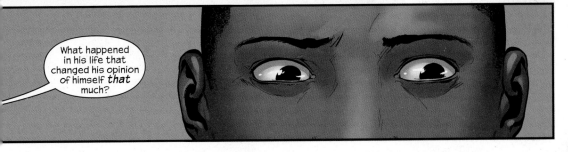

What happened in his life that changed his opinion of himself *that* much?

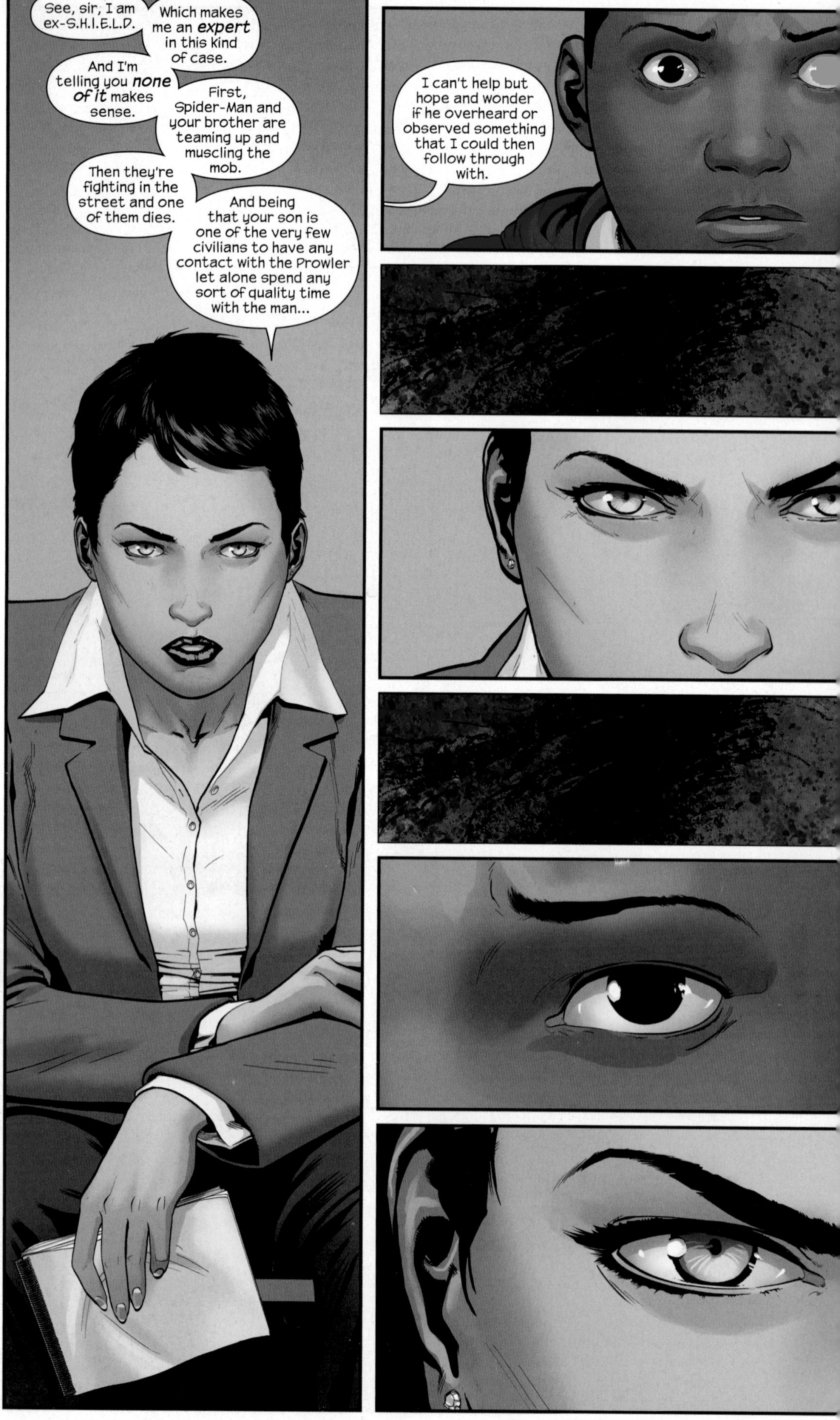

See, sir, I am ex-S.H.I.E.L.D.
Which makes me an *expert* in this kind of case.
And I'm telling you *none of it* makes sense.
First, Spider-Man and your brother are teaming up and muscling the mob.
Then they're fighting in the street and one of them dies.
And being that your son is one of the very few civilians to have any contact with the Prowler let alone spend any sort of quality time with the man...
I can't help but hope and wonder if he overheard or observed something that I could then follow through with.

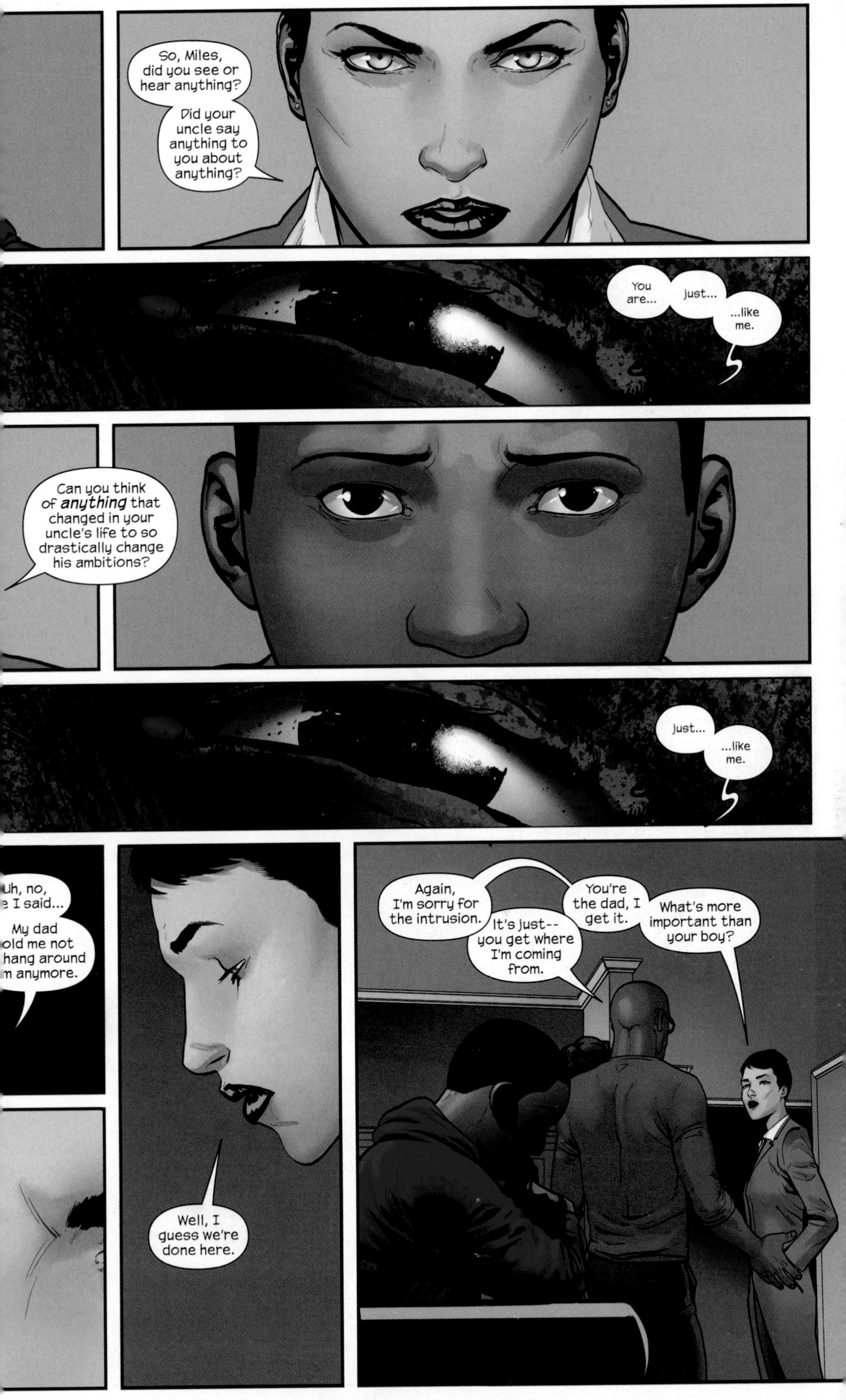
So, Miles, did you see or hear anything?
Did your uncle say anything to you about anything?
You are...
just...
...like me.
Can you think of *anything* that changed in your uncle's life to so drastically change his ambitions?
just...
...like me.
uh, no,
I said...
My dad
old me not
hang around
n anymore.
Well, I guess we're done here.
Again, I'm sorry for the intrusion.
It's just-- you get where I'm coming from.
You're the dad, I get it.
What's more important than your boy?

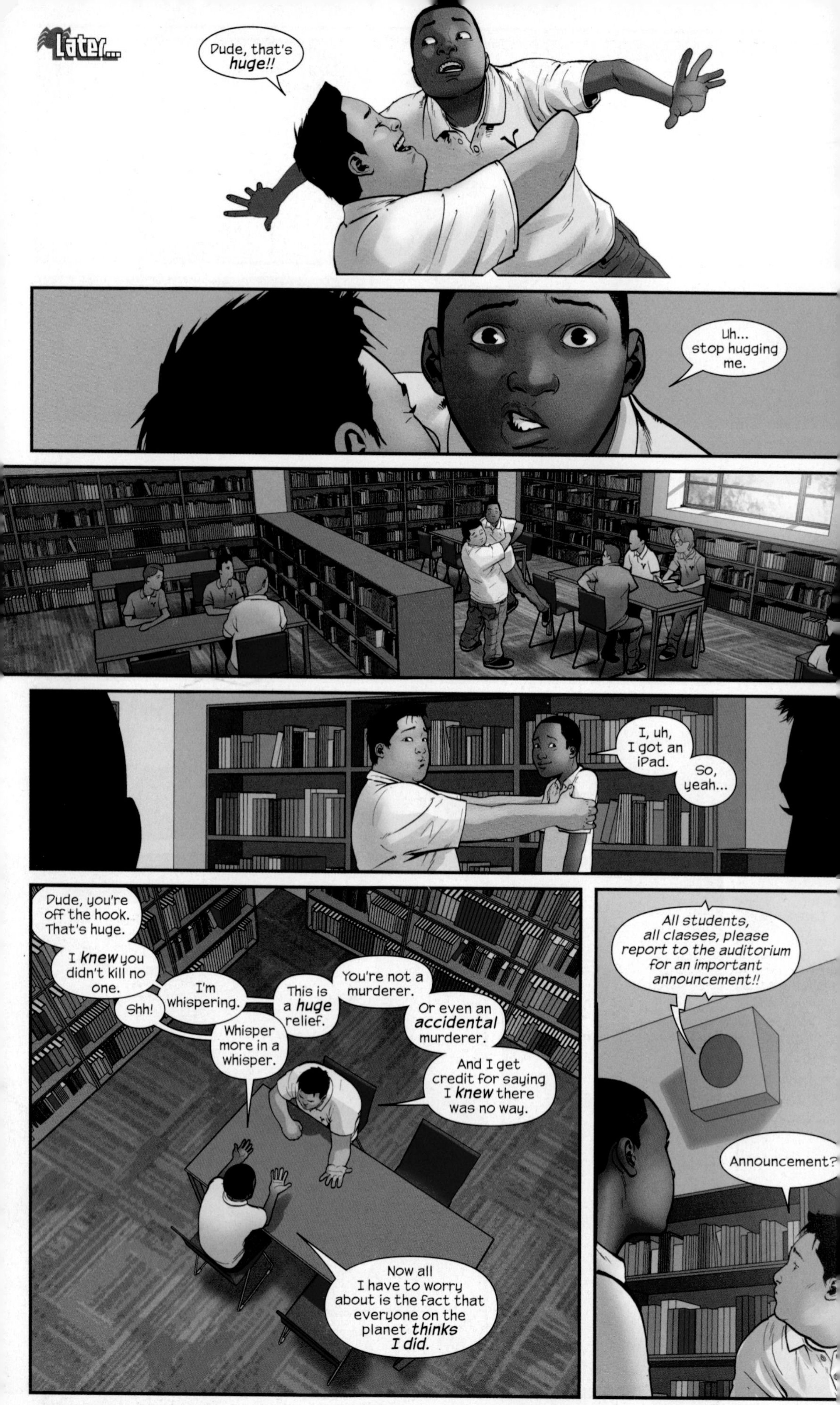

Later...
Dude, that's huge!!
Uh... stop hugging me.
I, uh, I got an iPad.
So, yeah...
Dude, you're off the hook. That's huge.
I knew you didn't kill no one.
I'm whispering.
Shh!
Whisper more in a whisper.
This is a huge relief.
You're not a murderer.
Or even an accidental murderer.
And I get credit for saying I knew there was no way.
Now all I have to worry about is the fact that everyone on the planet thinks I did.
All students, all classes, please report to the auditorium for an important announcement!!
Announcement?

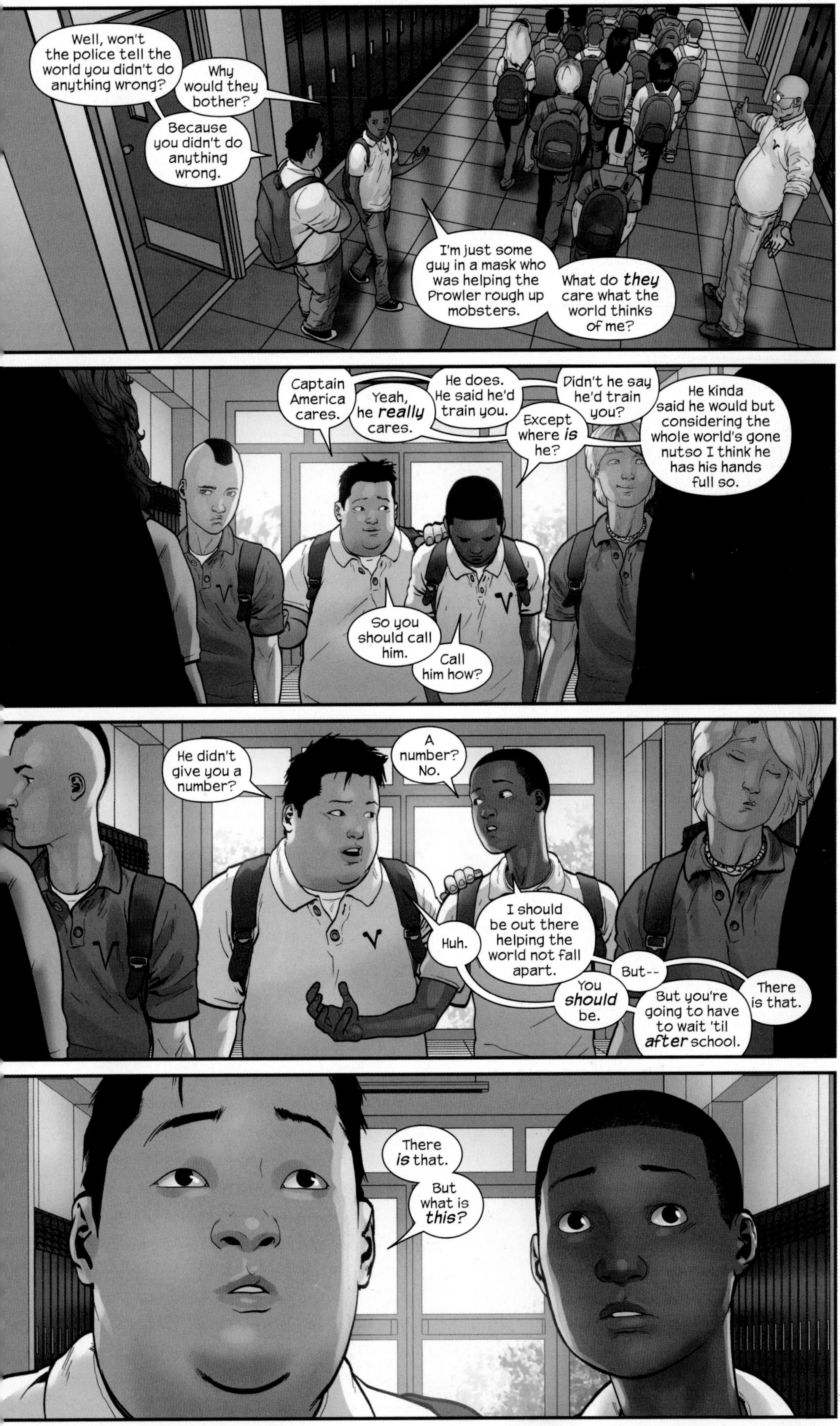
Well, won't the police tell the world you didn't do anything wrong?
Why would they bother?
Because you didn't do anything wrong.
I'm just some guy in a mask who was helping the Prowler rough up mobsters.
What do *they* care what the world thinks of me?
Captain America cares.
Yeah, he *really* cares.
He does. He said he'd train you.
Didn't he say he'd train you?
Except where *is* he?
He kinda said he would but considering the whole world's gone nutso I think he has his hands full so.
So you should call him.
Call him how?
He didn't give you a number?
A number? No.
Huh.
I should be out there helping the world not fall apart.
But--
You *should* be.
But you're going to have to wait 'til *after* school.
There is that.
There *is* that.
But what is *this?*

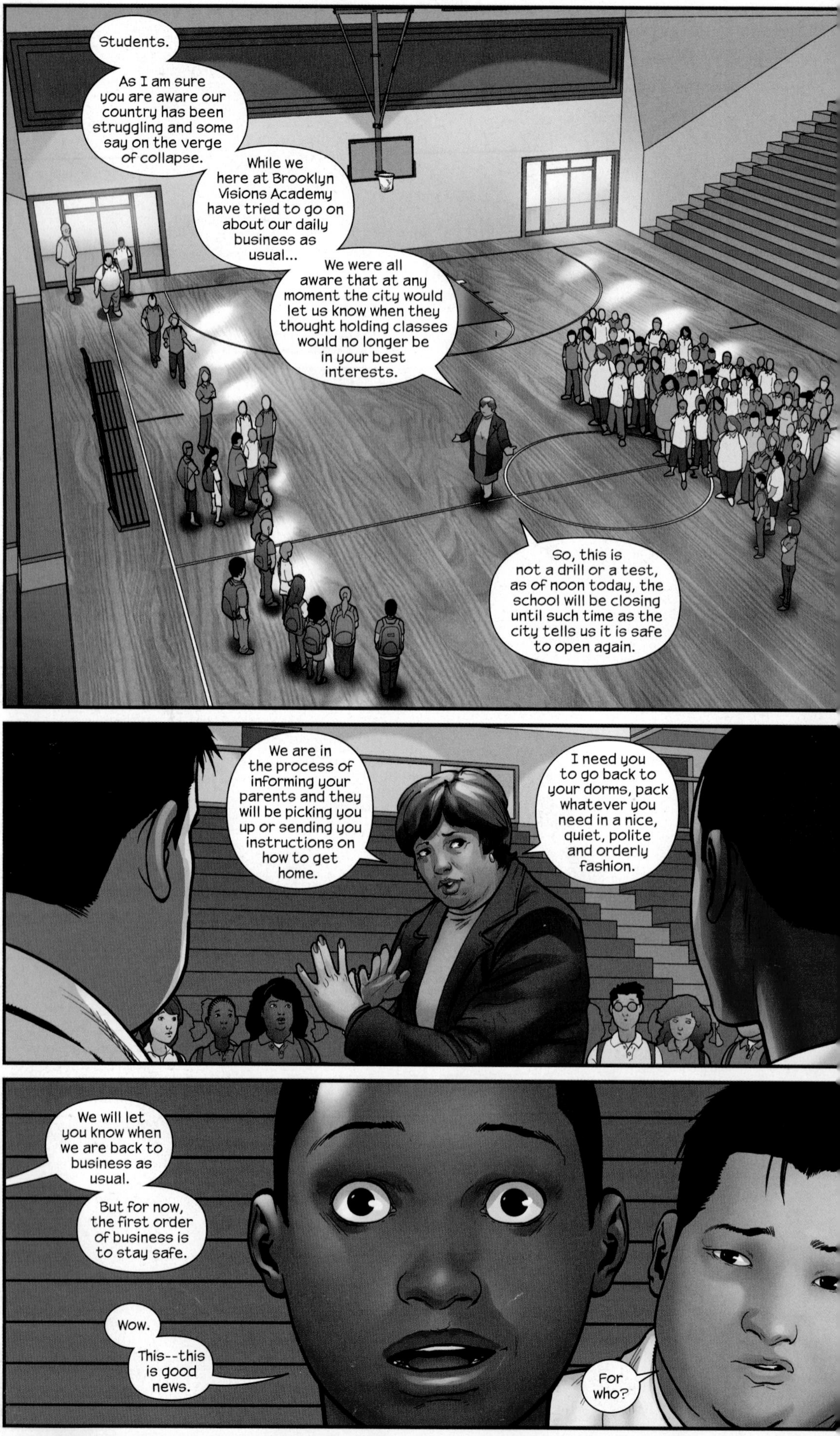
Students.
As I am sure you are aware our country has been struggling and some say on the verge of collapse.
While we here at Brooklyn Visions Academy have tried to go on about our daily business as usual...
We were all aware that at any moment the city would let us know when they thought holding classes would no longer be in your best interests.
So, this is not a drill or a test, as of noon today, the school will be closing until such time as the city tells us it is safe to open again.
We are in the process of informing your parents and they will be picking you up or sending you instructions on how to get home.
I need you to go back to your dorms, pack whatever you need in a nice, quiet, polite and orderly fashion.
We will let you know when we are back to business as usual.
But for now, the first order of business is to stay safe.
Wow.
This--this is good news.
For who?

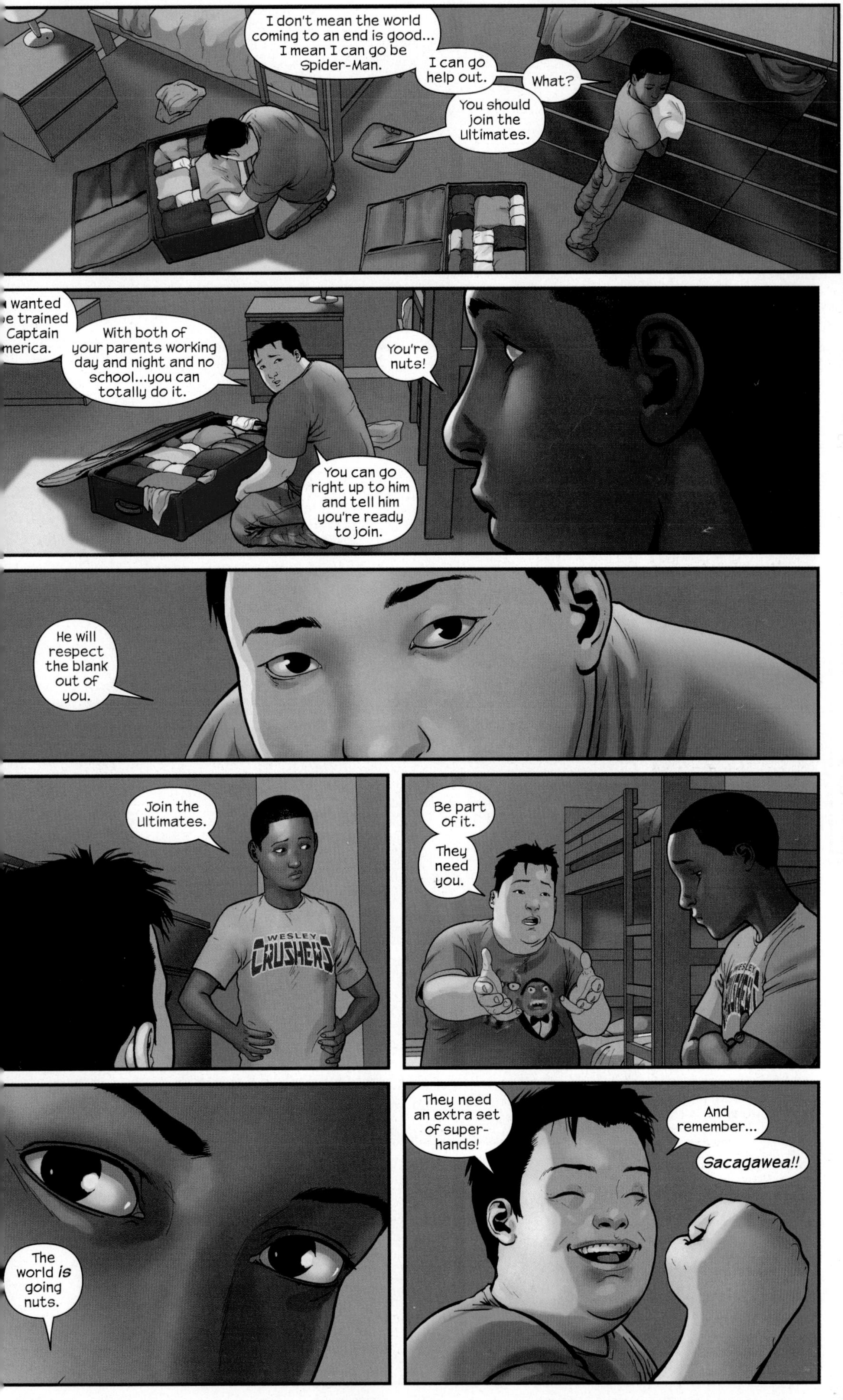
I don't mean the world coming to an end is good... I mean I can go be Spider-Man.
I can go help out.
What?
You should join the Ultimates.
wanted e trained Captain merica.
With both of your parents working day and night and no school...you can totally do it.
You're nuts!
You can go right up to him and tell him you're ready to join.
He will respect the blank out of you.
Join the Ultimates.
WESLEY CRUSHERS
Be part of it.
They need you.
The world *is* going nuts.
They need an extra set of super-hands!
And remember...
Sacagawea!!

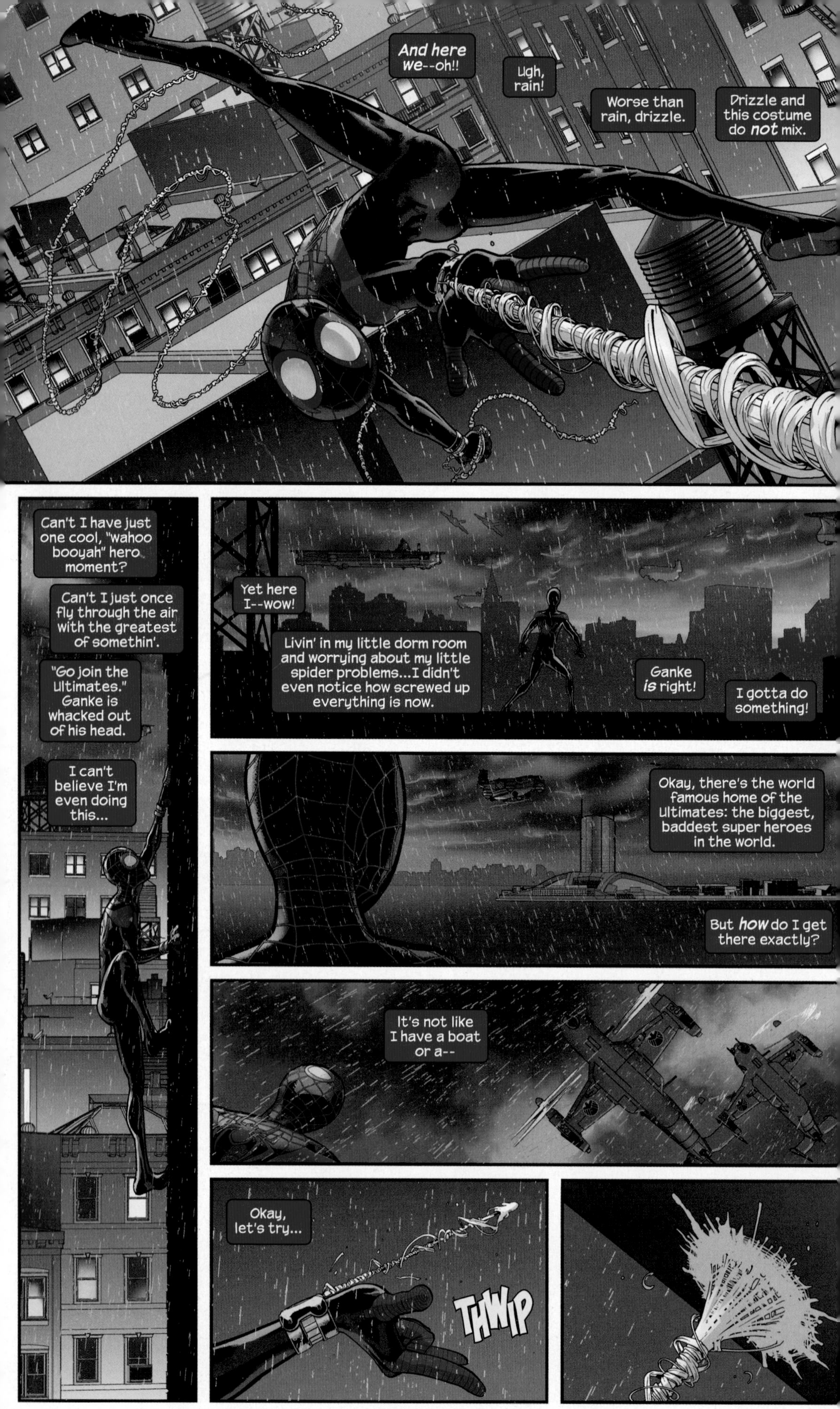
And here we--oh!!
Ugh, rain!
Worse than rain, drizzle.
Drizzle and this costume do not mix.
Can't I have just one cool, "wahoo booyah" hero moment?
Can't I just once fly through the air with the greatest of somethin'.
"Go join the Ultimates." Ganke is whacked out of his head.
I can't believe I'm even doing this...
Yet here I--wow!
Livin' in my little dorm room and worrying about my little spider problems...I didn't even notice how screwed up everything is now.
Ganke is right!
I gotta do something!
Okay, there's the world famous home of the Ultimates: the biggest, baddest super heroes in the world.
But how do I get there exactly?
It's not like I have a boat or a--
Okay, let's try...
THWIP

Whaaaatttt was I thinking??

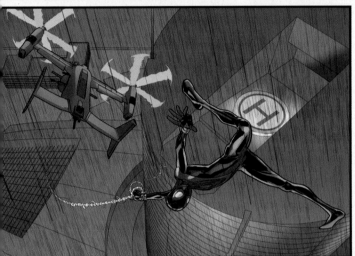

Whoa! Wahhaa!!

SSQQQQQQAAAAAAAAA

Whoa, sorry!!

Sorry everyone, I just wanted to--

We have a breach.

Um...

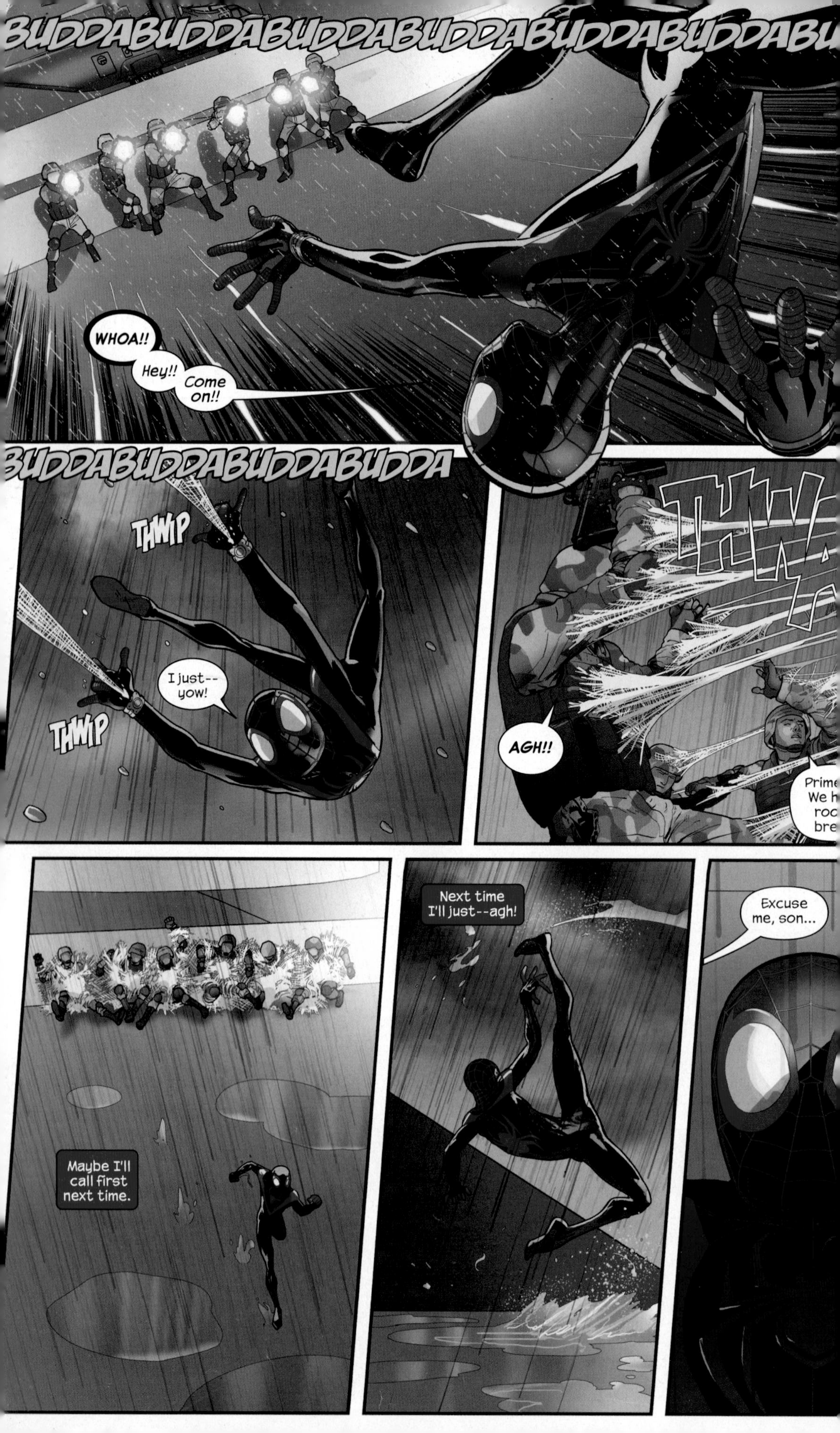
BUDDABUDDABUDDABUDDABUDDABUDDABU
WHOA!!
Hey!!
Come on!!
BUDDABUDDABUDDABUDDA
THWIP
I just-- yow!
THWIP
AGH!!
Maybe I'll call first next time.
Next time I'll just--agh!
Excuse me, son...

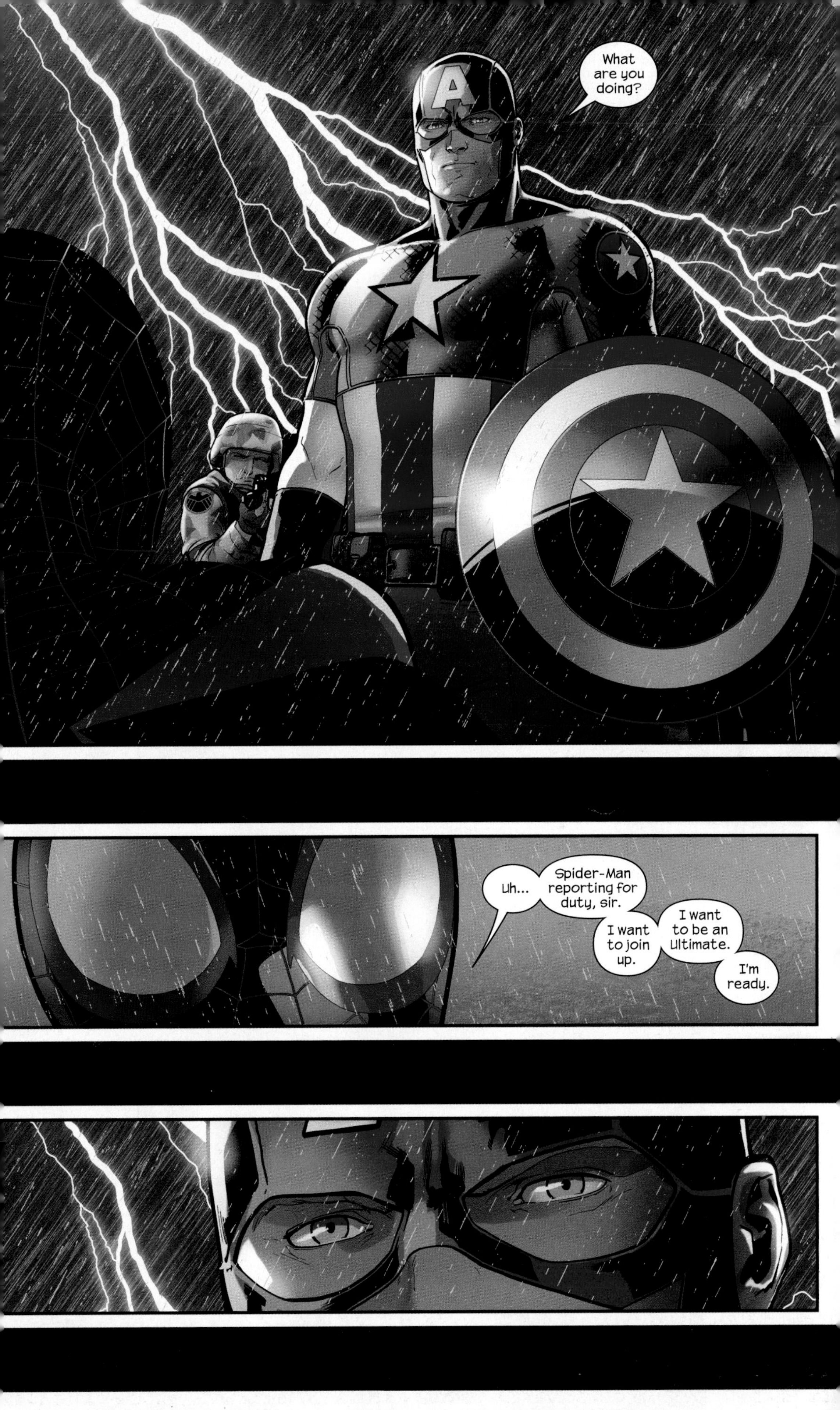
What are you doing?
Uh...
Spider-Man reporting for duty, sir.
I want to join up.
I want to be an Ultimate.
I'm ready.

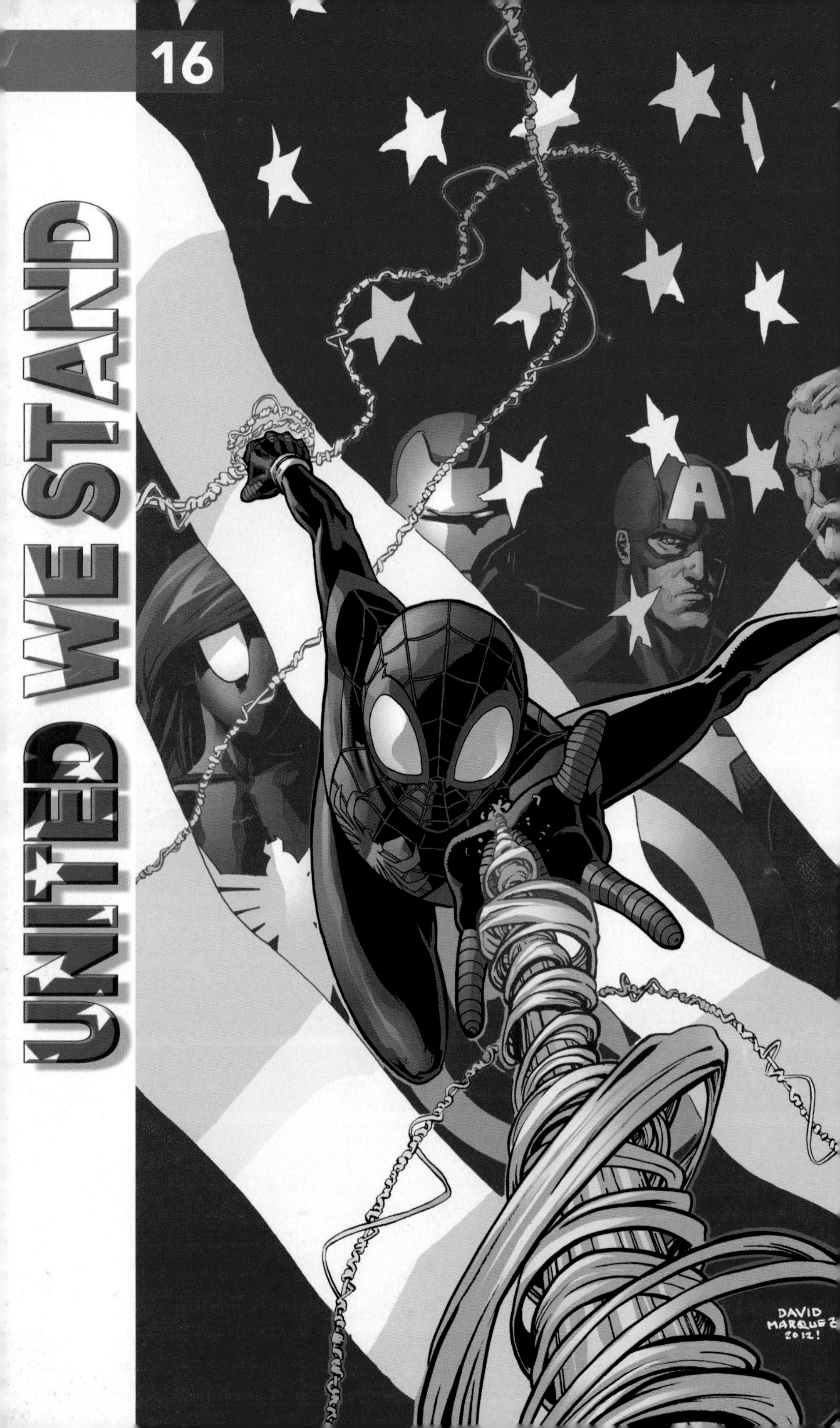
16
UNITED WE STAND
DAVID MARQUEZ 2012!

.H.I.E.L.D. SITUATION MAP:

ti-government militia hot spots]

aho, Montana,
Dakota, S. Dakota,
izona, New Mexico,
Carolina,
Carolina, Georgia

[Eastern seaboard control zone]

New England,
New York,
New Jersey,
Delaware,
Washington, D.C.,
Maryland,
Pennsylvania,
Virginia

secured by National Guard under emergency powers committee

he West Coast Nation]

alifornia, Oregon,
ashington

ndependent nation

Wyoming

status unknown

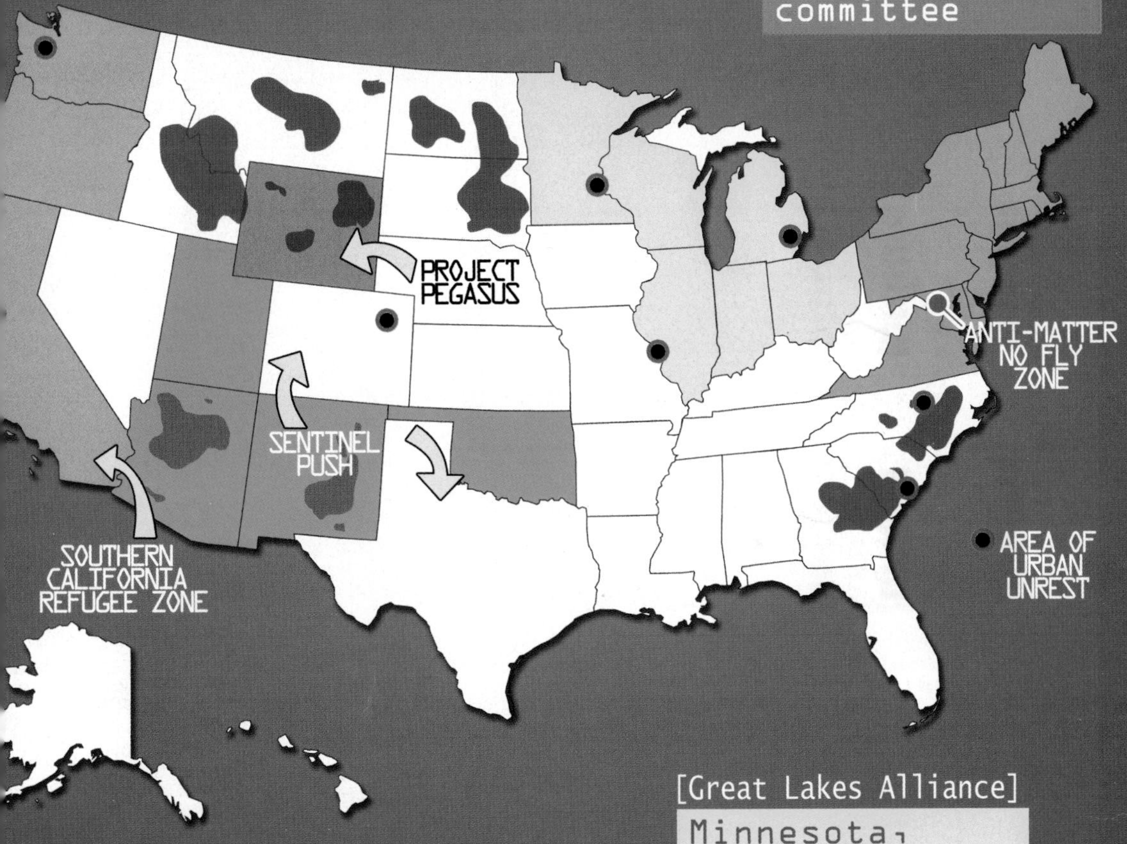

PROJECT PEGASUS
SENTINEL PUSH
SOUTHERN CALIFORNIA REFUGEE ZONE
ANTI-MATTER NO FLY ZONE
AREA OF URBAN UNREST

[Great Lakes Alliance]

Minnesota,
Wisconsin,
Michigan,
Illinois,
Indiana, Ohio

Independent nation

entinel-controlled no-man's-land]

w Mexico, Arizona,
ah, Oklahoma

bandoned by the
.S. government

ALL STATES SHOWN IN WHITE ARE U.S. GOVERNMENT-CONTROLLED ZONES

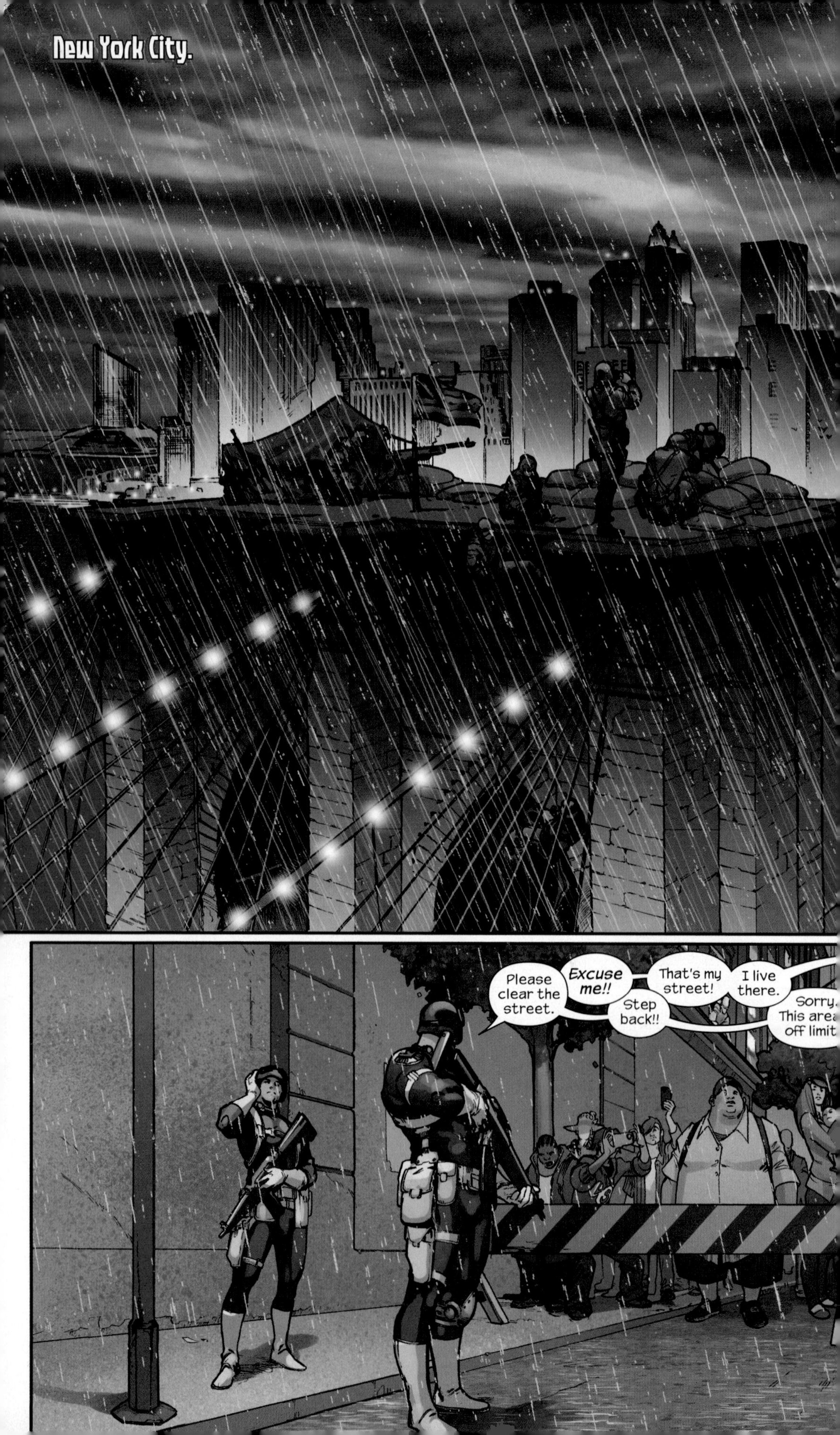
New York City.
Please clear the street.
Excuse me!!
That's my street!
I live there.
Step back!!
Sorry. This area off limit

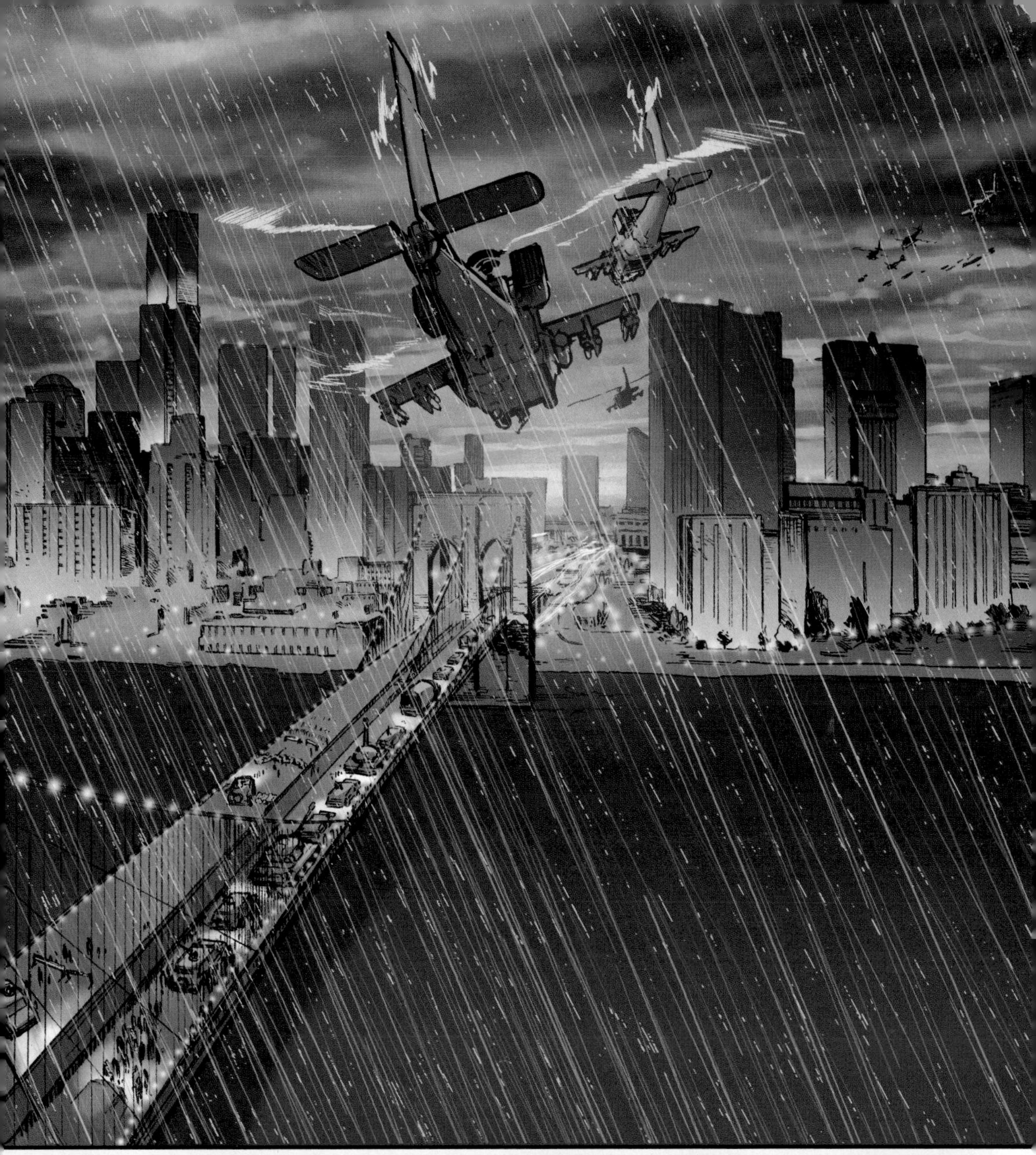

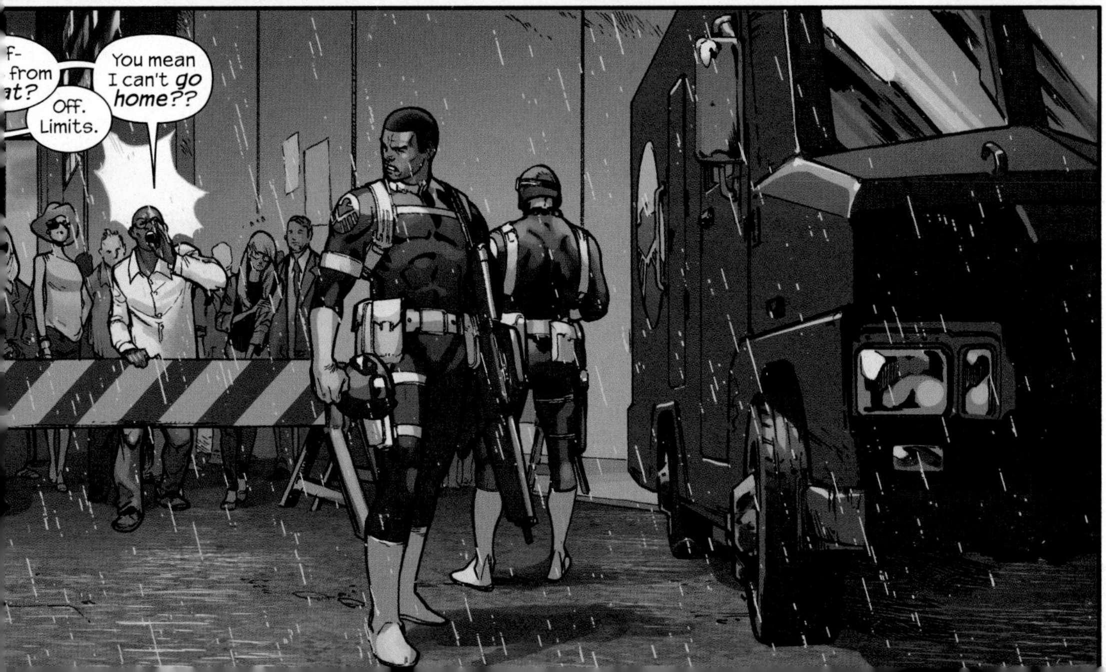
Off. Limits.
You mean I can't *go home*??

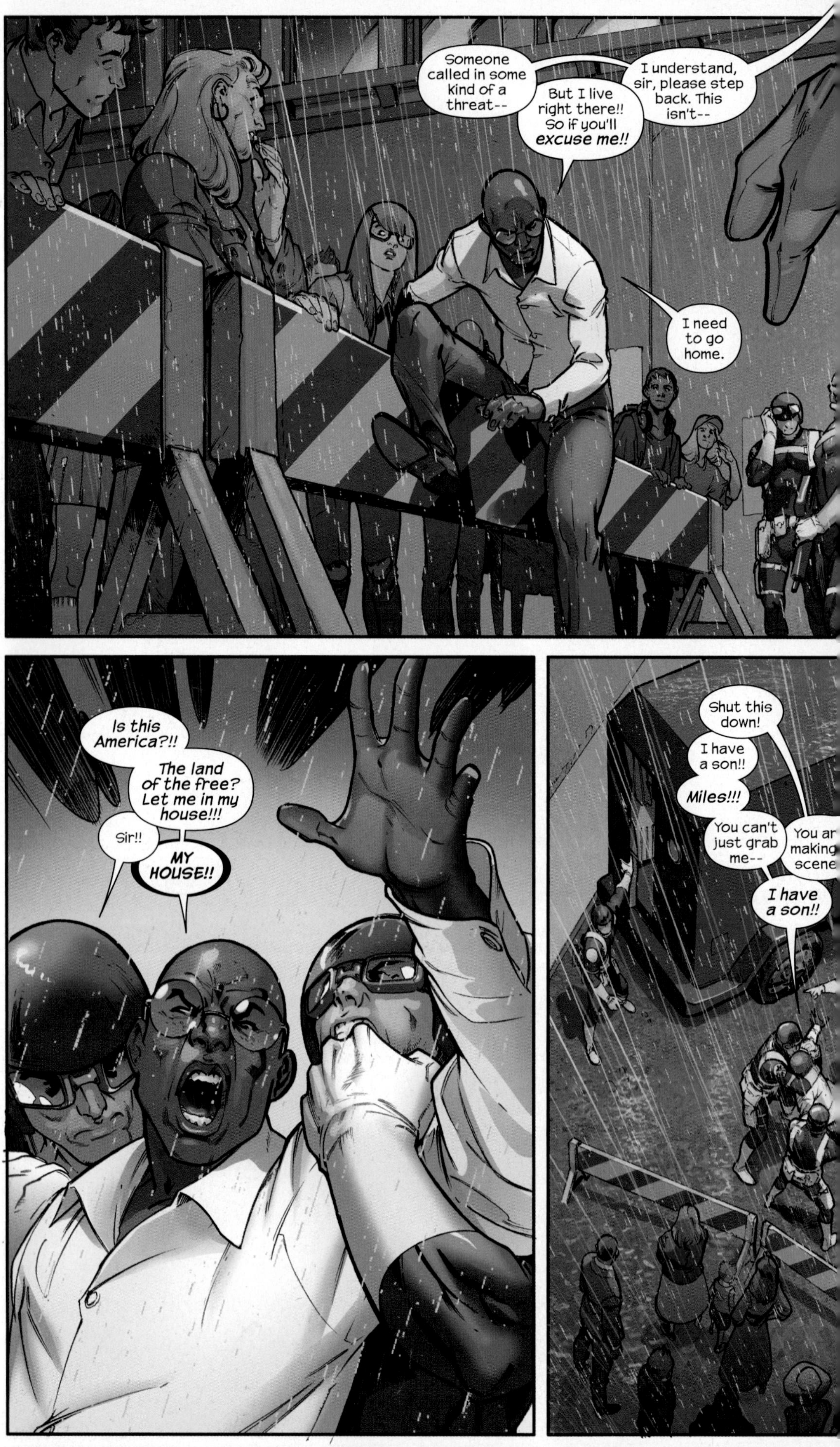
Someone called in some kind of a threat--
I understand, sir, please step back. This isn't--
But I live right there!! So if you'll *excuse me!!*
I need to go home.
Is this America?!!
The land of the free? Let me in my house!!!
Sir!!
MY HOUSE!!
Shut this down!
I have a son!!
Miles!!!
You can't just grab me--
I have a son!!

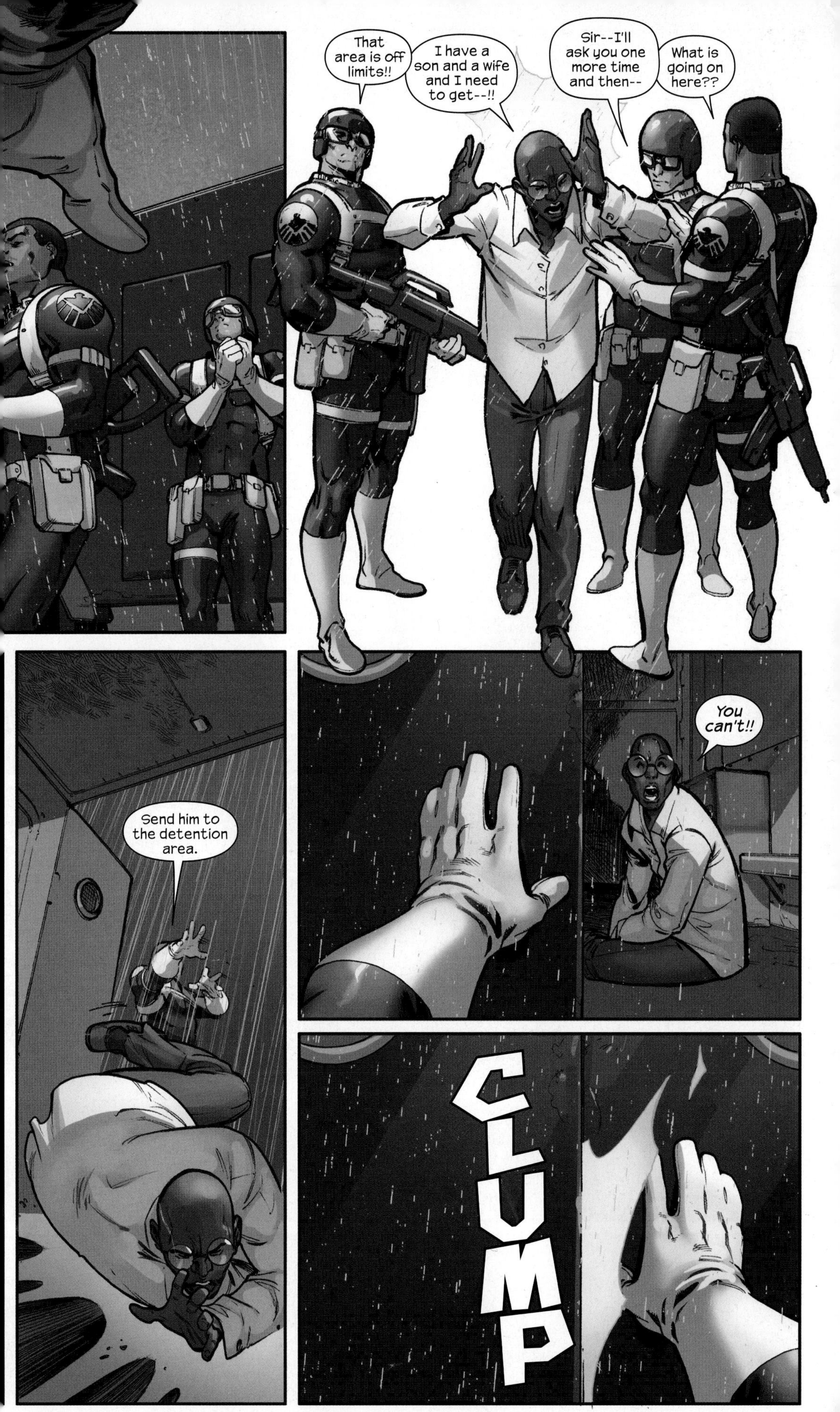

That area is off limits!!
I have a son and a wife and I need to get--!!
Sir--I'll ask you one more time and then--
What is going on here??
Send him to the detention area.
You can't!!
CLUMP

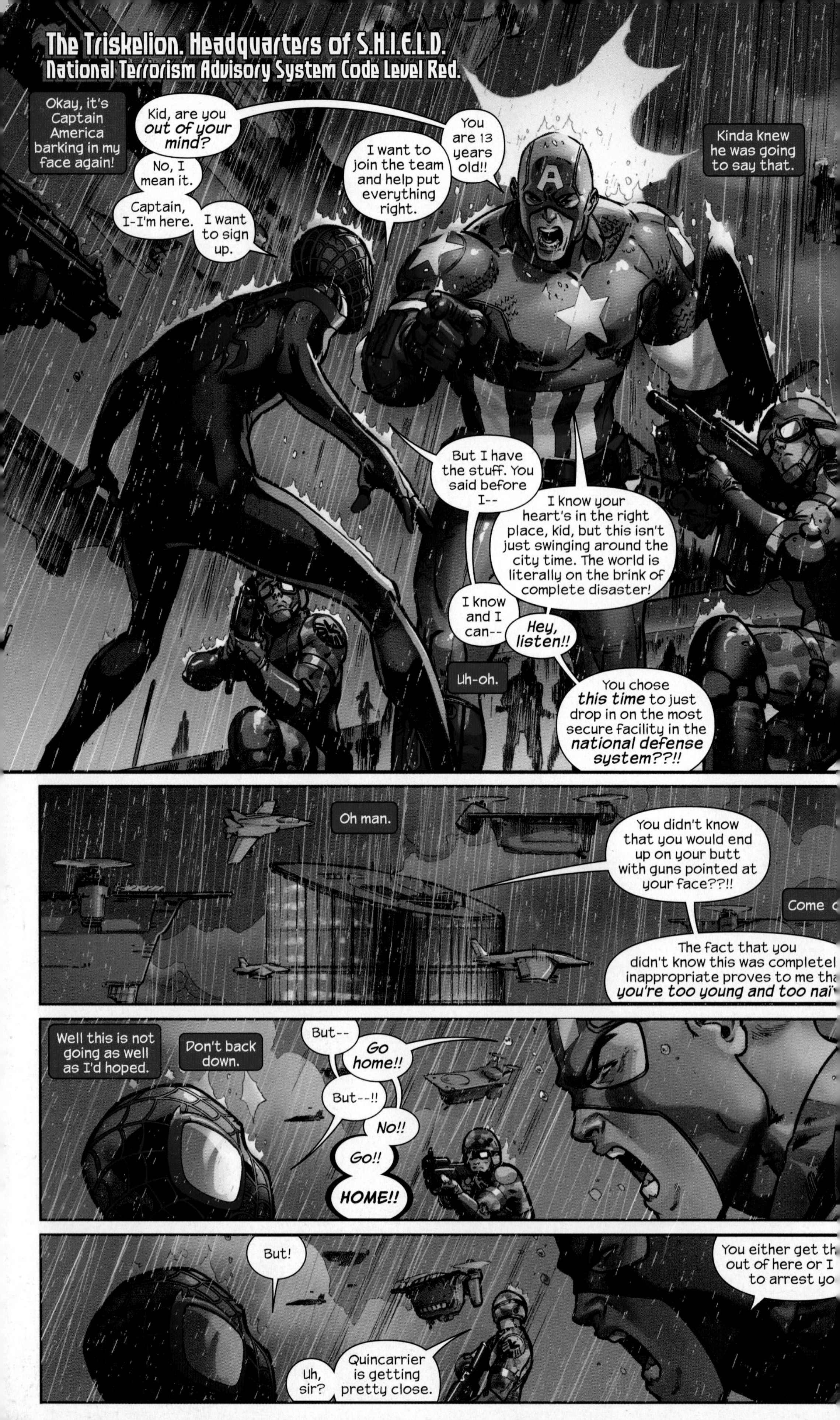
The Triskelion. Headquarters of S.H.I.E.L.D.
National Terrorism Advisory System Code Level Red.
Okay, it's Captain America barking in my face again!
Kid, are you *out of your mind?*
No, I mean it.
Captain, I-I'm here.
I want to sign up.
I want to join the team and help put everything right.
You are 13 years old!!
Kinda knew he was going to say that.
But I have the stuff. You said before I--
I know your heart's in the right place, kid, but this isn't just swinging around the city time. The world is literally on the brink of complete disaster!
I know and I can--
Hey, listen!!
Uh-oh.
You chose *this time* to just drop in on the most secure facility in the *national defense system??!!*
Oh man.
You didn't know that you would end up on your butt with guns pointed at your face??!!
Come
The fact that you didn't know this was completel inappropriate proves to me tha *you're too young and too nai*
Well this is not going as well as I'd hoped.
Don't back down.
But--
Go home!!
But--!!
No!!
Go!!
HOME!!
But!
You either get th out of here or I to arrest yo
Uh, sir?
Quincarrier is getting pretty close.

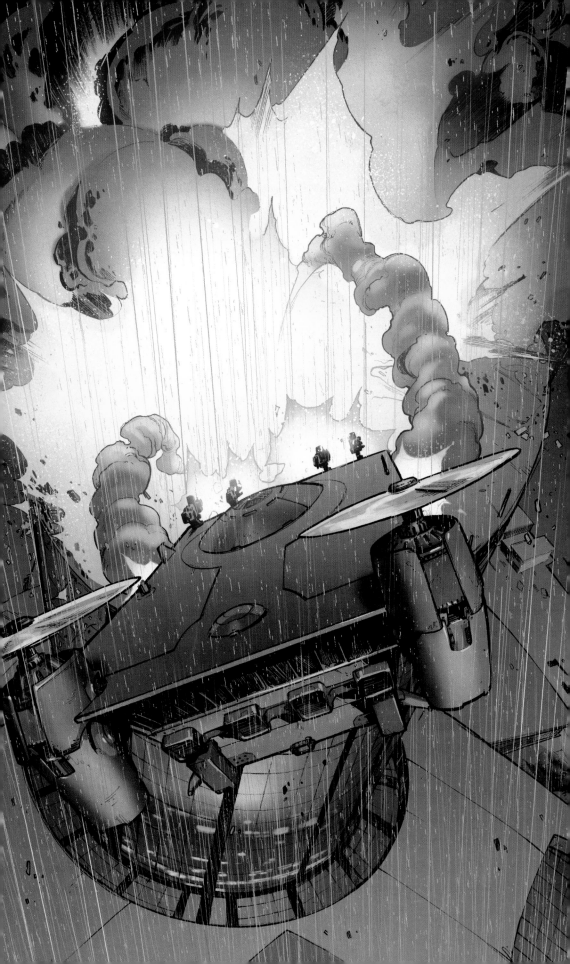

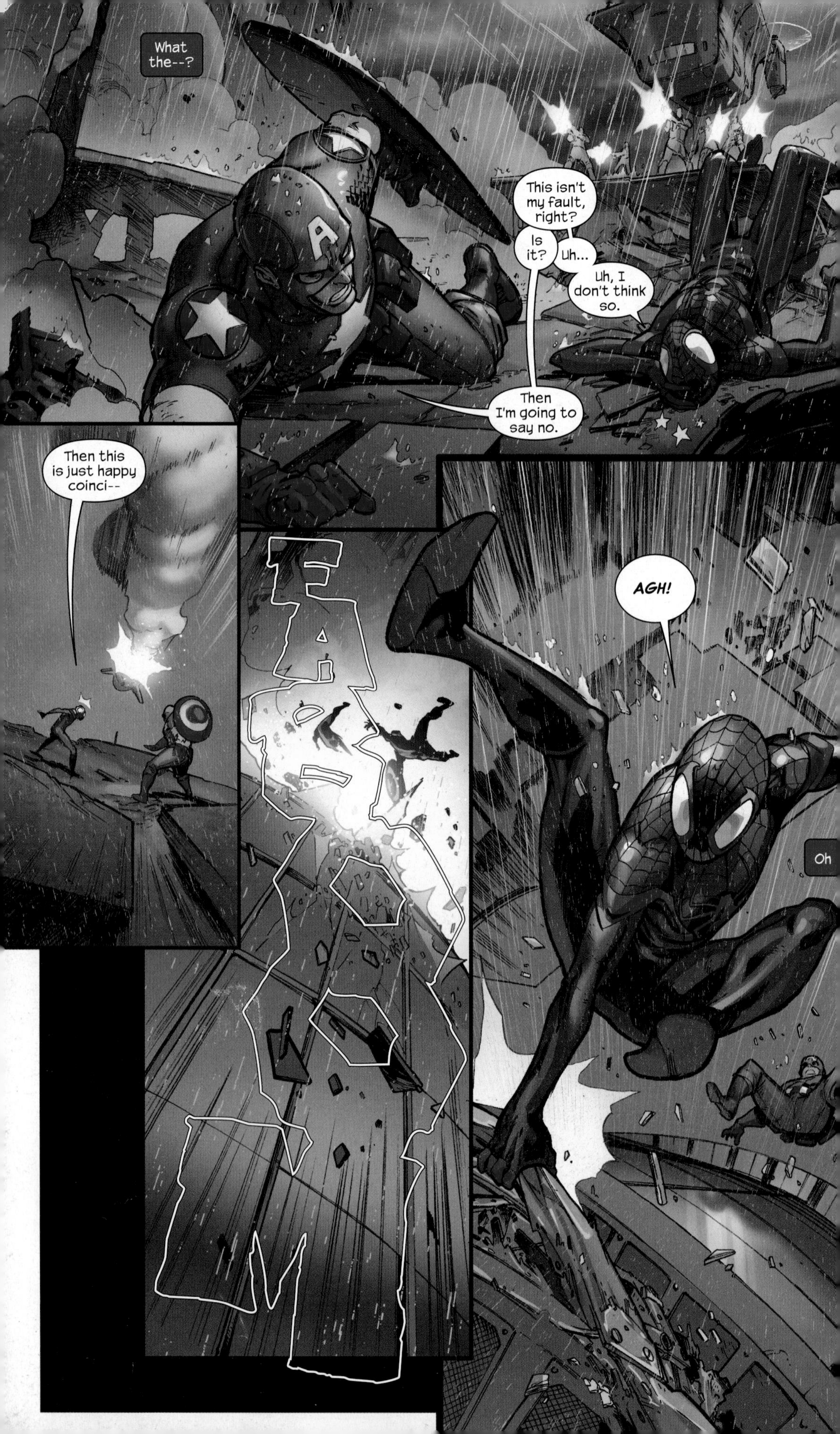
What the--?
This isn't my fault, right?
Is it?
Uh...
Uh, I don't think so.
Then I'm going to say no.
Then this is just happy coinci--
AGH!
Oh

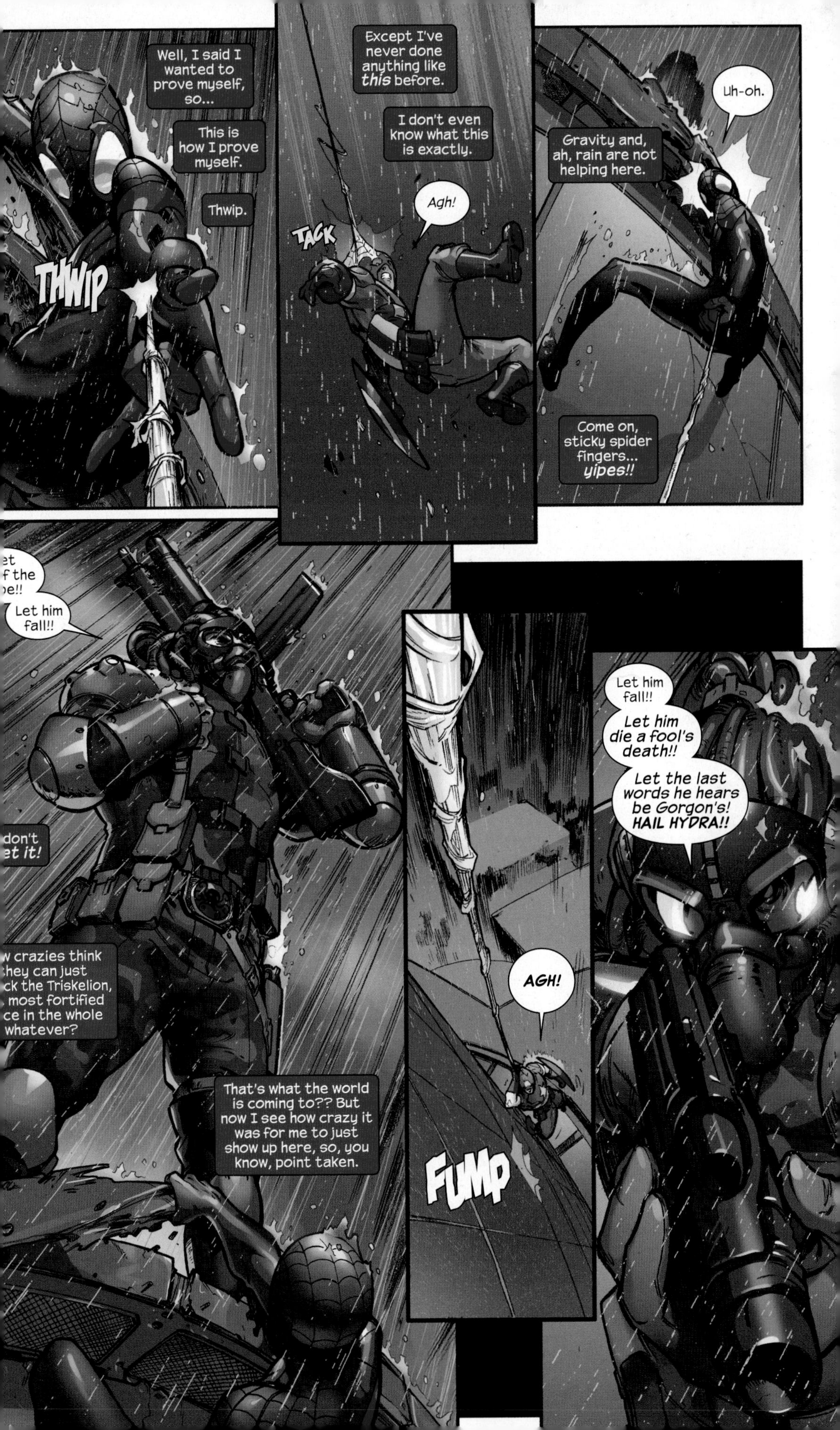

Well, I said I wanted to prove myself, so...
This is how I prove myself.
Thwip.
THWIP
Except I've never done anything like *this* before.
I don't even know what this is exactly.
Agh!
TACK
Uh-oh.
Gravity and, ah, rain are not helping here.
Come on, sticky spider fingers... *yipes!!*
et f the e!!
Let him fall!!
don't et it!
w crazies think hey can just ck the Triskelion, most fortified ce in the whole whatever?
That's what the world is coming to?? But now I see how crazy it was for me to just show up here, so, you know, point taken.
AGH!
FUMP
Let him fall!!
Let him die a fool's death!!
Let the last words he hears be Gorgon's! HAIL HYDRA!!

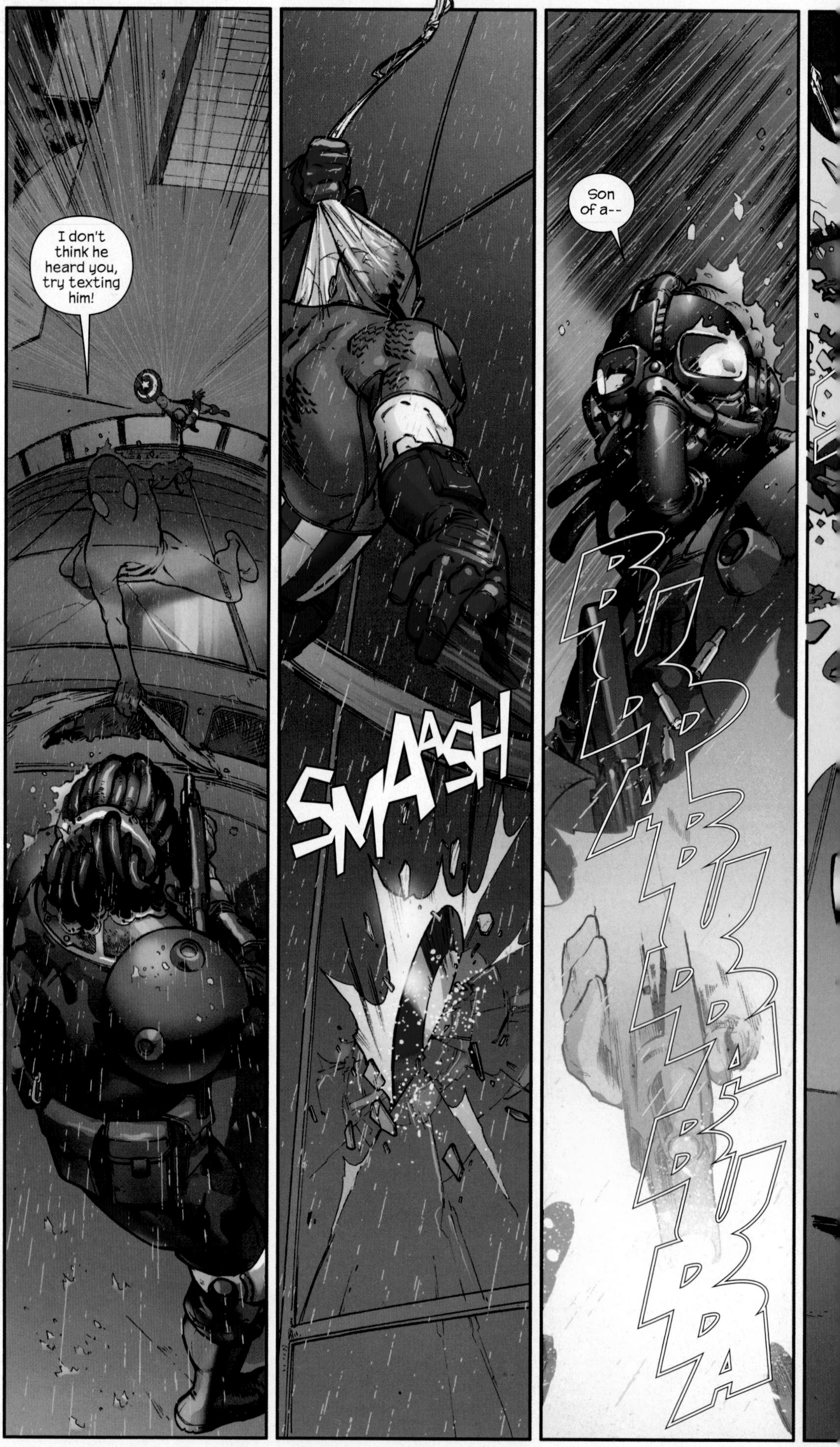
I don't think he heard you, try texting him!
SMAASH
Son of a--
BUDDA BUDDA BUDDA BUDDA

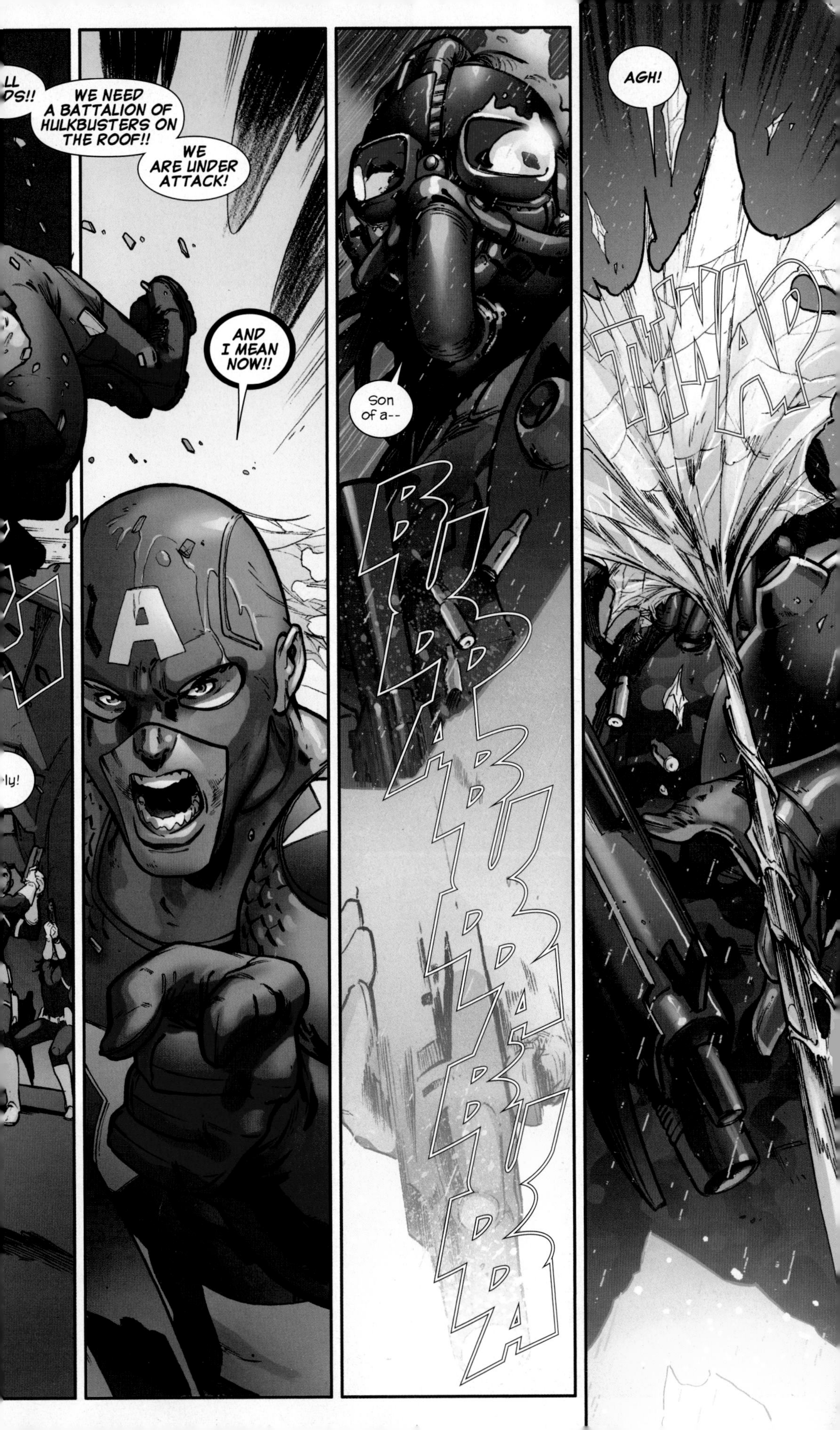
WE NEED A BATTALION OF HULKBUSTERS ON THE ROOF!!
WE ARE UNDER ATTACK!
AND I MEAN NOW!!
Son of a--
AGH!

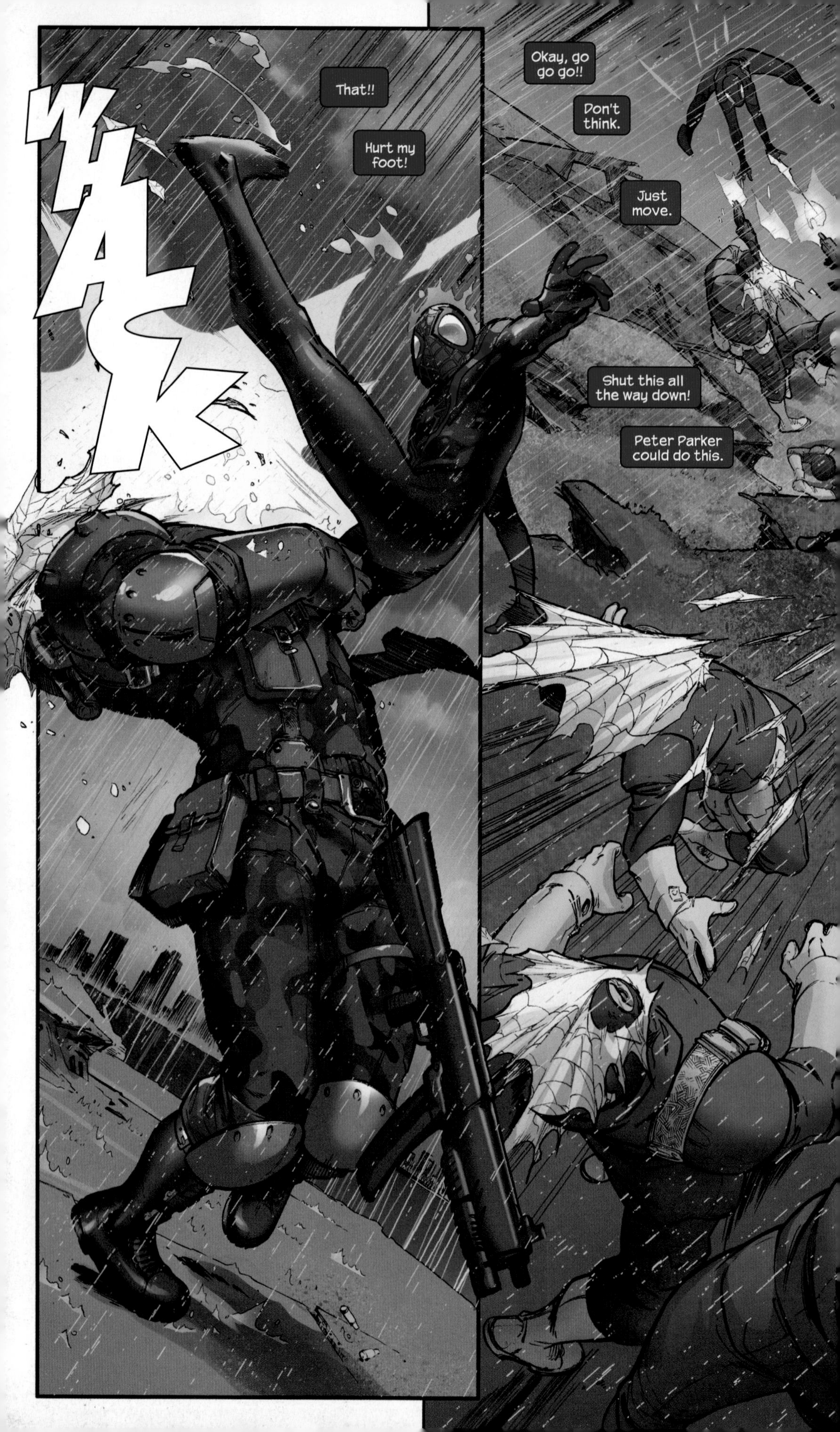
WHACK
That!!
Hurt my foot!
Okay, go go go!!
Don't think.
Just move.
Shut this all the way down!
Peter Parker could do this.

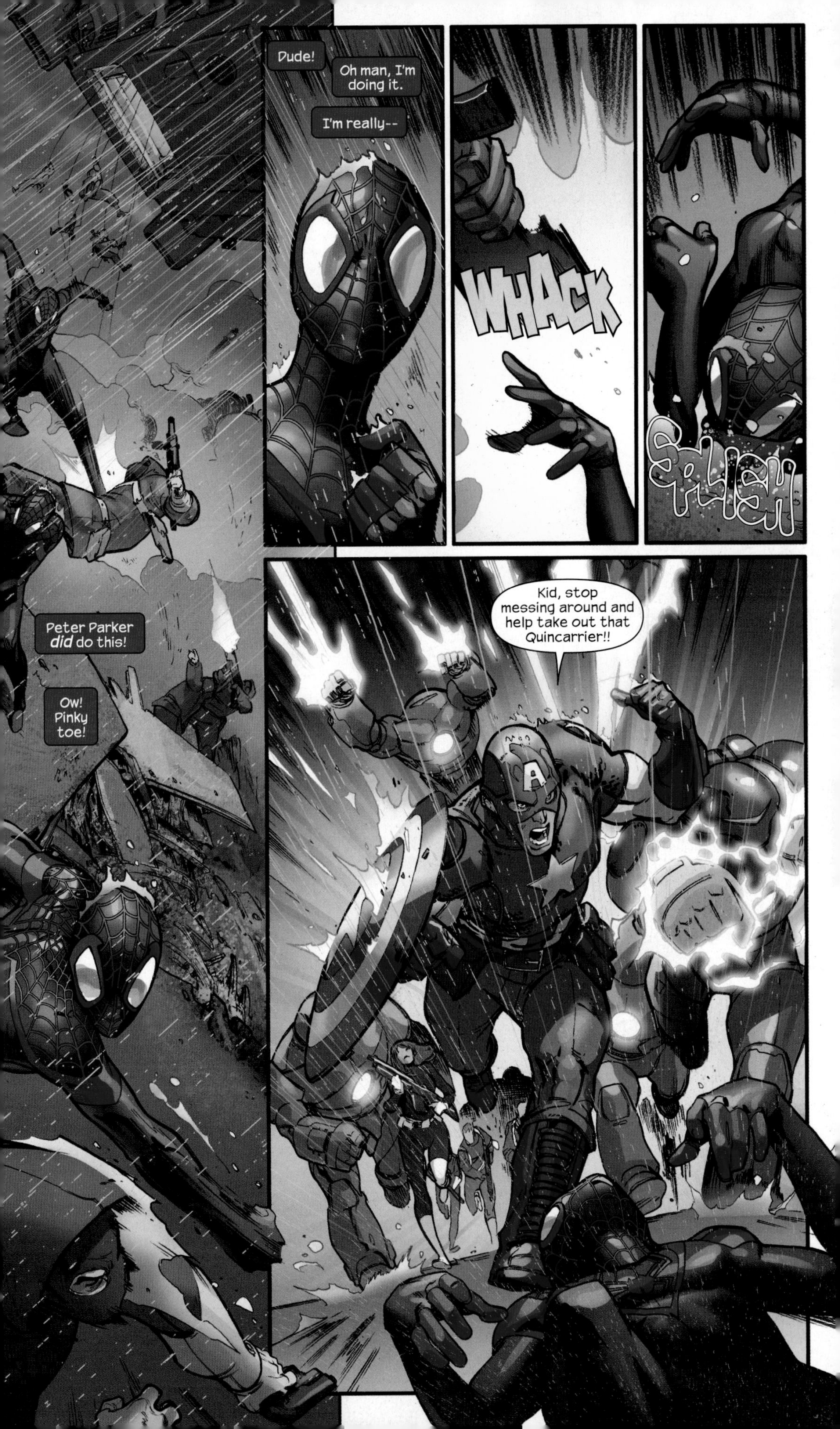
Dude!
Oh man, I'm doing it.
I'm really--
WHACK
SPLISH
Peter Parker *did* do this!
Ow! Pinky toe!
Kid, stop messing around and help take out that Quincarrier!!

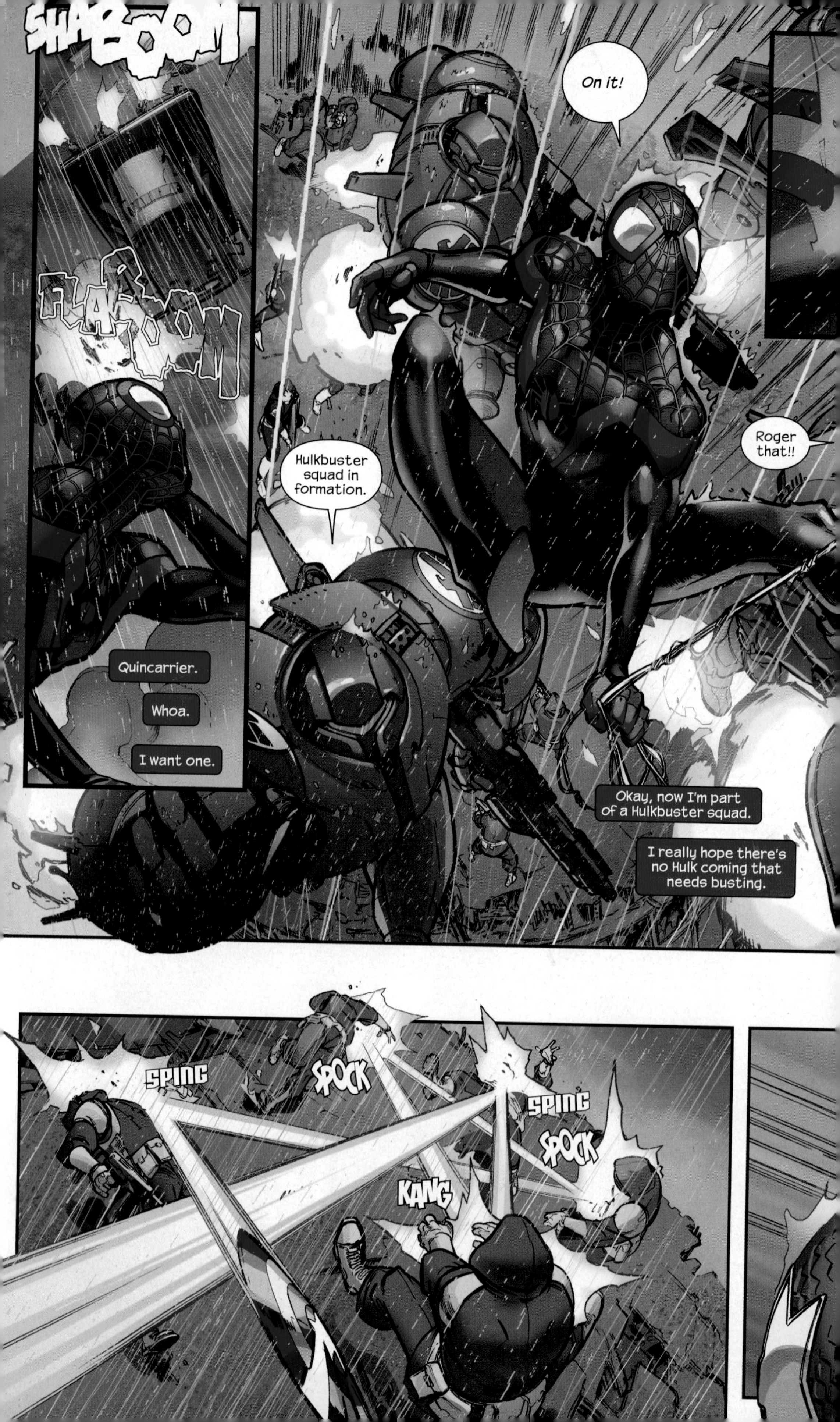
SHABOOM
FLARAOOOM
Quincarrier.
Whoa.
I want one.
On it!
Hulkbuster squad in formation.
Roger that!!
Okay, now I'm part of a Hulkbuster squad.
I really hope there's no Hulk coming that needs busting.
SPING
SPOCK
SPING
SPOCK
KANG

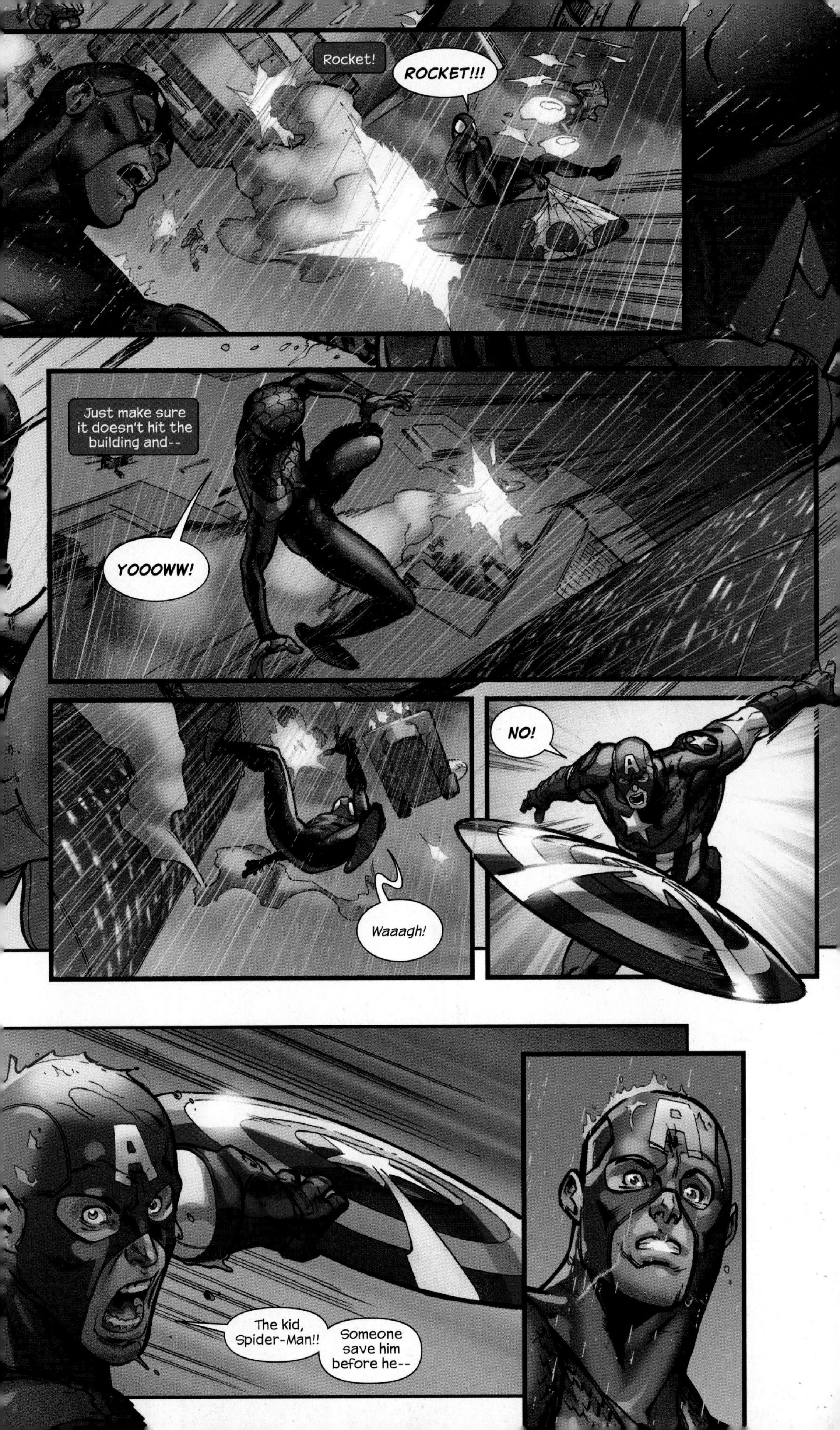
Rocket!
ROCKET!!!
Just make sure it doesn't hit the building and--
YOOOWW!
Waaagh!
NO!
The kid, Spider-Man!!
Someone save him before he--

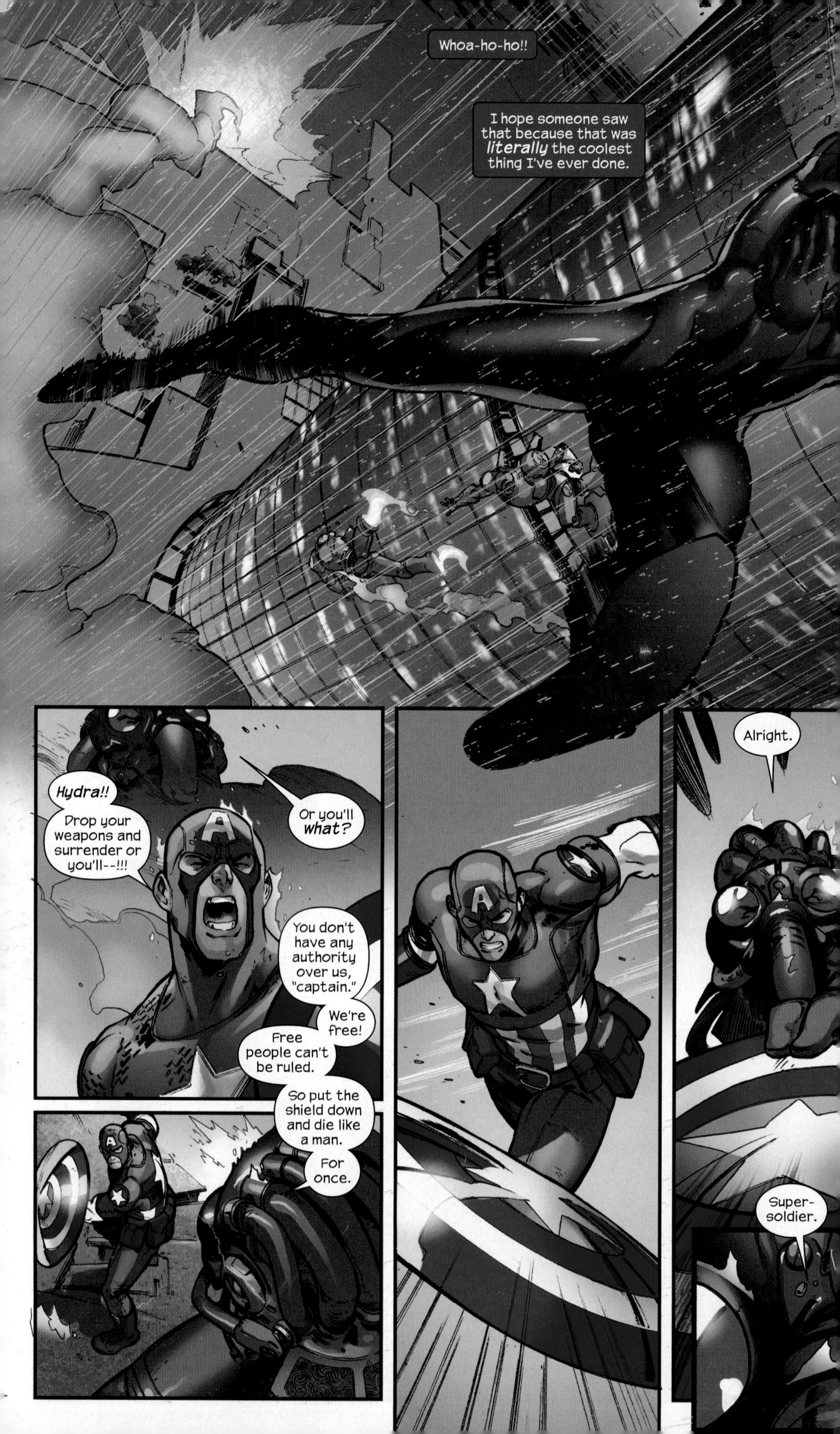
Whoa-ho-ho!!
I hope someone saw that because that was *literally* the coolest thing I've ever done.
Hydra!!
Drop your weapons and surrender or you'll--!!!
Or you'll *what?*
You don't have any authority over us, "captain."
We're free!
Free people can't be ruled.
So put the shield down and die like a man.
For once.
Alright.
Super-soldier.

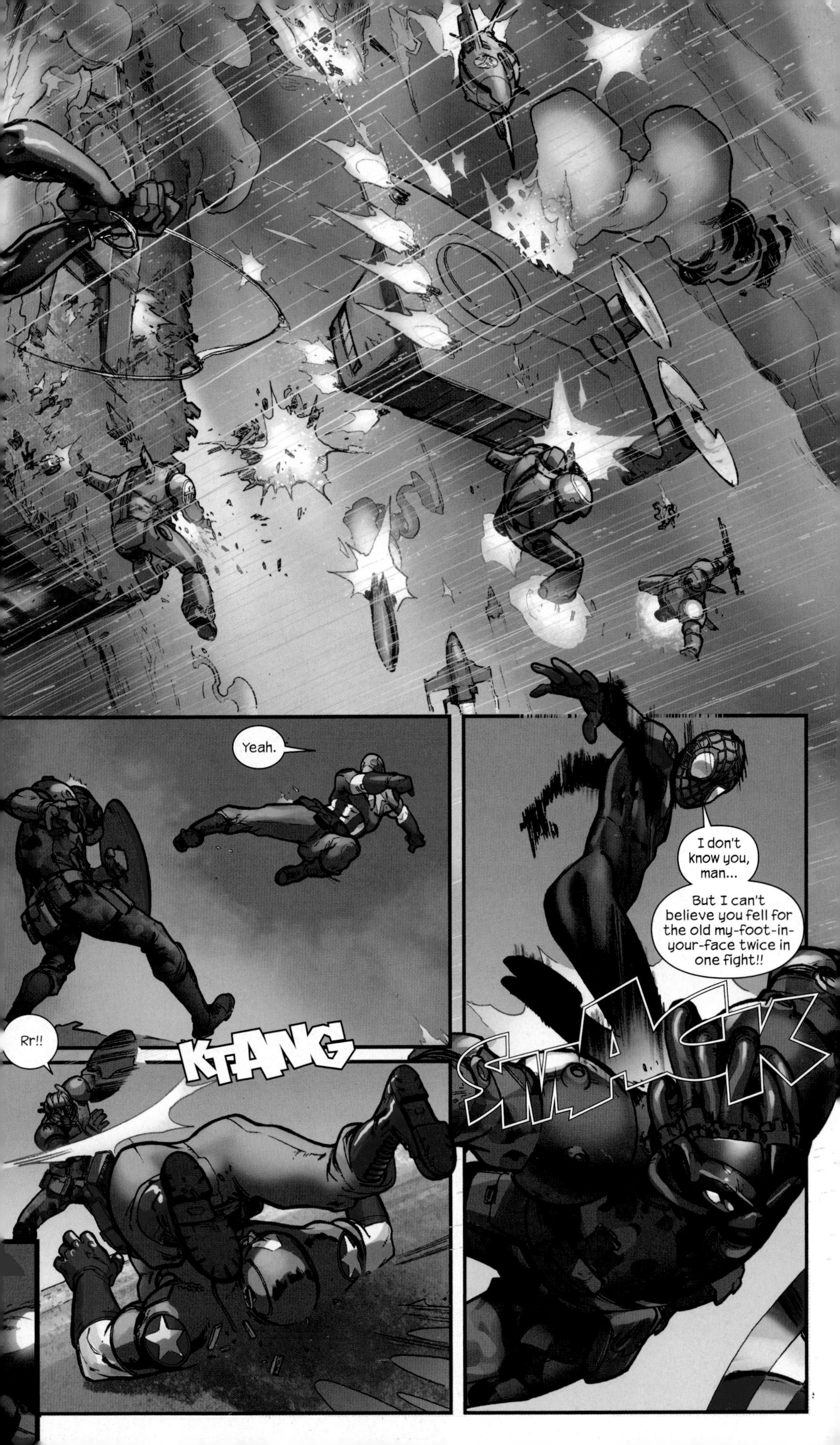

Yeah.
Rr!!
KTANG
I don't know you, man...
But I can't believe you fell for the old my-foot-in-your-face twice in one fight!!
SMACK

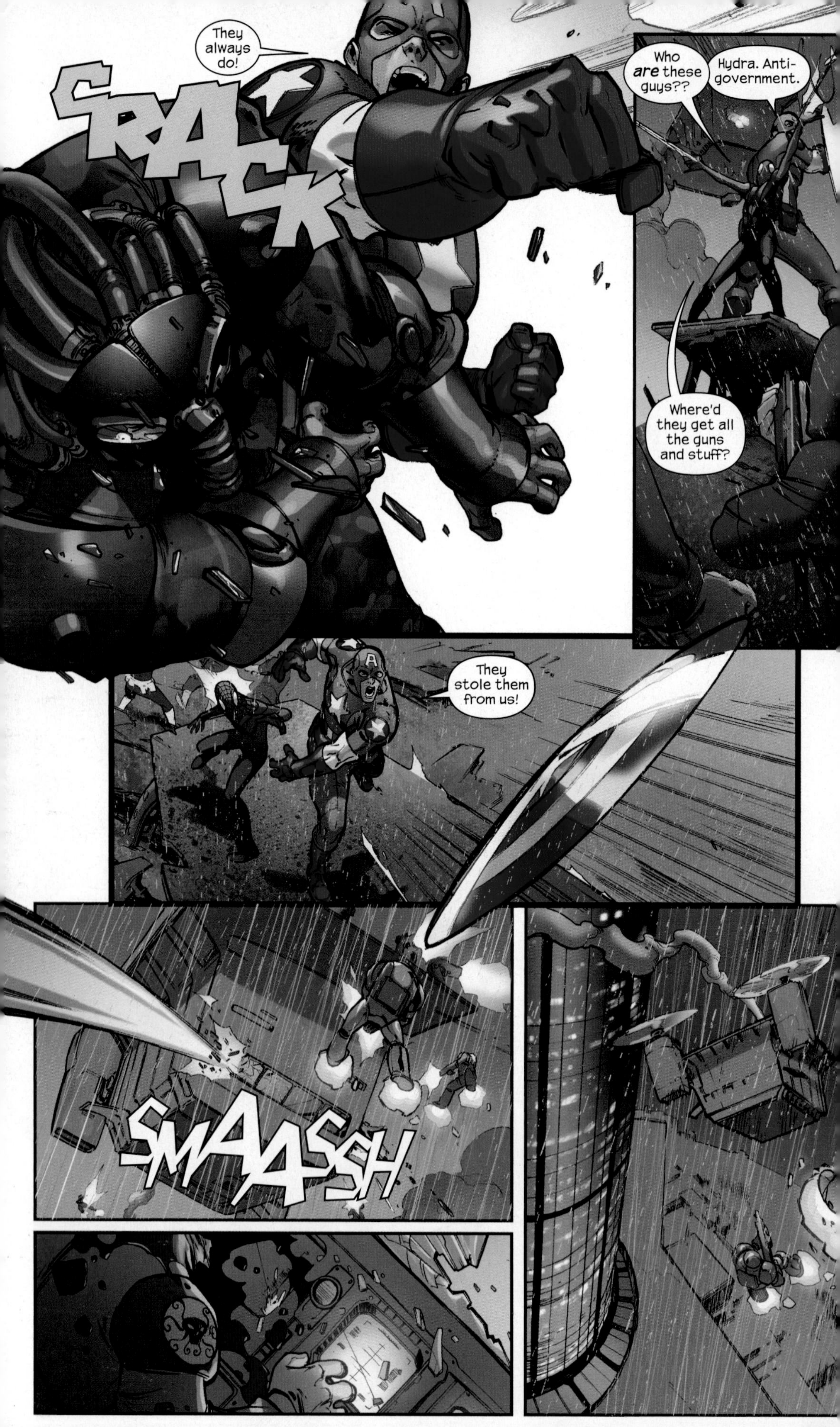
They always do!
CRACK
Who are these guys??
Hydra. Anti-government.
Where'd they get all the guns and stuff?
They stole them from us!
SMAASSH

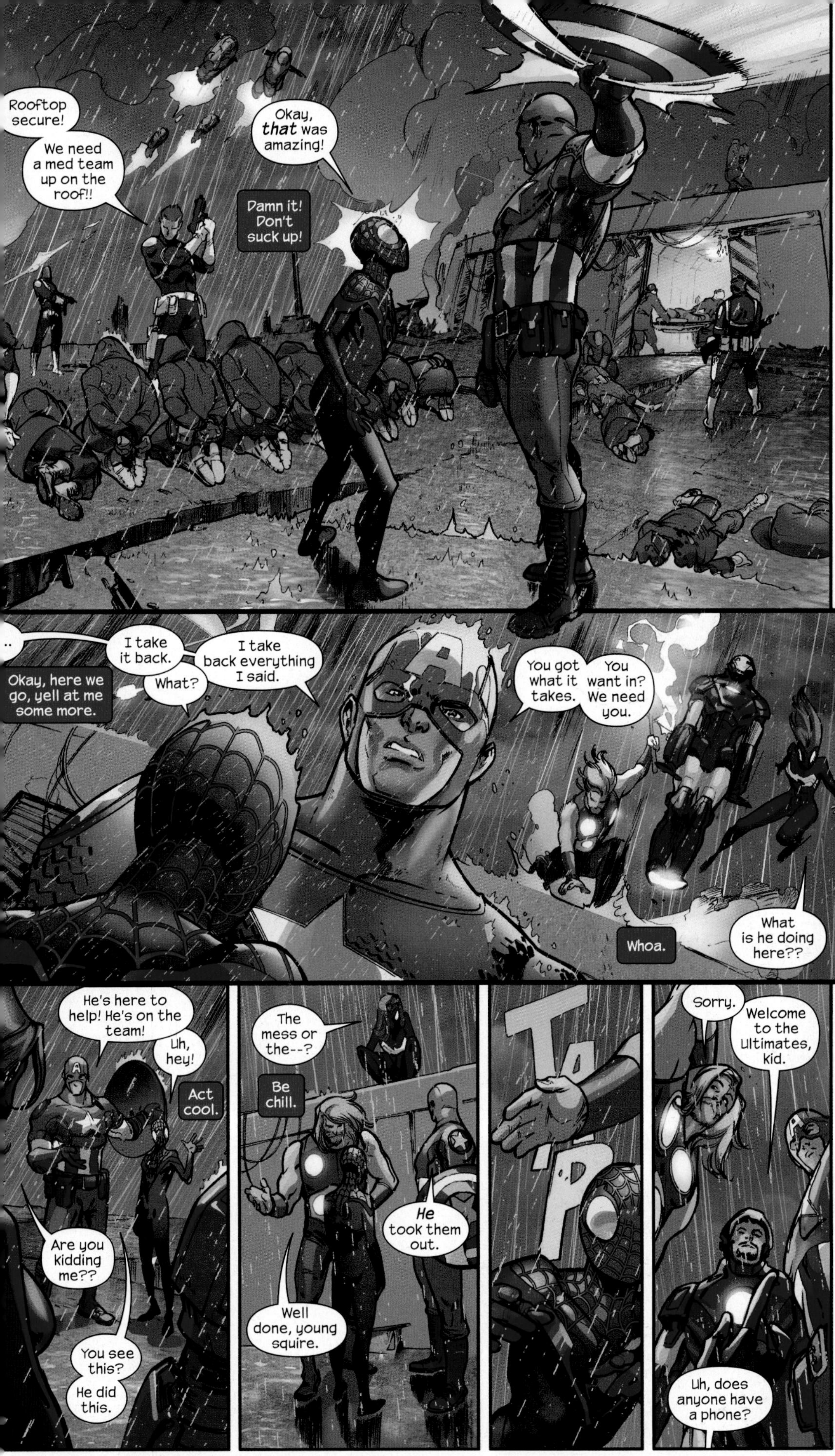
Rooftop secure!
We need a med team up on the roof!!
Okay, that was amazing!
Damn it! Don't suck up!
..
I take it back.
I take back everything I said.
Okay, here we go, yell at me some more.
What?
You got what it takes.
You want in? We need you.
Whoa.
What is he doing here??
He's here to help! He's on the team!
Uh, hey!
Act cool.
Are you kidding me??
You see this?
He did this.
The mess or the--?
Be chill.
He took them out.
Well done, young squire.
Sorry.
Welcome to the Ultimates, kid.
Uh, does anyone have a phone?

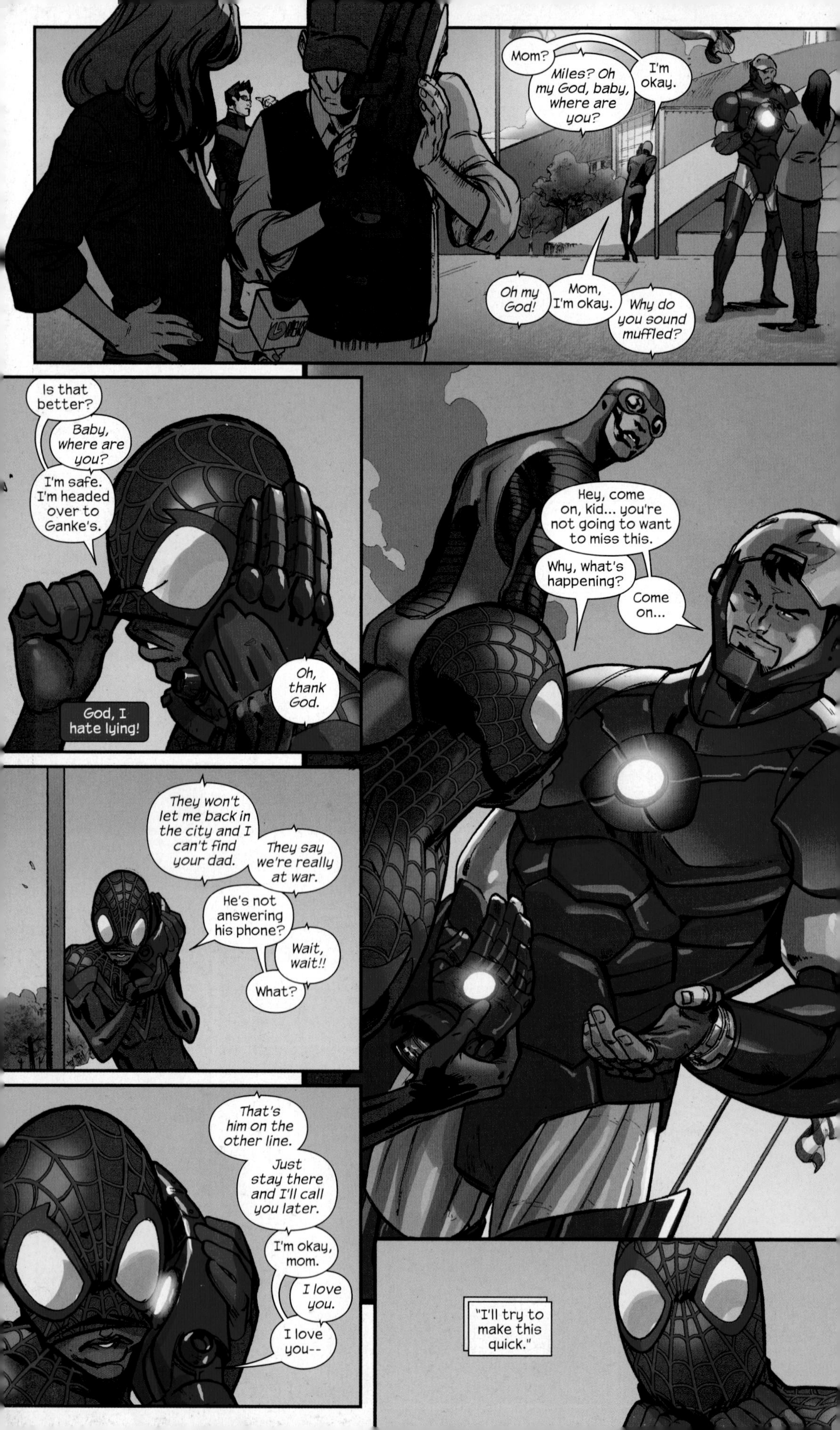
Mom?
Miles? Oh my God, baby, where are you?
I'm okay.
Oh my God!
Mom, I'm okay.
Why do you sound muffled?
Is that better?
Baby, where are you?
I'm safe. I'm headed over to Ganke's.
Oh, thank God.
God, I hate lying!
Hey, come on, kid... you're not going to want to miss this.
Why, what's happening?
Come on...
They won't let me back in the city and I can't find your dad.
They say we're really at war.
He's not answering his phone?
Wait, wait!!
What?
That's him on the other line.
Just stay there and I'll call you later.
I'm okay, mom.
I love you.
I love you--
"I'll try to make this quick."

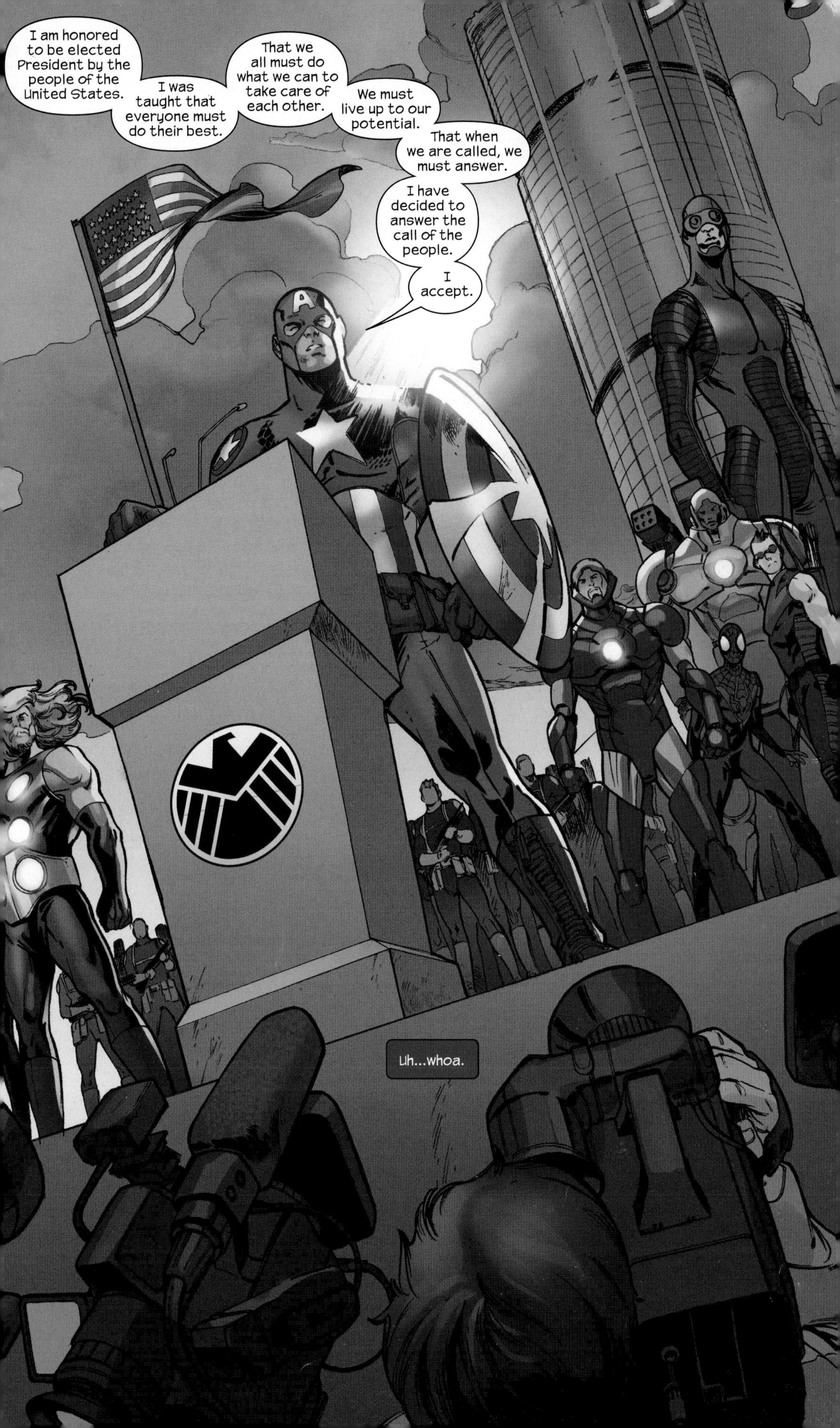
I am honored to be elected President by the people of the United States.
I was taught that everyone must do their best.
That we all must do what we can to take care of each other.
We must live up to our potential.
That when we are called, we must answer.
I have decided to answer the call of the people.
I accept.
Uh...whoa.

17

UNITED WE STAND

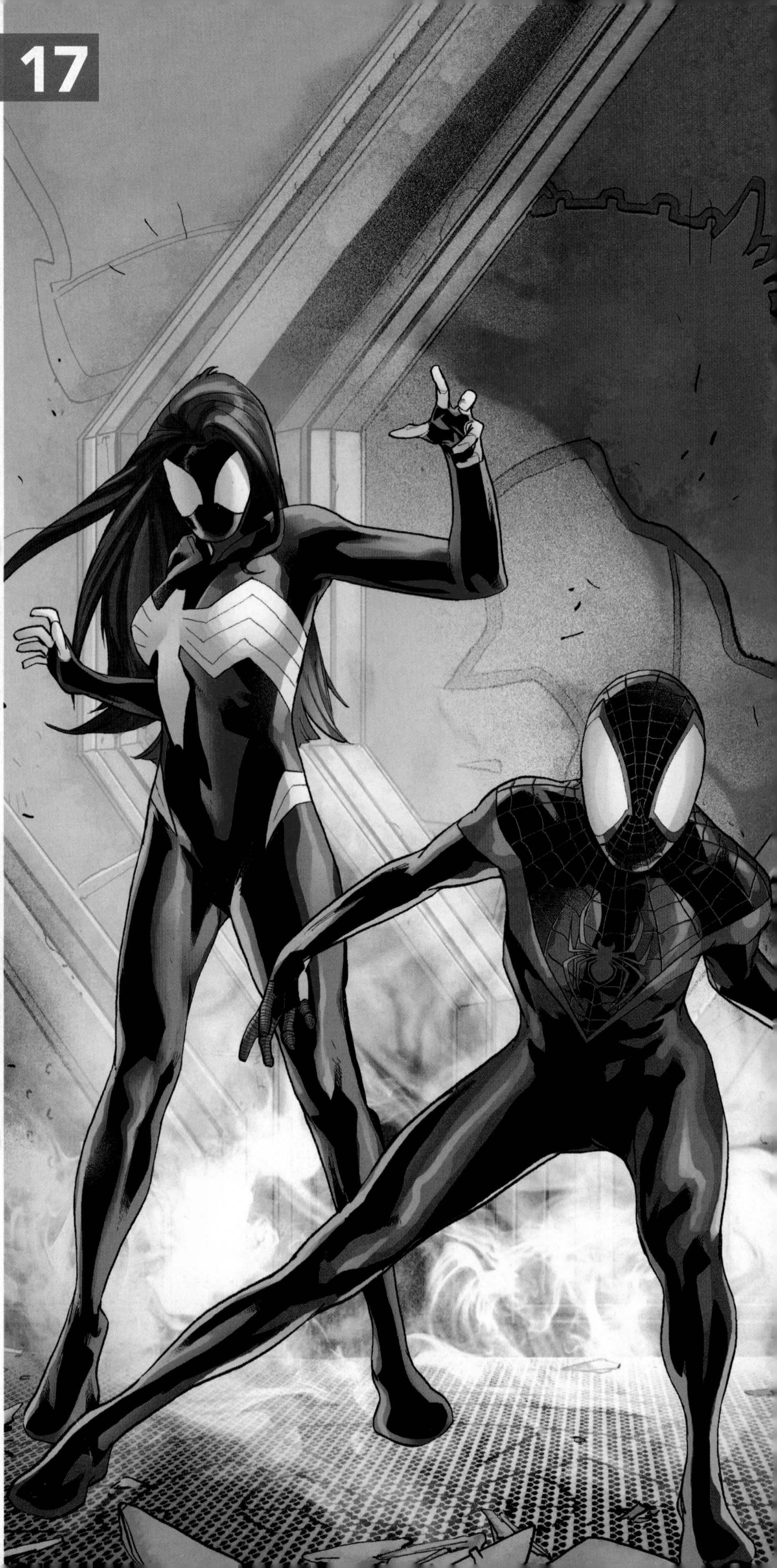

.H.I.E.L.D. SITUATION MAP:

[i-government militia hot spots]

aho, Montana,
Dakota, S.Dakota,
izona, Wyoming

Wyoming
status unknown

[Eastern seaboard control zone]

New England,
New York,
New Jersey,
Delaware,
Washington, D.C.,
Maryland,
Pennsylvania,
Virginia

secured by
National Guard
under emergency
powers
committee

PROJECT
PEGASUS

ANTI-MATTER
NO FLY
ZONE

AREA OF
URBAN
UNREST

[Great Lakes Alliance]

Minnesota,
Wisconsin,
Michigan,
Illinois,
Indiana, Ohio

Independent
nation

ALL STATES
SHOWN IN WHITE
ARE U.S. GOVERNMENT-
CONTROLLED ZONES

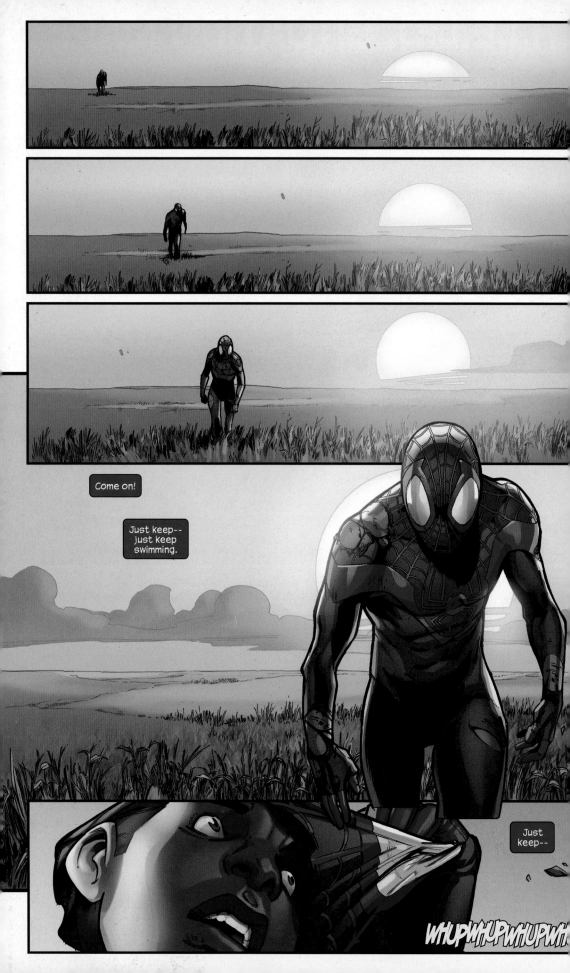

Come on!

Just keep--
just keep
swimming.

Just
keep--

WHUPWHUPWHUPWH

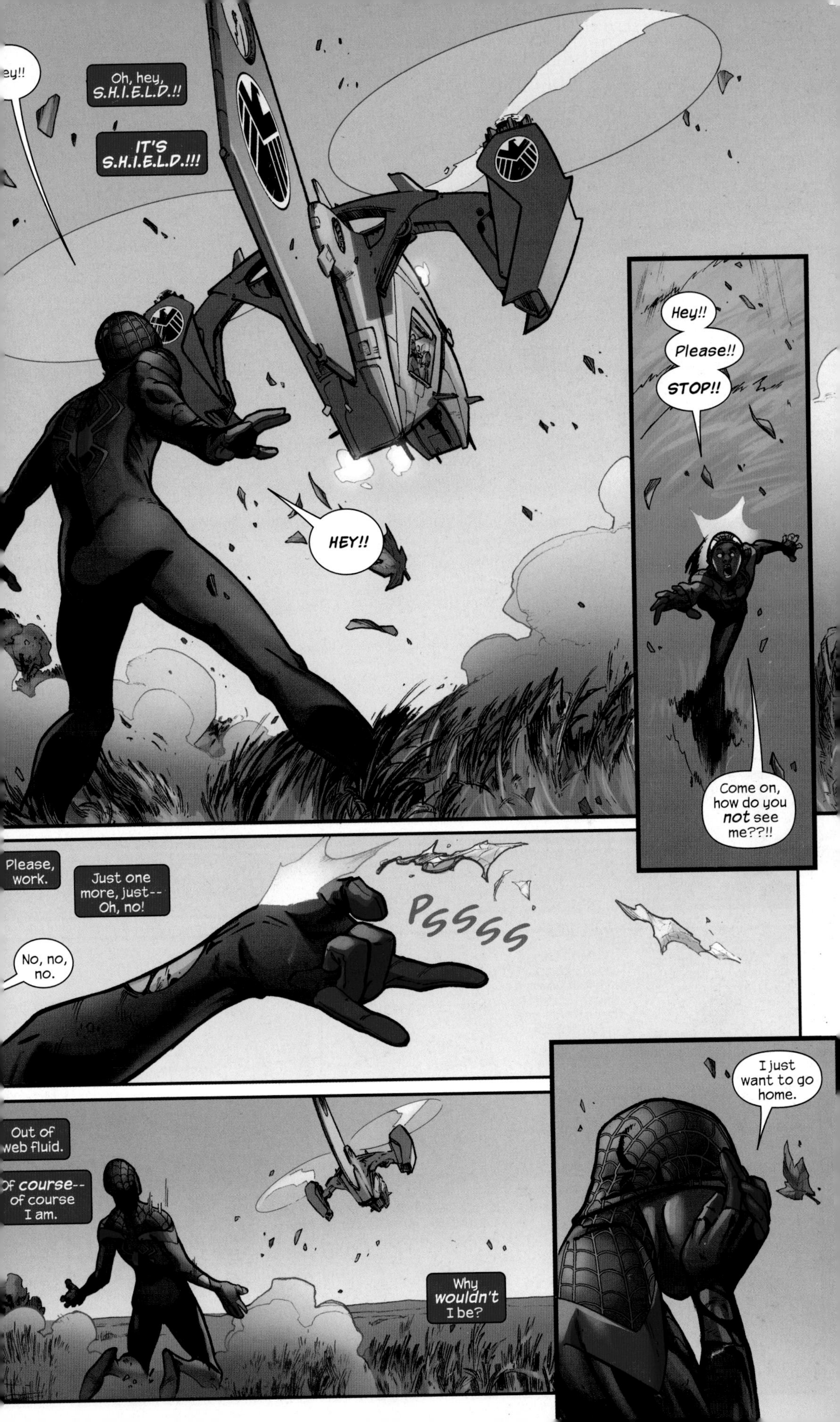
ey!!
Oh, hey, S.H.I.E.L.D.!!
IT'S S.H.I.E.L.D.!!!
HEY!!
Hey!!
Please!!
STOP!!
Come on, how do you *not* see me??!!
Please, work.
Just one more, just-- Oh, no!
PSSSS
No, no, no.
Out of web fluid.
Of *course*-- of course I am.
Why *wouldn't* I be?
I just want to go home.

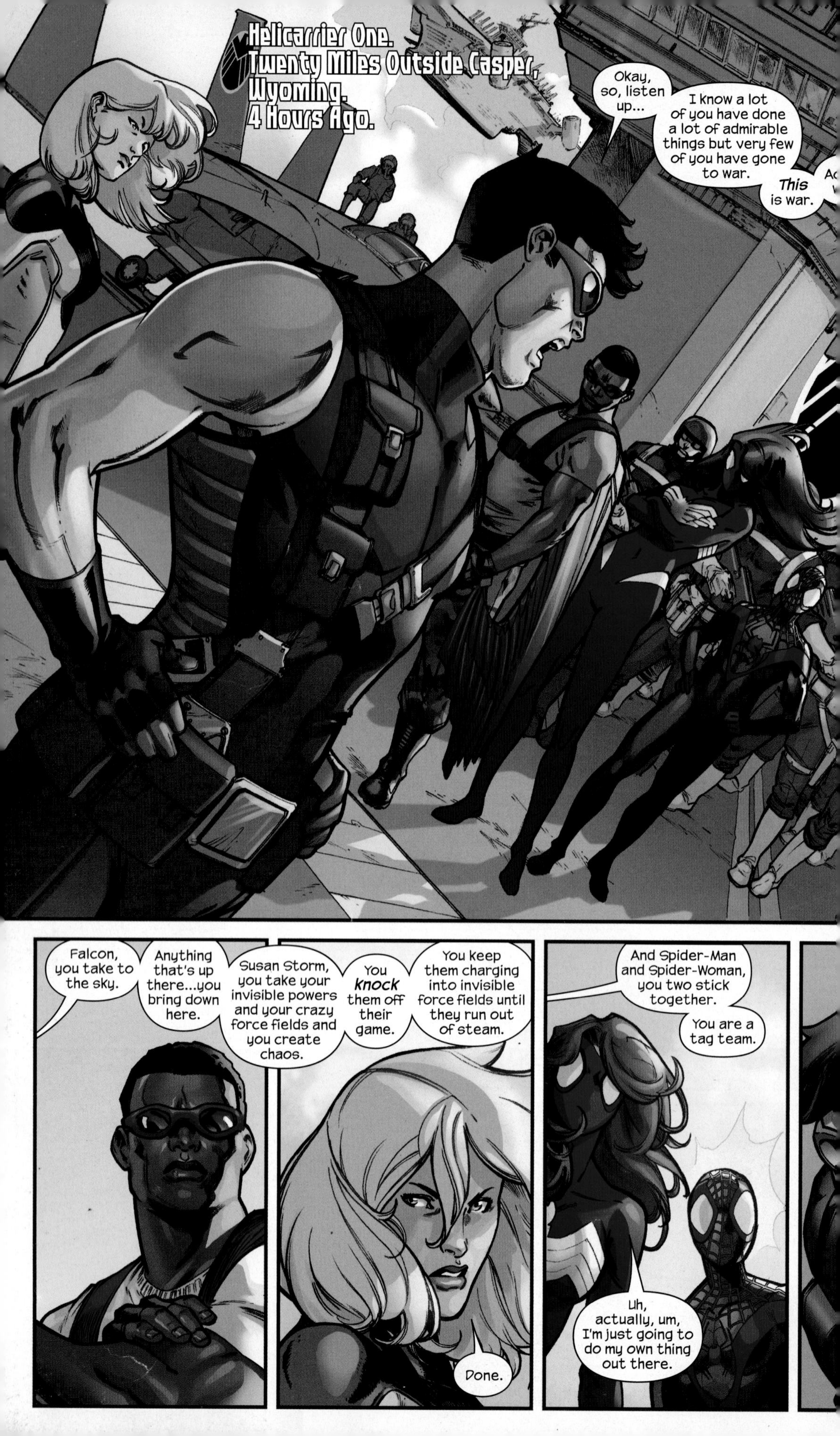
Helicarrier One.
Twenty Miles Outside Casper, Wyoming.
4 Hours Ago.
Okay, so, listen up...
I know a lot of you have done a lot of admirable things but very few of you have gone to war.
This is war.
Falcon, you take to the sky.
Anything that's up there...you bring down here.
Susan Storm, you take your invisible powers and your crazy force fields and you create chaos.
You *knock* them off their game.
You keep them charging into invisible force fields until they run out of steam.
Done.
And Spider-Man and Spider-Woman, you two stick together.
You are a tag team.
Uh, actually, um, I'm just going to do my own thing out there.

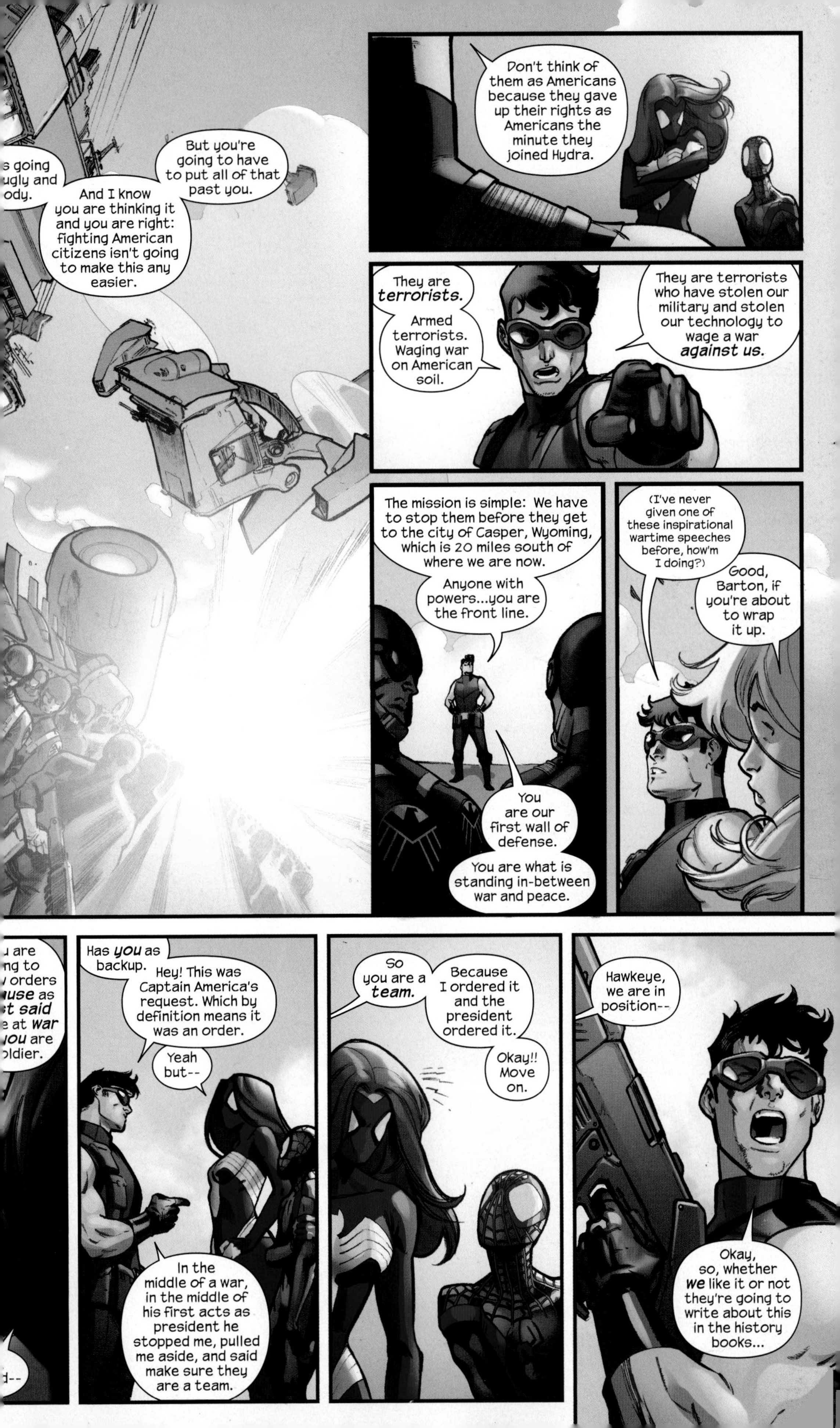
And I know you are thinking it and you are right: fighting American citizens isn't going to make this any easier.
But you're going to have to put all of that past you.
Don't think of them as Americans because they gave up their rights as Americans the minute they joined Hydra.
They are *terrorists.*
Armed terrorists. Waging war on American soil.
They are terrorists who have stolen our military and stolen our technology to wage a war ***against us.***
The mission is simple: We have to stop them before they get to the city of Casper, Wyoming, which is 20 miles south of where we are now.
Anyone with powers...you are the front line.
You are our first wall of defense.
You are what is standing in-between war and peace.
(I've never given one of these inspirational wartime speeches before, how'm I doing?)
Good, Barton, if you're about to wrap it up.
Has ***you*** as backup.
Hey! This was Captain America's request. Which by definition means it was an order.
Yeah but--
In the middle of a war, in the middle of his first acts as president he stopped me, pulled me aside, and said make sure they are a team.
So you are a ***team.***
Because I ordered it and the president ordered it.
Okay!! Move on.
Hawkeye, we are in position--
Okay, so, whether ***we*** like it or not they're going to write about this in the history books...

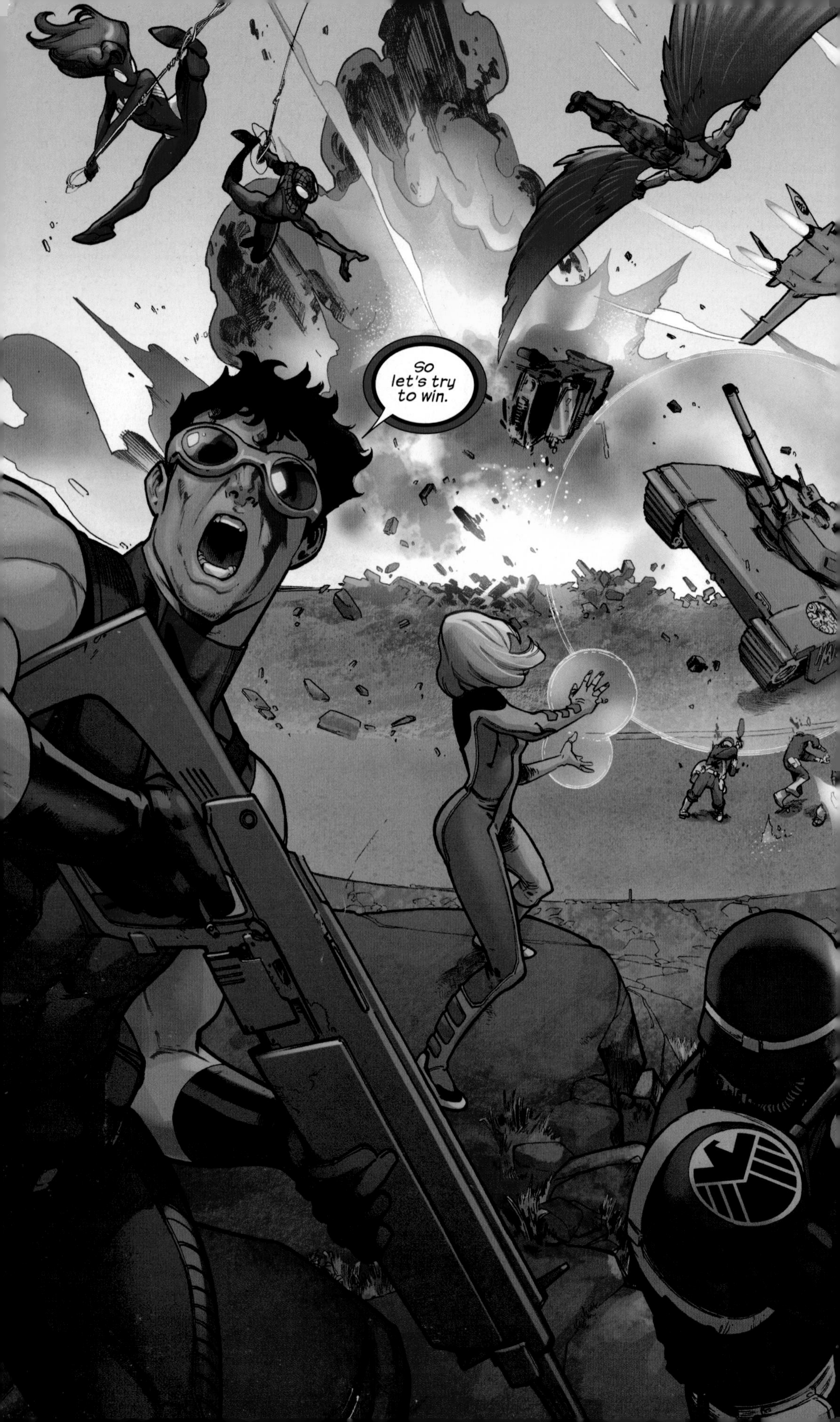
So let's try to win.

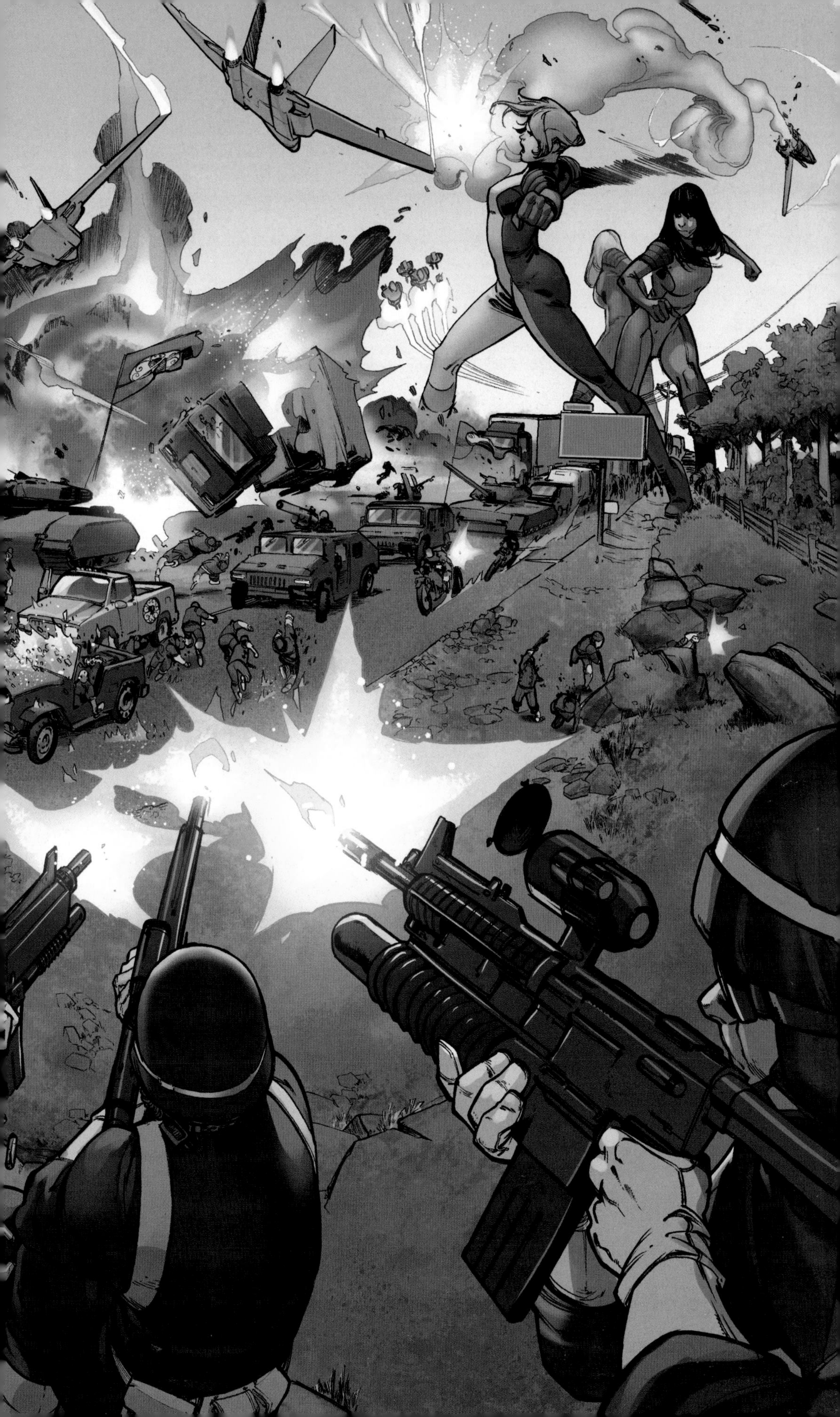

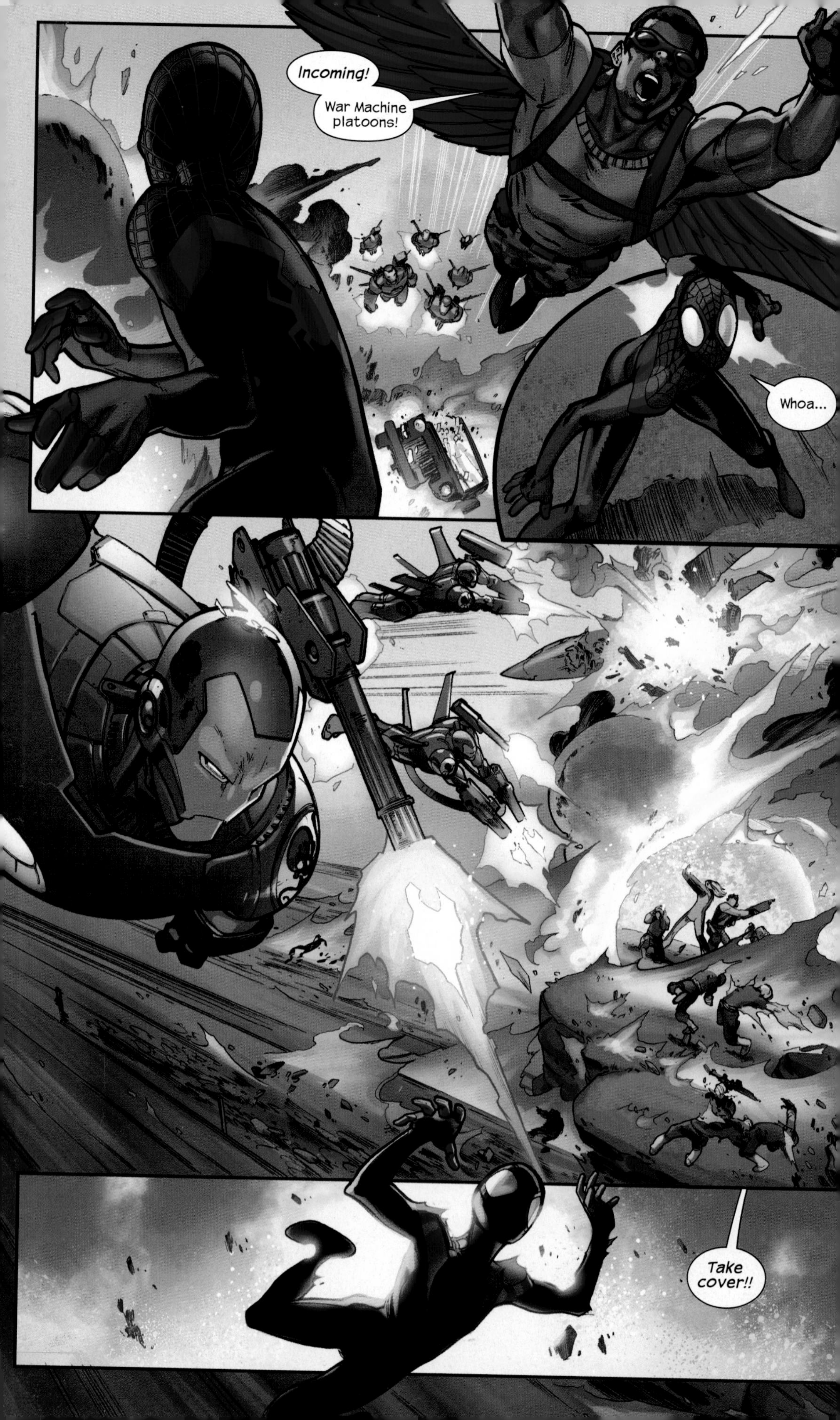
Incoming!
War Machine platoons!
Whoa...
Take cover!!

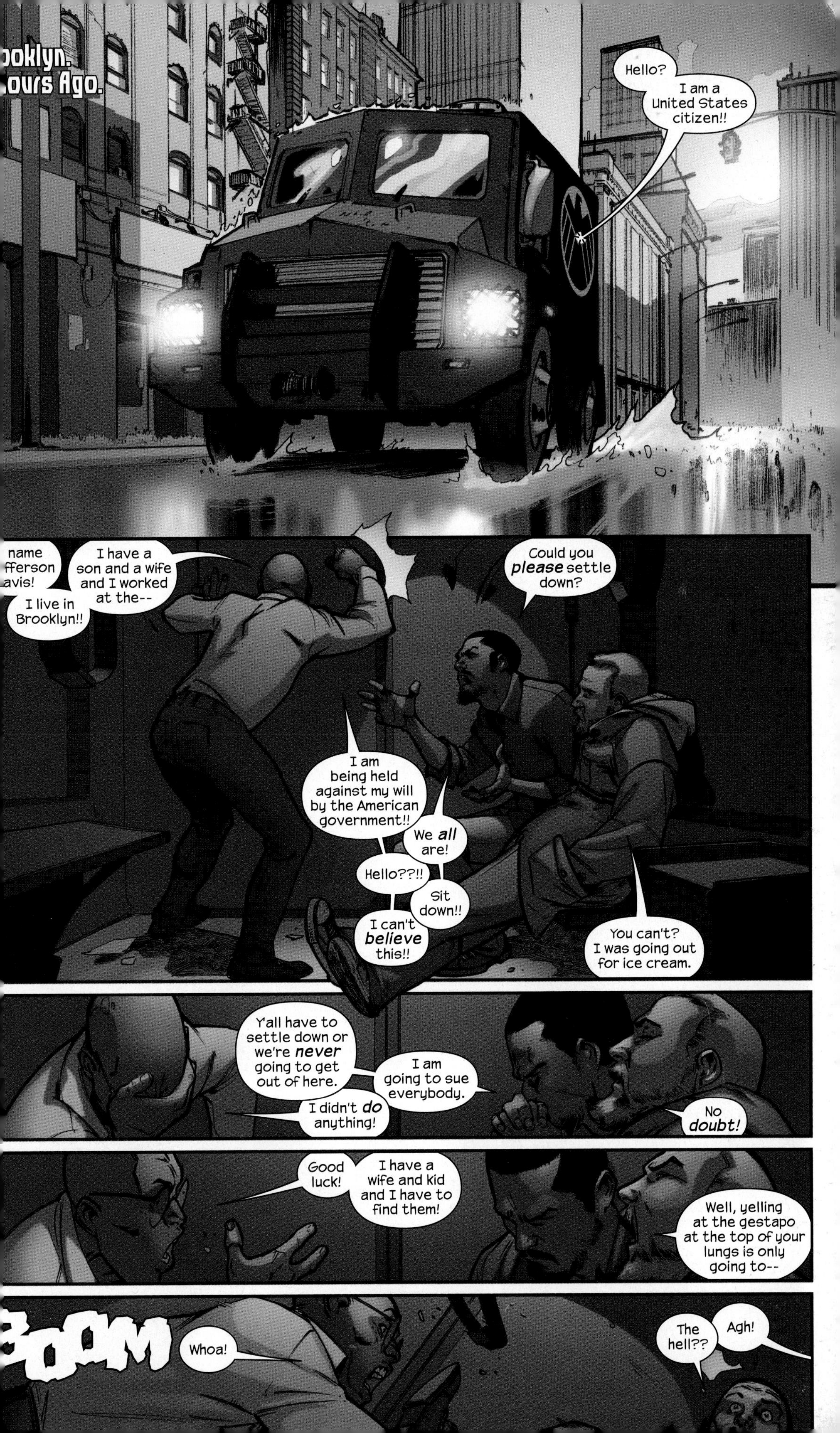

ooklyn.
ours Ago.
Hello?
I am a United States citizen!!
name fferson avis!
I live in Brooklyn!!
I have a son and a wife and I worked at the--
Could you *please* settle down?
I am being held against my will by the American government!!
We *all* are!
Hello??!!
Sit down!!
I can't *believe* this!!
You can't? I was going out for ice cream.
Y'all have to settle down or we're *never* going to get out of here.
I am going to sue everybody.
I didn't *do* anything!
No *doubt!*
Good luck!
I have a wife and kid and I have to find them!
Well, yelling at the gestapo at the top of your lungs is only going to--
BOOM
Whoa!
The hell??
Agh!

SHABOOM SHABOOM SHABOOM SHABU

HAIL HYDRA!!

Oh my God!

Off me!

Please don't *touch* me!!

I'm leaving this city!

Suing *everyone*!

Is everyone all right?

Sorry for the bumpy ride!

Come on out!

What *the hell*, man?

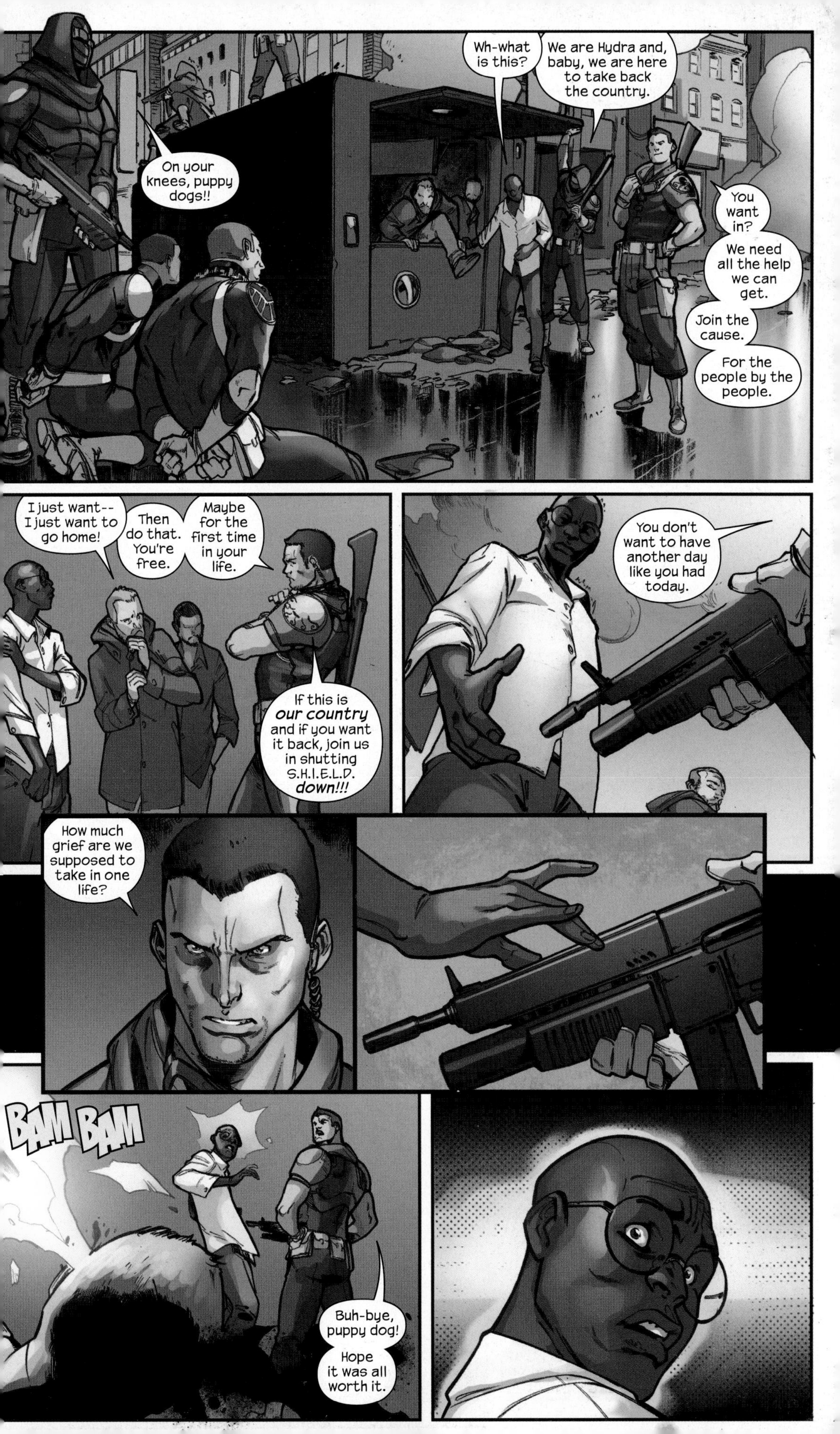

On your knees, puppy dogs!!
Wh-what is this?
We are Hydra and, baby, we are here to take back the country.
You want in?
We need all the help we can get.
Join the cause.
For the people by the people.
I just want-- I just want to go home!
Then do that. You're free.
Maybe for the first time in your life.
If this is *our country* and if you want it back, join us in shutting S.H.I.E.L.D. *down!!!*
You don't want to have another day like you had today.
How much grief are we supposed to take in one life?
BAM BAM
Buh-bye, puppy dog!
Hope it was all worth it.

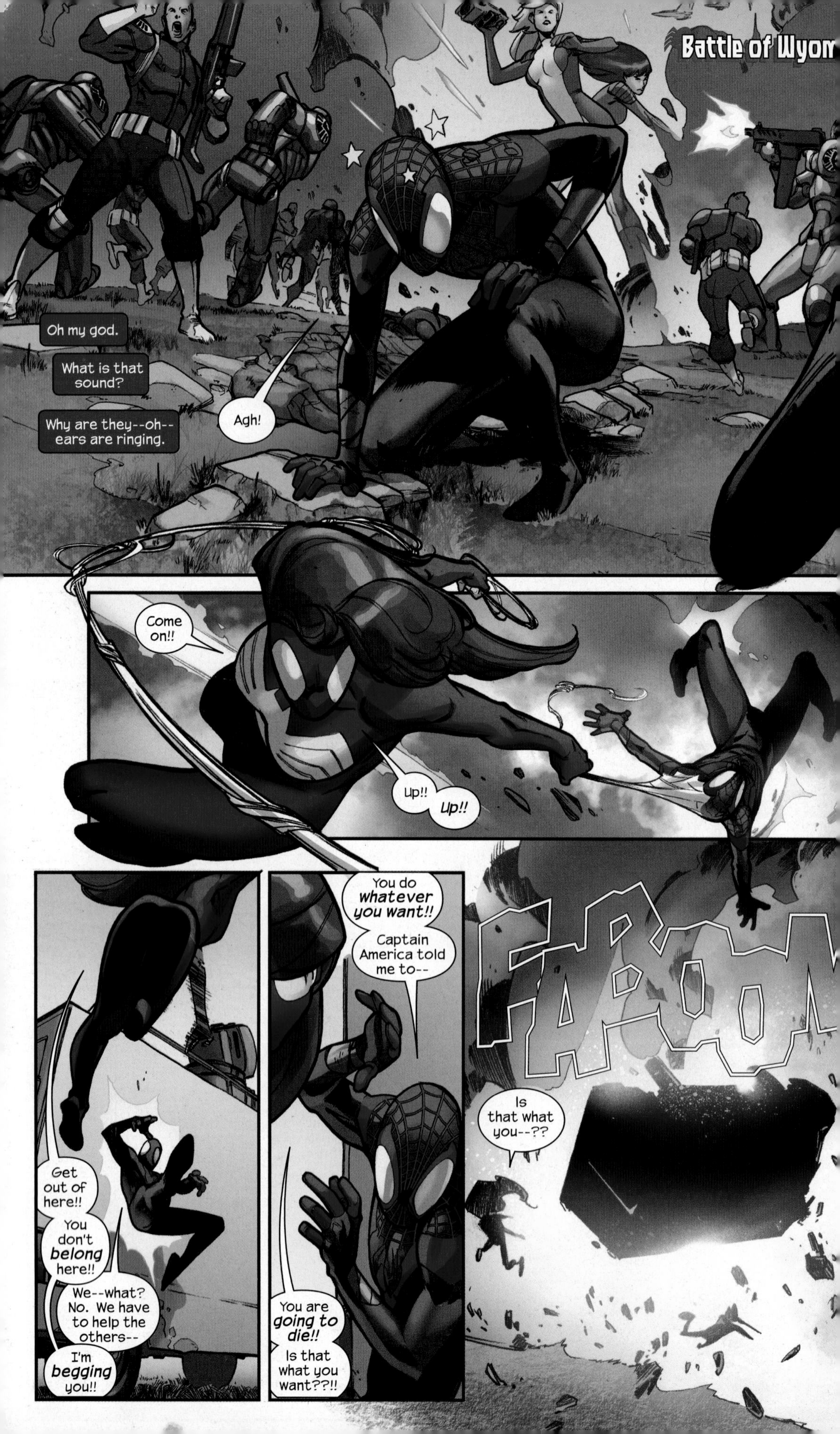
Battle of Wyom
Oh my god.
What is that sound?
Why are they--oh-- ears are ringing.
Agh!
Come on!!
Up!! Up!!
Get out of here!!
You don't belong here!!
We--what? No. We have to help the others--
I'm begging you!!
You do whatever you want!!
Captain America told me to--
You are going to die!!
Is that what you want??!!
FABOOM
Is that what you--??

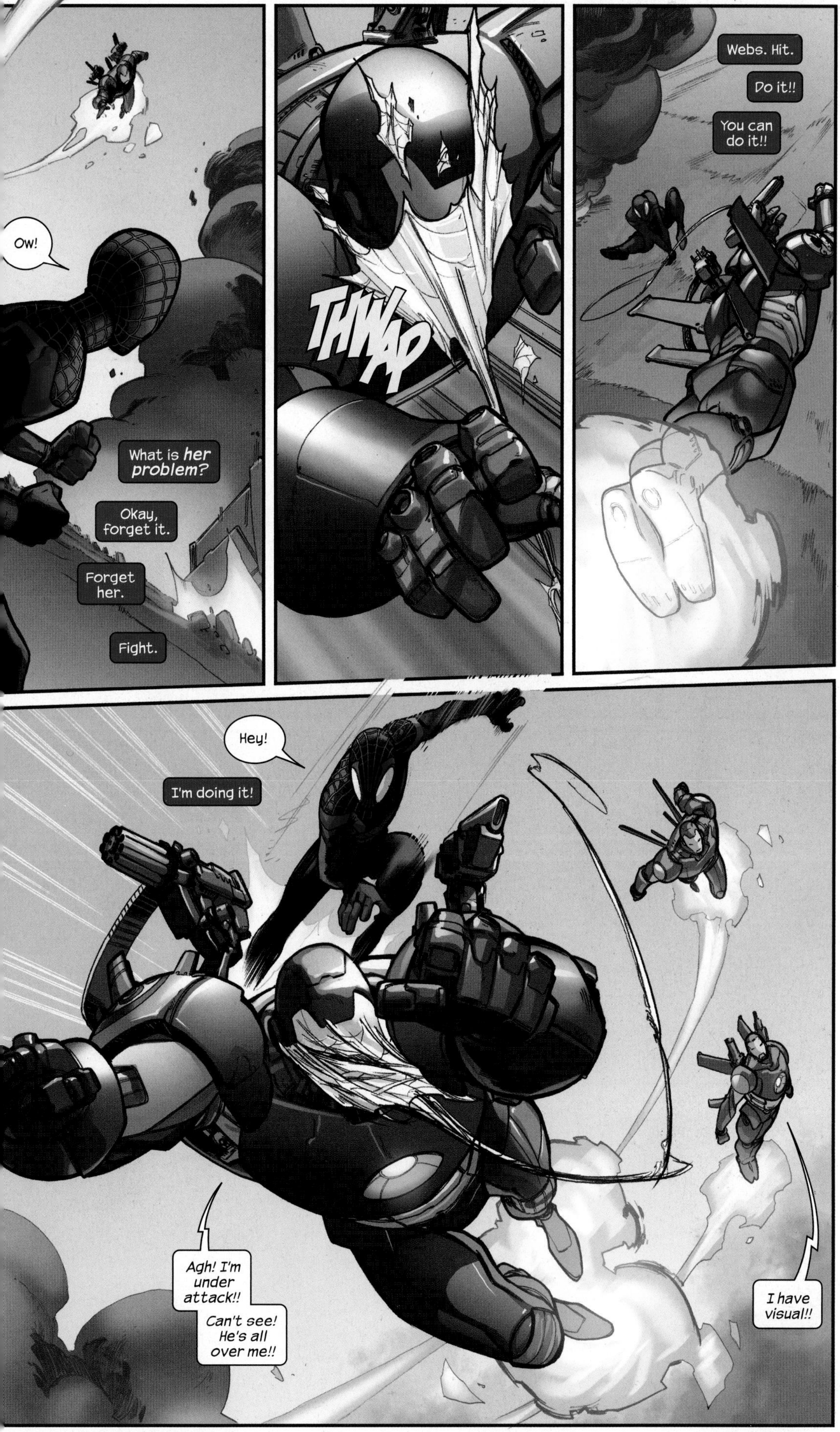
Ow!
What is her problem?
Okay, forget it.
Forget her.
Fight.
THWAP
Webs. Hit.
Do it!!
You can do it!!
Hey!
I'm doing it!
Agh! I'm under attack!!
Can't see! He's all over me!!
I have visual!!

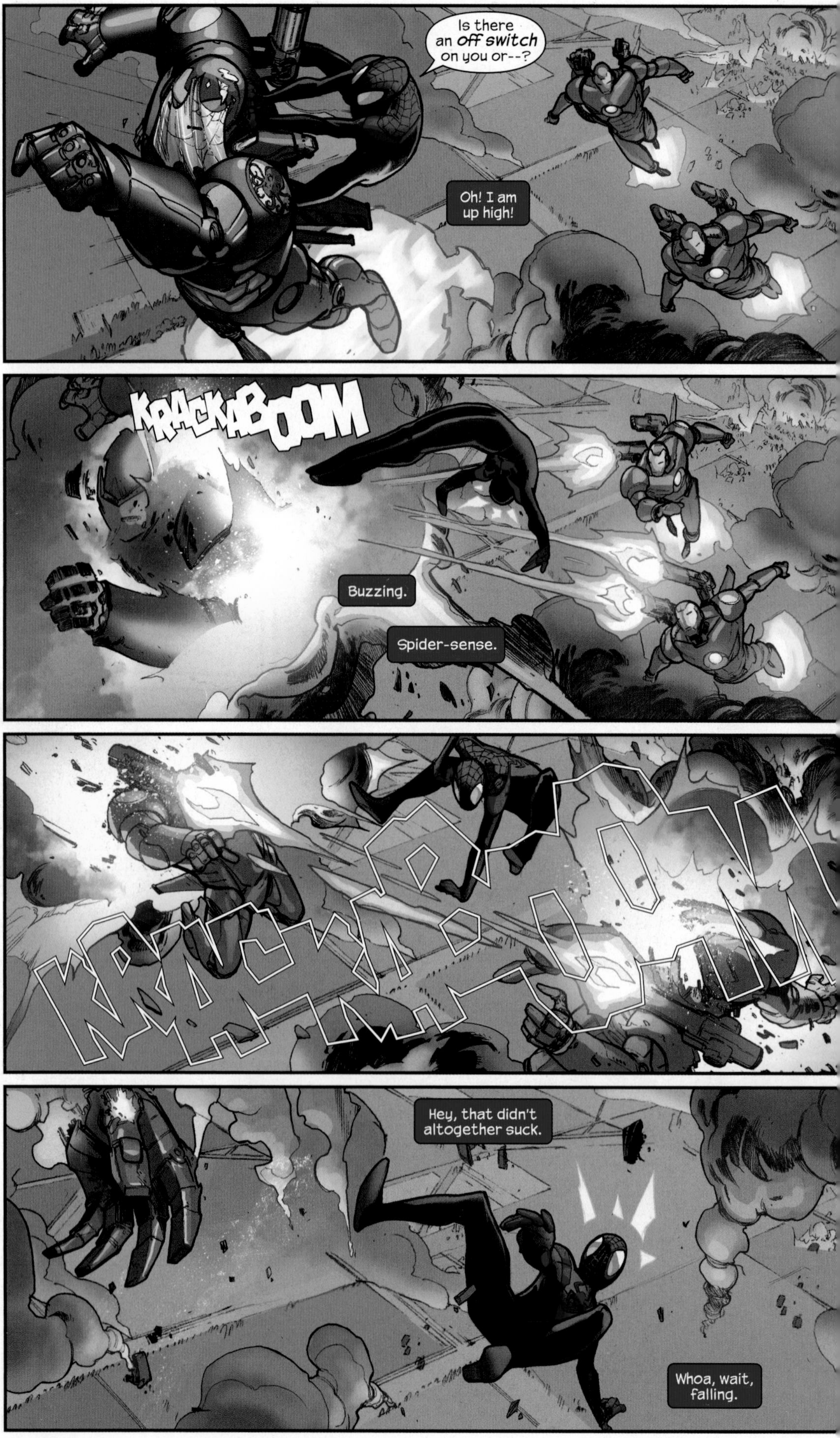

Is there an off switch on you or--?
Oh! I am up high!
KRACKABOOM
Buzzing.
Spider-sense.
Hey, that didn't altogether suck.
Whoa, wait, falling.

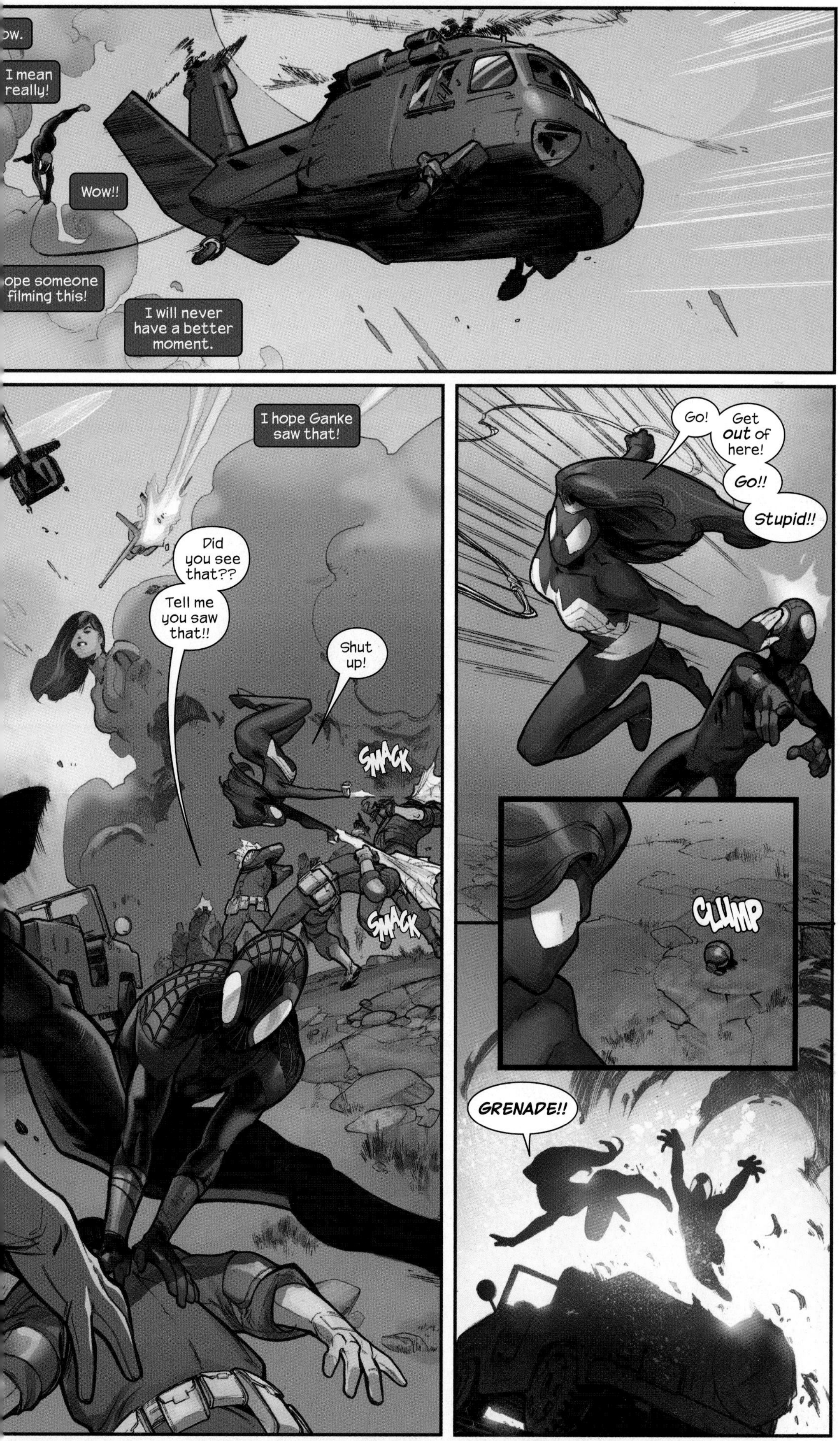

ow.
I mean really!
Wow!!
ope someone filming this!
I will never have a better moment.
I hope Ganke saw that!
Did you see that??
Tell me you saw that!!
Shut up!
SMACK
SMACK
Go!
Get out of here!
Go!!
Stupid!!
CLUMP
GRENADE!!

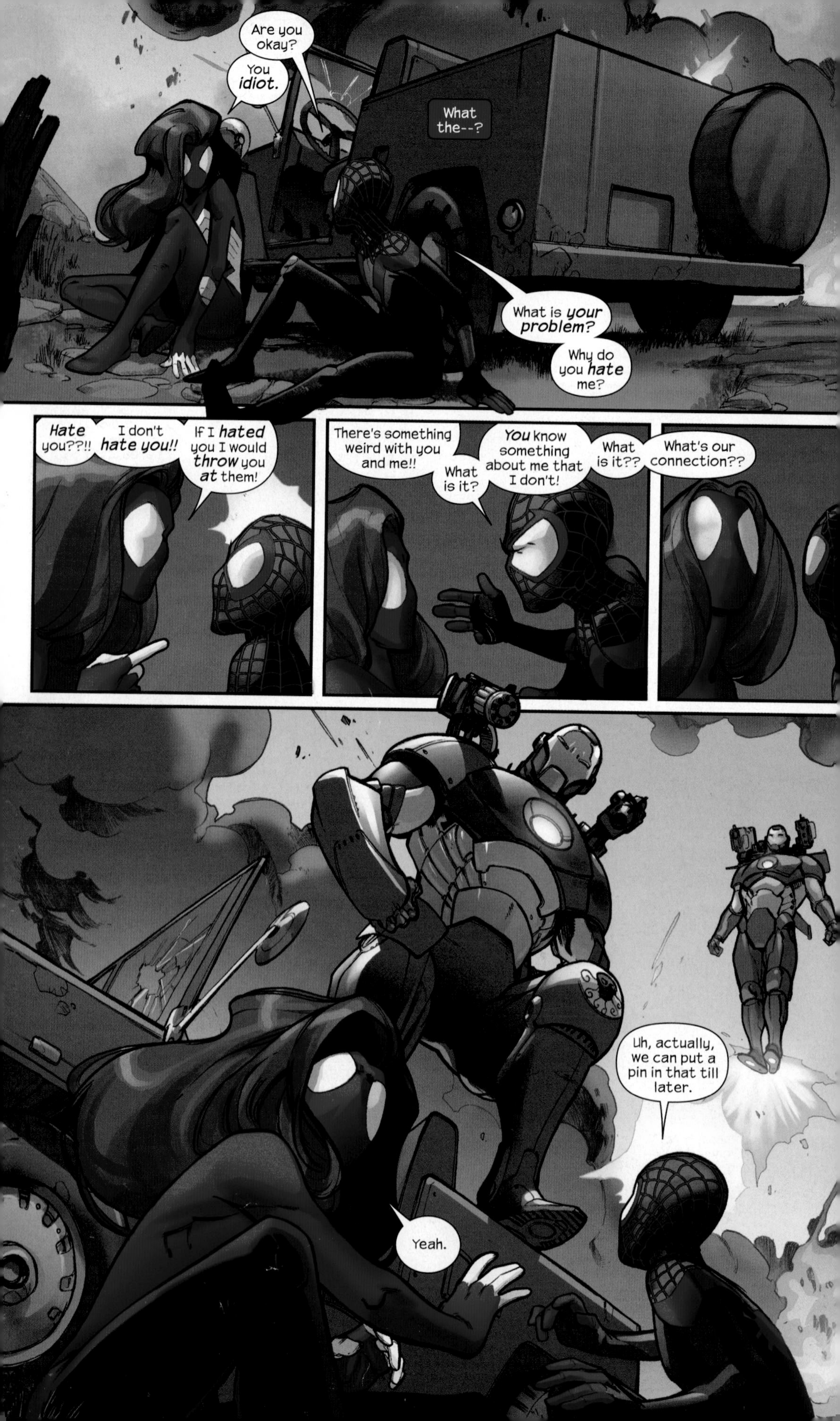
Are you okay?
You idiot.
What the--?
What is your problem?
Why do you hate me?
Hate you??!!
I don't hate you!!
If I hated you I would throw you at them!
There's something weird with you and me!!
What is it?
You know something about me that I don't!
What is it??
What's our connection??
Uh, actually, we can put a pin in that till later.
Yeah.

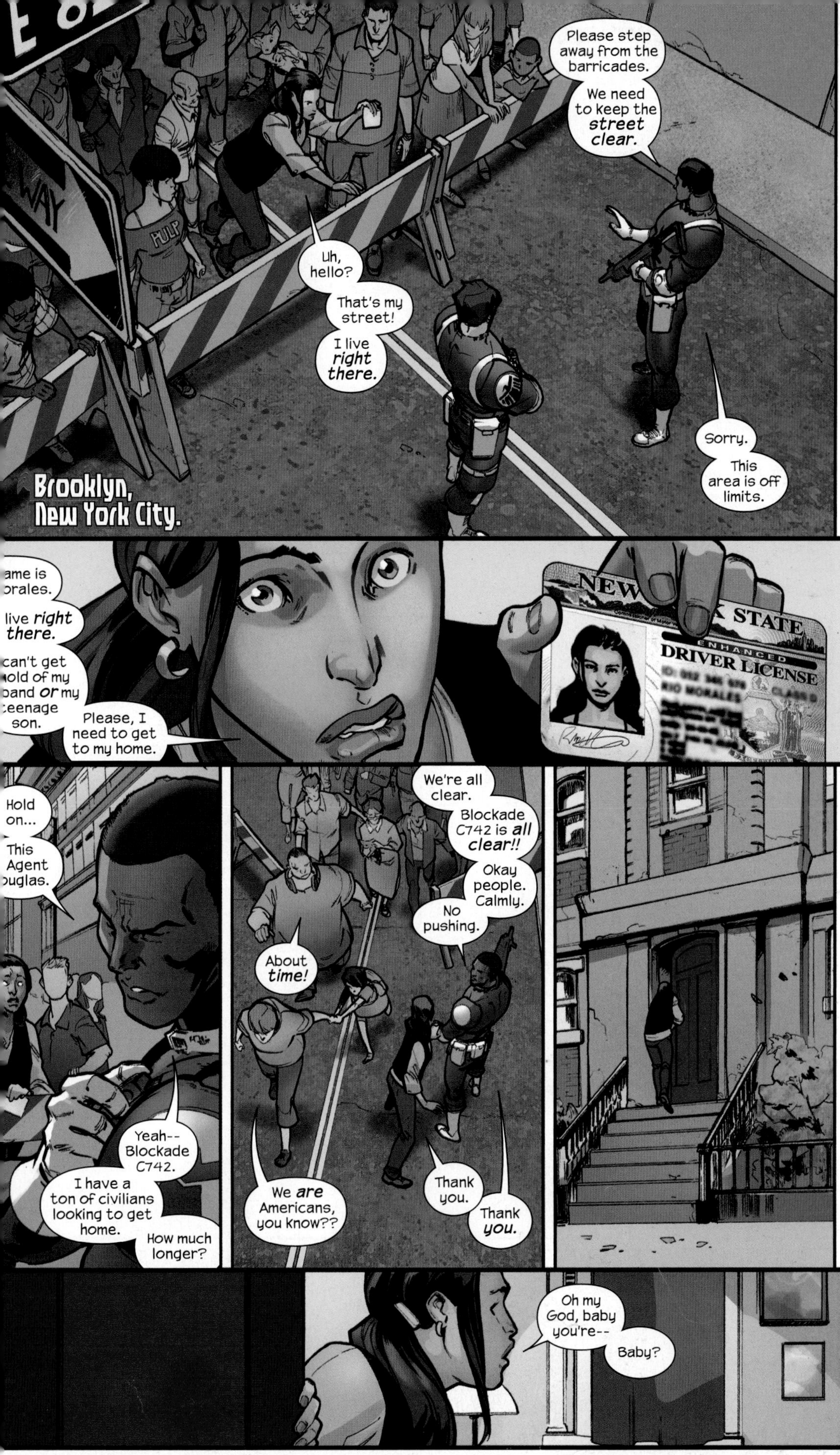

Please step away from the barricades.
We need to keep the *street clear.*
Uh, hello?
That's my street!
I live *right there.*
Sorry.
This area is off limits.
Brooklyn, New York City.
ame is orales.
live *right there.*
can't get lold of my band *or* my teenage son.
Please, I need to get to my home.
NEW STATE
ENHANCED
DRIVER LICENSE
Hold on...
This Agent ouglas.
Yeah-- Blockade C742.
I have a ton of civilians looking to get home.
How much longer?
We're all clear.
Blockade C742 is *all clear!!*
Okay people. Calmly.
No pushing.
About *time!*
We *are* Americans, you know??
Thank you.
Thank *you.*
Oh my God, baby you're--
Baby?

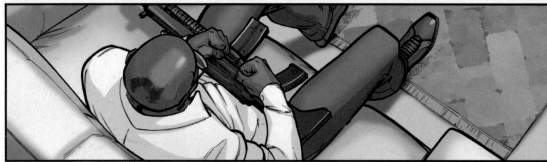

Baby, what happened?

Where--where did you get that gun?

Hey!

Oh! I didn't--

I didn't hear you...

What *happened*?

Are you hurt?

Wher did you the gu

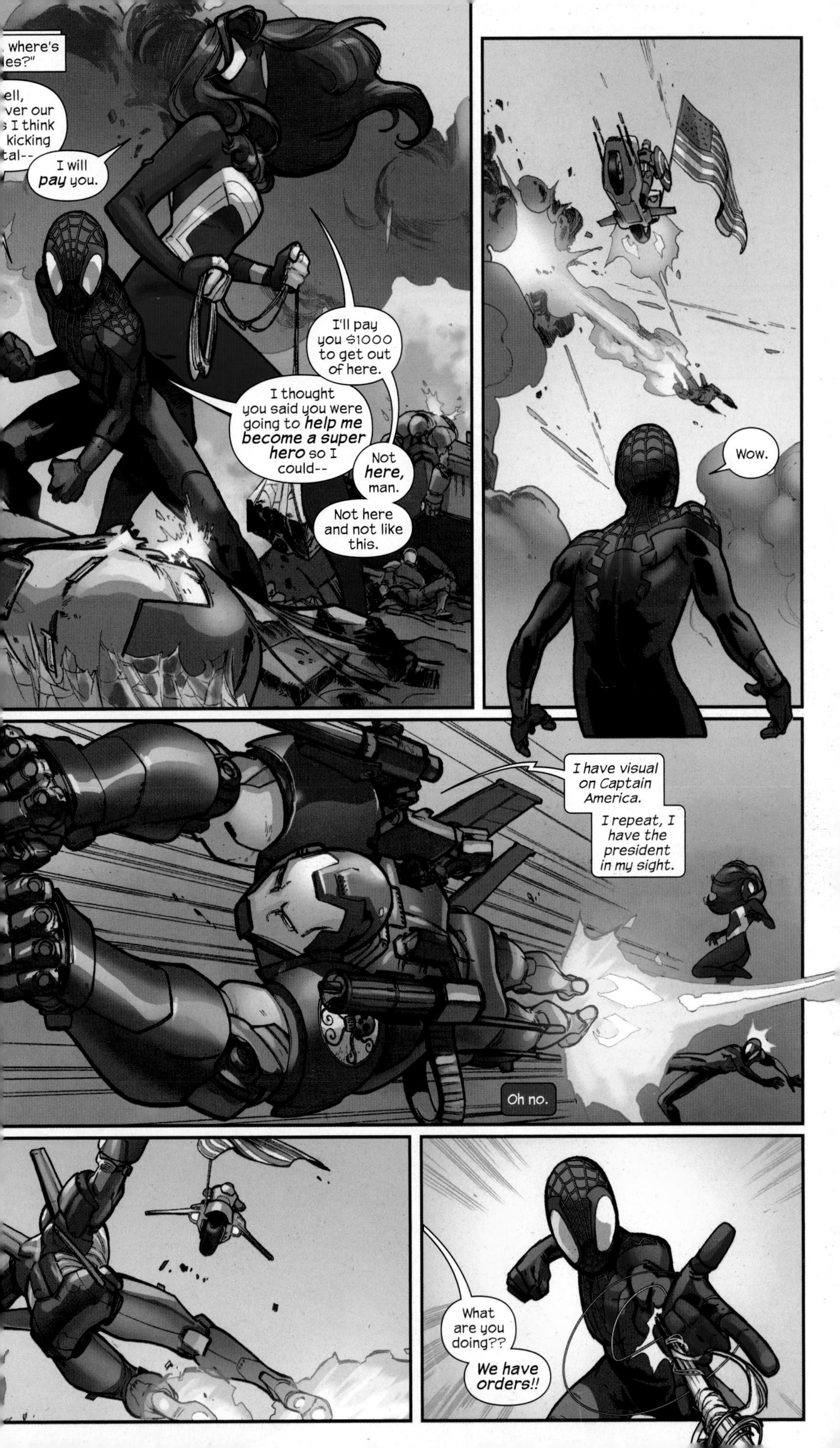

where's
es?"
ell,
ver our
I think
kicking
tal--
I will *pay* you.
I'll pay you $1000 to get out of here.
I thought you said you were going to ***help me become a super hero*** so I could--
Not ***here,*** man.
Not here and not like this.
Wow.
I have visual on Captain America.
I repeat, I have the president in my sight.
Oh no.
What are you doing??
We have orders!!

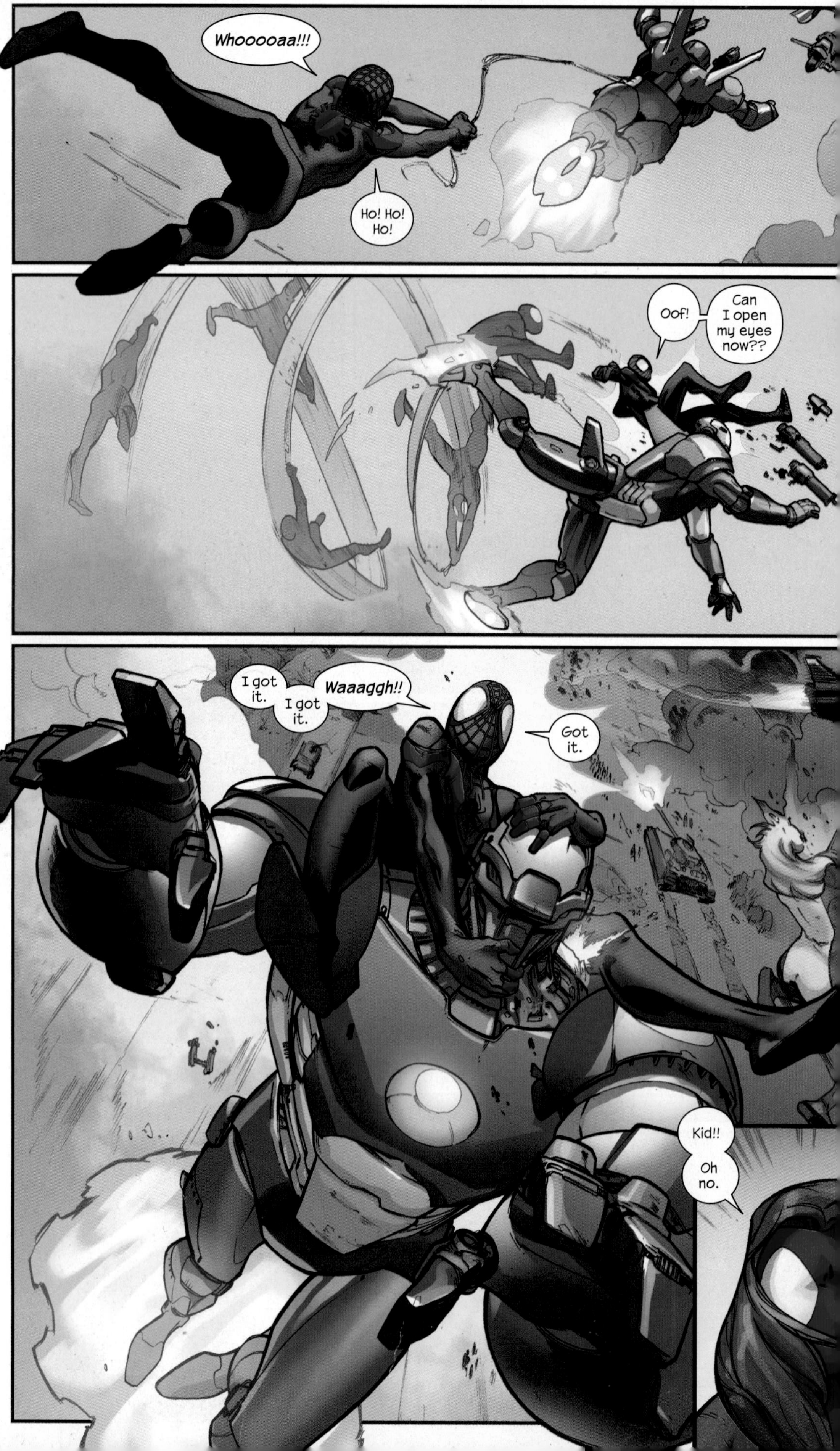
Whoooooa!!!
Ho! Ho! Ho!
Oof!
Can I open my eyes now??
I got it.
I got it.
Waaagh!!
Got it.
Kid!!
Oh no.

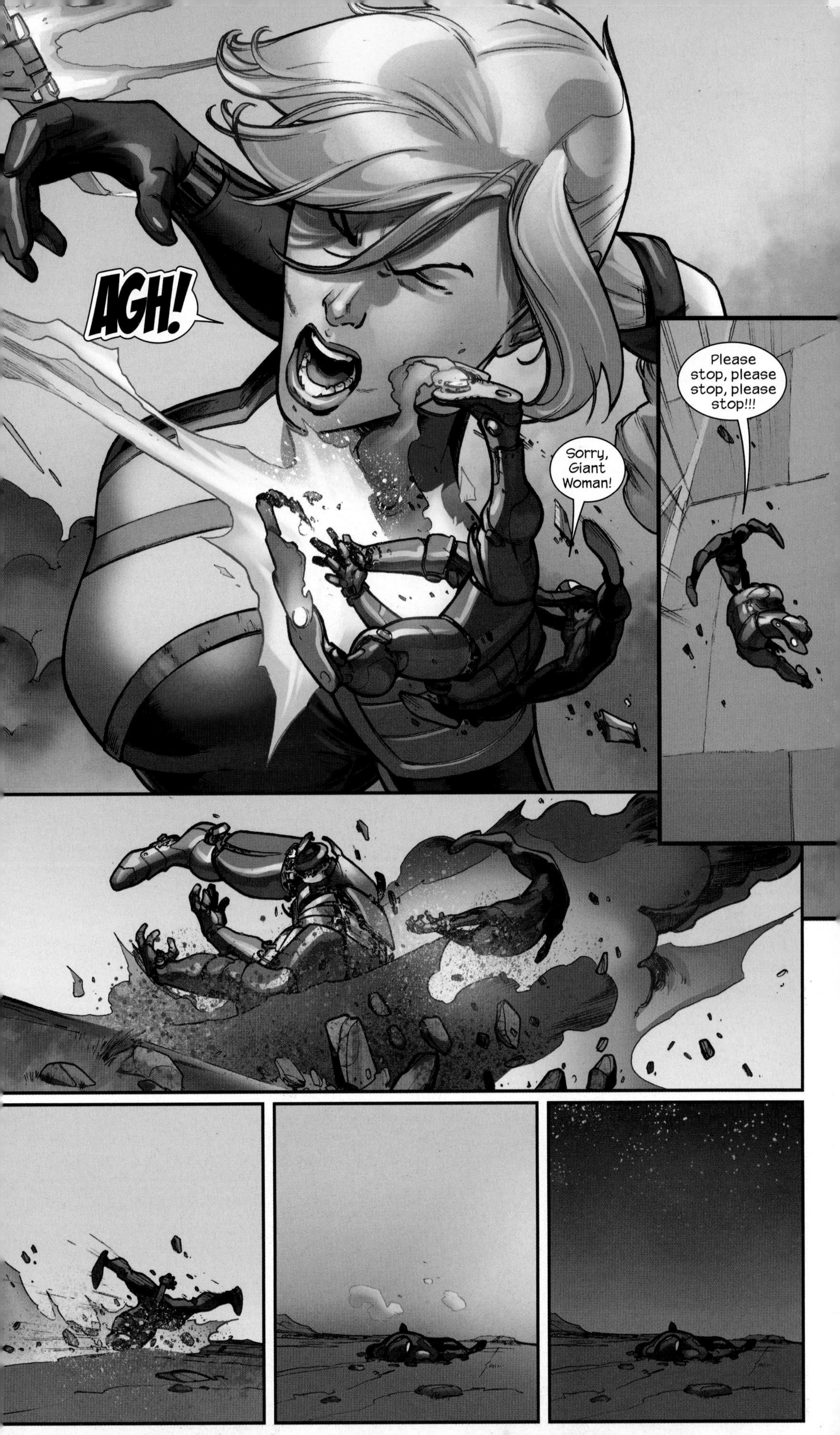
AGH!
Sorry, Giant Woman!
Please stop, please stop, please stop!!!

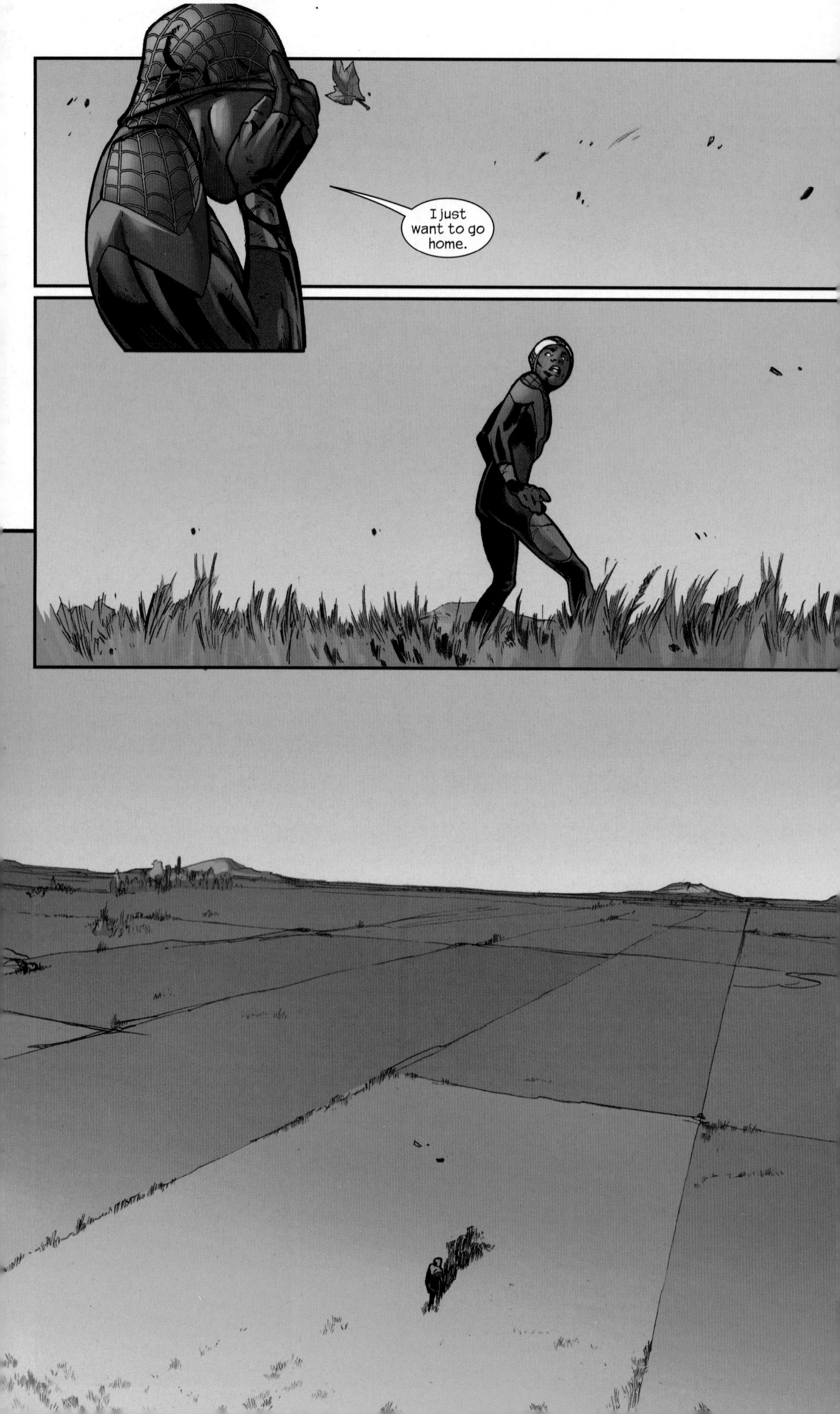
I just want to go home.

18

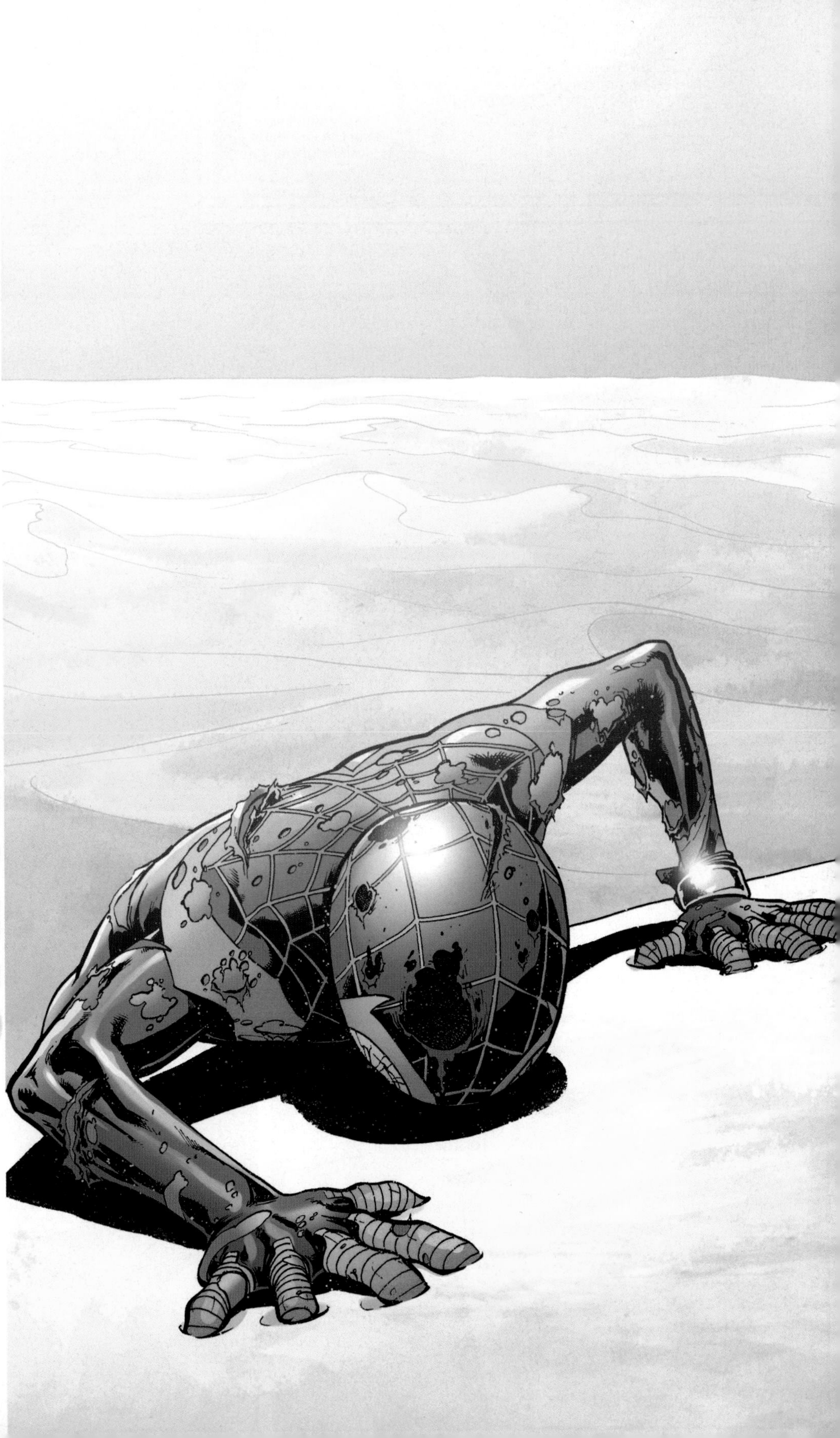

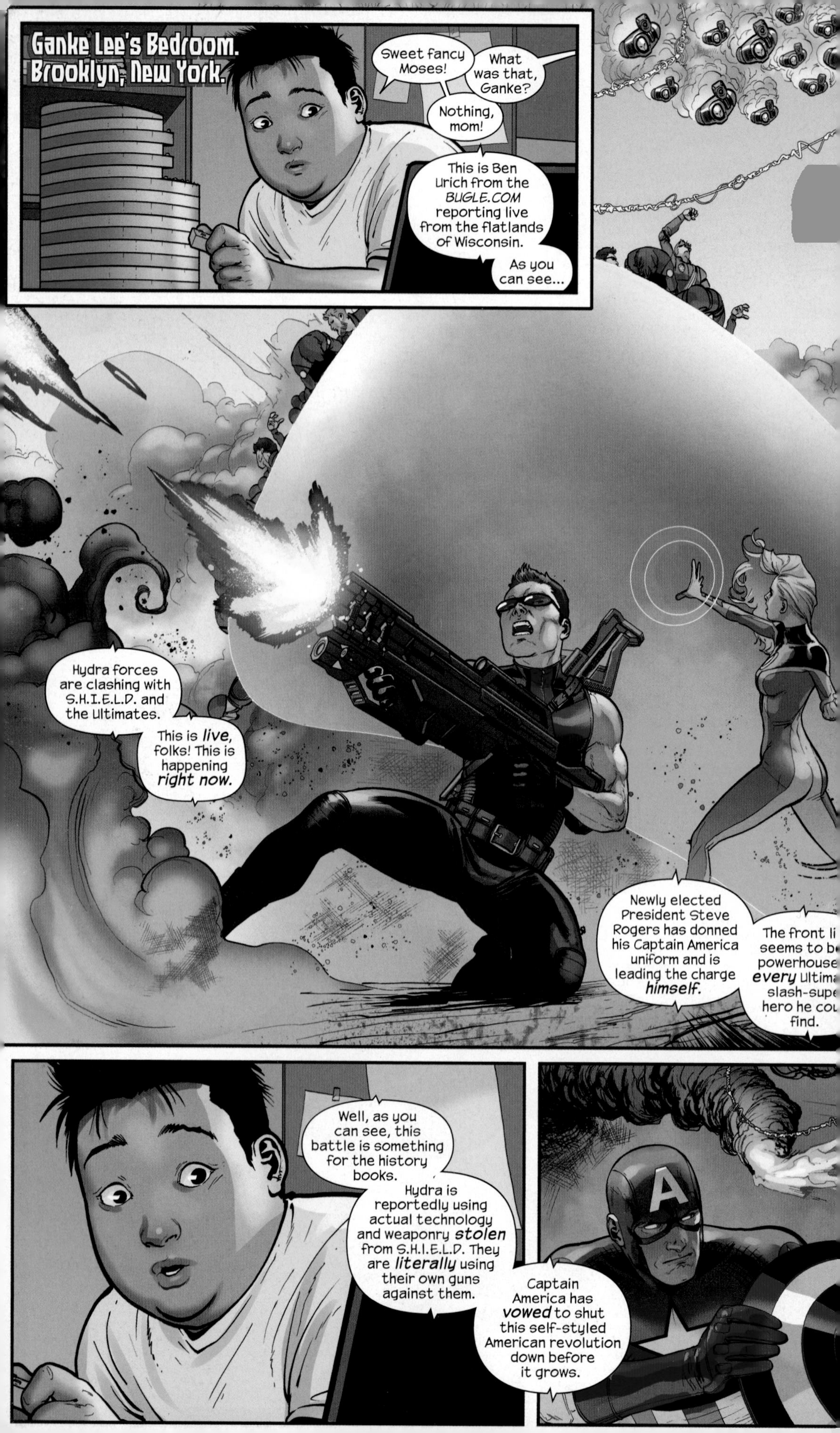
Ganke Lee's Bedroom. Brooklyn, New York.
Sweet fancy Moses!
What was that, Ganke?
Nothing, mom!
This is Ben Urich from the BUGLE.COM reporting live from the flatlands of Wisconsin.
As you can see...
Hydra forces are clashing with S.H.I.E.L.D. and the Ultimates.
This is live, folks! This is happening right now.
Newly elected President Steve Rogers has donned his Captain America uniform and is leading the charge himself.
Well, as you can see, this battle is something for the history books.
Hydra is reportedly using actual technology and weaponry stolen from S.H.I.E.L.D. They are literally using their own guns against them.
Captain America has vowed to shut this self-styled American revolution down before it grows.

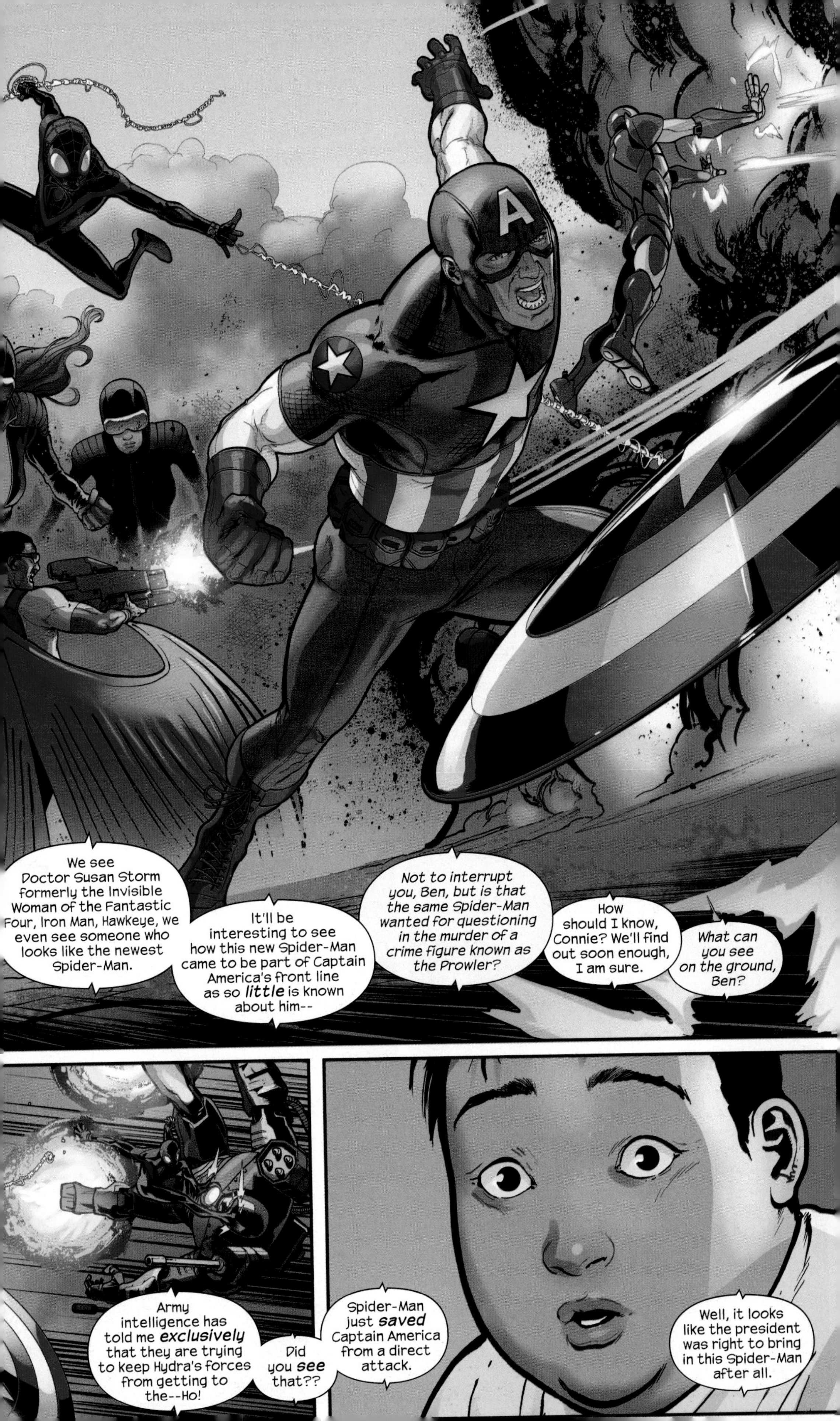
We see Doctor Susan Storm formerly the Invisible Woman of the Fantastic Four, Iron Man, Hawkeye, we even see someone who looks like the newest Spider-Man.
It'll be interesting to see how this new Spider-Man came to be part of Captain America's front line as so *little* is known about him--
Not to interrupt you, Ben, but is that the same Spider-Man wanted for questioning in the murder of a crime figure known as the Prowler?
How should I know, Connie? We'll find out soon enough, I am sure.
What can you see on the ground, Ben?
Army intelligence has told me ***exclusively*** that they are trying to keep Hydra's forces from getting to the--Ho!
Did you ***see*** that??
Spider-Man just ***saved*** Captain America from a direct attack.
Well, it looks like the president was right to bring in this Spider-Man after all.

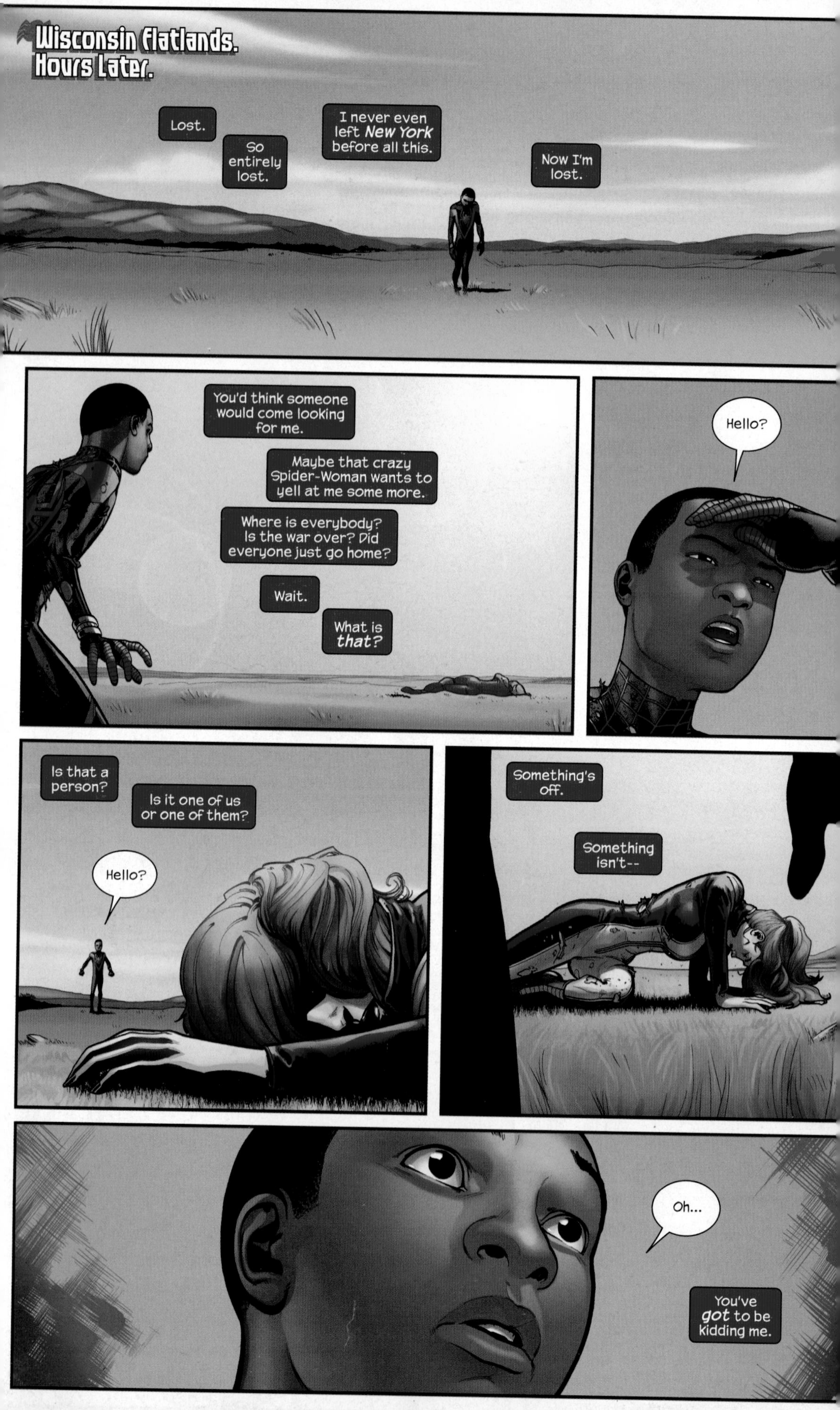
Wisconsin Flatlands.
Hours Later.
Lost.
So entirely lost.
I never even left New York before all this.
Now I'm lost.
You'd think someone would come looking for me.
Maybe that crazy Spider-Woman wants to yell at me some more.
Where is everybody? Is the war over? Did everyone just go home?
Wait.
What is that?
Hello?
Is that a person?
Is it one of us or one of them?
Hello?
Something's off.
Something isn't--
Oh...
You've got to be kidding me.

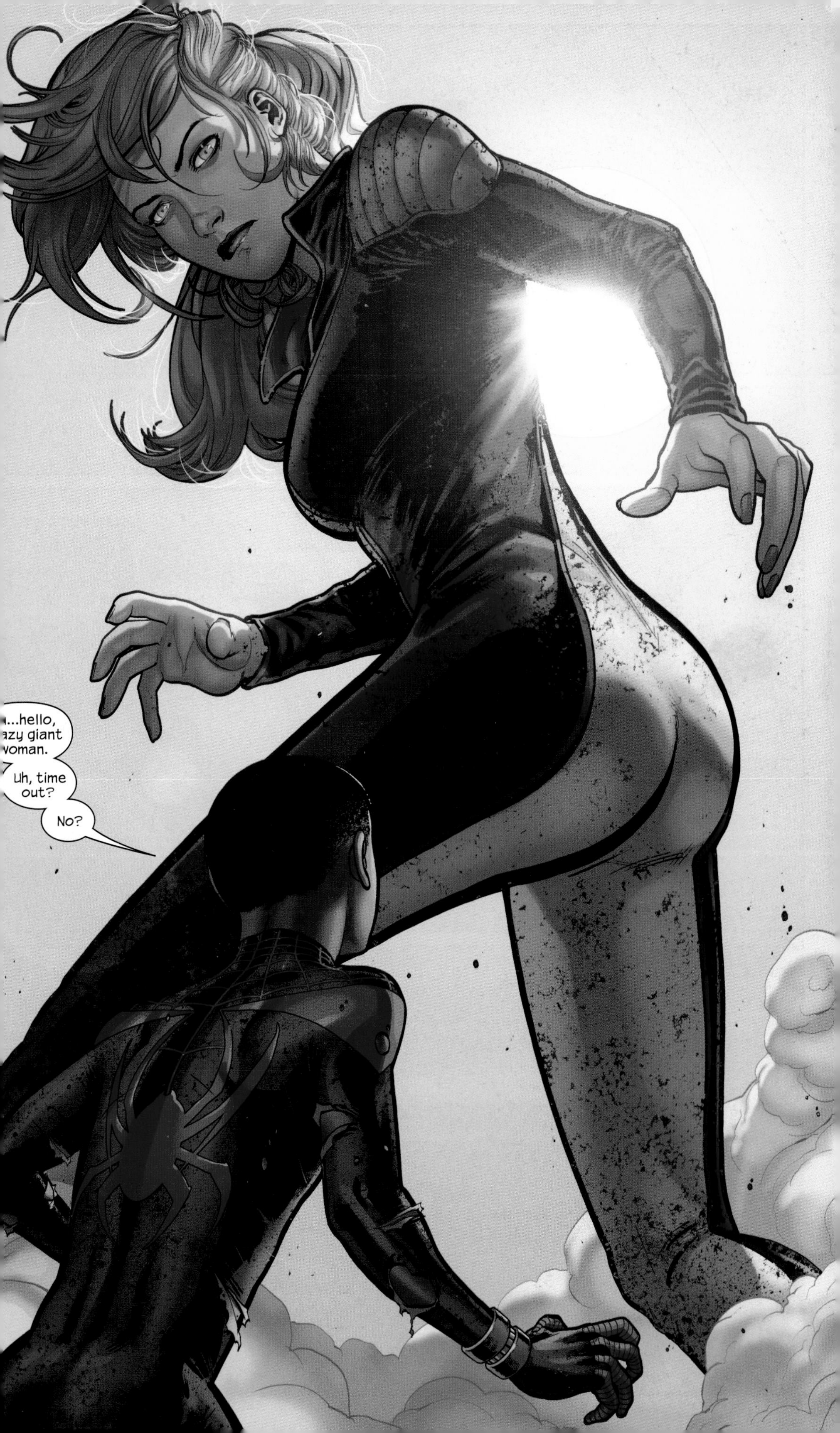
...hello,
azy giant
woman.
Uh, time
out?
No?

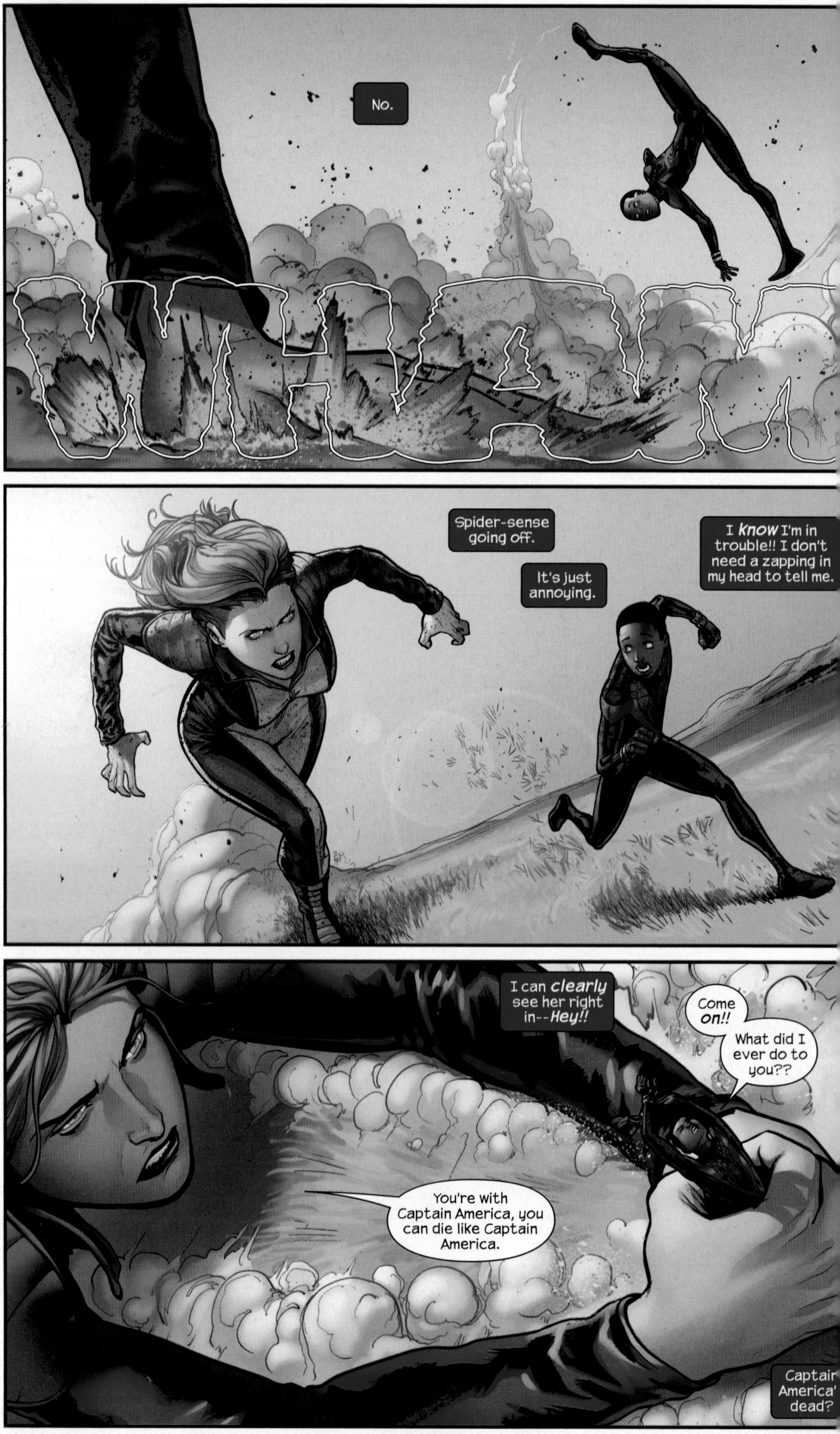
No.
WHAM
Spider-sense going off.
It's just annoying.
I *know* I'm in trouble!! I don't need a zapping in my head to tell me.
I can *clearly* see her right in--*Hey!!*
Come *on!!*
What did I ever do to you??
You're with Captain America, you can die like Captain America.
Captain America' dead?

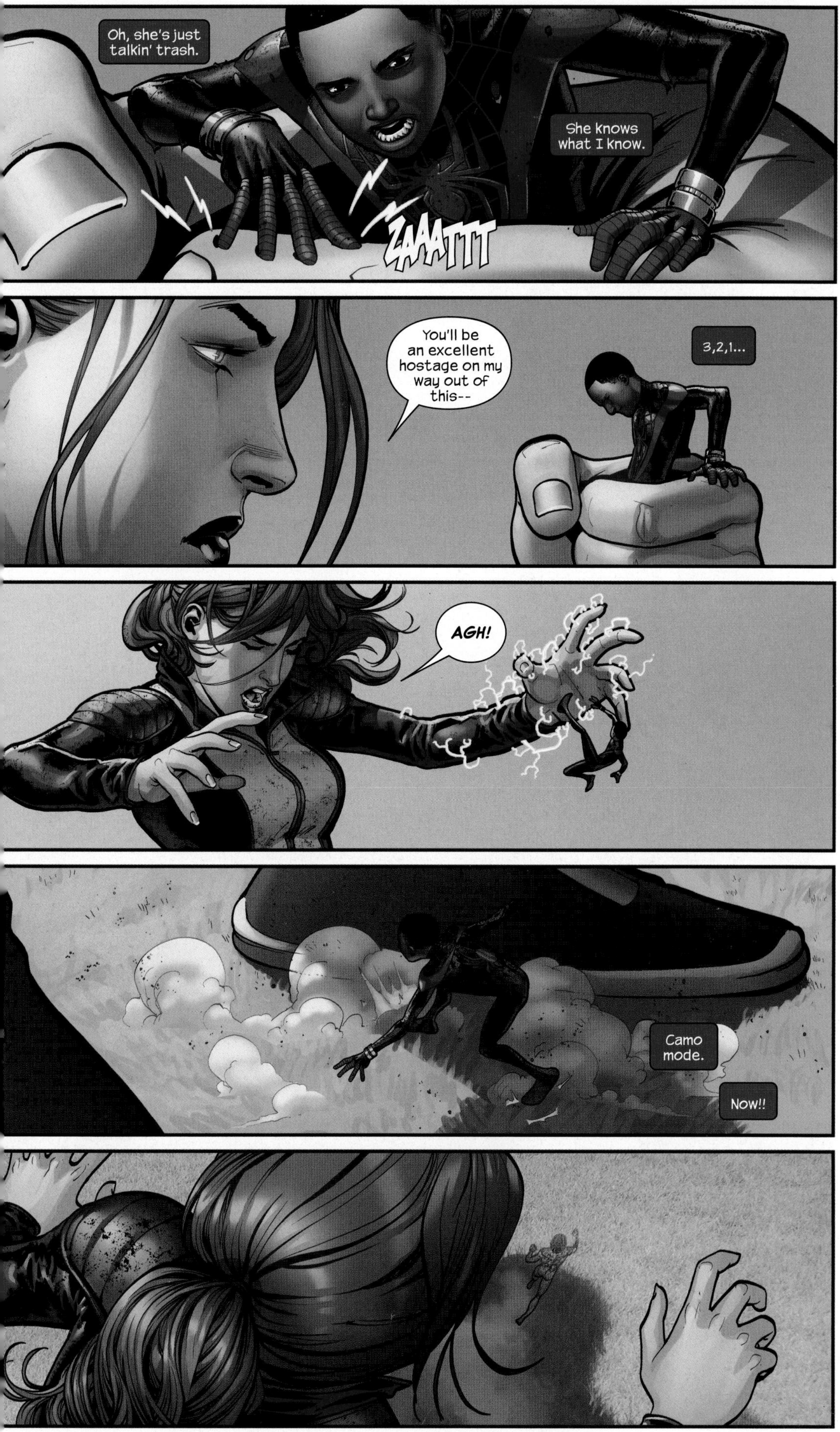
Oh, she's just talkin' trash.
She knows what I know.
ZAAATTT
You'll be an excellent hostage on my way out of this--
3,2,1...
AGH!
Camo mode.
Now!!

What the hell?

I'm embarrassed that I find her so hot.

Gotta tiptoe.

Can't let her see me.

Just get out of here and find the rest of the war that I seem to have misplaced.

I didn't just imagine him, did I?

You're a *coward!!*

You *know* that, right?

Running away from a fight. Some big hero.

I'm a coward for not getting into i with a giant craz terrorist girl?

I'm *not* goin to hit a girl. E a *giant* girl.

My mo would *kill* me

Seriously, how did you--?

Gotcha.

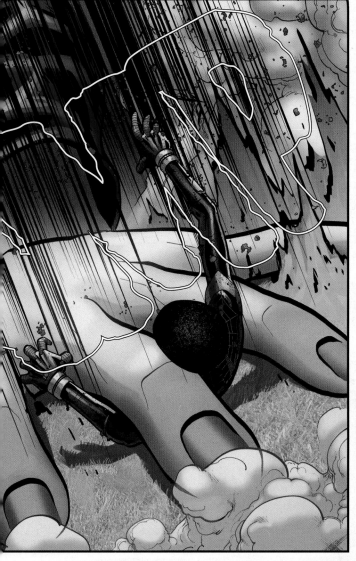

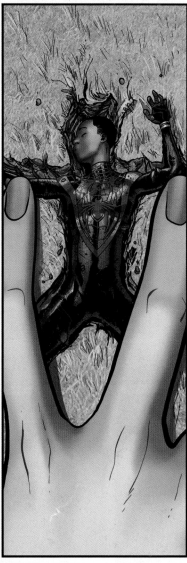

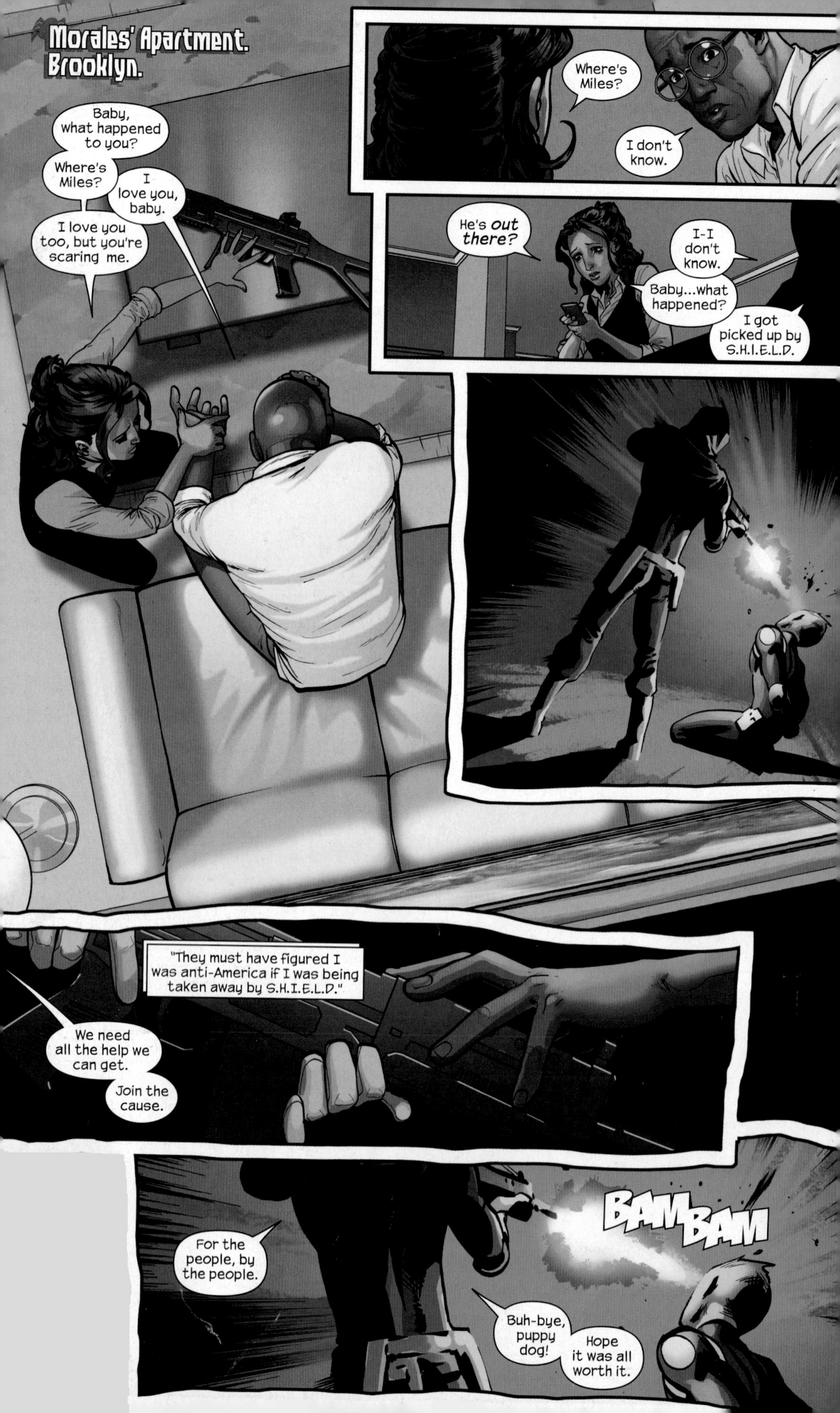
Morales' Apartment. Brooklyn.
Baby, what happened to you?
Where's Miles?
I love you, baby.
I love you too, but you're scaring me.
Where's Miles?
I don't know.
He's out there?
I-I don't know.
Baby...what happened?
I got picked up by S.H.I.E.L.D.
"They must have figured I was anti-America if I was being taken away by S.H.I.E.L.D."
We need all the help we can get.
Join the cause.
For the people, by the people.
BAM BAM
Buh-bye, puppy dog!
Hope it was all worth it.

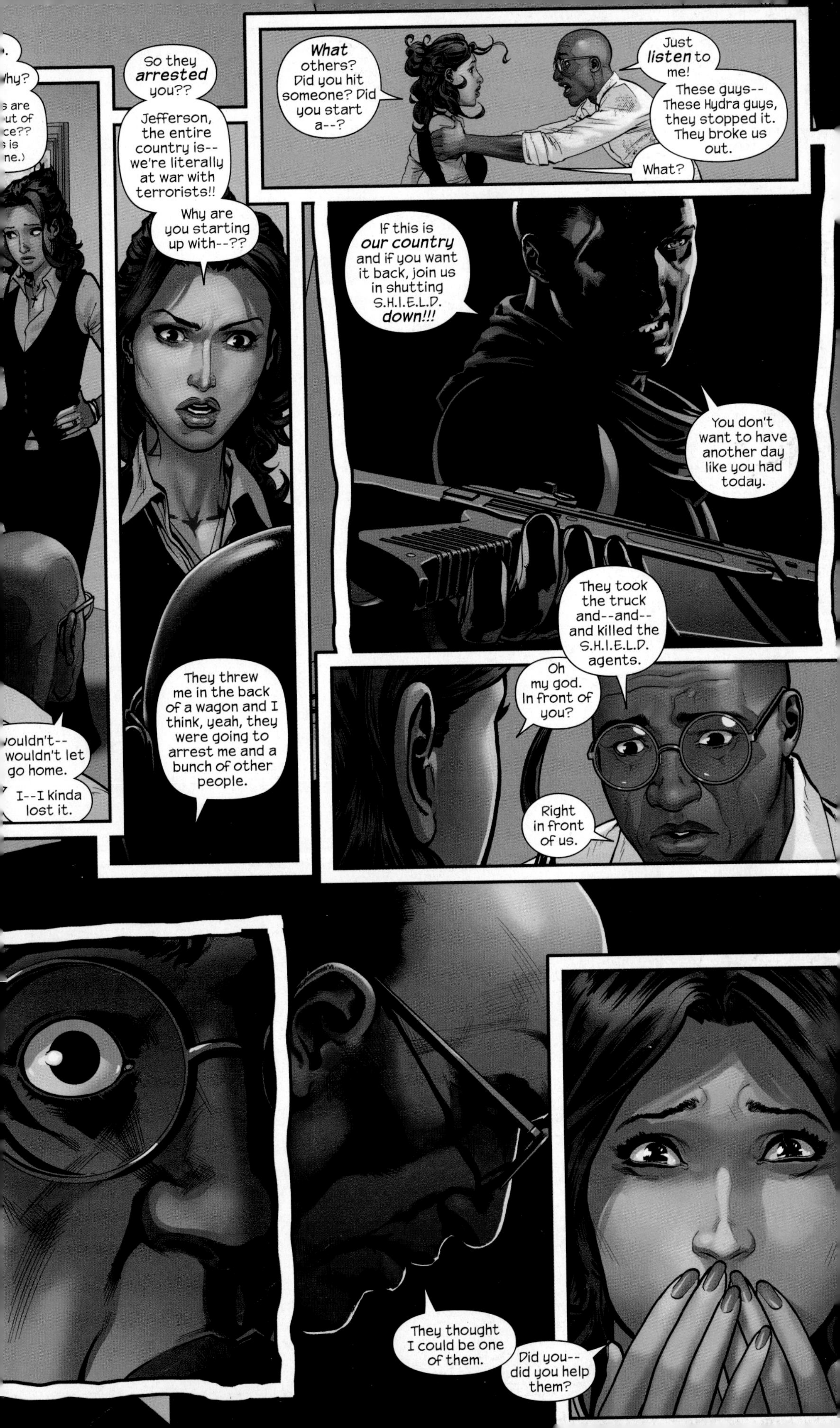
wouldn't let go home.
I--I kinda lost it.
So they *arrested* you??
Jefferson, the entire country is--we're literally at war with terrorists!!
Why are you starting up with--??
They threw me in the back of a wagon and I think, yeah, they were going to arrest me and a bunch of other people.
What others? Did you hit someone? Did you start a--?
Just *listen* to me!
These guys--These Hydra guys, they stopped it. They broke us out.
What?
If this is *our country* and if you want it back, join us in shutting S.H.I.E.L.D. *down!!!*
You don't want to have another day like you had today.
They took the truck and--and--and killed the S.H.I.E.L.D. agents.
Oh my god. In front of you?
Right in front of us.
They thought I could be one of them.
Did you--did you help them?

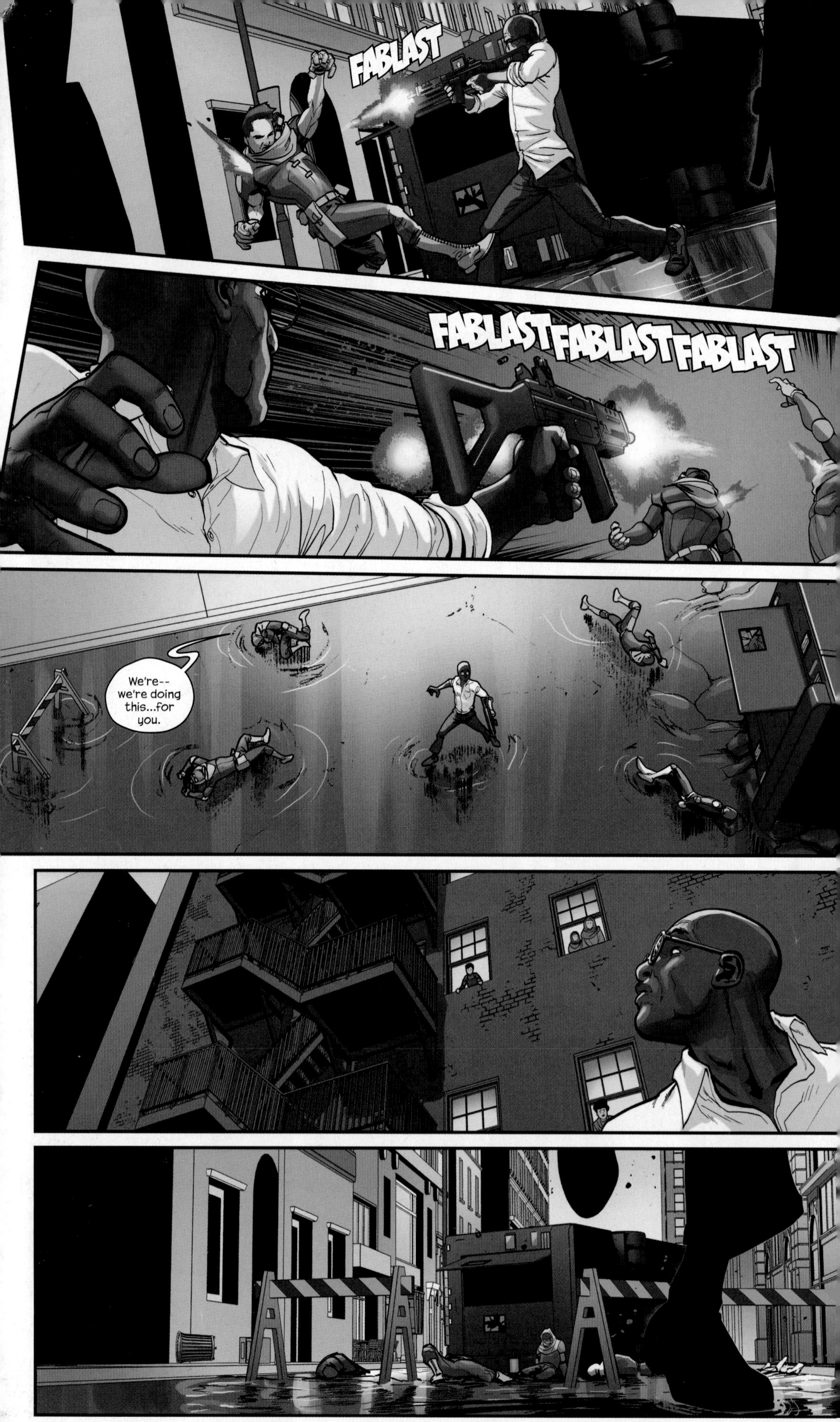
FABLAST
FABLAST FABLAST FABLAST
We're--
we're doing
this...for
you.

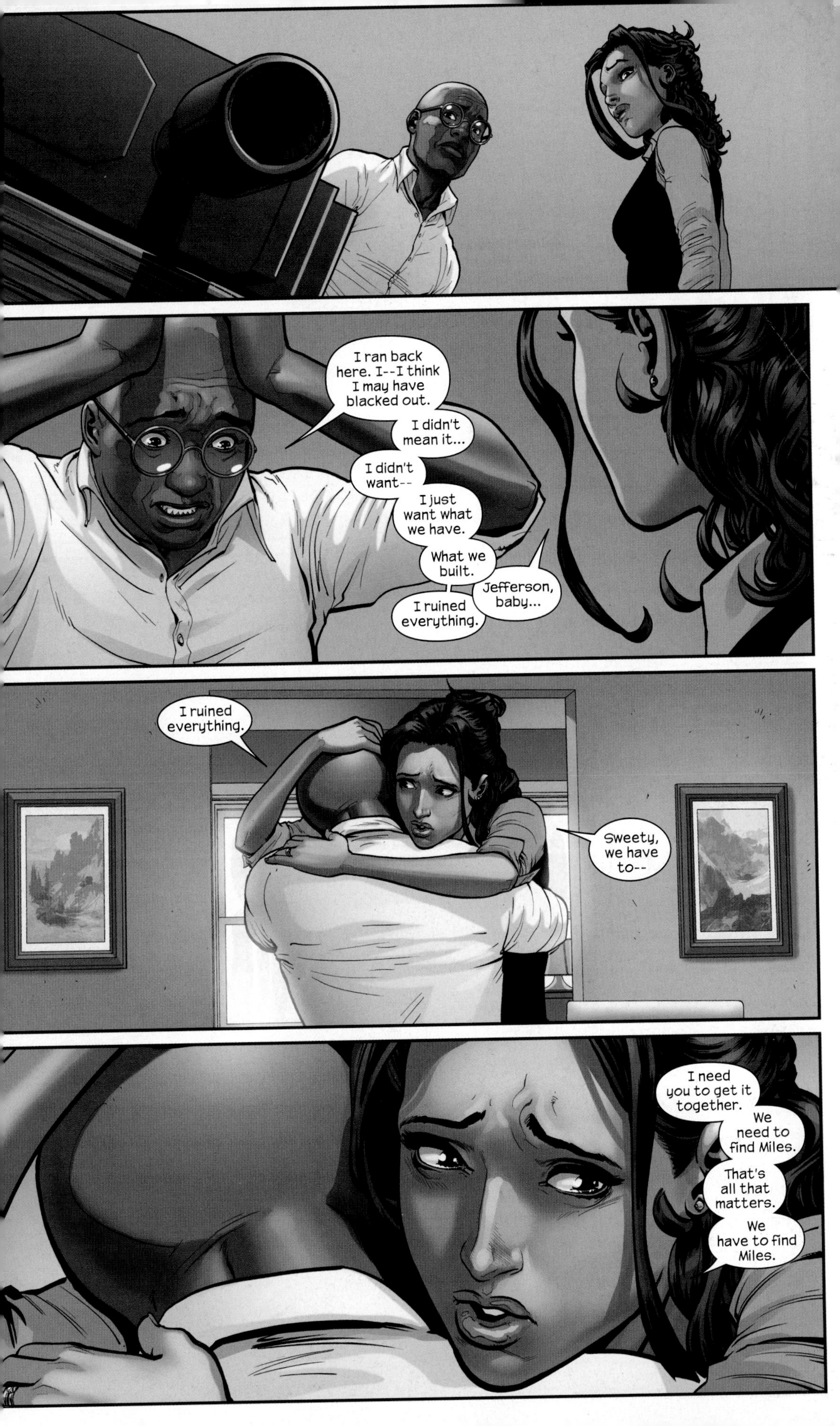
I ran back here. I--I think I may have blacked out.
I didn't mean it...
I didn't want--
I just want what we have.
What we built.
Jefferson, baby...
I ruined everything.
I ruined everything.
Sweety, we have to--
I need you to get it together.
We need to find Miles.
That's all that matters.
We have to find Miles.

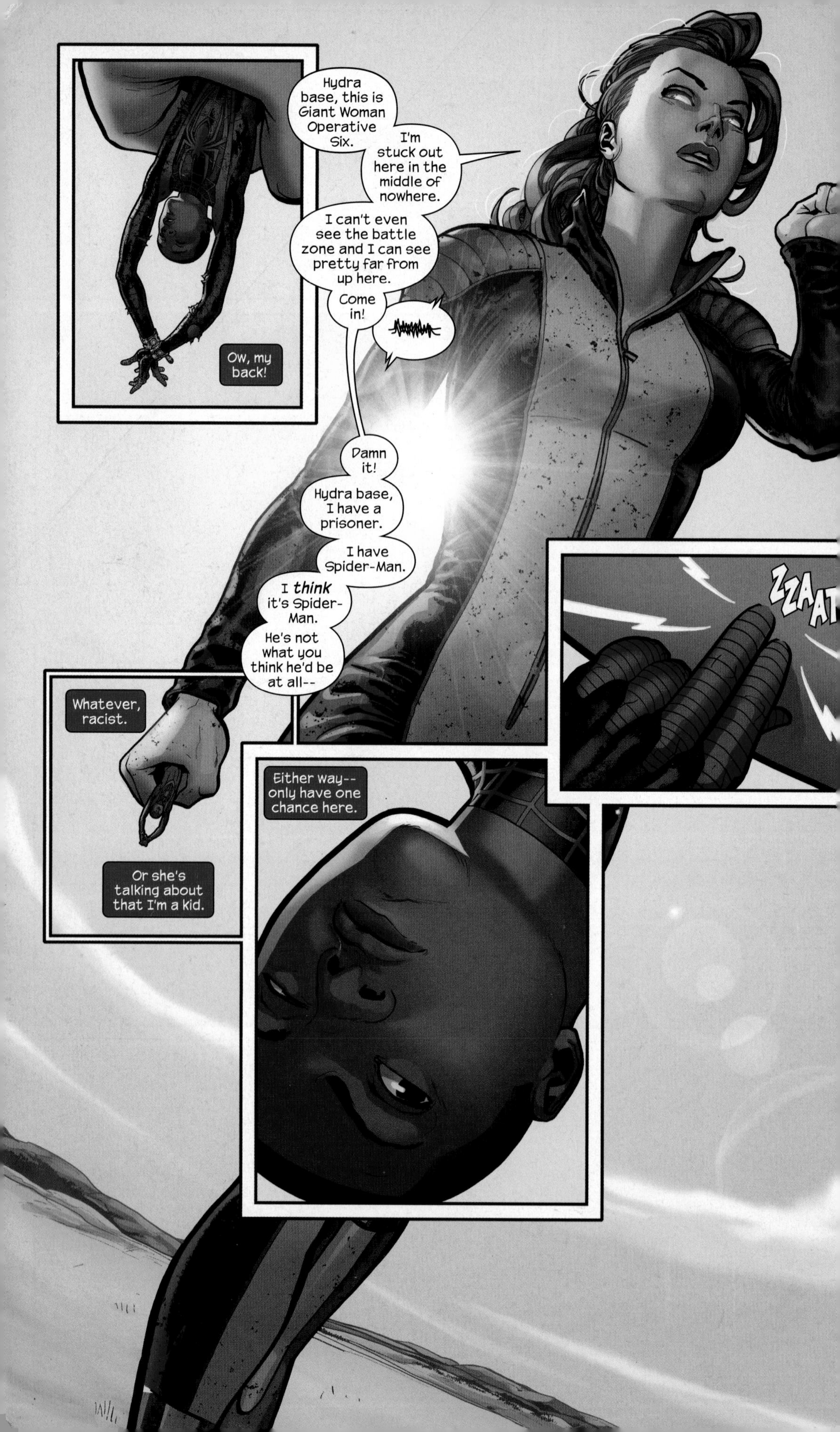
Hydra base, this is Giant Woman Operative Six.
I'm stuck out here in the middle of nowhere.
I can't even see the battle zone and I can see pretty far from up here.
Come in!
Ow, my back!
Damn it!
Hydra base, I have a prisoner.
I have Spider-Man.
I *think* it's Spider-Man.
He's not what you think he'd be at all--
Whatever, racist.
Or she's talking about that I'm a kid.
ZZAAT
Either way-- only have one chance here.

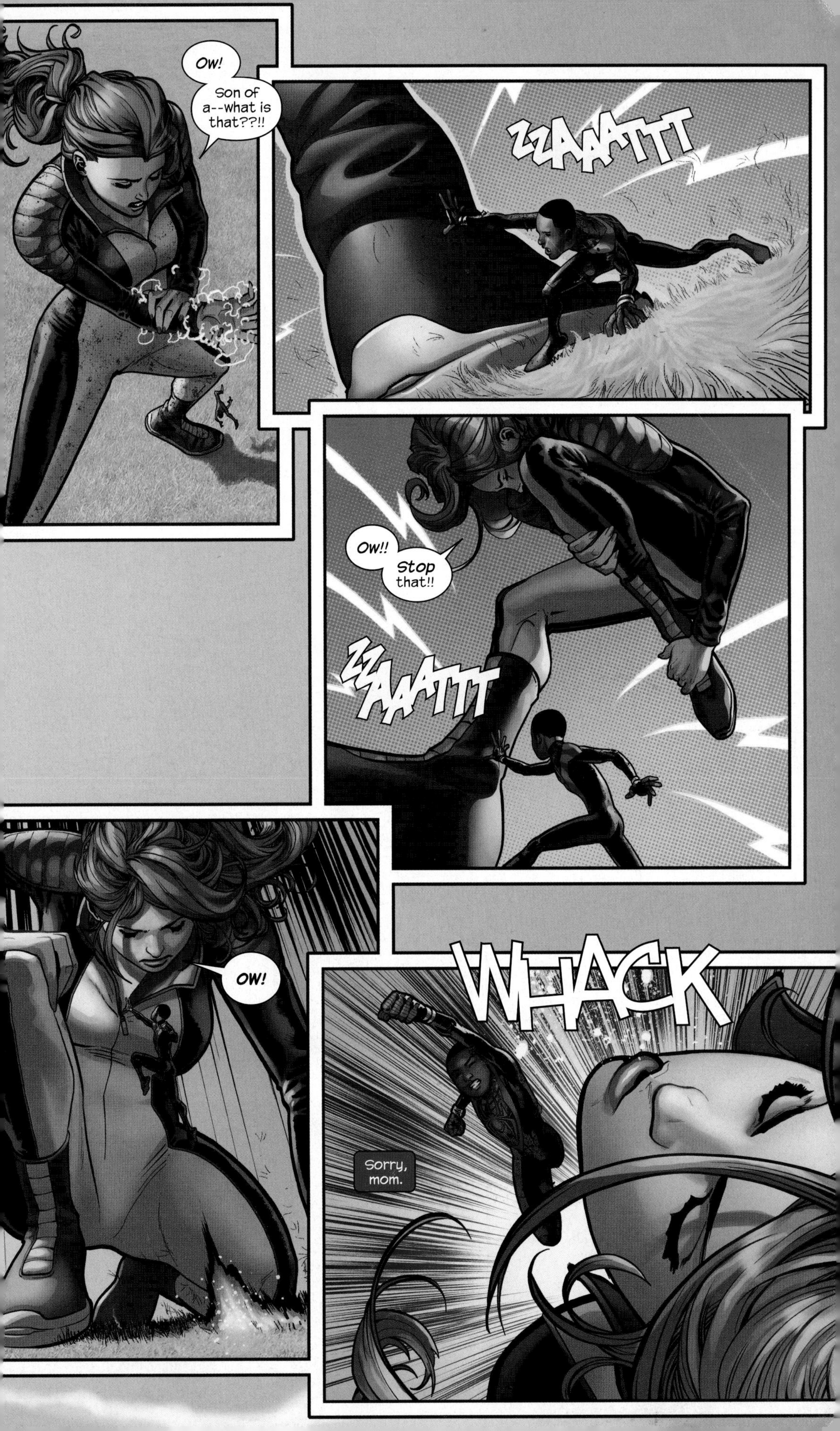
Ow!
Son of a--what is that??!!
ZZAAATTT
Ow!! Stop that!!
ZZAAATTT
OW!
WHACK
Sorry, mom.

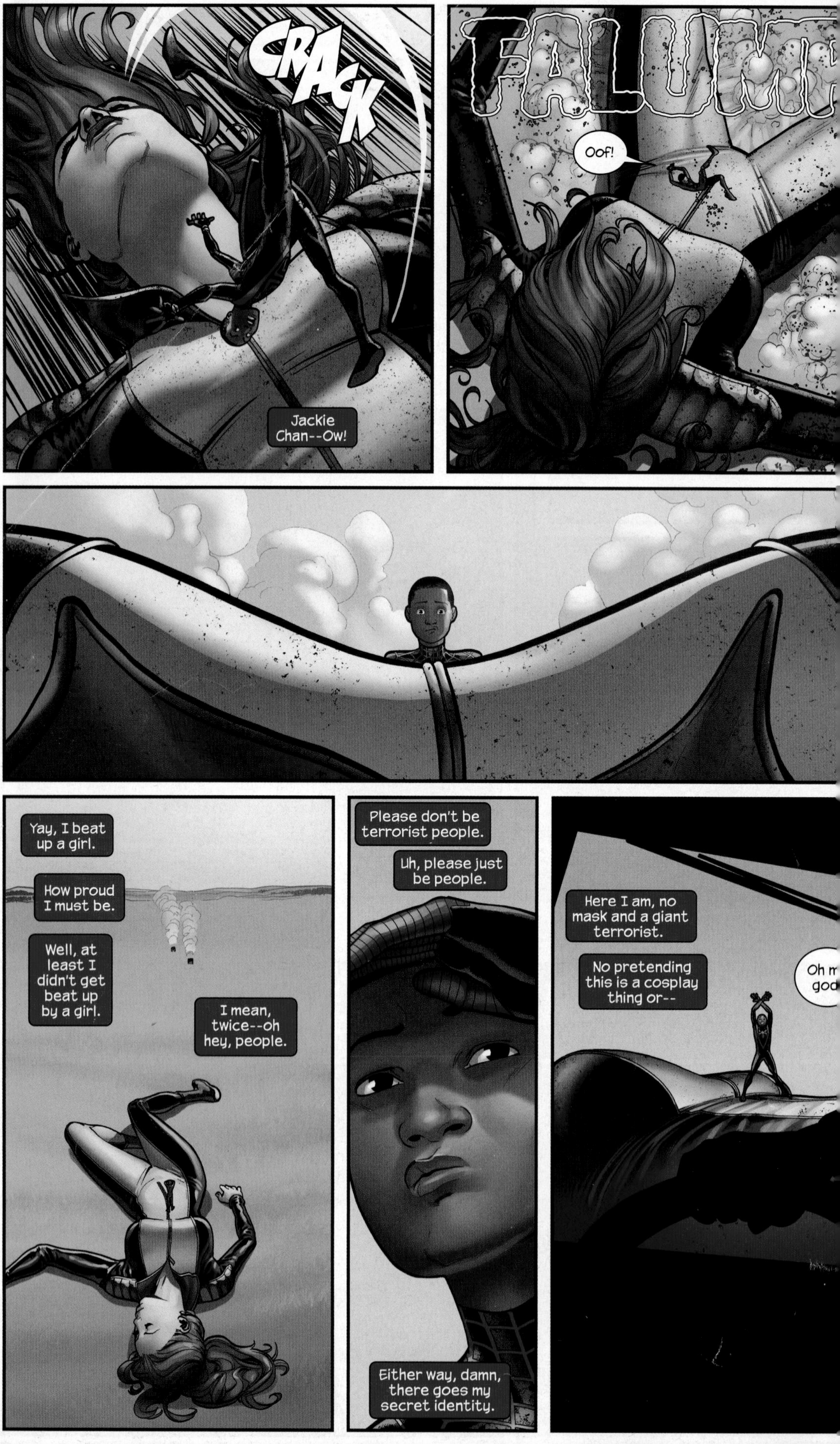
CRACK
Jackie Chan--Ow!
FALUMP
Oof!
Yay, I beat up a girl.
How proud I must be.
Well, at least I didn't get beat up by a girl.
I mean, twice--oh hey, people.
Please don't be terrorist people.
Uh, please just be people.
Either way, damn, there goes my secret identity.
Here I am, no mask and a giant terrorist.
No pretending this is a cosplay thing or--

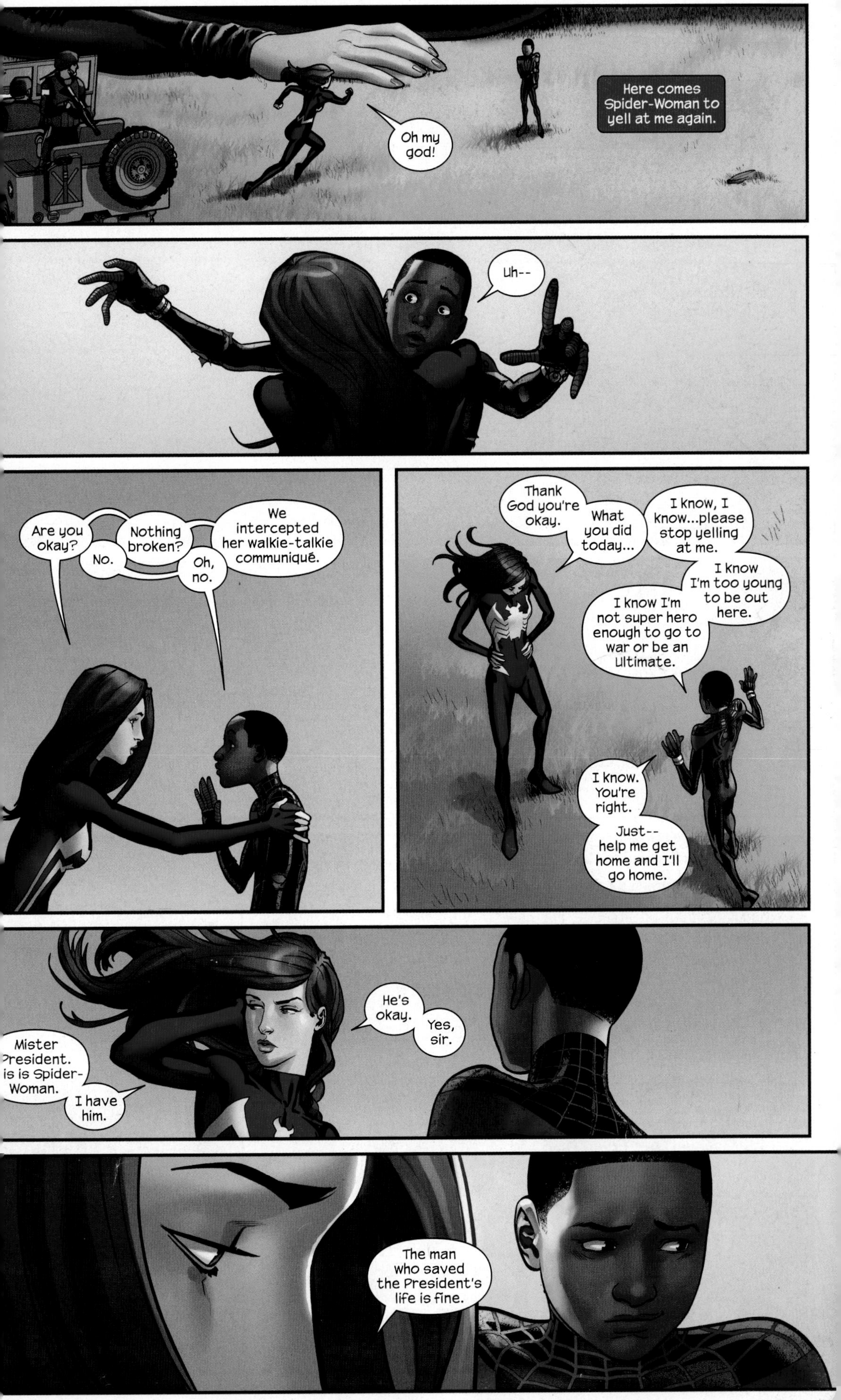
Here comes Spider-Woman to yell at me again.
Oh my god!
Uh--
Are you okay?
Nothing broken?
No.
Oh, no.
We intercepted her walkie-talkie communiqué.
Thank God you're okay.
What you did today...
I know, I know...please stop yelling at me.
I know I'm too young to be out here.
I know I'm not super hero enough to go to war or be an Ultimate.
I know. You're right.
Just-- help me get home and I'll go home.
Mister President. is is Spider-Woman.
I have him.
He's okay.
Yes, sir.
The man who saved the President's life is fine.

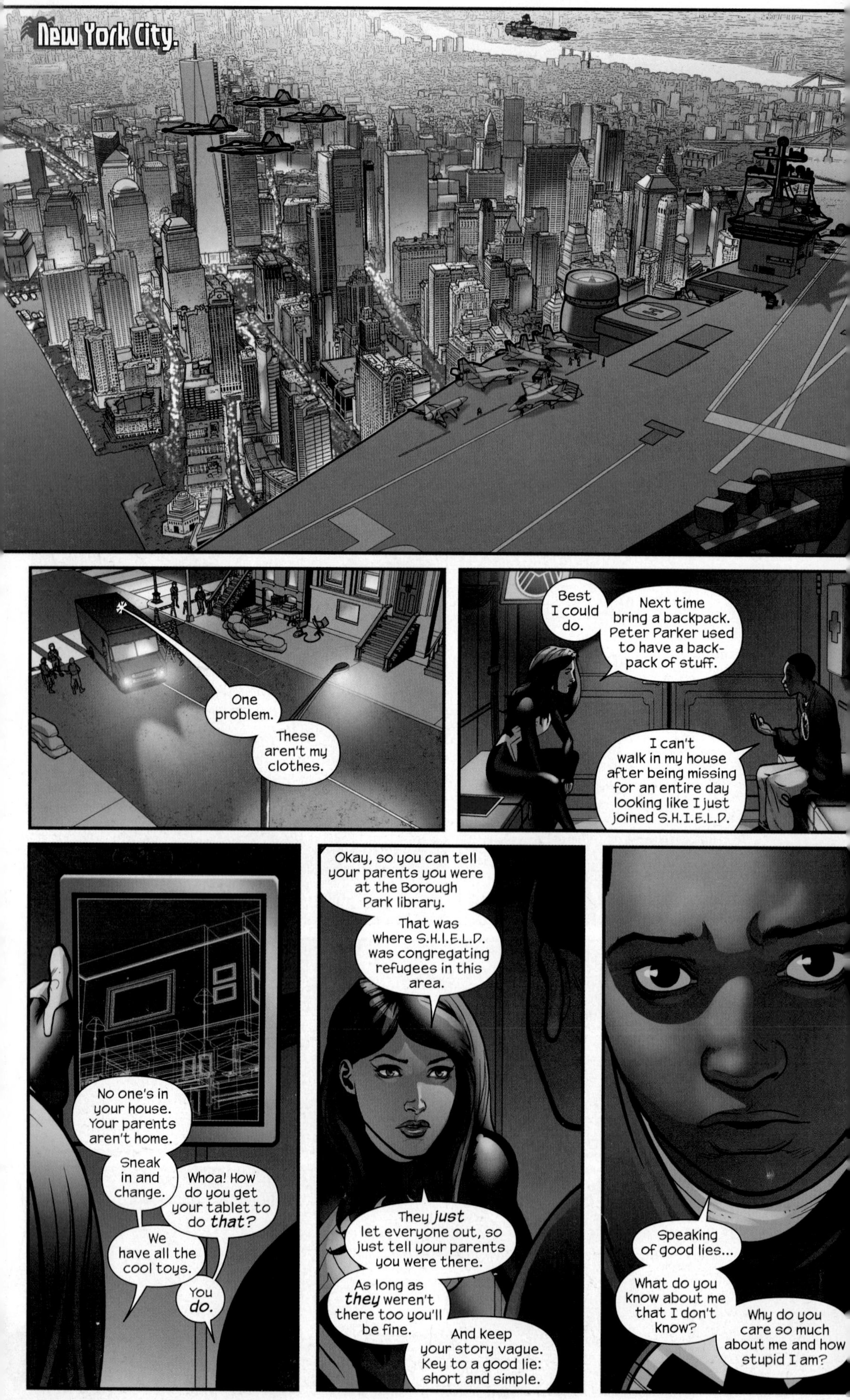
New York City.
One problem.
These aren't my clothes.
Best I could do.
Next time bring a backpack. Peter Parker used to have a back-pack of stuff.
I can't walk in my house after being missing for an entire day looking like I just joined S.H.I.E.L.D.
No one's in your house. Your parents aren't home.
Sneak in and change.
Whoa! How do you get your tablet to do *that?*
We have all the cool toys.
You *do.*
Okay, so you can tell your parents you were at the Borough Park library.
That was where S.H.I.E.L.D. was congregating refugees in this area.
They *just* let everyone out, so just tell your parents you were there.
As long as *they* weren't there too you'll be fine.
And keep your story vague. Key to a good lie: short and simple.
Speaking of good lies...
What do you know about me that I don't know?
Why do you care so much about me and how stupid I am?

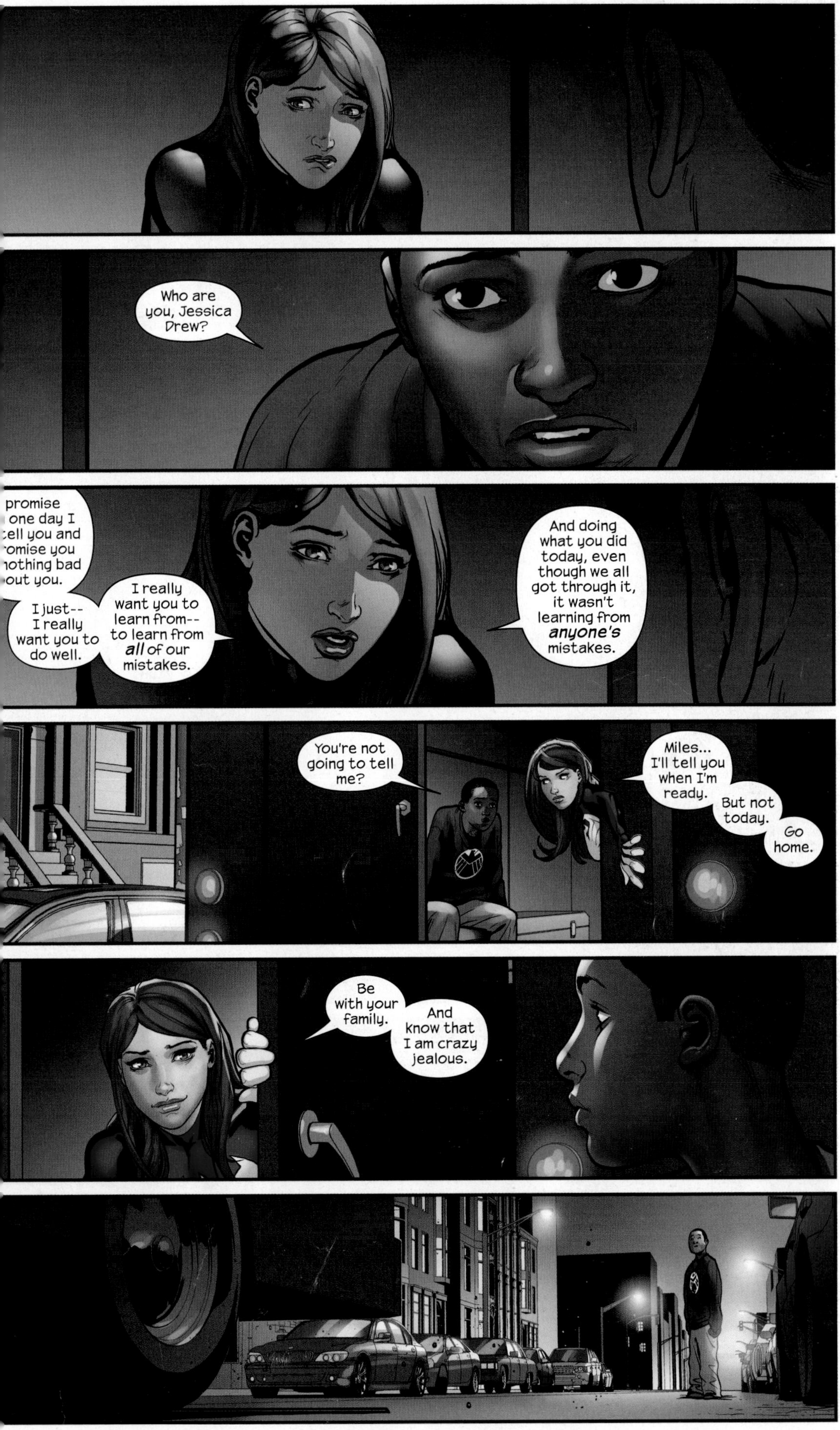
Who are you, Jessica Drew?
promise one day I ell you and omise you othing bad out you.
I just-- I really want you to do well.
I really want you to learn from-- to learn from *all* of our mistakes.
And doing what you did today, even though we all got through it, it wasn't learning from *anyone's* mistakes.
You're not going to tell me?
Miles... I'll tell you when I'm ready.
But not today.
Go home.
Be with your family.
And know that I am crazy jealous.

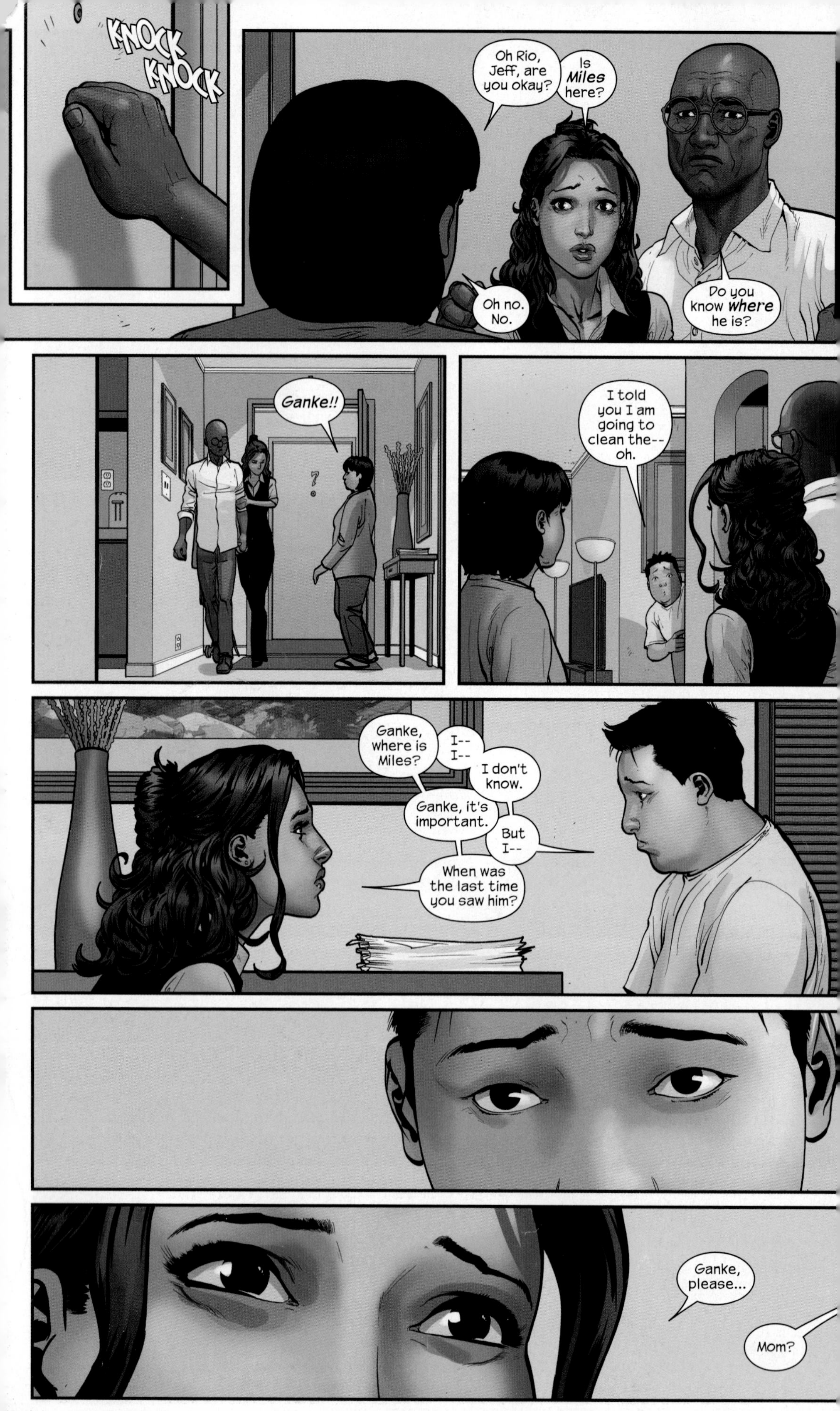
KNOCK KNOCK
Oh Rio, Jeff, are you okay?
Is Miles here?
Oh no. No.
Do you know where he is?
Ganke!!
?
I told you I am going to clean the-- oh.
Ganke, where is Miles?
I-- I--
I don't know.
Ganke, it's important.
But I--
When was the last time you saw him?
Ganke, please...
Mom?

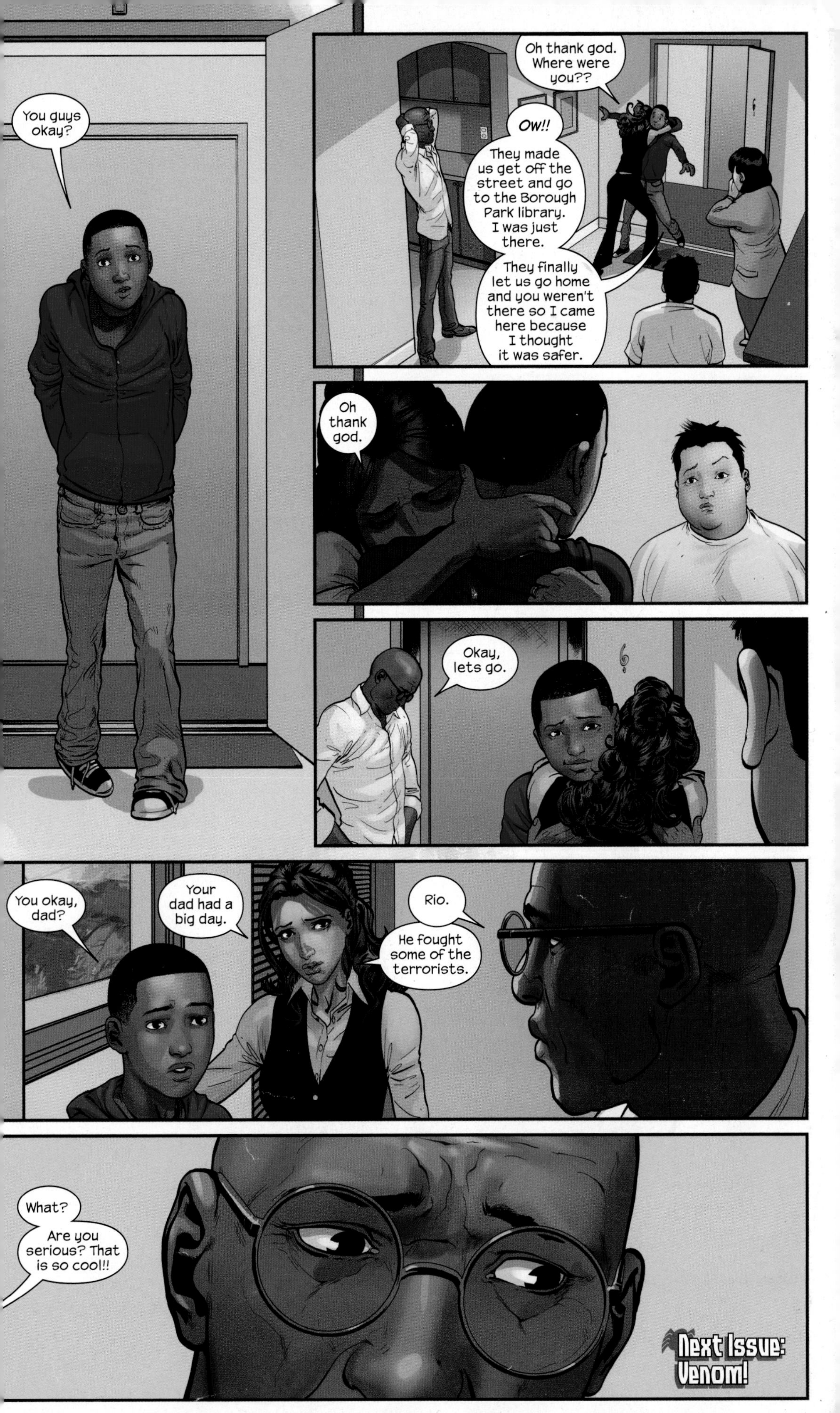
You guys okay?
Oh thank god. Where were you??
OW!!
They made us get off the street and go to the Borough Park library. I was just there.
They finally let us go home and you weren't there so I came here because I thought it was safer.
Oh thank god.
Okay, lets go.
You okay, dad?
Your dad had a big day.
Rio.
He fought some of the terrorists.
What?
Are you serious? That is so cool!!
Next Issue: Venom!

#13 VARIANT
BY ADI GRANOV

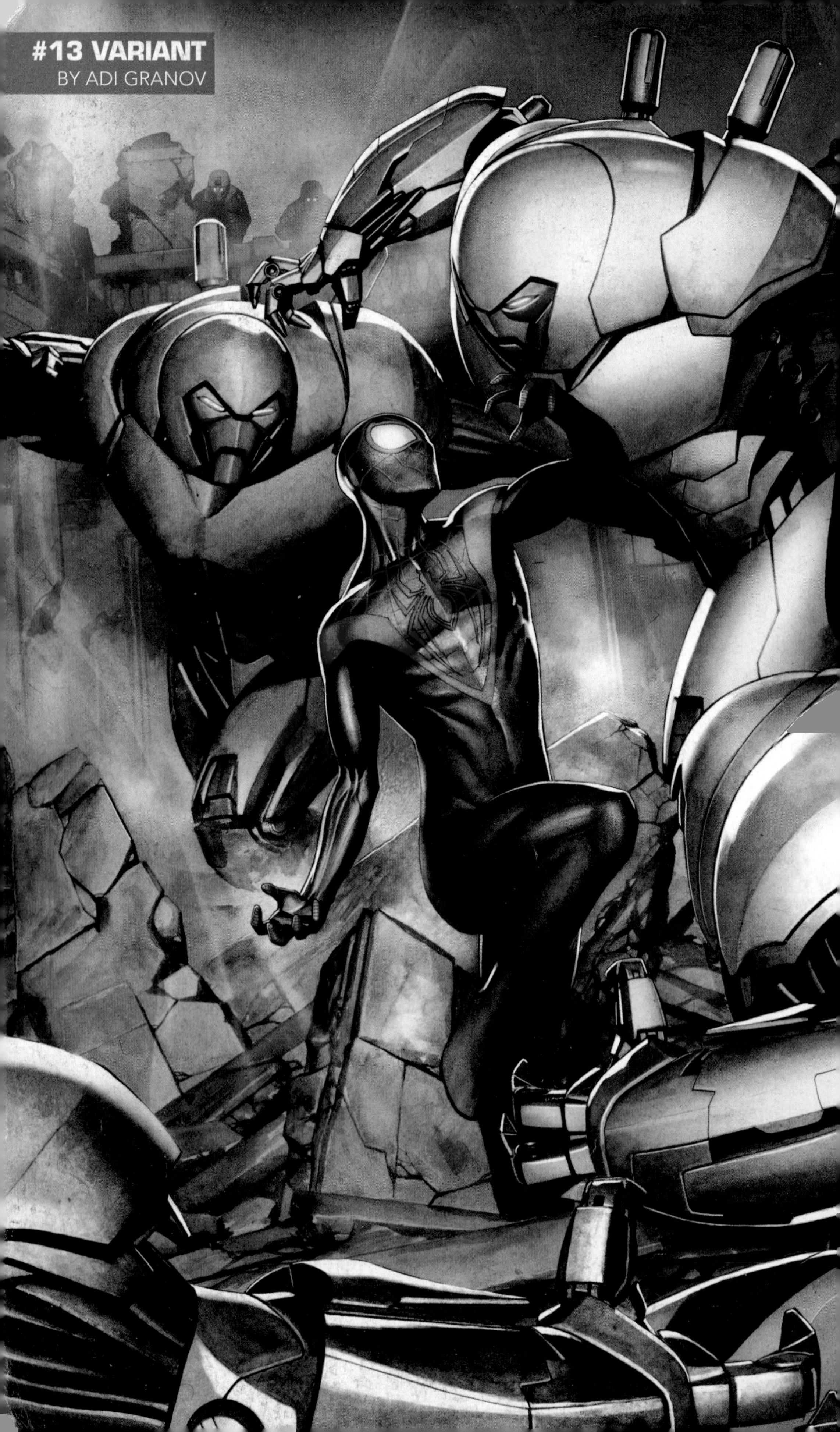

#16 COVER INKS BY DAVID MARQUEZ

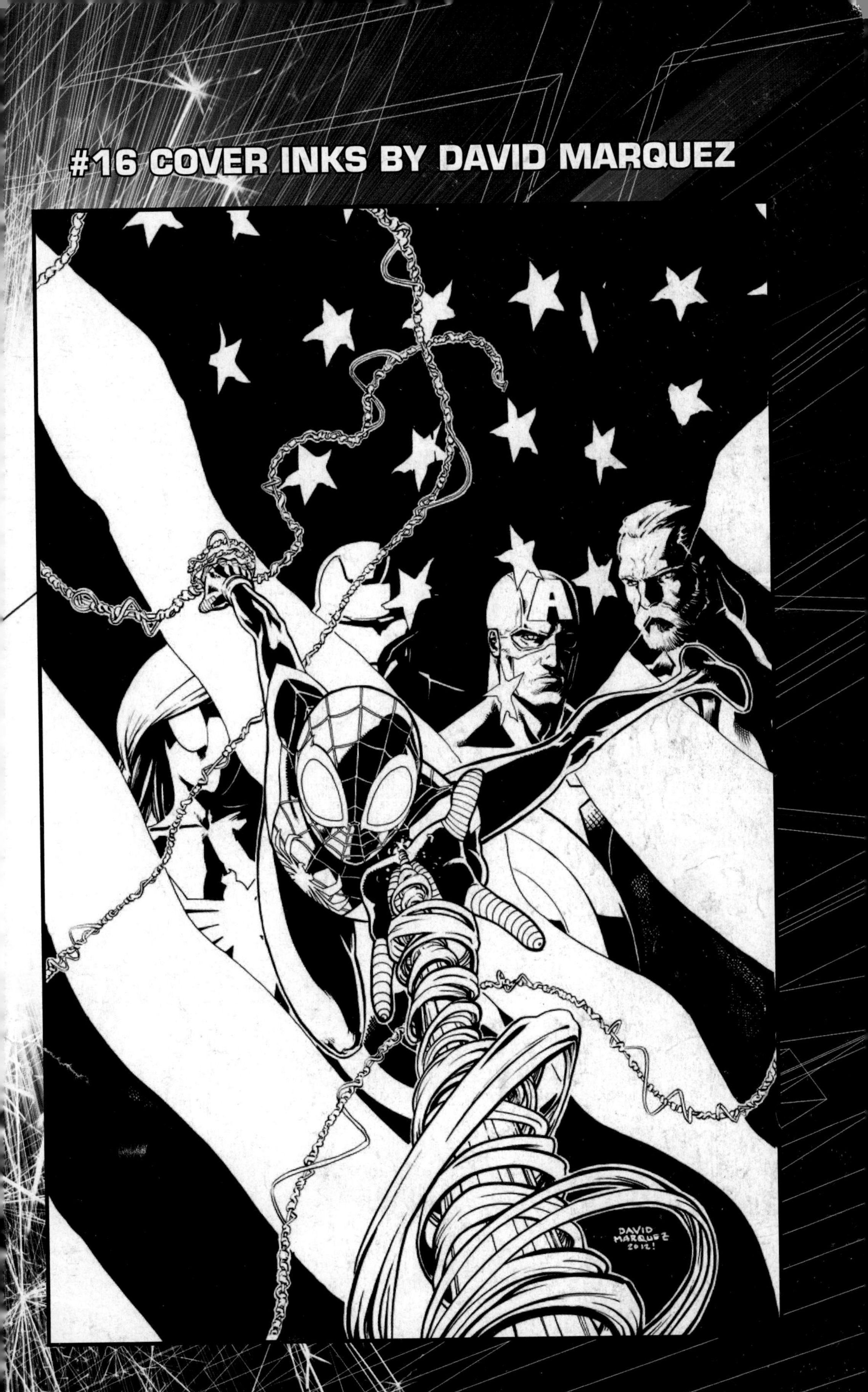
DAVID MARQUEZ 2012!

#18 COVER PROCESS BY DAVID MARQUEZ

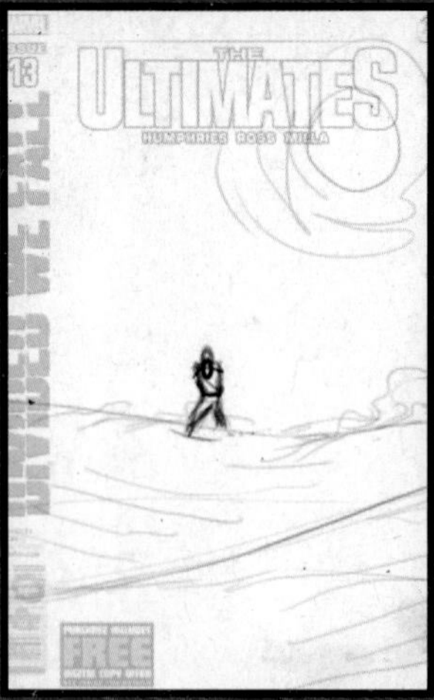
ISSUE 13
THE ULTIMATES
HUMPHRIES ROSS MILLA
DIVIDED WE FALL
FREE

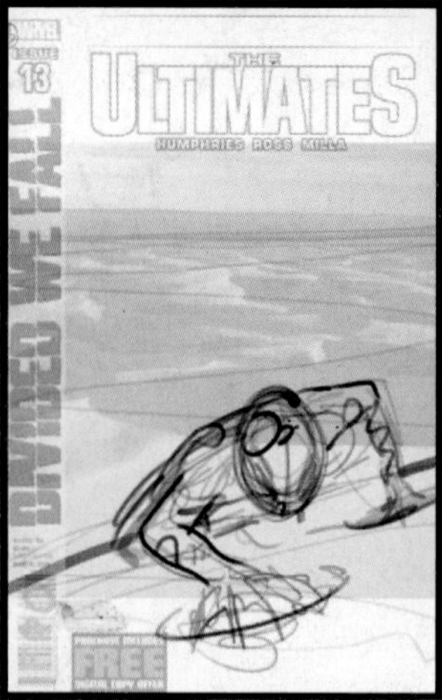
ISSUE 13
THE ULTIMATES
HUMPHRIES ROSS MILLA
DIVIDED WE FALL
FREE

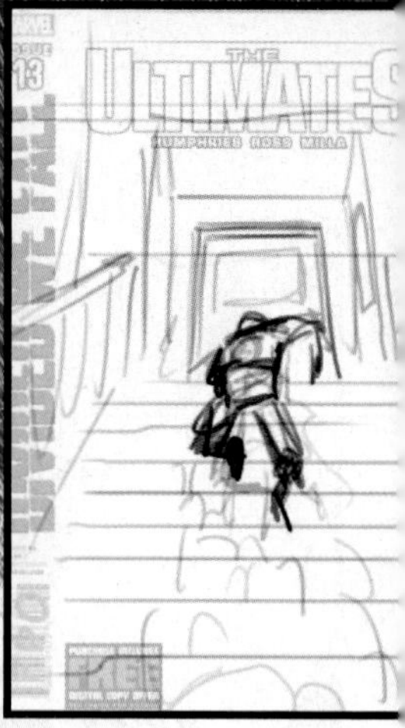
ISSUE 13
THE ULTIMATES
HUMPHRIES ROSS MILLA
FREE

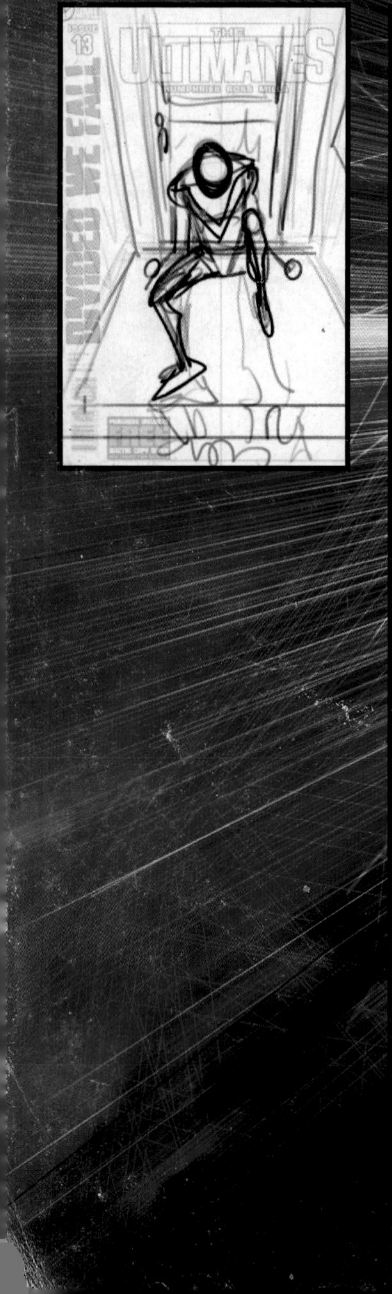
ISSUE 13
THE ULTIMATES
HUMPHRIES ROSS MILLA
DIVIDED WE FALL

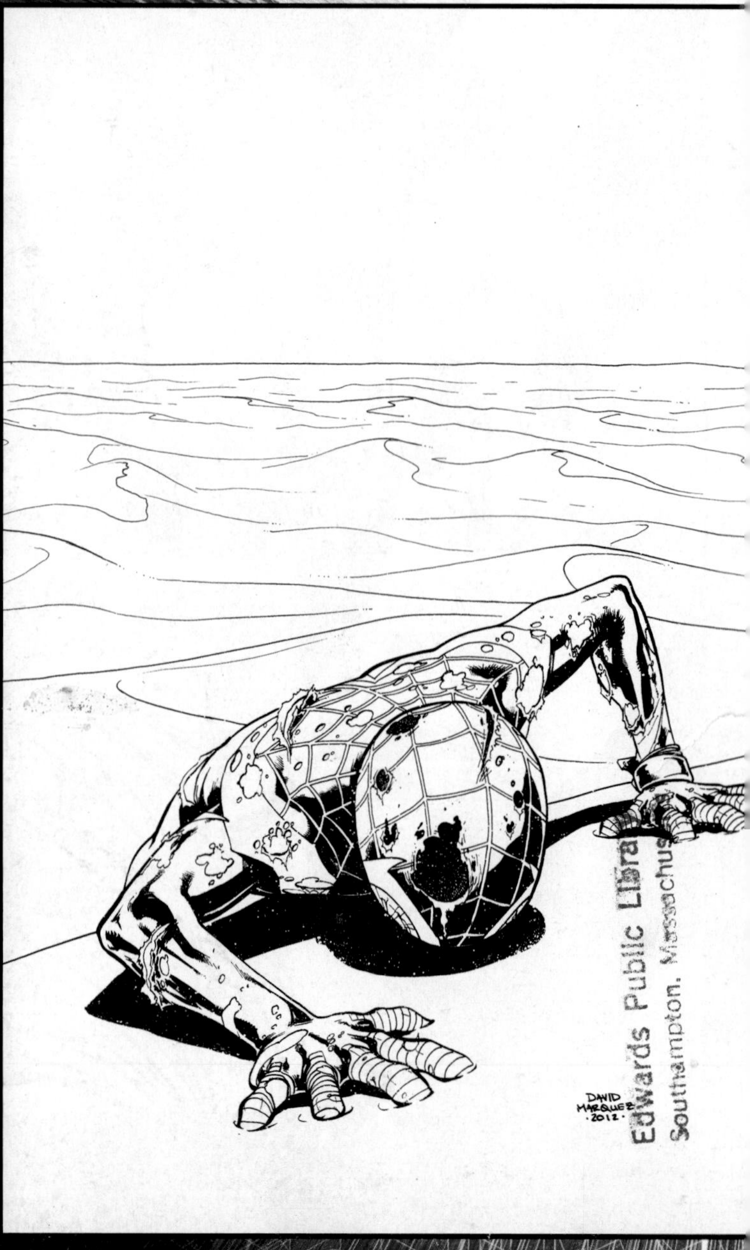
DAVID MARQUEZ ·2012·

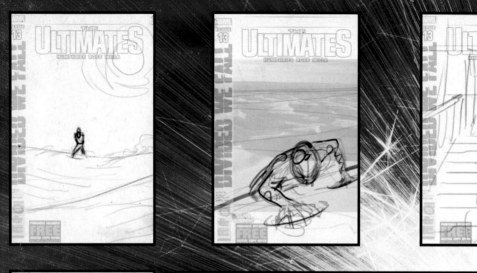